Beyond Disney

THE *unofficial* **GUIDE**®
TO Universal Orlando,®
SeaWorld,® & the Best
of Central Florida

7TH EDITION

Beyond Disney

THE *unofficial* GUIDE®

TO Universal Orlando,® SeaWorld,® & the Best of Central Florida

7TH EDITION

BOB SEHLINGER *with* ROBERT N. JENKINS

WILEY

Please note that prices fluctuate in the course of time and that travel information changes under the impact of many factors that influence the travel industry. We therefore suggest that you write or call ahead for confirmation when making your travel plans. Every effort has been made to ensure the accuracy of information throughout this book, and the contents of this publication are believed to be correct at the time of printing. Nevertheless, the publishers cannot accept responsibility for errors or omissions, for changes in details given in this guide, or for the consequences of any reliance on the information provided by the same. Assessments of attractions and so forth are based upon the authors' own experiences; therefore, descriptions given in this guide necessarily contain an element of subjective opinion, which may not reflect the publisher's opinion or dictate a reader's own experience on another occasion. Readers are invited to write the publisher with ideas, comments, and suggestions for future editions.

Published by:
John Wiley & Sons, Inc.
111 River St.
Hoboken, NJ 07030-5774

Produced by Menasha Ridge Press

Cover design by Paul Dinovo

Interior design by Vertigo Design

For information on our other products and services or to obtain technical support, please contact our Customer Care Department from within the United States at 800-762-2974, from outside the United States at 317-572-3993, or by fax at 317-572-4002.

John Wiley & Sons, Inc., also publishes its books in a variety of electronic formats. Some content that appears in print may not be available in electronic formats.

ISBN 978-0-470-88608-3

Manufactured in the United States of America

5 4 3 2 1

CONTENTS

LIST *of* MAPS

ABOUT
the AUTHORS

BOB SEHLINGER is the author of *The Unofficial Guide to Walt Disney World* and the executive publisher of the *Unofficial Guide* series.

ROBERT N. JENKINS, a native of Washington, D.C., earned a B.A. in journalism at Michigan State University, then worked at the *Grand Rapids* (Michigan) *Press* and at *Newsday* on Long Island before moving to St. Petersburg, Florida, in 1969.

In a 39-year career at the *St. Petersburg Times,* he served as editor of national news, state news, feature news, and, for 19 years, travel. While in that last assignment, *The Times* and his own writing won eight first-, second-, or third-place honors in the Society of American Travel Writers Foundation Lowell Thomas Travel Journalism Competition.

He is now a freelance writer; his website is **bobjenkinswrites.com**.

INTRODUCTION

WHY "UNOFFICIAL"?

THE AUTHORS AND RESEARCHERS OF THIS GUIDE specifically and categorically declare that they are and always have been totally independent. The material in this guide originated with the authors and has not been reviewed, edited, or in any way approved by the companies whose travel products are discussed. The purpose of this guide is to provide you with the information necessary to tour central Florida with the greatest efficiency and economy and with the least hassle and stress. In this guide we represent and serve you, the consumer. If a restaurant serves bad food, or a gift item is overpriced, or a certain ride isn't worth the wait, we can say so, and in the process we hope to make your visit more fun, efficient, and economical.

THERE'S *Another* WORLD *Out* THERE

IF YOU THINK THAT CENTRAL FLORIDA consists only of Walt Disney World, you're wrong. What's more, you're passing up some great fun and amazing sights. Admittedly, it's taken a while, but Walt Disney World now has plenty of competition that measures up toe-to-toe. And though it may sound blasphemous to suggest a whole vacation in central Florida without setting foot on Disney property, it's not only possible but also in many ways a fresh and appealing idea.

The big four non-Disney theme parks are Universal Studios Florida, Universal Islands of Adventure, SeaWorld, and Busch Gardens. Each is unique. Universal Studios Florida, a longtime rival of Disney's Hollywood Studios, draws its inspiration from movies and television and is every bit the equal of the Disney movie-themed park. Universal Islands of Adventure is arguably the most modern, high-tech theme park in the United States, featuring an all-star lineup of thrill rides that make it the best park in Florida for older kids and young-at-heart adults. SeaWorld provides an incomparable glimpse into the world of marine mammals and fish, served up in a way that (for the most part) eliminates those never-ending lines. Finally, Busch Gardens, with its shows, zoological exhibits, and knockout coasters, offers the most eclectic entertainment mix of any theme park we know. All four parks approximate, equal, or exceed the Disney standard without imitating Disney, successfully blending distinctive presentations and personalities into every attraction.

In addition to the big four, there are several specialty parks that are also worthy of your attention. The Kennedy Space Center Visitor Complex at Cape Canaveral provides an inside look at the past, present, and future of America's space program, and Gatorland showcases the alligator, one of the most ancient creatures on Earth. After closing for several years, SeaWorld's Discovery Cove offers central Florida's first-ever dolphin swim, and The Holy Land Experience is the first Christian theme park in the state and quite likely the most elaborate one in the world. All of these places offer an experience that is different from a day at one of the big theme parks, including a respite from standing in line, all of the walking, and the frenetic pace.

But these are just for starters. In central Florida, you'll also find a vibrant dinner-theater scene, two excellent non-Disney water parks, nightlife, and great shopping, all surrounded by some of the best hiking, biking, fishing, and canoeing available anywhere.

The ATTRACTION *that* ATE FLORIDA

BEFORE WALT DISNEY WORLD, Florida was a happy peninsula of many more or less equal tourist attractions. Distributed around the state in great profusion, these attractions constituted the nation's most perennially appealing vacation opportunity. There were the Monkey Jungle, the Orchid Jungle, venerable Marineland, the St. Augustine Alligator Farm, Silver Springs, the Miami Wax Museum, the Sunken Gardens, the Coral Castle, and the Conch Train Tour. These, along with the now-defunct Cypress Gardens, Busch Gardens, and others, were the attractions that ruled Florida. Now, like so many dinosaurs, those remaining survive precariously on the leavings of the greatest beast of them all, Walt Disney World. Old standbys continue to welcome tourists, but when was the last time you planned your vacation around a visit to Jungle Larry's Safari Park?

When Walt Disney World arrived on the scene, Florida tourism changed forever. Before Disney (BD), southern Florida was the state's and the nation's foremost tourist destination. Throngs sunned on the beaches of Miami, Hollywood, and Fort Lauderdale and patronized such nearby attractions as the Miami Serpentarium and the Parrot Jungle. Attractions in the Ocala and St. Augustine areas upstate hosted road travelers in great waves as they journeyed to and from southern Florida. At the time, Orlando was a sleepy central Florida town an hour's drive from Cypress Gardens, with practically no tourist appeal whatsoever.

Then came Disney, snapping up acres of farm- and swampland before anyone even knew who the purchaser was. Bargaining hard, Walt demanded improved highways, tax concessions, bargain financing, and community support. So successful had been his California Disneyland that whatever he requested, he received.

Generally approving, and hoping for a larger aggregate market, the existing Florida attractions failed to discern the cloud on the horizon. Walt had tipped his hand early, however, and all the cards were on the table. When Disney bought 27,500 central Florida acres, it was evident that he didn't intend to raise cattle.

The Magic Kingdom opened on October 1, 1971, and was immediately successful. Hotel construction boomed in Orlando, Kissimmee, and around Walt Disney World. Major new attractions popped up along recently completed I-4 to cash in on the tide of tourists arriving at Disney's latest wonder. Walt Disney World became a destination, and suddenly nobody cared as much about going to the beach. The Magic Kingdom was good for two days, and then you could enjoy the rest of the week at SeaWorld, Cypress Gardens, Circus World, Gatorland, Busch Gardens, the Stars Hall of Fame Wax Museum, and the Kennedy Space Center.

These attractions, all practically new and stretching from Florida's east to west coasts, formed what would come to be called the Orlando Wall. Tourists no longer poured into Miami and Fort Lauderdale. Instead they stopped at the Orlando Wall and exhausted themselves and their dollars in the shiny attractions arrayed between Cape Canaveral and Tampa. In southern Florida, venerable attractions held on by a parrot feather, and more than a few closed their doors. Flagship hotels on the fabled Gold Coast went bust or were converted into condominiums.

When Walt Disney World opened, the very definition of a tourist attraction changed. Setting new standards for cleanliness, size, scope, grandeur, variety, and attention to detail, Walt Disney World relegated the majority of Florida's headliner attractions to comparative insignificance almost overnight. Newer attractions such as SeaWorld and the vastly enlarged Busch Gardens successfully matched the standard Disney set. Cypress Gardens, Weeki Wachi, and Silver Springs expanded and modernized. Most other attractions, however, slipped into a limbo of diminished status. Far from being headliners or tourist destinations, they plugged along as local diversions, pulling in the curious, the bored, and the sunburned for mere 2-hour excursions.

Many of the affected attractions were and are wonderful places to spend a day, but even collectively they don't command sufficient appeal to lure many tourists beyond the Orlando Wall. We recommend them, however, not only for a variety of high-quality offerings but also as a glimpse of Florida's golden age, a time of less sophisticated, less plastic pleasures before the Mouse. Take a day or two and drive 3.5 hours south of Orlando. Visit the Miami Seaquarium, Vizcaya Museum and Gardens, Fairchild Tropical Botanic Garden, and Lion Country Safari. Drive Collins Avenue along the Gold Coast. You'll be glad you did.

When Epcot (then EPCOT Center) opened in Walt Disney World on October 1, 1982, another seismic shock reverberated throughout the Florida attractions industry. This time it wasn't only the smaller and more vulnerable attractions that were affected but the newer large-scale attractions along the Orlando Wall. Suddenly, Disney World swallowed up another one or two days of each tourist's vacation week. When the Magic Kingdom stood alone, most visitors had three or four days remaining to sample other attractions. With the addition of Epcot, that time was cut to one or two days.

Disney ensured its market share by creating multiday admission passes, which allowed unlimited access to both the Magic Kingdom and Epcot. More cost-efficient than a one-day pass to a single park, these passes kept the guest on Disney turf for three to five days.

Kennedy Space Center and SeaWorld, by virtue of their very specialized products, continued to prosper after Epcot opened. Most other attractions were forced to focus on local markets. Some, like Busch Gardens, did very well, with increased local support replacing the decreased numbers of Walt Disney World tourists coming over for the day. Others, like Circus World and the Hall of Fame Wax Museum, passed into history.

Though long an innovator, Disney turned in the mid-1980s to copying existing successful competitors. Except copying is not exactly the right word. What Disney did was to take a competitor's concept, improve it, and reproduce it in Disney style and on a grand scale.

The first competitor to feel the heat was SeaWorld, when Disney added the Living Seas Pavilion to the Future World section of Epcot. SeaWorld, however, had killer whales, the Shark Encounter, and sufficient corporate resources to remain preeminent among marine exhibits. Still, many Disney patrons willingly substituted a visit to the Living Seas for a visit to SeaWorld.

One of Disney's own products was threatened when the Wet 'n Wild water park took aim at the older and smaller but more aesthetically pleasing River Country. Never one to take a challenge sitting down, Disney responded in 1989 with the opening of Typhoon Lagoon, then the world's largest swimming theme park.

Also in 1989, Disney opened Pleasure Island, a single-cover multi-nightclub entertainment complex patterned on Orlando's successful Church Street Station. Tourist traffic around the theme parks started gravitating to Pleasure Island for nightlife rather than traveling to Church Street.

The third big Disney opening of 1989 was Disney-MGM Studios (now Disney's Hollywood Studios), a combination working motion picture and television production complex and theme park. Copying the long-lauded Universal Studios tour in Southern California, Disney-MGM Studios was speeded into operation after Universal announced its plans for a central Florida park.

Disney-MGM Studios, however, affected much more than Universal's plans. With the opening of Disney-MGM, the Three-Day World Passport was discontinued. Instead, Disney patrons were offered a single-day pass or the more economical multiday passports, good for either four or five days. With three theme parks on a multi-day pass, plus two swimming parks, several golf courses, various lakes, and a nighttime entertainment complex, Disney effectively swallowed up the average family's entire vacation. Break away to SeaWorld or the Kennedy Space Center for the day? How about a day at the ocean (remember the ocean)? Fat chance.

In 1995, Disney opened Blizzard Beach, a third swimming theme park, and began plans for a fourth major theme park, the Animal Kingdom, designed to compete directly with Busch Gardens. During the same year, the first phase of Disney's All-Star resorts came online, featuring (by Disney standards) budget accommodations. The location and rates of the All-Star resorts were intended to capture the market of the smaller independent and chain hotels along US 192 (Irlo Bronson Memorial Highway). Disney even discussed constructing a monorail to the airport so that visitors wouldn't have to set foot in Orlando.

As time passed, Disney continued to consolidate its hold. With the openings in 1996 of Disney's BoardWalk, Fantasia Gardens miniature golf, and the Walt Disney World Speedway; in 1997 of Disney's Wide World of Sports, Disney's West Side shopping and entertainment district, and a new convention center; and in 1998 of the Animal Kingdom, Disney attracted armies of central Floridians to compensate for decreased tourist traffic during off-season. For people who can never get enough, there is the town of Celebration, a Disney residential land-development project where home buyers can live in Disney-designed houses in Disney-designed neighborhoods, protected by Disney-designed security.

In 1999, however, for the first time in many years, the initiative passed to Disney's competitors. Universal Studios Florida became a bona fide destination with the opening of its second major theme park (Islands of Adventure), on-property hotels, and the CityWalk dining and entertainment complex that directly competed with Pleasure Island (and Church Street Station, which was promptly forced out of business). SeaWorld announced the 2000 debut of its Discovery Cove park, and Busch Gardens turned up the heat with the addition of new roller coasters. The latest additions bring Busch Gardens' total to seven coasters, making them the roller-coaster capital of Florida. Giving Disney some of its own medicine, Busch Gardens, SeaWorld, and Universal combined with Wet 'n Wild to offer multiday passes good at any of the parks. Although it may be too early to say that Disney's hegemony is at an end, one thing's for sure: Disney's not the only 800-pound gorilla on the block anymore.

The tourism slump that began during the collapse of the Internet bubble economy and worsened during post-9/11 paranoia, continues with the current troubled economic times. While the big boys are tightening their belts and cutting corners where they can, some have had to call it quits. The classic Ocean World in Fort Lauderdale was shut down for good shortly after the turn of the millennium. Splendid China—a vast, landscaped garden filled with miniature re-creations of Chinese buildings, monuments, palaces, cities, temples, and landmarks—closed its doors in 2003; Water Mania, a swimming park, followed in 2006; and Cypress Gardens said good-bye in 2009 after a valiant attempt at staying open.

Even with these recent bad patches, most attractions and theme parks in central Florida are just learning how to become more adaptive and creative. Those that survive will be leaner, cleaner, and even more competitive than ever before. All this competition, of course, is good for central Florida, and it's good for you. The time, money, and energy invested in developing ever-better parks and attractions boggle the mind. Nobody, including Disney, can rest on their laurels in this market. And as for you, you're certain to find something new and amazing on every visit.

TRYING TO REASON WITH THE TOURIST SEASON

CENTRAL FLORIDA THEME PARKS and attractions are busiest Christmas Day through New Year's Day. Thanksgiving weekend, the week of Washington's birthday, Martin Luther King Jr. holiday weekend, spring break for colleges, plus the two weeks around Easter are also extremely busy. What does "busy" mean? More than 90,000 people can tour one of the larger theme parks on a single day during these peak times! Although this level of attendance isn't typical, it is possible, and only the ignorant or foolish challenge the major Florida theme parks at their peak periods.

The least busy time extends from after the Thanksgiving weekend until the week before Christmas. The next slowest times are November up to the weekend preceding Thanksgiving, January 4 through the first week of February, and the week after Easter through early June. Late February, March, and early April are dicey. Crowds ebb and flow according to spring break schedules and the timing of Presidents' Day weekend. Though crowds have grown markedly in September and October as a result of special promotions aimed at locals and the international market, these months continue to be good for weekday touring.

IT TAKES MORE *than* ONE BOOK *to* DO *the* JOB RIGHT

WE'VE BEEN COVERING CENTRAL FLORIDA TOURISM for more than 25 years. We began by lumping everything into one guidebook, but that was when the Magic Kingdom was the only theme park at Walt Disney World, at the very beginning of the boom that has made central Florida the most visited tourist destination on Earth. As central Florida grew, so did our guide, until eventually we needed to split the tome into smaller, more in-depth (and more portable) volumes. The result is a small library of seven titles, designed to work both individually and together. All seven provide specialized information tailored to very specific central Florida and Walt Disney World visitors. Although some tips (such as arriving at the theme parks early) are echoed or elaborated in all the guides, most of the information in each book is unique.

The Unofficial Guide to Walt Disney World is the centerpiece of our central Florida coverage because, well, Walt Disney World is the centerpiece of most central Florida vacations. *The Unofficial Guide to Walt Disney World* is evaluative, comprehensive, and instructive—the ultimate planning tool for a successful Walt Disney World vacation. *The Unofficial Guide to Walt Disney World* is supplemented by five additional titles, including this guide:

Mini-Mickey: The Pocket-Sized Unofficial Guide to Walt Disney World, by Bob Sehlinger and Len Testa

The Unofficial Guide Color Companion to Walt Disney World, by Bob Sehlinger and Len Testa

The Unofficial Guide to Walt Disney World with Kids, by Bob Sehlinger and Liliane J. Opsomer with Len Testa

The Unofficial Guide to Walt Disney World for Grown-Ups, by Eve Zibart

Mini-Mickey is a nifty, portable, *Cliffs Notes* version of *The Unofficial Guide to Walt Disney World.* Updated semiannually, it distills information from this comprehensive guide to help short-stay or last-minute visitors decide quickly how to plan their limited hours at Disney World. *The Unofficial Guide Color Companion to Walt Disney World* is a visual feast that proves a picture is worth 1,000 words. *The Unofficial Guide to Walt Disney World for Grown-Ups* helps adults traveling without children make the most of their Disney vacation, and *The Unofficial Guide to Walt Disney World with Kids* presents a wealth of planning and touring tips for a successful Disney family vacation. Finally, this guide, *Beyond Disney,* is a complete consumer guide to the non-Disney attractions, hotels, restaurants, and nightlife in Orlando and central Florida. All of the guides are available from Wiley Publishing and at most bookstores.

LETTERS AND COMMENTS FROM READERS

MANY OF THOSE WHO USE *The Unofficial Guides* write us to make comments or share their own strategies for visiting central Florida. We appreciate all such input, both positive and critical, and encourage our readers to continue writing. Readers' comments and observations are frequently incorporated into revised editions of *The Unofficial Guides* and have contributed immeasurably to their improvement. If you write us, you can rest assured that we won't release your name and address to any mailing lists, direct-mail advertisers, or other third party.

How to Write the Authors

Bob Sehlinger and Robert N. Jenkins
The Unofficial Guides
P.O. Box 43673
Birmingham, AL 35243
UnofficialGuides@menasharidge.com

When you write by mail, put your address on both your letter and envelope, as sometimes the two get separated. It is also a good idea to include your phone number. And remember, as travel writers, we're often out of the office for long periods of time, so forgive us if our response is slow.

PART ONE

ACCOMMODATIONS

❗ ORLANDO LODGING OPTIONS

SELECTING AND BOOKING A HOTEL

LODGING COSTS IN ORLANDO vary incredibly. If you shop around, you can find a clean motel with a pool for as low as $40 a night. Because of hot competition, discounts abound, particularly for AAA and AARP members. There are four primary areas to consider:

1. INTERNATIONAL DRIVE AREA This area, about 5 minutes from Universal, parallels I-4 on its eastern side and offers a wide selection of hotels and restaurants. Prices range $56–$400 per night. The chief drawbacks of this area are its terribly congested roads, countless traffic signals, and inadequate access to westbound I-4. While the area's biggest bottleneck is its intersection with Sand Lake Road, the mile between Kirkman and Sand Lake roads is almost always gridlocked.

Regarding traffic on International Drive (known locally as I-Drive), these comments are representative. From a Seattle mom:

> After spending half our trip sitting in traffic on International Drive, those Disney hotels didn't sound so expensive after all.

A convention-goer from Islip, New York, weighed in with this:

> When I visited Orlando last summer, we wasted huge chunks of time in traffic on International Drive. Our hotel was in the section between the big McDonald's [at Sand Lake Road] and Wet 'n Wild [at Universal Boulevard]. There are practically no left-turn lanes in this section, so anyone turning left can hold up traffic for a long time.

Traffic aside, a man from Ottawa, Ontario, sings the praises of his I-Drive experience:

> International Drive is the place to stay in Orlando. Your single-paragraph description of this location failed to point out that several

continued on page 16

South Orlando & Walt Disney World Area

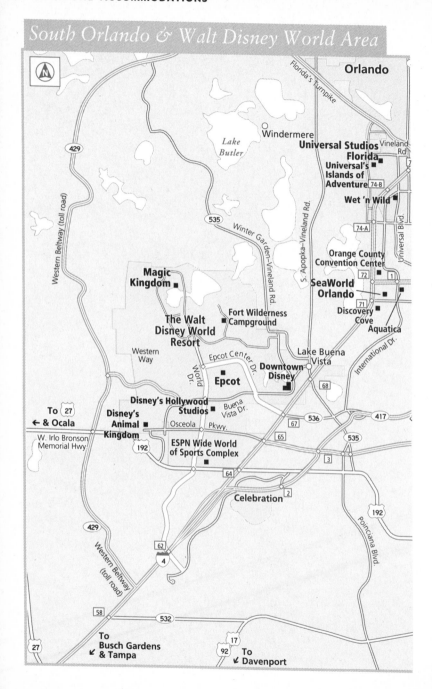

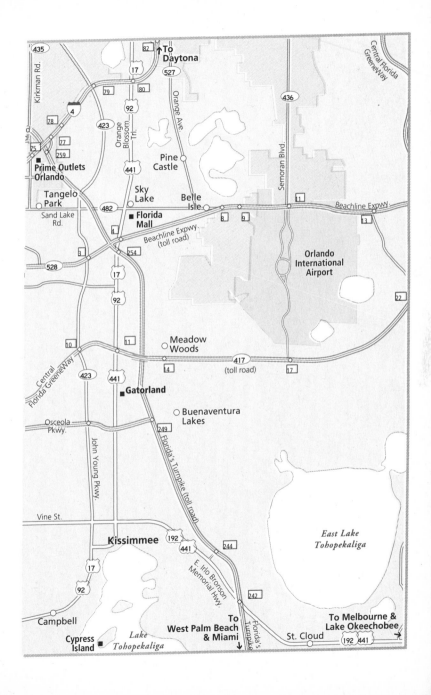

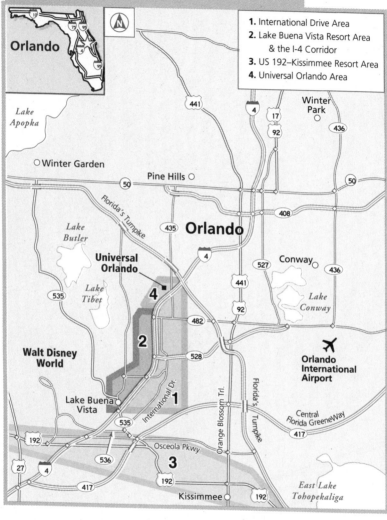

Hotel Concentrations around Orlando Area Attractions

1. International Drive Area
2. Lake Buena Vista Resort Area
   & the I-4 Corridor
3. US 192–Kissimmee Resort Area
4. Universal Orlando Area

International Drive & Universal Areas

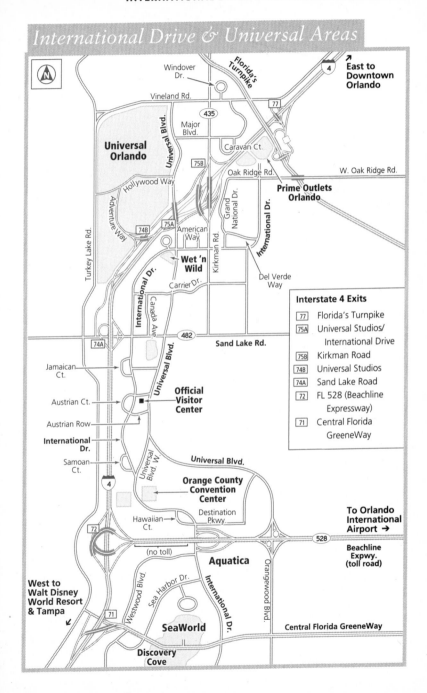

East to
Downtown
Orlando

Windover Dr.

Florida's Turnpike

Vineland Rd.

435

Major Blvd.

Caravan Ct.

Universal Blvd.

Universal Orlando

75B

Hollywood Way

Oak Ridge Rd.

W. Oak Ridge Rd.

Prime Outlets Orlando

Adventure Way

Grand National Dr.

International Dr.

74B

75A

American Way

Turkey Lake Rd.

Kirkman Rd.

Wet 'n Wild

Del Verde Way

International Dr.

Carrier Dr.

Canada Ave.

74A

482

Sand Lake Rd.

Interstate 4 Exits

77	Florida's Turnpike
75A	Universal Studios/ International Drive
75B	Kirkman Road
74B	Universal Studios
74A	Sand Lake Road
72	FL 528 (Beachline Expressway)
71	Central Florida GreeneWay

Jamaican Ct.

Austrian Ct.

Austrian Row

International Dr.

Samoan Ct.

Universal Blvd.

Official Visitor Center

4

Universal Blvd. W.

Universal Blvd.

Orange County Convention Center

Destination Pkwy.

Hawaiian Ct.

To Orlando International Airport →

72

528

(no toll)

Aquatica

Orangewood Blvd.

Beachline Expwy. (toll road)

West to Walt Disney World Resort & Tampa

71

Westwood Blvd.

Sea Harbor Dr.

International Dr.

SeaWorld

Central Florida GreeneWay

Discovery Cove

Lake Buena Vista Resort Area & the I-4 Corridor

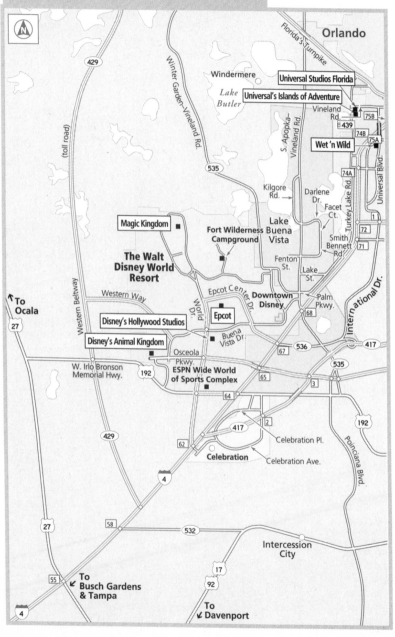

US 192–Kissimmee Resort Area

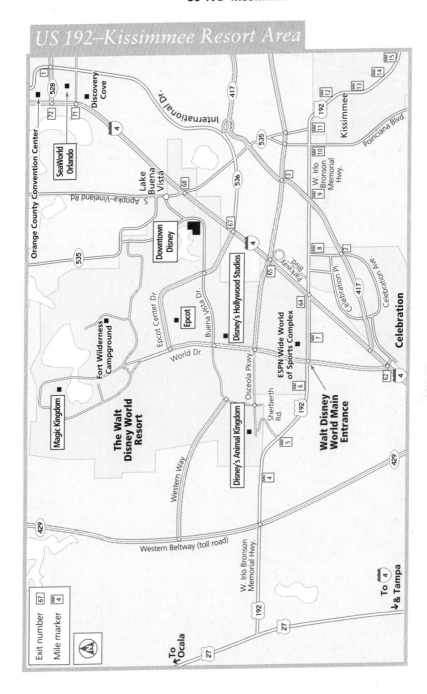

continued from page 9

discount stores, boutiques, restaurants, mini-putts, and other enter-
tainment facilities are all within walking distance of remarkably inex-
pensive accommodations and a short drive away from the attractions.
Many of the chain motels and hotels are in this area, and the local
merchants have created a mini-resort to cater to the tourists. It's the
ideal place to unwind after a hard day visiting the theme parks.

I-Drive hotels are listed in the *Official Vacation Guide,* published
by the Orlando–Orange County Convention and Visitors Bureau. For
a copy, call ☎ 800-972-3304 or 407-363-5872, or see **orlandoinfo.com.**

2. LAKE BUENA VISTA AND THE I-4 CORRIDOR A number of hotels are
along FL 535 and west of I-4 between Disney World and I-4's intersection with Florida's Turnpike. They're easily reached from the interstate and are near many restaurants, including those on International
Drive. The *Official Vacation Guide* (see above) lists most of them.
Traffic on I-4 can be a real slog, with construction projects both on the
highway itself and at the interchanges, so avoid it during rush hours.

3. US 192 (IRLO BRONSON MEMORIAL HIGHWAY) This is the highway
to Kissimmee to the south of Disney World. In addition to large, full-
service hotels, there are many small, privately owned motels that are
often a good value. Several dozen properties on US 192 are nearer
Disney parks than are more expensive hotels inside the World. The
number and variety of restaurants on US 192 has increased markedly,
compensating for the area's primary shortcoming. Locally, US 192 is
called Irlo Bronson Memorial Highway. The section to the west of
I-4 and the Disney "Maingate" is designated Irlo Bronson Memorial
Highway West, while the section from I-4 running southeast toward
Kissimmee is Irlo Bronson Memorial Highway East.

A senior citizen from Brookfield, Connecticut, was pleased with
lodging in the US 192–Kissimmee area:

We were amazed to find that from our cheaper and superior accom-
modations in Kissimmee it took only 5 minutes longer to reach the
park turnstiles than it did from the Disney accommodations.

Hotels on US 192 and in Kissimmee are listed in the *Kissimmee*
Visitor's Guide. Order a copy by calling ☎ 800-327-9159, or view it
online at **floridakiss.com.**

4. UNIVERSAL STUDIOS AREA In the triangular area bordered by I-4 on
the southeast, Vineland Road on the north, and Turkey Lake Road on
the west are Universal Orlando and the hotels most convenient to it.
Running north–south through the middle of the triangle is Kirkman
Road, which connects to I-4. On the east side of Kirkman are a number of independent hotels and restaurants. Universal hotels, theme
parks, and CityWalk are west of Kirkman. Traffic in this area is not
nearly as congested as on nearby International Drive, and there are
good interstate connections in both directions.

GETTING A GOOD DEAL ON A ROOM

HOTEL DEVELOPMENT AT WALT DISNEY WORLD has sharpened competition among lodgings throughout the Walt Disney World–Orlando–Kissimmee area. Hotels outside the World struggle to fill their rooms, and the economy has only made things worse. Unable to compete with Disney resorts for convenience or perks, off-World hotels lure patrons with bargain rates. In high season, during holiday periods, and during large conventions at the Orange County Convention Center, even the most modest property is sold out.

Following are our strategies for getting a good deal on a room in Orlando. The list may refer to travel-market players unfamiliar to you, but many tips for lodging deals will work equally well almost anyplace you need a hotel. Once you understand these strategies, you will routinely be able to obtain rooms at the lowest possible rates.

1. ORLANDO MAGICARD Orlando Magicard is a discount program sponsored by the Orlando–Orange County Convention and Visitors Bureau. Cardholders are eligible for discounts of 12–50% at about 50 hotels. The Magicard is also good for discounts at some area attractions, three dinner theaters, museums, performing-arts venues, restaurants, shops, and more. Valid for up to six persons, the card isn't available for larger groups or conventions.

To obtain a free Magicard and a list of participating hotels and attractions, call ☎ 800-643-9492 or 407-363-5872. On the Web, go to **orlandoinfo.com/magicard,** where you can print Magicard and the accompanying brochure. Or obtain one at the Convention and Visitors Bureau Information Center at 8723 International Dr. When you call for your Magicard, also request the *Official Vacation Guide.*

2. FLORIDA ROOMSAVER GUIDE This book of coupons for discounts at hotels statewide is free in many restaurants and motels on main highways leading to Florida. Because most travelers make reservations before leaving home, picking up the book en route doesn't help much. If you call and use a credit card, you'll receive the guide first-class for $3 ($5 U.S. for Canadian delivery). Call ☎ 352-371-3948 or 800-332-3948, or visit **travelerdiscountguide.com.**

3. HOTEL SHOPPING ON THE INTERNET Hotels use the Internet to fill rooms during slow periods and to advertise limited-time specials. Hotels also use more-traditional communication avenues, such as promoting specials through travel agents. If you enjoy cybershopping, have at it, but hotel shopping on the Internet isn't as quick or convenient as handing the task to your travel agent. When we bump into a great deal on the Web, we call our agent. Often she can beat the deal or improve on it (perhaps with an upgrade). A good agent working with a savvy, helpful client can work wonders.

See the chart at the top of the next page for websites we've found most dependable for discounts on Orlando-area hotels.

OUR FAVORITE ONLINE HOTEL RESOURCES

mousesavers.com Best site for hotels in Disney World.

dreamsunlimitedtravel.com Excellent for both Disney and non-Disney hotels.

2000orlando-florida.com Comprehensive hotel site.

valuetrips.com Specializes in budget accommodations.

travelocity.com Multidestination travel superstore.

roomsaver.com Provides discount coupons for hotels.

floridakiss.com Primarily US 192–Kissimmee area hotels.

orlandoinfo.com Good info; not user-friendly for booking.

orlandovacation.com Great rates for condos and home rentals.

expedia.com Largest of the multidestination travel sites.

hotels.com Largest Internet hotel-booking service; many other sites link to this site and its subsidiary, **hoteldiscounts.com.**

The secret to shopping on the Internet is, well, shopping. When we're really looking for a deal, we check all the sites listed in the chart. Flexibility on dates and location are helpful, and we always give our travel agent the opportunity to beat any deal we find.

We recommend choosing a hotel based on location, room quality, price, and commuting times to the various attractions, plus any features important to you. Next, check each of the applicable sites above. You'll be able to ferret out the best Internet deal in about 30 minutes. Then call the hotel to see if you can save more by booking directly. Start by asking the hotel for specials. If their response doesn't beat the Internet deal, tell them what you've found and ask if they can do better.

4. IF YOU MAKE YOUR OWN RESERVATION Always call the hotel in question, not the chain's national toll-free number. Often, reservationists at the toll-free number are unaware of local specials. Always ask about specials before you inquire about corporate rates. Don't hesitate to bargain, but do it before you check in. If you're buying a hotel's weekend package and want to extend your stay, for example, you can often obtain at least the corporate rate for the extra days.

CONDOMINIUMS AND VACATION HOMES

VACATION HOMES ARE FREESTANDING, while condominiums are essentially one- to three-bedroom accommodations in a larger building housing a number of similar units. Because condos tend to be part of large developments (frequently time-shares), amenities such as swimming pools, playgrounds, game arcades, and fitness centers often rival those found in the best hotels. Generally speaking, condo developments don't have restaurants, lounges, or spas. In a condo, if something goes wrong, someone will be on hand to fix the problem. Vacation homes rented from a property-management company likewise will have someone to come to the rescue, though responsiveness varies vastly from company to company. If you rent directly from an owner, correcting problems is often more difficult, particularly when the owner doesn't live in the same area as the rental home.

In a vacation home, all the amenities are contained in the home (though community amenities may be available in planned developments). Depending on the specific home, you might find a small swimming pool, hot tub, two-car garage, family room, game room, and even a home theater. Features found in both condos and vacation homes include full kitchens, laundry rooms, TVs, DVD players, and frequently stereos. Interestingly, though almost all freestanding vacation homes have private pools, very few have backyards. This means that, except for swimming, the kids are pretty much relegated to playing in the house.

Time-share condos are clones when it comes to furniture and decor, but single-owner condos and vacation homes are furnished and decorated in a style that reflects the owner's taste. Vacation homes, usually one- to two-story houses in a subdivision, rarely afford interesting views (though some overlook lakes or natural areas), while condos, especially the high-rise variety, sometimes offer exceptional ones.

The Price Is Nice

The best deals in lodging in the Orlando area are vacation homes and single-owner condos. Prices range from about $65 a night for two-bedroom condos and town homes to $200–$500 a night for three- to seven-bedroom vacation homes. Forgetting about taxes to keep the comparison simple, let's compare renting a vacation home to staying at a Disney's Value resort. A family of two parents, two teens, and two grandparents would need three hotel rooms at Disney's Pop Century Resort. At the lowest rate obtainable, that would run you $82 per night, per room, or $246 total. Rooms are 260 square feet each, so you'd have a total of 780 square feet. Each room has a private bath and a TV.

Renting at the same time of year from **All Star Vacation Homes** (no relation to Disney's All-Star Resorts), you can stay at a 2,053-square-foot, four-bedroom, three-bath vacation home with a private pool 3 miles from Walt Disney World for $269—not quite as economical as Disney's Value resorts, but plenty of value all the same: with four bedrooms, each of the teens can have his or her own room. Further, for the dates we checked, All Star Vacation Homes was running a special in which they threw in a free rental car with a one-week home rental.

But that's not all—the home comes with the following features and amenities: a big-screen TV with PlayStation, DVD player, and VCR (assorted games and DVDs available for complimentary checkout at the rental office); a CD player; a heatable private pool; five additional TVs (one in each bedroom and one in the family room); a fully equipped kitchen; a two-car garage; a hot tub; a laundry room with full-size washer and dryer; a fully furnished private patio; and a child-safety fence.

The home is in a community with a 24-hour gated entrance.

Available at the community center are a large swimming pool; a hot tub; tennis, volleyball, and half-court basketball courts; a playground; a gym; a convenience store; and a 58-seat cinema.

One thing we like about All Star Vacation Homes is that its website (**allstarvacationhomes.com**) offers detailed information, including a dozen or more photos of each specific home. When you book, the home you've been looking at is the actual one you're reserving. (If you want to see how the home previously described is furnished, for instance, go to the home page, scroll down to "Select Code," and choose property code **2-8137 SP-WP** in the pull-down menu. You'll be taken to another page with a description of the home, a slide show, a floor plan, a virtual tour, and more.)

On the other hand, some vacation-home companies, like rental-car agencies, don't assign you a specific home until the day you arrive. These companies provide photos of a "typical home" instead of making information available on each of the individual homes in their inventory. In this case, you have to take the company's word that the typical home pictured is representative and that the home you'll be assigned will be just as nice.

How the Vacation-home Market Works

In the Orlando area, there are more than 25,000 rental homes, including stand-alone homes, single-owner condos (that is, not time-shares), and town homes. The same area has about 114,000 hotel rooms. Almost all the rental homes are owned by individuals who occupy them for at least a week or two each year; the rest of the year, the owners make the homes available for rent. Some owners deal directly with renters, while others enlist the assistance of a property-management company.

Incredibly, about 700 property-management companies operate in the Orlando market. Most of these are mom-and-pop outfits that manage an inventory of 10 homes or less (probably fewer than 70 companies oversee more than 100 rental homes).

Homeowners pay these companies to maintain and promote their properties and handle all rental transactions. Some homes are made available to wholesalers, vacation packagers, and travel agents in deals negotiated either directly by the owners or by property-management companies on the owners' behalf. A wholesaler or vacation packager will occasionally drop its rates to sell slow-moving inventory, but more commonly the cost to renters is higher than when dealing directly with owners or management companies: because most wholesalers and packagers sell their inventory through travel agents, both the wholesaler/packager's markup and the travel agent's commission are passed along to the renter. These costs are in addition to the owner's cut and/or the fee for the property manager.

Along similar lines, logic may suggest that the lowest rate of all can be obtained by dealing directly with owners, thus eliminating middlemen. Although this is sometimes true, it's more often the case that property-management companies offer the best rates. With their marketing expertise and larger customer base, these companies can produce a higher occupancy rate than can the owners themselves. What's more, management companies, or at least the larger ones, can achieve economies of scale not available to owners in regard to maintenance, cleaning, linens, even acquiring furniture and appliances (if a house is not already furnished). The combination of higher occupancy rates and economies of scale adds up to a win–win situation for owners, management companies, and renters alike.

Location, Location, Location

The best vacation home is one that is within easy commuting distance of the theme parks. If you plan to spend some time at SeaWorld and the Universal parks, you'll want something just to the northeast of Walt Disney World (between the World and Orlando). If you plan to spend most of your time in the World or Legoland Florida, the best selection of vacation homes is along US 192 to the south of the park.

Disney World is mostly in Orange County but has a small southern tip that dips into Osceola County, which, along with Polk County to the west of the World, is where most vacation homes and single-owner condos and town houses are. Zoning laws in Orange County (which also includes most of Orlando, Universal Studios, SeaWorld, Lake Buena Vista, and the International Drive area) used to prohibit short-term rentals of homes and single-owner condos, but in recent years the county has loosened its zoning restrictions in a few predominantly tourist-oriented areas. So far, practically all of the vacation-rental homes in Orange County are in the **Floridays** and **Vista Cay** developments.

By our reckoning, about half the rental homes in Osceola County and all the rental homes in Polk County are too far away from the major attractions for commuting to be practical. You might be able to save a few bucks by staying farther out, but the most desirable homes to be found are in Vista Cay and in developments no more than 4 miles from Disney World's main entrance on US 192 (Irlo Bronson Memorial Highway), in Osceola County.

To get the most from a vacation home, you need to be close enough to commute in 20 minutes or less to your Orlando destination. This will allow for naps, quiet time, swimming, and dollar-saving meals you prepare yourself.

Shopping for a Vacation Home

The only practical way to shop for a rental home is on the Web. This makes it relatively easy to compare different properties and rental companies; on the downside, there are so many owners, rental companies, and individual homes to choose from that you could research yourself into a stupor. There are three main types of websites in the home-rental game: those for property-management companies, which showcase a given company's homes and are set up for direct bookings; individual owner sites; and third-party listings sites, which

Rental-home Developments

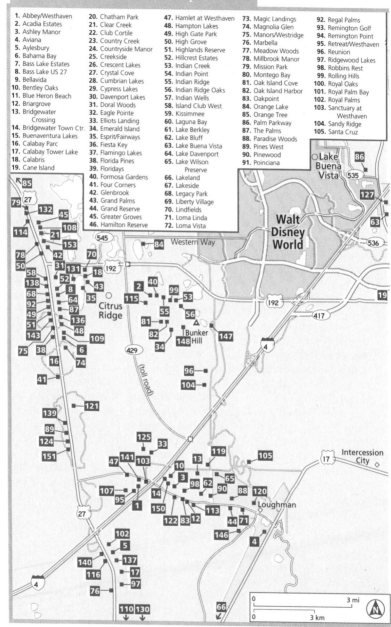

1. Abbey/Westhaven
2. Acadia Estates
3. Ashley Manor
4. Aviana
5. Aylesbury
6. Bahama Bay
7. Bass Lake Estates
8. Bass Lake US 27
9. Bellavida
10. Bentley Oaks
11. Blue Heron Beach
12. Briargrove
13. Bridgewater Crossing
14. Bridgewater Town Ctr.
15. Buenaventura Lakes
16. Calabay Parc
17. Calabay Tower Lake
18. Calabris
19. Cane Island
20. Chatham Park
21. Clear Creek
22. Club Cortile
23. Country Creek
24. Countryside Manor
25. Creekside
26. Crescent Lakes
27. Crystal Cove
28. Cumbrian Lakes
29. Cypress Lakes
30. Davenport Lakes
31. Doral Woods
32. Eagle Pointe
33. Elliots Landing
34. Emerald Island
35. Esprit/Fairways
36. Fiesta Key
37. Flamingo Lakes
38. Florida Pines
39. Floridays
40. Formosa Gardens
41. Four Corners
42. Glenbrook
43. Grand Palms
44. Grand Reserve
45. Greater Groves
46. Hamilton Reserve
47. Hamlet at Westhaven
48. Hampton Lakes
49. High Gate Park
50. High Grove
51. Highlands Reserve
52. Hillcrest Estates
53. Indian Creek
54. Indian Point
55. Indian Ridge
56. Indian Ridge Oaks
57. Indian Wells
58. Island Club West
59. Kissimmee
60. Laguna Bay
61. Lake Berkley
62. Lake Bluff
63. Lake Buena Vista
64. Lake Davenport
65. Lake Wilson Preserve
66. Lakeland
67. Lakeside
68. Legacy Park
69. Liberty Village
70. Lindfields
71. Loma Linda
72. Loma Vista
73. Magic Landings
74. Magnolia Glen
75. Manors/Westridge
76. Marbella
77. Meadow Woods
78. Millbrook Manor
79. Mission Park
80. Montego Bay
81. Oak Island Cove
82. Oak Island Harbor
83. Oakpoint
84. Orange Lake
85. Orange Tree
86. Palm Parkway
87. The Palms
88. Paradise Woods
89. Pines West
90. Pinewood
91. Poinciana
92. Regal Palms
93. Remington Golf
94. Remington Point
95. Retreat/Westhaven
96. Reunion
97. Ridgewood Lakes
98. Robbins Rest
99. Rolling Hills
100. Royal Oaks
101. Royal Palm Bay
102. Royal Palms
103. Sanctuary at Westhaven
104. Sandy Ridge
105. Santa Cruz

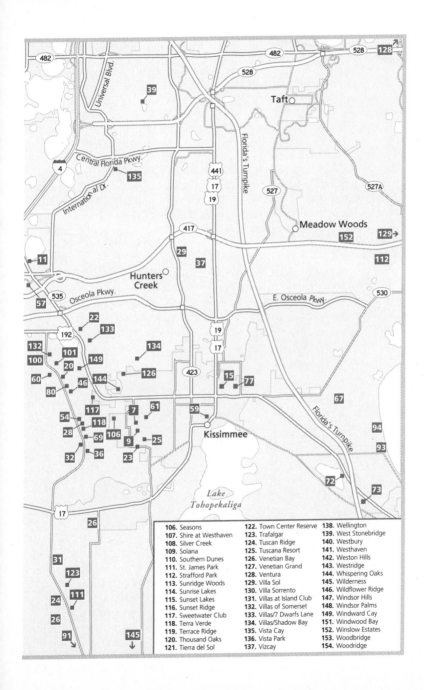

106. Seasons	122. Town Center Reserve	138. Wellington
107. Shire at Westhaven	123. Trafalgar	139. West Stonebridge
108. Silver Creek	124. Tuscan Ridge	140. Westbury
109. Solana	125. Tuscana Resort	141. Westhaven
110. Southern Dunes	126. Venetian Bay	142. Weston Hills
111. St. James Park	127. Venetian Grand	143. Westridge
112. Strafford Park	128. Ventura	144. Whispering Oaks
113. Sunridge Woods	129. Villa Sol	145. Wilderness
114. Sunrise Lakes	130. Villa Sorrento	146. Wildflower Ridge
115. Sunset Lakes	131. Villas at Island Club	147. Windsor Hills
116. Sunset Ridge	132. Villas of Somerset	148. Windsor Palms
117. Sweetwater Club	133. Villas/7 Dwarfs Lane	149. Windward Cay
118. Terra Verde	134. Villas/Shadow Bay	151. Windwood Bay
119. Terrace Ridge	135. Vista Cay	152. Winslow Estates
120. Thousand Oaks	136. Vista Park	153. Woodbridge
121. Tierra del Sol	137. Vizcay	154. Woodridge

advertise properties available through different owners and some-times management companies as well. Sites in the last category will usually refer prospective renters to an owner's or management com-pany's site for reservations.

We've found that most property-management sites are not very well designed and will test your patience to the max. You can practically click yourself into old age trying to see all the homes available or figure out where on earth they are. Nearly all claim to be "just minutes from Disney or Universal." (By that reasoning, we should list our homes; they're also just minutes from Disney . . . 570 minutes, to be exact!)

Many websites list homes according to towns (such as Auburndale, Clermont, Davenport, Haines City, and Winter Garden) or real estate developments (including Eagle Pointe, Formosa Gardens, Indian Ridge, and Windsor Palms) in the general Disney–Universal area, none of which you're likely to be familiar with. If you visit a site that lists homes by towns or real estate developments, begin by looking at our map on the previous pages, which shows where all these places are.

The best websites provide the following:

- Numerous photos and in-depth descriptions of individual homes to make comparisons quick and easy
- Overview maps or text descriptions that reflect how distant specific homes or developments are from Walt Disney World
- The ability to book the specific rental home of your choice on the site
- An easy-to-find phone number for non-Internet bookings and questions

The best sites are also easy to navigate, let you see what you're inter-ested in without your having to log in or divulge personal informa-tion, and list memberships in such organizations as the Better Business Bureau and the Central Florida Vacation Rental Managers Association (log on to **cfvrma.com** for the association's code of ethics).

Recommended Websites

After checking out dozens upon dozens of sites, here are the ones we recommend. All of them meet the criteria listed above. If you're stunned that there are so few of them, well, so were we. (For the record, we elected not to list some sites that met our criteria but whose homes are too far away from Orlando-area attractions.)

All Star Vacation Homes (**allstarvacationhomes.com**) is easily the best of the management-company sites, with photos and plenty of details about featured homes. All the company's rental properties are within either 4 miles of Disney World or 3 miles of Universal Studios.

Orlando's Finest Vacation Homes (**orlandosfinest.com**) represents both homeowners and vacation-home-management companies. Offer-ing a broad inventory, the website has photos and information on indi-vidual homes. Although the info is not as detailed as that offered by All Star Vacation Homes, friendly sales agents can fill in the blanks.

The website for the **Orlando–Orange County Convention and Visitors**

Bureau (orlandoinfo.com) is the place to go if you're interested in renting a condominium at one of the many time-share developments (click on "Places to Stay" at the site's home page). You can call the developments directly, but going through this website allows you to bypass sales departments and escape their high-pressure invitations to sit through sales presentations. The site also lists hotels and vacation homes.

Vacation Rentals by Owner (vrbo.com) is a nationwide vacation-homes listings service that puts prospective renters in direct contact with owners. The site is straightforward and always lists a large number of rental properties in Celebration, Disney's planned community situated about 8–10 minutes from the theme parks. Two similar listings services with good websites are **Vacation Rentals 411 (vacationrentals411.com)** and **Last Minute Villas (lastminutevillas.net)**.

Making Contact

Once you've found a vacation home you like, check around the website for a Frequently Asked Questions (FAQ) page. If there's not a FAQ page, here are some of the things you'll want to check out on the phone with the owner or rental company.

1. How close is the property to your vacation destination?
2. Is the home or condominium that I see on the Internet the one that I'll get?
3. Is the property part of a time-share development?
4. Are there any specials or discounts available?
5. Is everything included in the rental price, or are there additional charges? What about taxes?
6. How old is the home or condo I'm interested in? Has it been refurbished recently?
7. What is the view from the property?
8. Is the property near any noisy roads?
9. What is your smoking policy?
10. Are pets allowed? This consideration is as important to those who want to avoid pets as to those who want to bring them.
11. Is the pool heated?
12. Is there a fenced backyard where children can play?
13. How many people can be seated at the main dining table?
14. Is there a separate dedicated telephone at the property?
15. Is high-speed Internet access available?
16. Are linens and towels provided?
17. How far are the nearest supermarket and drugstore?
18. Are child-care services available?
19. Are there restaurants nearby?
20. Is transportation to the parks provided?
21. Will we need a car?

22. What is required to make a reservation?
23. What is your change/cancellation policy?
24. When is checkout time?
25. What will we be responsible for when we check out?
26. How will we receive our confirmation and arrival instructions?
27. What are your office hours?
28. What are the directions to your office?
29. What if we arrive after your office has closed?
30. Whom do we contact if something breaks or otherwise goes wrong during our stay?
31. How long have you been in business?
32. Are you licensed by the state of Florida?
33. Do you belong to the Better Business Bureau and/or the Central Florida Vacation Rental Managers Association?

We frequently receive letters from readers extolling the virtues of renting a condo or vacation home. This endorsement by a family from Ellington, Connecticut, is typical:

> Our choice to stay in a vacation home was based on cost and sanity. We've found over the last couple of years that our children can't share the same bed. We have also gotten tired of having to turn off the lights at 8 p.m. and lie quietly in the dark waiting for our children to fall asleep. With this in mind, we needed a condo/suite layout. We decided on the Sheraton Vistana Resort. We had a two-bedroom villa with full kitchen, living room, three TVs, and washer/dryer. I packed for half the trip and did laundry almost every night. The facilities offered a daily children's program and several pools, kiddie pools, and "playscapes." Located on FL 535, we had a 5- to 10-minute drive to most attractions, including SeaWorld, Disney, and Universal.

A St. Joe, Indiana, family also had a good experience, relating the following:

> We rented a home in Kissimmee this time, and we'll never stay in a hotel again. It was by far the nicest, most relaxing time we've ever had down there. Our rental home was within 10–15 minutes of all the Disney parks, and 25 minutes from SeaWorld. We had three bedrooms, two baths, and a pool out back. We paid $90 per night for the whole shootin' match. We did spring for the pool heating, $25 per night extra in February. We used AAA Dream Homes Rental Company and they did a great job by us. They provided us with detailed info before we went down so we'd know what we needed to bring.

From a New Jersey family of five:

> I cannot stress enough how important it is if you have a large family (more than two kids) to rent a house for your stay! We had visited Orlando several times in the past by ourselves when we were newlyweds. Fast-forward to 10 years later, when we took our three kids, ages

6 years, 4 years, and 20 months. We stayed at Windsor Hills Resort, which I booked through **globalresorthomes.com.** *I was able to see all the homes and check availability when I was reserving the house. This development is 1.5 miles from Walt Disney World. It took us about 10 minutes to drive there in the morning. We rented a brand-new four-bedroom, four-bathroom house with our own swimming pool. It was professionally decorated and just stunning! All for $215 a night! This was in October, but rental rates never climb above $300 even in the high season. We loved getting away from the hubbub of the theme parks and relaxing back at the house in "our" pool.*

#1 Dream Homes (**floridadreamhomes.com**) has a good reputation for customer service and now has photos of and information about the homes in its online inventory.

ORLANDO'S BEST HOTELS *for* FAMILIES

WHAT MAKES A SUPER FAMILY HOTEL? Roomy accommodations, in-room fridge, great pool, complimentary breakfast, child-care options, and programs for kids are a few of the things the *Unofficial Guide* team researched in selecting the top hotels for families from hundreds of properties in the Orlando area. Some of our picks are expensive, others are more reasonable, and some are a bargain. Regardless of price, be assured that these hotels understand a family's needs.

Though all of the following hotels offer some type of shuttle to the theme parks, some offer very limited service. Call the hotel before you book and ask what the shuttle schedule will be when you visit. Since families, like individuals, have different wants and needs, we haven't ranked the following properties here; they're listed by zone and alphabetically.

INTERNATIONAL DRIVE & UNIVERSAL AREAS

CoCo Key Hotel and Water Resort–Orlando   ★★★½

Rate per night $99–$149. **Pools** ★★★★. **Fridge in room** No. **Shuttle to parks** Yes (Aquatica, SeaWorld, Universal, Wet 'n Wild). **Maximum number of occupants per room** 4. **Special comments** $19/room fee charged for use of the water park; day guests may use the water park for a fee of $20/person ($15/person for Florida residents).

7400 International Dr.
Orlando
☎ 407-351-2626 or
877-875-4681
cocokeywaterresort.com

THE COCO KEY HOTEL AND WATER RESORT is on International Drive, not far from the Universal Orlando theme parks. It combines a tropical-themed hotel with a canopied water park featuring 3 pools and 14 waterslides, as well as poolside food and arcade entertainment. A full-service restaurant serves breakfast and dinner; a food court offers family favorites such as burgers, chicken fingers, and pizza. A unique feature of the resort is its cashless payment system. At check-in, families receive bar-coded wristbands that allow purchased items to be charged to the room.

The unusually spacious guest rooms include 37-inch flat-panel TVs, Wi-Fi, granite showers and countertops, and plenty of accessible outlets for guests' electronics.

DoubleTree Castle Hotel ★ ★ ★ ½

8629 International Dr.
Orlando
☎ 407-345-1511 or
800-952-2785
doubletreecastle.com

Rate per night $100–$230. **Pool** ★★★. **Fridge in room** Yes ($15/day). **Shuttle to parks** Yes (Disney and Universal; additional fee). **Maximum number of occupants per room** 4. **Special comments** For $13.95 adults, $7.95 kids, up to 4 people receive a full breakfast; 2 chocolate-chip cookies come with every room. Pets up to 75 pounds welcome for an additional $75.

YOU CAN'T MISS THIS ONE; it's the only castle on I-Drive. Inside you'll find royal colors, opulent fixtures, European art, Renaissance music, and a mystic Castle Creature at the door. The 216 guest rooms also receive the royal treatment in decor, though some guests may find them gaudy. All, however, are fairly large and well equipped with TV plus PlayStation, minibar (fridge is available at extra charge), three phones, coffeemaker, iron and board, hair dryer, and safe. The Castle Café off the lobby serves full or Continental breakfast. For lunch or dinner, you might walk next door to Vito's Chop House (dinner only) or Café Tu Tu Tango (an *Unofficial* favorite). The heated circular pool is 5 feet deep and features a fountain in the center, a poolside bar, and a whirlpool. There's no separate kiddie pool. Other amenities include a fitness center, gift shop, lounge, valet laundry service and facilities, and a guest-services desk with park passes for sale and babysitting recommendations. Security feature: elevators require an electronic key card.

DoubleTree Resort Orlando–International Drive ★ ★ ★ ★

10100 International Dr.
Orlando
☎ 407-352-1100 or
800-327-0363
doubletreeorlando
   idrive.com

Rate per night $89–$499. **Pools** ★★★½. **Fridge in room** Standard in some rooms; available in others for $10/day. **Shuttle to parks** Yes. **Maximum number of occupants per room** 4. **Special comments** A good option if visiting SeaWorld or Aquatica.

FORMERLY THE INTERNATIONAL PLAZA RESORT & SPA, this hotel has undergone a comprehensive $35 million renovation. Situated on 28 lush, tropical acres with a Balinese feel, the DoubleTree is adjacent to SeaWorld and Aquatica water park. All 1,094 rooms and suites—classified as "resort" or "tower"—have been completely refurbished and are equally suitable for business travelers or families. We recommend the tower rooms for good views and the resort rooms for maximum convenience. The Bamboo Grille serves steak and seafood along with breakfast; you can also get a quick bite at Bangli Lounge, the deli, or the pool bar. Relax and cool off at one of the three pools (there are three more just for kids), or indulge in a spa treatment. A fitness center, minigolf course, children's day camp, and game area afford even more diversions. The resort is about a 15-minute drive to Disney World, a 12-minute drive to Universal, or a short walk to SeaWorld.

Hard Rock Hotel ★★★★½

5800 Universal Blvd.
Orlando
☎ 407-503-2000
hardrockhotel
orlando.com

Rate per night $234–$724. **Pool** ★★★★. **Fridge in room** $15/ day. **Shuttle to parks** Yes (Universal, SeaWorld, Discovery Cove, Aquatica, and Wet 'n Wild). **Maximum number of occupants per room** 5 (double-queen) or 3 (king). **Special comments** Microwaves available for $15/day.

ON UNIVERSAL PROPERTY, the 650-room Hard Rock Hotel is nirvana for kids older than 8, especially those interested in music. Architecture is California Mission–style, and rock memorabilia is displayed throughout. If you plan to spend at least a few days at Universal parks, this is an excellent upscale option. Guests receive theme park privileges such as all-day access to the Universal Express line-breaking program, as well as delivery of packages to their rooms and priority seating at select Universal restaurants. The music-filled pool area has a white-sand beach, a 260-foot waterslide, a 12,000-square-foot pool, an underwater audio system, and a pool bar. You'll also find four restaurants and lounges, including the Palm Restaurant, a chic lounge, fitness center, and Hard Rock merchandise store. Guest rooms feature cutting-edge contemporary decor, a CD sound system, TV with pay-per-view movies and video games, coffeemaker, iron and board, minibar, robes, hair dryer, and two phones. A supervised activity center, Camp Lil' Rock, serves kids ages 4–14. Pet-friendly rooms are available.

Loews Portofino Bay Hotel ★★★★½

Rate per night $269–$714. **Pools** ★★★★. **Fridge in room** Minibar; fridge available for $15/day. **Shuttle to parks** Yes (Universal, SeaWorld, Discovery Cove, Wet 'n Wild). **Maximum number of occupants per room** 4. **Special comments** Character dinner on Friday.

5601 Universal Blvd.
Orlando
☎ 407-503-1000 or
888-273-1311
tinyurl.com/portofinobay

IN UNIVERSAL ORLANDO, the 750-room Portofino Bay Hotel is themed like an Italian Riviera village. Guests receive theme park privileges such as all-day access to the Universal Express line-breaking program, as well as delivery of packages to their room and priority seating at select Universal restaurants. The rooms are ultraluxurious, with Italian furnishings and opulent baths. Standard guest-room amenities include minibar, coffeemaker, iron and board, hair dryer, safe, and TV with pay-per-view movies. Campo Portofino offers supervised activities (movies, video games, crafts, and such) for children ages 4–14. The cost is $15 per hour plus $15 per meal, per child; hours vary. Trattoria del Porto restaurant offers a character dinner 6:30–9:30 p.m. on Friday, with characters such as Scooby-Doo and Woody Woodpecker. Portofino has four other Italian restaurants (with children's menus), an Italian bakery, and two bars. Three elaborate pools, gardens, jogging trails, pet-friendly rooms, and a spa and fitness center round out major amenities.

Nickelodeon Suites Resort Orlando ★★★½

Rate per night $159–$529. **Pools** ★★★★. **Fridge in room** Yes. **Shuttle to parks** Yes. **Maximum number of occupants per room** 8. **Special comments** Daily character breakfast; resort fee of $25/night.

14500 Continental Gateway
Orlando
☎ 407-387-5437 or
877-NICK-111; nickhotel.com

SPONGEBOB SQUAREPANTS, EAT YOUR HEART OUT. This resort is as kid-friendly as they come. Decked out in all themes Nickelodeon, the hotel is sure to please any fan of TV shows such as *SpongeBob, Dora the Explorer, Avatar: The Last Airbender,* and *iCarly,* to name a few. Nickelodeon characters from the channel's many shows hang out in the resort's lobby and mall area, greeting kids while parents check in. Guests can choose from among 777 suites—one-bedroom Family Suites and two- and three-bedroom KidSuites—executed in a number of different themes—all very brightly and creatively decorated. All suites include kitchenettes or full kitchens; also standard are a microwave, fridge, coffeemaker, TV, iron and board, hair dryer, and a safe. KidSuites feature a semiprivate kids' bedroom with bunk or twin beds, pull-out sleeper bed, 32-inch TV, CD player, and activity table. The master bedroom offers ample storage space that the kids' bedroom lacks. Additional amenities include a high-tech video arcade, Studio Nick—which hosts several game shows a night for the entertainment of a live studio audience, a buffet (kids 3 and younger eat free with a paying adult), a food court offering Subway and other choices, the full-service Nicktoons Cafe (offers character breakfasts), a convenience store, a lounge, a gift shop, a fitness center, a washer and dryer in each courtyard, and a guest-activities desk (buy Disney tickets and get babysitting recommendations). Not to be missed are the resort's two pools, Oasis and Lagoon. Oasis features a water park complete with water cannons, rope ladders, geysers, and dump buckets, as well as a hot tub for adults (with a view of the rest of the pool to keep an eye on little ones) and a smaller play area for younger kids. Kids will love the huge, zero-depth-entry Lagoon Pool, replete with 400-gallon dump bucket, plus nearby basketball court and nine-hole minigolf course. Pool activities for kids are scheduled several times a day, seasonally.

Rosen Shingle Creek ★★★★

Rate per night $99–$285. **Pools** ★★★★. **Fridge in room** Yes. **Shuttle to parks** Yes (Universal, Wet 'n Wild, Discovery Cove, Aquatica, and SeaWorld only). **Maximum number of occupants per room** 4.

9939 Universal Blvd.
Orlando
☎ 407-996-9939
or 866-996-9939
rosenshinglecreek.com

BEAUTIFUL ROOMS (east-facing ones have great views) and excellent restaurants distinguish this mostly meeting- and convention-oriented resort. The pools are large and lovely and include a lap pool, a family pool, and a kiddie wading pool. There's an 18-hole golf course on-site as well as a superior spa and an adequate fitness center. Child care is provided as well. Though a state-of-the-art video arcade will gobble up your kids' pocket change, the real kicker, especially for the 8 years-and-up crowd, is a natural area encompassing lily ponds, grassy wetlands, Shingle Creek, and an adjacent cypress swamp. Running through the area is a nature trail complete with signs to help you identify wildlife. Great blue herons, wood storks, egrets, mallard ducks, and ospreys are common, as are sliders (turtles), chameleons, and skinks (lizards). Oh yeah, there are alligators and snakes, too—real ones, but that's part of the fun. If you stay at Shingle Creek and plan to visit the theme parks, you'll want a car. Shuttle service is limited, departing and picking up at rather inconvenient times and stopping at other hotels before arriving at your destination.

LAKE BUENA VISTA & I-4 CORRIDOR

Buena Vista Palace Hotel & Spa ★ ★ ★ ½

Rate per night $99–$380. **Pools** ★ ★ ★ ½. **Fridge in room** Yes. **Shuttle to parks** Yes (Disney only). **Maximum number of occupants per room** 4. **Special comments** Sunday character brunch.

IN THE DOWNTOWN DISNEY RESORT AREA, the Buena Vista Palace is upscale and convenient. Surrounded by an artificial lake and plenty of palms, the spacious pool area contains three heated pools, the largest of which is partially covered; a whirlpool and sauna; a basketball court; and a sand volleyball court. Plus, a pool concierge will fetch your favorite magazine or fruity drink. On Sunday, the Watercress Café hosts a character brunch ($20 adults; $10 children). The 897 guest rooms are posh and spacious; each comes with a desk, coffeemaker, hair dryer, satellite TV with pay-per-view movies, iron and board, and minifridge. There are also 117 suites. In-room babysitting is available through All About Kids (**all-about-kids.com**). One lighted tennis court, a European-style spa offering 60 services, a fitness center, an arcade, a playground, and a beauty salon round out amenities. Two restaurants and a mini-market are on-site. Consider dropping by the Lobby Lounge or the full-menu sports bar for a nightcap. *Note:* All these amenities and services come at a price—a $15-per-night resort fee will be added to your bill.

1900 E. Buena Vista Dr.
Lake Buena Vista
☎ 407-827-2727 or
866-397-6516
buenavistapalace.com

Hilton in the Walt Disney World Resort ★ ★ ★ ★

Rate per night $99–$309. **Pools** ★ ★ ★ ½. **Fridge in room** Minibar; minifridge available free on request. **Shuttle to parks** Yes (Disney theme and water parks only). **Maximum number of occupants per room** 4. **Special comments** Sunday character breakfast and Disney Extra Magic Hours program.

THE HILTON OCCUPIES 23 ACRES in the Downtown Disney Resort Area. Since it's an official Walt Disney World hotel, guests can take advantage of the Disney Extra Magic Hours program, which allows entry to a selected Disney park 1 hour before official opening and late stays to a selected park up to 3 hours after official close. The Hilton's 814 guest rooms and suites are spacious, luxurious, and tasteful. Decorated in earth tones, all standard rooms have a granite bath, iron and board, hair dryer, two phones, desk, minibar, coffeemaker, and

1751 Hotel Plaza Blvd.
Lake Buena Vista
☎ 407-827-4000 or
800-782-4414
hilton-wdwv.com

cable TV with pay-per-view movies and video games. A character-breakfast buffet is served 8:30–11 a.m. on Sunday (reservations recommended). Five characters attend (only two are present at a time). Other important family amenities include babysitting services; an arcade and pool table; and two heated swimming pools, as well as a kiddie pool. Adults and older children can relax in the fitness center after a long day touring. Seven restaurants, including Benihana, add to the hotel's convenience.

Holiday Inn Resort Lake Buena Vista ★ ★ ★ ½

13351 FL 535
Lake Buena Vista
☎ 407-239-4500
or 866-808-8833
hiresortlbv.com

Rate per night $75–$80. **Pool** ★★★. **Fridge in room** Yes. **Shuttle to parks** Yes (Disney only). **Maximum number of occupants per room** 4–6. **Special comments** The first hotel in the world to offer KidSuites; resort fee of $6/night entitles guests to numerous perks, including use of fitness center and daily fountain drinks for kids.

THE BIG LURE HERE IS KIDSUITES—405-square-foot rooms, each with a separate children's area. Themes include a tree house, jail, space capsule, and fort, among others. The kids' area sleeps two to four children in one or two sets of bunk beds. The separate adult area has its own TV, safe, hair dryer, and mini-kitchenette with fridge, microwave, sink, and coffeemaker. Standard guest rooms offer these adult amenities. Other kid-friendly amenities include the tiny Castle Movie Theater, which shows movies all day, every day; a playground; an arcade with video games and air hockey, among its many games; and a basketball court. Other amenities include a fitness center for the grown-ups and a large free-form pool complete with kiddie pool and two whirlpools. Maxine's Kitchen serves breakfast and dinner buffets and offers an à la carte menu for dinner. There's also a minimart. More perks: kids age 12 and younger eat free from a special menu when dining with one paying adult (maximum four kids per adult), and "Dive-Inn" poolside movies are shown Saturday nights. Finally, pets up to 30 pounds are welcome for a $40 nonrefundable fee.

Hyatt Regency Grand Cypress ★ ★ ★ ★ ½

1 Grand Cypress Blvd.
Orlando
☎ 407-239-1234
grandcypress.hyatt.com

Rate per night $215–$355. **Pool** ★★★★★. **Fridge in room** Yes, plus minibar. **Shuttle to parks** Yes (Disney, Universal, SeaWorld). **Maximum number of occupants per room** 4.

THERE ARE MYRIAD REASONS to stay at this 1,500-acre resort, but the pool ranks as number one. The 800,000-gallon tropical paradise has two 45-foot waterslides, waterfalls, caves and grottos, and a suspension bridge. Your kids may never want to leave the pool to visit the theme parks. The Hyatt also is a golfer's paradise. With 45 holes of Jack Nicklaus–designed championship golf, a 9-hole pitch-and-putt course, and a golf academy, there's something for golfers of all abilities. Other recreational perks include a racquet facility with hard and clay courts, a private lake with beach, a fitness center, and miles of trails for biking, walking, and jogging. (Note: A daily $22.50 resort fee applies.) The 683 standard guest rooms are 360 square feet and have a Florida ambience, with green and reddish hues, touches of rattan, and private balconies. Amenities include minibar, iron and board, safe, hair dryer, ceiling fan, and cable/satellite TV with pay-per-view movies and video games. Suite and villa accommodations offer even more amenities. Camp Hyatt provides supervised programs for kids ages 3–12; in-room babysitting is available. Six restaurants offer dining options. Four lounges provide nighttime entertainment. If outdoor recreation is high on your family's list, Hyatt is an excellent high-end choice.

Marriott Village at Lake Buena Vista ★ ★ ★

Rate per night $119–$219. **Pools** ★★★. **Fridge in room** Yes. **Shuttle to parks** Disney only, $7. **Maximum number of occupants per room** 4 (Courtyard and Fairfield) or 5 (SpringHill). **Special comments** Free Continental breakfast at Fairfield and SpringHill.

8623 Vineland Ave.
Orlando
☎ 407-938-9001 or
877-682-8552
marriottvillage.com

THIS GATED HOTEL COMMUNITY INCLUDES a 388-room Fairfield Inn, a 400-suite SpringHill Suites, and a 312-room Courtyard. If you need a bit more space, book SpringHill Suites; if you're looking for value, try the Fairfield Inn; if you need limited business amenities, reserve at the Courtyard. Amenities at all three properties include fridge, cable TV, iron and board, hair dryer, and microwave. Cribs and roll-away beds are available at no extra charge at all locations. Swimming pools at all three hotels are attractive and medium-sized, featuring children's interactive splash zones and whirlpools; in addition, each property has its own fitness center. The Village Marketplace food court includes Pizza Hut, Village Grill, Village Coffee House, and a 24-hour convenience store. Bahama Breeze and Golden Corral full-service restaurants are within walking distance. Other services and amenities include a Disney planning station and ticket sales, an arcade, and a Hertz car-rental desk. Shoppers will find the Orlando Premium Outlets adjacent.

Sheraton Safari Hotel & Suites Lake Buena Vista ★ ★ ★ ★

Rate per night $89–$174. **Pool** ★★★. **Fridge in room** Standard in suites, $10/day in standard rooms. **Shuttle to parks** Yes (Disney free; other parks for a fee). **Maximum number of occupants per room** 4–6. **Special comments** Cool python waterslide. Dogs allowed.

12205 S. Apopka–
Vineland Rd.
Orlando
☎ 407-239-0444 or
800-325-3535
sheratonsafari.com

THE SAFARI THEME IS NICELY EXECUTED throughout the property—from the lobby dotted with African artifacts and native decor to the 79-foot python waterslide dominating the pool. The 393 guest rooms and 90 safari suites sport African-inspired art and tasteful animal-print soft goods in brown, beige, and jewel tones. Amenities include cable TV, coffeemaker, iron and board, hair dryer, and safe. Suites are a good option for families since they provide added space with a separate sitting room and a kitchenette with a fridge, microwave, and sink. The python waterslide is pretty impressive, but as one *Unofficial Guide* researcher pointed out, it's somewhat of a letdown: the python doesn't actually spit you out of its mouth. Instead you're deposited below its chin. Other on-site amenities include a restaurant (children's menu available), lounge, arcade, and fitness center.

Sheraton Vistana Resort Villas ★★★★

8800 Vistana Centre Dr.
Orlando
☎ 407-239-3100 or
866-208-0003
sheraton.com

Rate per night $139–$279. **Pools** ★★★½. **Fridge in room** Yes. **Shuttle to parks** Yes (Disney free; other parks for a fee). **Maximum number of occupants per room** 4–8. **Special comments** Though time-shares, the villas are rented nightly as well.

THE SHERATON VISTANA IS DECEPTIVELY LARGE. Because Sheraton's emphasis is on selling the time-shares, the rental angle is little known. But families should consider it; the Vistana is one of Orlando's best off-Disney properties. If you want a serene retreat from your days in the theme parks, this is an excellent base. The spacious villas come in one-bedroom, two-bedroom, and two-bedroom-with-lock-off models (which can be reconfigured as one studio room and a one-bedroom suite). All are decorated in beachy pastels. Each villa has a full kitchen (including fridge/freezer, microwave, oven/range, dishwasher, toaster, and coffeemaker, with an option to prestock with groceries and laundry products), washer and dryer, TVs in the living room and each bedroom (one with DVD player), stereo with CD player in some villas, separate dining area, and private patio or balcony in most. Grounds offer seven swimming pools (three with bars), four playgrounds, two restaurants, game rooms, fitness centers, a minigolf course, sports equipment rental (including bikes), and courts for basketball, volleyball, tennis, and shuffleboard. An array of activities ranges from crafts to games and sports tournaments. Of special note: Vistana is highly secure, with locked gates bordering all guest areas, so kids can have the run of the place without parents worrying about them wandering off.

Waldorf Astoria Orlando ★★★★½

14200 Bonnet Creek
Resort Lane
Lake Buena Vista
☎ 407-597-5500
waldorfastoria
orlando.com

Rate per night $199–$379. **Pool** ★★★★. **Fridge in room** Yes. **Shuttle to parks** Yes. **Maximum number of occupants per room** 4, plus child in crib. **Special comments** A good alternative to Disney's Deluxe properties.

OPENED IN 2009, the Waldorf Astoria is between I-4 and Disney's Pop Century Resort, near the Hilton Orlando at the back of the Bonnet Creek Resort property. Getting here requires a GPS or good directions, so be prepared with those before you travel. Beautifully decorated and well manicured, the Waldorf is more elegant than any Disney resort. Service is excellent, and the staff-to-guest ratio is far lower than at Disney properties.

At just under 450 square feet, standard rooms feature either two queen beds or one king. A full-size desk allows you to get work done if necessary, and rooms also have flat-panel TVs, high-speed Internet, and Wi-Fi. The bathrooms are spacious and gorgeous, with cool marble floors, glass-walled showers, separate tubs, and lots of counter space. This space is so nice that when we stayed here in 2009, we debated whether we'd rather stay at Pop Century with three others or sleep in a Waldorf bathroom by ourselves.

Amenities include a fitness center, a golf course, six restaurants, and two pools (including one zero-entry for kids). Pool-size cabanas are available for rent. The resort offers shuttle service to the Disney parks about every half hour, but check with the front desk for the exact schedule when you arrive. Runners will enjoy the relative solitude—it's about a 1-mile round-trip to the nearest busy road, and the route is flat as a pancake.

US 192 AREA

Comfort Suites Maingate ★ ★ ★ ½

7888 W. Irlo Bronson
  Memorial Hwy.

Rate per night $70–$170. **Pool** ★★★. **Fridge in room** Yes. **Shuttle to parks** Yes (Disney, Universal, and SeaWorld). **Maximum number of occupants per room** 6 for most suites. **Special comments** Complimentary Continental breakfast daily.

Kissimmee
☎ 407-390-9888 or
888-390-9888
comfortsuites
kissimmee.com

THIS PROPERTY HAS 150 SPACIOUS one-room suites, each with double sofa bed, microwave, fridge, coffeemaker, TV, hair dryer, and safe. The suites aren't lavish, but they're clean and contemporary. Extra bathroom counter space is especially convenient for larger families. The heated pool is large and has plenty of lounge chairs and moderate landscaping. A kiddie pool, whirlpool, and poolside bar complete the courtyard. Other amenities include an arcade and a gift shop. But Maingate's big plus is its location next door to a shopping center. There, you'll find 10 dining options, including Outback Steakhouse, Red Lobster, Subway, T.G.I. Friday's, and Chinese, Italian, and Japanese eateries; a Winn-Dixie Marketplace; a liquor store; a bank; a dry cleaner; and a tourist-information center with park passes for sale, among other services. All this a short walk from your room.

Gaylord Palms Hotel and Convention Center ★ ★ ★ ★ ½

Rate per night $129–$279. **Pool** ★★★★. **Fridge in room** Yes. **Shuttle to parks** Disney only. **Maximum number of occupants per room** 4. **Special comments** Probably the closest you'll get off-World to Disney-level extravagance. Resort fee of $15/day.

6000 W. Osceola Pkwy.
Kissimmee
☎ 407-586-0000
gaylordpalms.com

THIS DECIDEDLY UPSCALE RESORT has a colossal convention facility and caters strongly to business clientele, but it's still a nice (if pricey) family resort. Hotel wings are defined by the three themed, glass-roofed atriums they overlook. Key West's design is reminiscent of island life in the Florida Keys; Everglades is an overgrown spectacle of shabby swamp chic, with piped-in cricket noise and a robotic alligator; and the immense, central St. Augustine harks back to Spanish Colonial Florida. Lagoons, streams, and waterfalls cut through and connect all three, and walkways and bridges abound. Rooms reflect the colors of their respective areas, though there's no particular connection in decor (St. Augustine atrium-view rooms are the most opulent, but they're not Spanish). A fourth wing, Emerald Bay Tower, overlooks the Emerald Plaza shopping and dining area of the St. Augustine atrium. These rooms are the nicest and most expensive, and are mostly used by convention-goers. Though rooms have fridges and alarm clocks with CD players (as well as high-speed Internet), the rooms themselves really work better as retreats for adults than for kids. However, children will enjoy wandering the themed areas and playing in the family pool (with water-squirting octo-pus); in-room child care is provided by Kid's Nite Out (**kidsniteout.com**).

Orange Lake Resort ★ ★ ★ ★ ½

8505 W. Irlo Bronson
  Memorial Hwy.
Kissimmee
☎ 407-586-2000 or
800-877-6522
orangelake.com

Rate per night $126–$270 (2-bedroom summer rate). **Pools** ★★★★. **Fridge in room** Yes. **Shuttle to parks** Yes (fee varies depending on destination). **Maximum number of occupants per room** Varies. **Special comments** This is a time-share property, but if you rent directly through the resort (as opposed to the sales office), you can avoid time-share sales pitches.

YOU COULD SPEND YOUR ENTIRE VACATION never leav-ing this property, about 6–10 minutes from the Disney theme parks. From its 10 pools and two mini–water parks to its golfing opportunities (36 holes of championship greens plus two 9-hole executive courses), Orange Lake offers an extensive menu of amenities and recreational opportunities. If you tire of lazing by the pool, try waterskiing, wake-boarding, tubing, fishing, or other activities on the 80-acre lake. There's also a live alligator show, exercise programs, organized competitive sports and games, arts-and-crafts sessions, and miniature golf. Activities don't end when the sun goes down. Karaoke, live music, a Hawaiian luau, and movies at the resort cinema are some of the evening options.

The 2,412 units are tastefully decorated and comfortably furnished, rang-ing from suites and studios to three-bedroom villas, all containing fully equipped kitchens. If you'd rather not cook on vacation, try one of the seven restaurants scattered across the resort: two cafés, three grills, one pizzeria, and a fast-food eatery. Babysitters are available to come to your villa, accom-pany your family on excursions, or take your children to attractions for you.

Radisson Resort Orlando-Celebration ★ ★ ★ ★

2900 Parkway Blvd.
Kissimmee
☎ 407-396-7000
or 800-634-4774
radissonorlando
resort.com

Rate per night $107–$168. **Pool** ★★★★½. **Fridge in room** Yes. **Shuttle to parks** Yes (Disney, Universal, SeaWorld). **Maximum number of occupants per room** 5. **Special comments** $12.50/day resort fee; kids age 10 and younger eat free with paying adult at Mandolin's restaurant.

THE POOL ALONE IS WORTH A STAY HERE, but the Radisson Resort gets high marks in all areas. The free-form pool is huge, with a waterfall and waterslide surrounded by palms, plus a smaller heated pool, two whirlpools, and a kiddie pool. Other outdoor amenities include two lighted tennis courts, sand volleyball, a playground, and jogging areas. Kids can also blow off steam at the arcade, while adults might visit the fit-ness center. Rooms are elegant, featuring Italian furnishings and marble baths. They're of ample size and include a minibar (some rooms), coffee-maker, TV, iron and board, hair dryer, and safe. Dining options include Mandolin's for breakfast (buffet) and dinner, and a 1950s-style diner serv-ing burgers, sandwiches, shakes, and Pizza Hut pizza, among other fare. A sports lounge with an 1126-foot TV offers nighttime entertainment. Guest services can help with tours, park passes, car rental, and babysitting. While there are no children's programs per se, there are plenty of activities such as face painting by a clown, juggling classes, bingo, and arts and crafts.

Wyndham Bonnet Creek Resort ★ ★ ★ ★

Rate per night $179–$359. **Pool** ★★★★. **Fridge in room** Yes. **Shuttle to parks** Disney only. **Maximum number of occupants per room** 4–12 depending on room/suite. **Special comments** A non-Disney suite hotel within Walt Disney World.

9560 Via Encinas
Lake Buena Vista
☎ 407-238-3500
wyndham
bonnetcreek.com

THIS CONDO HOTEL LIES ON THE SOUTH side of Buena Vista Drive. The property has an interesting history: When Walt Disney began secretly buying up real estate in the 1960s under the names of numerous front companies, the land on which this resort stands was the last holdout and was never sold to Disney, though the company tried repeatedly to acquire it through the years. (The owners reportedly took issue with the way Disney went about acquiring land and preferred to see the site languish undeveloped.) The 482-acre site was ultimately bought by Marriott, which put up a Fairfield Inn time-share development in 2004. The Wyndham is part of a luxury-hotel complex on the same site that includes a 500-room Waldorf Astoria (see page 34) and a 1,000-room Hilton. The development is surrounded on three sides by Disney property and on one side by I-4.

The Bonnet Creek Resort offers upscale, family-friendly accommodations: one- and two-bedroom condos with fully equipped kitchens, washer-dryers, jetted tubs, and balconies. Activities and amenities on-site include two outdoor swimming pools, a "lazy river" float stream, a children's activities program, a game room, a playground, and miniature golf. One-bedroom units are equipped with a king bed in the bedroom and a sleeper sofa in the living area; two-bedroom condos have two double beds in the second bedroom, a sleeper sofa in the living area, and an additional bath.

HOTELS *and* MOTELS:
Rated and Ranked

IN THIS SECTION, WE COMPARE HOTELS in four main areas outside Walt Disney World (see page 9) with those inside the World.

In addition to Disney properties, we rate hotels in the four lodging areas defined earlier in this chapter. Additional hotels can be found at the intersection of US 27 and I-4, on US 441 (Orange Blossom Trail), and in downtown Orlando. Most of these require more than 30 minutes of commuting to Disney World and thus are not rated. We also haven't rated lodging east of Siesta Lago Drive on US 192.

WHAT'S IN A ROOM?

EXCEPT FOR CLEANLINESS, state of repair, and decor, travelers pay little attention to hotel rooms. There is, of course, a clear standard of quality and luxury that differentiates Motel 6 from Holiday Inn, Holiday Inn from Marriott, and so on. Many guests, however, fail to appreciate that some rooms are better engineered than others. Making the room usable to its occupants is an art that combines both form and function.

Decor and taste are important. No one wants to stay in a room that's dated, garish, or ugly. But beyond decor, how "livable" is the room? In Orlando, for example, we've seen some beautifully appointed rooms that aren't well designed for human habitation. The next time you stay in a hotel, note your room's details and design elements. Even more than decor, these are the things that will make you feel comfortable and at home.

ROOM RATINGS

TO EVALUATE PROPERTIES FOR THEIR QUALITY, tastefulness, state of repair, cleanliness, and size of their standard rooms, we have grouped the hotels and motels into classifications denoted by stars—the overall star rating. Star ratings in this guide apply only to Orlando-area properties and don't necessarily correspond to ratings awarded by *Frommer's,* Mobil, AAA, or other travel critics. Because stars have little relevance when awarded in the absence of recognized standards of comparison, we have tied our ratings to expected levels of quality established by specific American hotel corporations.

Overall star ratings apply only to room quality and describe the property's standard accommodations. For most hotels, a standard accommodation is a room with one king bed or two queen beds. In an all-suite property, the standard accommodation is either a studio or one-bedroom suite. In addition to standard accommodations, many hotels offer luxury rooms and special suites, which aren't rated in this guide. Star ratings for rooms are assigned without regard to whether a property has restaurant(s), recreational facilities, entertainment, or other extras.

OVERALL STAR RATINGS		
★★★★★	Superior rooms	Tasteful and luxurious by any standard
★★★★	Extremely nice rooms	What you'd expect at a Hyatt Regency or Marriott
★★★	Nice rooms	Holiday Inn or comparable quality
★★	Adequate rooms	Clean, comfortable, and functional without frills—like a Motel 6
★	Super-budget	These exist but are not included in our coverage

In addition to stars (which delineate broad categories), we use a numerical rating system—the room-quality rating. Our scale is 0–100, with 100 being the best possible rating and zero (0) the worst. Numerical ratings show the difference we perceive between one property and another. For instance, rooms at both the Courtyard Orlando Lake Buena Vista at Vista Centre and the Courtyard Orlando I-Drive are rated 3½ stars (★★★½). In the numerical ratings, the former is an 82 and the latter a 76. This means that within the 3½-star category, the first Courtyard Orlando has slightly nicer rooms than its sibling.

The location column identifies the area where you'll find a particular property. The designation **WDW** means the property is inside Walt Disney World. A **1** means it's on or near International Drive. Properties on or near US 192 (aka Irlo Bronson Memorial Highway, Vine Street, and Space Coast Parkway) are indicated by a **3;** those in the vicinity of Universal Orlando as **4.** All others are marked with **2** and for the most part are along FL 535 and the I-4 corridor, though some are in nearby locations that don't meet any other criteria.

LODGING AREAS			
WDW	Walt Disney World	3	US 192 (Irlo Bronson
1	International Drive		Memorial Highway)
2	I-4 Corridor	4	Universal Orlando Area

Names of properties along US 192 also designate location (for example, Holiday Inn Maingate West). The consensus in Orlando seems to be that the main entrance to Disney World is the broad interstate-type road that runs off US 192. This is called the **Maingate.** Properties along US 192 call themselves Maingate East or West to differentiate their positions along the highway. So, driving southeast from Clermont or Florida's Turnpike, the properties before you reach the Maingate turnoff are called Maingate West, while the properties after you pass the Maingate turnoff are called Maingate East.

Cost estimates are based on the hotel's published rack rates for standard rooms. Each **$** represents $50. Thus a cost symbol of **$$$** means that a room (or suite) at that hotel will be about $150 a night.

We've focused on room quality and excluded consideration of location, services, recreation, or amenities. In some instances, a one- or two-room suite is available for the same price or less than that of a single standard hotel room.

If you've used an earlier edition of this guide, you'll notice that new properties have been added and many ratings and rankings have changed, some because of room renovation or improved maintenance or housekeeping. Failure to maintain rooms or lax housekeeping can bring down ratings.

Before you shop for a hotel, consider this letter from a man in Hot Springs, Arkansas:

We canceled our room reservations to follow the advice in your book and reserved a hotel highly ranked by the Unofficial Guide. *We wanted inexpensive, but clean and cheerful. We got inexpensive, but also dirty, grim, and depressing. I really felt disappointed in your advice and the room. It was the pits. That was the one real piece of information I needed from your book! The room spoiled the holiday for me aside from our touring.*

This letter was as unsettling to us as the bad room was to our reader. Our integrity as travel journalists is based on the quality of the information we provide. When rechecking the hotel our reader disliked, we found our rating was representative, but he had been assigned one of a small number of threadbare rooms scheduled for renovation.

Note that some chains use the same guest-room photo in promotional literature for all its hotels and that the room in a specific property may not resemble the photo. When you or your travel agent calls, ask how old the property is and when the guest room you're being assigned was last renovated. If you're assigned a room inferior to expectations, demand to be moved.

A WORD ABOUT TOLL-FREE TELEPHONE NUMBERS

IT'S ESSENTIAL TO COMMUNICATE with the hotel directly when shopping for deals and stating room preferences. Most toll-free numbers are routed directly to a hotel chain's central reservations office, and the customer-service agents there typically have little or no knowledge of the individual hotels in the chain or of any special offers. In our Hotel Information Chart (pages 48–62), therefore, we list the toll-free number only if it connects directly to the hotel in question; otherwise, we provide the hotel's local phone number. We also provide local numbers for the Disney resorts in the Hotel Information Chart; while cast members can answer questions about amenities and such, note that these hotels must be booked through the Disney Reservation Center (☎ 407-W-DISNEY). After you've reserved your room, however, it's a good idea to call the hotel directly about two weeks before you arrive to make sure the reservation is in order.

> *unofficial* **TIP**
> The key to avoiding disappointment is to snoop in advance. Ask how old the hotel is and when its guest rooms were last renovated.

THE 30 BEST HOTEL VALUES

LET'S LOOK AT THE BEST COMBINATIONS of quality and value in a room. Rankings are made without consideration for location or the availability of restaurant(s), recreational facilities, entertainment, and/or amenities.

A reader recently wrote to complain that he had booked one of our top-ranked rooms in terms of value and had been very disappointed in the room. We noticed that the room the reader occupied had a quality rating of ★★½. Remember that the list of top deals is intended to give you some sense of value received for dollars spent. A ★★½ room at $40 may have the same value as a ★★★★ room at $115, but that doesn't mean the rooms will be of comparable quality. Regardless of whether it's a good deal, a ★★½ room is still a ★★½ room.

The Top 30 Best Deals

HOTEL	LOCATION	RATING	QUALITY	($ = $50)
1. Holiday Inn Main Gate East	3	★★★★½	90	$+
2. Liki Tiki Village	3	★★★★½	90	$+
3. Champions World Resort	3	★★★	66	$−
4. Westgate Lakes Resort & Spa	2	★★★★½	92	$+
5. Monumental Hotel	1	★★★★½	94	$$−
6. Ramada Gateway Kissimmee(tower)	3	★★★	71	$−
7. Super 8 Kissimmee/Orlando Area	3	★★★	70	$−
8. Orlando Vista Hotel	2	★★★★	83	$+
9. Seralago Hotel & Suites Main Gate East	3	★★★	71	$−
10. CoCo Key Water Resort–Orlando	1	★★★½	90	$$−
11. Hawthorn Suites Lake Buena Vista	2	★★★★	87	$+
12. Vacation Village at Parkway	3	★★★★½	91	$$−
13. Rodeway Inn Maingate	3	★★½	59	$−
14. Celebrity Resorts Lake Buena Vista	2	★★★★	85	$+
15. Ramada Gateway Kissimmee(garden)	3	★★½	64	$−
16. Country Inn & Suites Orlando Maingate at Calypso	3	★★★½	82	$+
17. Extended Stay America Universal	4	★★★½	75	$
18. Westgate Vacation Villas(town center)	2	★★★★½	93	$$−
19. Holiday Inn Resort Lake Buena Vista	2	★★★½	79	$+
20. DoubleTree Resort Orlando– I-Drive (resort)	1	★★★★	92	$$−
21. Super 8 Orlando/Kissimmee/Lakeside	3	★★½	58	$−
22. Hawthorn Suites Orlando Convention Center	1	★★★½	80	$+
23. Shades of Green	WDW	★★★★½	91	$$−
24. Comfort Inn Universal Studios Area	1	★★★	66	$
25. Motel 6 Main Gate West	3	★★	52	$−
26. Peabody Orlando	1	★★★★½	90	$$
27. Motel 6 Orlando–I-Drive	1	★★½	61	$−
28. Days Inn Orlando/I-Drive	1	★★½	61	$−
29. DoubleTree Resort Orlando– I-Drive (tower)	1	★★★★	92	$$
30. Extended Stay Deluxe Orlando Lake Buena Vista	2	★★★★	83	$$−

How the Hotels Compare

HOTEL	LOCATION	STARS	QUALITY	($ = $50)
Omni Orlando Resort at ChampionsGate	2	★★★★★	96	$$$
Royale Parc Suites	3	★★★★½	95	$$+
Sheraton Vistana Resort Villas	2	★★★★½	95	$$+
Animal Kingdom Villas (Kidani Village)	WDW	★★★★½	95	$$$$$$$–
Bay Lake Tower at Contemporary Resort	WDW	★★★★½	95	$$$$$$$$–
Monumental Hotel	1	★★★★½	94	$$–
The Ritz-Carlton Orlando, Grande Lakes	1	★★★★½	94	$$$$$
Westgate Vacation Villas (town center)	2	★★★★½	93	$$–
Orange Lake Resort	3	★★★★½	93	$$$+
JW Marriott Orlando Grande Lakes	1	★★★★½	93	$$$$$–
Waldorf Astoria Orlando	WDW	★★★★½	93	$$$$$–
Hard Rock Hotel	4	★★★★½	93	$$$$$
Contemporary Resort	WDW	★★★★½	93	$$$$$$–
Grand Floridian Resort & Spa	WDW	★★★★½	93	$$$$$$$$+
Westgate Lakes Resort & Spa	2	★★★★½	92	$+
DoubleTree Resort Orlando–I-Drive (resort)	1	★★★★½	92	$$–
DoubleTree Resort Orlando–I-Drive (tower)	1	★★★★½	92	$$
Marriott's Grande Vista	1	★★★★½	92	$$$
Loews Portofino Bay Hotel	4	★★★★½	92	$$$$$
Polynesian Resort	WDW	★★★★½	92	$$$$$$$+
Shades of Green	WDW	★★★★½	91	$$–
Vacation Village at Parkway	3	★★★★½	91	$$–
Animal Kingdom Villas (Jambo House)	WDW	★★★★½	91	$$$$$$$–
Holiday Inn Main Gate East	3	★★★★½	90	$+
Liki Tiki Village	3	★★★★½	90	$+
CoCo Key Water Resort–Orlando	1	★★★★½	90	$$–
Four Points by Sheraton Orlando Studio City	1	★★★★½	90	$$
Holiday Inn in the Walt Disney World Resort	WDW	★★★★½	90	$$
Peabody Orlando	1	★★★★½	90	$$
Westgate Vacation Villas (villas)	2	★★★★½	90	$$+
Marriott's Harbour Lake	2	★★★★½	90	$$$–
Rosen Plaza Hotel	1	★★★★½	90	$$$
Rosen Centre Hotel	1	★★★★½	90	$$$+
Bohemian Celebration Hotel	2	★★★★½	90	$$$$–
Hyatt Regency Grand Cypress	2	★★★★½	90	$$$$–
Gaylord Palms Hotel & Convention Center	3	★★★★½	90	$$$$
Swan	WDW	★★★★½	90	$$$$+
Dolphin	WDW	★★★★½	90	$$$$$
Loews Royal Pacific Resort at Universal Orlando	4	★★★★½	90	$$$$$

HOTEL	LOCATION	STARS	QUALITY	($ = $50)
Disney's Old Key West Resort	WDW	★★★★½	90	$$$$$$
Disney's Saratoga Springs Resort & Spa	WDW	★★★★½	90	$$$$$$
Beach Club Resort	WDW	★★★★½	90	$$$$$$$−
BoardWalk Villas	WDW	★★★★½	90	$$$$$$$−
Wilderness Lodge Villas	WDW	★★★★½	90	$$$$$$$−
Treehouse Villas at Disney's Saratoga Springs Resort & Spa	WDW	★★★★½	90	$$$$$$$$$$$
Beach Club Villas	WDW	★★★★½	90	$$$$$$$$$$$$$$
DoubleTree Universal Orlando	4	★★★★	89	$$+
Hilton Grand Vacations Club at SeaWorld International	1	★★★★	89	$$$−
Renaissance Orlando SeaWorld	1	★★★★	89	$$$$−
Animal Kingdom Lodge	WDW	★★★★	89	$$$$$−
Orlando World Center Marriott Resort	2	★★★★	89	$$$$$+
BoardWalk Inn	WDW	★★★★	89	$$$$$$$−
Yacht Club Resort	WDW	★★★★	89	$$$$$$$−
Hilton Grand Vacations Club on I-Drive	1	★★★★	88	$$+
Wyndham Bonnet Creek Resort	WDW	★★★★	88	$$$$$−
Rosen Shingle Creek	1	★★★★	88	$$$$$$−
Caribe Royale All-Suite Hotel & Convention Center	1	★★★★	88	$$$$$$$+
Hawthorn Suites Lake Buena Vista	2	★★★★	87	$+
Mystic Dunes Resort & Golf Club	3	★★★★	87	$$
Hilton in the Walt Disney World Resort	WDW	★★★★	87	$$$
Royal Plaza(tower)	WDW	★★★★	87	$$$
Wyndham Cypress Palms	3	★★★★	87	$$$
Westin Imagine Orlando	1	★★★★	87	$$$$−
DoubleTree Guest Suites	WDW	★★★★	86	$$$−
Radisson Resort Orlando-Celebration	3	★★★★	86	$$$−
Marriott Cypress Harbour Villas	1	★★★★	86	$$$$$−
Wilderness Lodge	WDW	★★★★	86	$$$$$−
Fort Wilderness Resort(cabins)	WDW	★★★★	86	$$$$$+
Marriott Imperial Palm Villas	1	★★★★	86	$$$$$$+
Celebrity Resorts Lake Buena Vista	2	★★★★	85	$+
Best Western Lake Buena Vista Resort Hotel	WDW	★★★★	85	$$+
Marriott Residence Inn Orlando SeaWorld/International Center	2	★★★★	85	$$$+
Extended Stay Deluxe Orlando Convention Center	1	★★★★	84	$$−
Star Island Resort & Club	3	★★★★	84	$$
Hyatt Place Orlando/Universal	4	★★★★	84	$$+

How the Hotels Compare (continued)

HOTEL	LOCATION	STARS	QUALITY	($ = $50)
Port Orleans Resort (French Quarter)	WDW	★★★★	84	$$$
Orlando Vista Hotel	2	★★★★	83	$+
Extended Stay Deluxe Orlando Lake Buena Vista	2	★★★★	83	$$–
Sheraton Safari Hotel & Suites Lake Buena Vista	2	★★★★	83	$$–
Wyndham Orlando Resort	1	★★★★	83	$$$–
Coronado Springs Resort	WDW	★★★★	83	$$$
Port Orleans Resort (Riverside)	WDW	★★★★	83	$$$
Polynesian Isles Resort (Phase 1)	3	★★★★	83	$$$$–
Buena Vista Suites	1	★★★★	83	$$$$$+
Country Inn & Suites Orlando Maingate at Calypso	3	★★★½	82	$+
Courtyard Orlando LBV in Marriott Village	2	★★★½	82	$$–
Hawthorn Suites Universal	1	★★★½	82	$$–
Parkway International Resort	3	★★★½	82	$$–
Courtyard Orlando Lake Buena Vista at Vista Centre	2	★★★½	82	$$
DoubleTree Castle Hotel	1	★★★½	82	$$+
Hilton Garden Inn Orlando at SeaWorld	1	★★★½	82	$$+
Hilton Garden Inn Orlando I-Drive North	1	★★★½	82	$$+
Radisson Hotel Orlando Lake Buena Vista	2	★★★½	82	$$+
Nickelodeon Suites Resort Orlando	1	★★★½	82	$$$+
Westgate Vacation Villas (towers)	2	★★★½	81	$+
Embassy Suites Orlando–Lake Buena Vista	2	★★★½	81	$$+
Homewood Suites by Hilton I-Drive	1	★★★½	81	$$+
Hawthorn Suites Orlando Convention Center	1	★★★½	80	$+
Holiday Inn Express Lake Buena Vista	2	★★★½	80	$$–
SpringHill Suites Orlando Convention Center	1	★★★½	80	$$–
Celebrity Resorts Orlando	3	★★★½	80	$$+
Embassy Suites Orlando I-Drive/ Jamaican Court	1	★★★½	80	$$+
Residence Inn Orlando Convention Center	1	★★★½	80	$$+
Saratoga Resort Villas	3	★★★½	80	$$+
Buena Vista Palace Hotel & Spa	WDW	★★★½	80	$$$–
Caribbean Beach Resort	WDW	★★★½	80	$$$
Holiday Inn Resort Lake Buena Vista	2	★★★½	79	$+
Country Inn & Suites Orlando Lake Buena Vista (rooms)	2	★★★½	78	$+

HOTEL	LOCATION	STARS	QUALITY	($ = $50)
Country Inn & Suites Orlando Lake Buena Vista (suites)	2	★★★½	78	$+
Radisson Resort Worldgate	3	★★★½	77	$$−
Hampton Inn Orlando/Lake Buena Vista	2	★★★½	76	$+
Comfort Suites Maingate	3	★★★½	76	$$−
Grand Lake Resort	3	★★★½	76	$$+
Palms Hotel & Villas	3	★★★½	76	$$+
Courtyard Orlando I-Drive	1	★★★½	76	$$$$−
Extended Stay America Universal	4	★★★½	75	$
Extended Stay Deluxe Orlando Universal	4	★★★½	75	$+
Holiday Inn Main Gate to Universal Orlando	4	★★★½	75	$$−
Rosen Inn at Pointe Orlando	1	★★★½	75	$$−
Staybridge Suites Orlando	1	★★★½	75	$$+
Fairfield Inn & Suites LBV in Marriott Village	2	★★★½	75	$$$−
Residence Inn Orlando Lake Buena Vista	2	★★★½	75	$$$
Embassy Suites Orlando I-Drive	1	★★★½	75	$$$$−
Residence Inn Orlando I-Drive	1	★★★½	75	$$$$
Wyndham Lake Buena Vista Resort	WDW	★★★½	75	$$−
Quality Suites Orlando	2	★★★	74	$+
Galleria Palms Kissimmee Hotel	3	★★★	74	$+
Hampton Inn I-Drive/Convention Center	1	★★★	74	$$−
Holiday Inn Hotel & Suites Orlando Convention Center	1	★★★	74	$$−
Quality Suites Orlando Lake Buena Vista	2	★★★	74	$$
La Quinta Inn Orlando I-Drive	1	★★★	73	$+
All-Star Resorts	WDW	★★★	73	$$−
Fairfield Inn & Suites Near Universal Orlando	4	★★★	73	$$−
International Palms Resort & Conference Center	1	★★★	73	$$
Extended Stay America Convention Center	1	★★★	72	$+
Ramada Inn Orlando I-Drive Lakefront	1	★★★	72	$$$−
Staybridge Suites Lake Buena Vista	2	★★★	72	$$$−
Ramada Gateway Kissimmee (tower)	3	★★★	71	$−
Seralago Hotel & Suites Main Gate East	3	★★★	71	$−
Pop Century Resort	WDW	★★★	71	$$−
SpringHill Suites LBV in Marriott Village	2	★★★	71	$$+
Royal Plaza (garden)	WDW	★★★	71	$$$−
Super 8 Kissimmee/Orlando Area	3	★★★	70	$−
Best Western Orlando Gateway Hotel	1	★★★	70	$+

How the Hotels Compare (continued)

HOTEL	LOCATION	STARS	QUALITY	($ = $50)
Holiday Inn Express at Summer Bay Resort	3	★★★	70	$+
Monumental MovieLand Hotel	1	★★★	68	$+
Westgate Palace	1	★★★	68	$$+
Best Western Lakeside	3	★★★	67	$
Enclave Suites	1	★★★	67	$+
Hampton Inn Universal	4	★★★	67	$$−
Champions World Resort	3	★★★	66	$−
Comfort Inn Universal Studios Area	1	★★★	66	$
Comfort Suites Universal Studios Area	4	★★★	66	$$−
Destiny Palms Hotel Maingate West	3	★★★	65	$
Orlando Palm Hotel	3	★★★	65	$$−
Ramada Inn Convention Center I-Drive	1	★★★	65	$$−
Ramada Gateway Kissimmee (garden)	3	★★½	64	$−
Inn Nova Kissimmee	3	★★½	64	$
Clarion Inn Lake Buena Vista	2	★★½	64	$+
Clarion Inn & Suites at International Drive	1	★★½	64	$$−
Hampton Inn Kirkman	1	★★½	64	$$−
Silver Lake Resort	3	★★½	64	$$−
Orlando Metropolitan Express	1	★★½	63	$
Baymont Inn & Suites	1	★★½	63	$+
Best Western Universal Inn	1	★★½	63	$+
Country Inn & Suites Orlando Universal	1	★★½	63	$+
La Quinta Inn Orlando–Universal Studios	4	★★½	63	$+
The Inn at Summer Bay	3	★★½	63	$$−
Days Inn Clermont South	3	★★½	62	$−
Econo Lodge Inn & Suites I-Drive	1	★★½	62	$
Days Inn Orlando/I-Drive	1	★★½	61	$−
Motel 6 Orlando–I-Drive	1	★★½	61	$−
Imperial Swan Hotel & Suites	1	★★½	61	$
Celebration Suites	3	★★½	61	$+
Days Inn Orlando/Universal Maingate	4	★★½	60	$−
Super 8 Main Gate	3	★★½	60	$−
Days Inn Orlando/Convention Center	1	★★½	60	$
Ramada Maingate West Kissimmee	3	★★½	60	$
Clarion Hotel Maingate	3	★★½	60	$+
Comfort Inn I-Drive	1	★★½	60	$+
Lexington Suites Orlando	1	★★½	60	$+
Royal Celebration Inn	3	★★½	60	$+
Continental Plaza Hotel Kissimmee	3	★★½	60	$$−

HOTEL	LOCATION	STARS	QUALITY	($ = $50)
Howard Johnson Enchanted Land Hotel	3	★★½	59	$–
Howard Johnson Inn Maingate East	3	★★½	59	$–
Rodeway Inn Maingate	3	★★½	59	$–
Westgate Inn & Suites	3	★★½	59	$–
Howard Johnson Inn Orlando I-Drive	1	★★½	59	$
Blue Palm Hotel	1	★★½	58	$–
Super 8 Orlando/Kissimmee/Lakeside	3	★★½	58	$–
Travelodge Suites East Gate Orange	3	★★½	58	$–
Extended Stay Deluxe Pointe Orlando	1	★★½	58	$+
Red Roof Inn Orlando Convention Center	1	★★½	58	$+
HomeSuiteHome Eastgate	3	★★½	57	$$$
Knights Inn Maingate Kissimmee	3	★★	55	$–
Masters Inn Kissimmee	3	★★	55	$–
Quality Inn & Suites	3	★★	55	$+
Quality Inn & Suites Eastgate	3	★★	55	$+
Golden Link Resort Motel	3	★★	54	$–
Orlando Sleep Inn Hotel	1	★★	54	$+
Sun Inn & Suites	3	★★	53	$–
Motel 6 Main Gate West	3	★★	52	$–
Baymont Inn & Suites Celebration	3	★★	51	$
Rosen Inn at Universal	1	★★	51	$
Central Motel	3	★★	51	$–
Key Motel	3	★★	51	$–
Fun Spots Hotel at Fountain Park	3	★★	50	$–
Howard Johnson Express Inn & Suites	3	★★	50	$–
Magic Castle Inn & Suites	3	★★	50	$–
La Quinta Inn Orlando I-Drive North	1	★★	50	$+
Quality Inn International Hotel	1	★★	50	$+
Best Western I-Drive	1	★★	50	$$
Monte Carlo Motel	3	★★	48	$–
HomeSuiteHome Kissimmee Maingate	3	★★	48	$$$
Motel 6 Main Gate East	3	★★	47	$–
Orlando Continental Plaza Hotel	1	★★	47	$–
Red Roof Inn Kissimmee	3	★★	47	$–
America's Best Value Inn Maingate	3	★½	46	$
InTown Suites Orlando Central	1	★½	40	$$$$+

Hotels Information Chart

All-Star Resorts ★★★
1701–1901 W. Buena Vista Dr.
Orlando, FL 32830
☎ 407-934-7639
disneyworld.com

LOCATION	WDW
ROOM RATING	73
COST ($ = $50)	$$−

**America's Best Inn
Main Gate East** ★★
5150 W. US 192*
Kissimmee, FL 34746
☎ 407-396-1111
FAX 407-396-1607
americasbestinnkissimmee.com

LOCATION	US 192
ROOM RATING	50
COST ($ = $50)	$−

**America's Best Value Inn
Maingate** ★½
7514 W. US 192*
Kissimmee, FL 34747
☎ 407-396-2000
FAX 407-396-2832
abvimaingate.com

LOCATION	US 192
ROOM RATING	46
COST ($ = $50)	$

**Bay Lake Tower at
Contemporary Resort**
★★★★½
4600 N. World Dr.
Lake Buena Vista, FL 32830
☎ 407-824-1000
FAX 407-824-3539
disneyworld.com

LOCATION	WDW
ROOM RATING	95
COST ($ = $50)	$$$$$$$$−

**Baymont Inn &
Suites** ★★½
7531 Canada Ave.
Orlando, FL 32819
☎ 407-226-9887
FAX 407-226-9877
baymontinns.com

LOCATION	I-Drive
ROOM RATING	63
COST ($ = $50)	$+

**Baymont Inn & Suites
Celebration** ★★
7601 Black Lake Rd.
Kissimmee, FL 34747
☎ 407-396-1100
FAX 407-396-0689
baymontinns.com

LOCATION	US 192
ROOM RATING	51
COST ($ = $50)	$

**Best Western Lake Buena
Vista Resort Hotel** ★★★★
2000 Hotel Plaza Blvd.
Lake Buena Vista, FL 32830
☎ 407-828-2424
FAX 407-827-6390
lakebuenavistaresorthotel.com

LOCATION	WDW
ROOM RATING	85
COST ($ = $50)	$$+

**Best Western Lake-
side** ★★★
7769 W. US 192*
Kissimmee, FL 34747
☎ 407-396-2222
FAX 407-396-7087
bestwesternflorida.com

LOCATION	US 192
ROOM RATING	67
COST ($ = $50)	$

**Best Western Orlando
Gateway Hotel** ★★★
7299 Universal Dr.
Orlando, FL 32819
☎ 407-351-5009
FAX 407-352-7277
bworlando.com

LOCATION	I-Drive
ROOM RATING	70
COST ($ = $50)	$+

BoardWalk Villas ★★★★½
2101 Epcot Resorts Blvd.
Lake Buena Vista, FL 32830
☎ 407-939-5100
FAX 407-939-5150
disneyworld.com

LOCATION	WDW
ROOM RATING	90
COST ($ = $50)	$$$$$$$−

**Bohemian Celebration
Hotel** ★★★★½
700 Bloom St.
Celebration, FL 34747
☎ 407-566-6000
FAX 407-566-1844
celebrationhotel.com

LOCATION	I-4 Corridor
ROOM RATING	90
COST ($ = $50)	$$$$−

**Buena Vista Palace
Hotel & Spa** ★★★½
1900 E. Buena Vista Dr.
Lake Buena Vista, FL 32830
☎ 407-827-2727
FAX 407-827-6034
buenavistapalace.com

LOCATION	WDW
ROOM RATING	80
COST ($ = $50)	$$$−

**Celebration Suites at
Old Town** ★★½
5820 W. US 192*
Kissimmee, FL 34746
☎ 407-396-7900
FAX 407-396-1789
suitesatoldtown.com

LOCATION	US 192
ROOM RATING	61
COST ($ = $50)	$+

**Celebrity Resorts
Lake Buena Vista** ★★★★
8451 Palm Pkwy.
Lake Buena Vista, FL 32836
☎ 407-238-1700
FAX 407-238-0255
celebrityresorts.com

LOCATION	I-4 Corridor
ROOM RATING	85
COST ($ = $50)	$+

**Celebrity Resorts
Orlando** ★★★½
2800 N. Poinciana Blvd.
Kissimmee, FL 34746
☎ 407-997-5000
FAX 407-997-5998
celebrityresorts.com

LOCATION	US 192
ROOM RATING	80
COST ($ = $50)	$$+

Animal Kingdom Lodge ★★★★
2901 Osceola Pkwy.
Lake Buena Vista, FL 32830
☎ 407-938-3000
FAX 407-938-4799
disneyworld.com

LOCATION	WDW
ROOM RATING	89
COST ($ = $50)	$$$$$–

Animal Kingdom Villas
(Jambo House) ★★★★½
2901 Osceola Pkwy.
Lake Buena Vista, FL 32830
☎ 407-938-3000
FAX 407-938-4799
disneyworld.com

LOCATION	WDW
ROOM RATING	91
COST ($ = $50)	$$$$$$–

Animal Kingdom Villas
(Kidani Village) ★★★★½
2901 Osceola Pkwy.
Lake Buena Vista, FL 32830
☎ 407-938-3000
FAX 407-938-4799
disneyworld.com

LOCATION	WDW
ROOM RATING	95
COST ($ = $50)	$$$$$$$–

Beach Club Resort ★★★★½
1800 Epcot Resorts Blvd.
Lake Buena Vista, FL 32830
☎ 407-934-8000
FAX 407-934-3850
disneyworld.com

LOCATION	WDW
ROOM RATING	90
COST ($ = $50)	$$$$$$–

Beach Club Villas ★★★★½
1900 Epcot Resorts Blvd.
Lake Buena Vista, FL 32830
☎ 407-934-2175
FAX 407-934-3850
disneyworld.com

LOCATION	WDW
ROOM RATING	90
COST ($ = $50)	$$$$$$$$$$$$

Best Western I-Drive ★★
8222 Jamaican Ct.
Orlando, FL 32819
☎ 407-345-1172
FAX 407-352-2801
bestwestern.com

LOCATION	I-Drive
ROOM RATING	50
COST ($ = $50)	$$

Best Western Universal Inn ★★½
5618 Vineland Rd.
Orlando, FL 32819
☎ 407-226-9119
FAX 407-370-2448
bestwestern.com

LOCATION	I-Drive
ROOM RATING	63
COST ($ = $50)	$+

Blue Palm Hotel ★★½
5859 American Way
Orlando, FL 32819
☎ 407-345-8880
FAX 407-363-9366
bluepalmhotel.com

LOCATION	I-Drive
ROOM RATING	58
COST ($ = $50)	$–

BoardWalk Inn ★★★★
2101 Epcot Resorts Blvd.
Lake Buena Vista, FL 32830
☎ 407-939-5100
FAX 407-939-5150
disneyworld.com

LOCATION	WDW
ROOM RATING	89
COST ($ = $50)	$$$$$$–

Buena Vista Suites ★★★★
8203 World Center Dr.
Orlando, FL 32821
☎ 407-239-8588
FAX 407-239-1401
thecaribeorlando.com

LOCATION	I-Drive
ROOM RATING	83
COST ($ = $50)	$$$$$+

Caribbean Beach Resort ★★★½
900 Cayman Way
Lake Buena Vista, FL 32830
☎ 407-934-3400
FAX 407-934-3288
disneyworld.com

LOCATION	WDW
ROOM RATING	80
COST ($ = $50)	$$$

Caribe Royale All-Suite Hotel & Convention Center ★★★★
8101 World Center Dr.
Orlando, FL 32821
☎ 407-238-8000
FAX 407-238-8050
thecaribeorlando.com

LOCATION	I-Drive
ROOM RATING	88
COST ($ = $50)	$$$$$$$+

Central Motel ★★
4698 W. US 192*
Kissimmee, FL 34746
☎ 407-396-2333
FAX 407-997-7550

LOCATION	US 192
ROOM RATING	51
COST ($ = $50)	$–

Champions World Resort ★★★
8660 W. US 192*
Kissimmee, FL 34747
☎ 407-396-4500
FAX 407-997-4503
championsworldresort.com

LOCATION	US 192
ROOM RATING	66
COST ($ = $50)	$–

Clarion Hotel Maingate ★★½
7675 W. US 192*
Kissimmee, FL 34747
☎ 407-396-4000
FAX 407-396-0714
clarionhotelmaingate.com

LOCATION	US 192
ROOM RATING	60
COST ($ = $50)	$+

Hotels Information Chart (continued)

Clarion Inn & Suites at International Drive ★★½
9956 Hawaiian Ct.
Orlando, FL 32819
☎ 407-351-5100
FAX 407-352-7188
clarionhotel.com

LOCATION	I-Drive
ROOM RATING	64
COST ($ = $50)	$$–

Clarion Inn Lake Buena Vista ★★½
8442 Palm Pkwy.
Lake Buena Vista, FL 32836
☎ 407-239-7300
FAX 407-996-1475
comfortinn.com

LOCATION	I-4 Corridor
ROOM RATING	64
COST ($ = $50)	$+

CoCo Key Water Resort–Orlando ★★★★½
7400 International Dr.
Orlando, FL 32819
☎ 877-875-4681
cocokeywaterresort.com

LOCATION	I-Drive
ROOM RATING	90
COST ($ = $50)	$$–

Comfort Suites Universal Studios Area ★★★
5617 Major Blvd.
Orlando, FL 32819
☎ 407-363-1967
FAX 407-363-6873
comfortsuites.com

LOCATION	Universal
ROOM RATING	66
COST ($ = $50)	$$–

Contemporary Resort ★★★★½
4600 N. World Dr.
Lake Buena Vista, FL 32830
☎ 407-824-1000
FAX 407-824-3539
disneyworld.com

LOCATION	WDW
ROOM RATING	93
COST ($ = $50)	$$$$$$–

Continental Plaza Hotel Kissimmee ★★½
7785 W. US 192*
Kissimmee, FL 34747
☎ 407-396-1828
FAX 407-396-1305
continentalplazahotels.com

LOCATION	US 192
ROOM RATING	60
COST ($ = $50)	$$–

Country Inn & Suites Orlando Maingate at Calypso ★★★½
5001 Calypso Cay Way
Kissimmee, FL 34746
☎ 407-997-1400
FAX 407-997-1401
countryinns.com

LOCATION	US 192
ROOM RATING	82
COST ($ = $50)	$+

Country Inn & Suites Orlando Universal ★★½
7701 Universal Blvd.
Orlando, FL 32819
☎ 407-313-4200
FAX 407-313-4201
countryinns.com

LOCATION	I-Drive
ROOM RATING	63
COST ($ = $50)	$+

Courtyard Orlando I-Drive ★★★½
8600 Austrian Ct.
Orlando, FL 32819
☎ 407-351-2244
FAX 407-351-3306
tinyurl.com/courtyardidrive

LOCATION	I-Drive
ROOM RATING	76
COST ($ = $50)	$$$$–

Days Inn Orlando/Convention Center ★★½
9990 International Dr.
Orlando, FL 32819
☎ 407-352-8700
FAX 407-363-3965
daysinnorlandohotel.com

LOCATION	I-Drive
ROOM RATING	60
COST ($ = $50)	$

Days Inn Orlando/I-Drive ★★½
5858 International Dr.
Orlando, FL 32819
☎ 407-351-4410
FAX 407-351-2481
daysinn.com

LOCATION	I-Drive
ROOM RATING	61
COST ($ = $50)	$–

Days Inn Orlando/Universal Maingate ★★½
5827 Caravan Ct.
Orlando, FL 32819
☎ 407-351-3800
FAX 407-363-2793
daysinn.com

LOCATION	Universal
ROOM RATING	60
COST ($ = $50)	$–

Dolphin ★★★★½
1500 Epcot Resorts Blvd.
Lake Buena Vista, FL 32830
☎ 407-934-4000
FAX 407-934-4009
swandolphin.com

LOCATION	WDW
ROOM RATING	90
COST ($ = $50)	$$$$$

DoubleTree Castle Hotel ★★★½
8629 International Dr.
Orlando, FL 32819
☎ 407-345-1511
FAX 407-248-8181
doubletreecastle.com

LOCATION	I-Drive
ROOM RATING	82
COST ($ = $50)	$$+

DoubleTree Guest Suites ★★★★
2305 Hotel Plaza Blvd.
Lake Buena Vista, FL 32830
☎ 407-934-1000
FAX 407-934-1015
doubletreeguestsuites.com

LOCATION	WDW
ROOM RATING	86
COST ($ = $50)	$$$–

Comfort Inn I-Drive ★★½
8134 International Dr.
Orlando, FL 32819
☎ 407-313-4000
FAX 407-313-4001
comfortinn.com

LOCATION	I-Drive
ROOM RATING	60
COST ($ = $50)	$+

Comfort Inn Universal Studios Area ★★★
6101 Sand Lake Rd.
Orlando, FL 32919
☎ 407-363-7886
FAX 407-345-0670
comfortinn.com

LOCATION	I-Drive
ROOM RATING	66
COST ($ = $50)	$

Comfort Suites Maingate ★★★½
7888 W. US 192*
Kissimmee, FL 34747
☎ 407-390-9888
FAX 407-390-0981
comfortsuiteskissimmee.com

LOCATION	US 192
ROOM RATING	76
COST ($ = $50)	$$−

Coronado Springs Resort ★★★★
1000 W. Buena Vista Dr.
Orlando, FL 32830
☎ 407-939-1000
FAX 407-939-1001
disneyworld.com

LOCATION	WDW
ROOM RATING	83
COST ($ = $50)	$$$

Country Inn & Suites Orlando Lake Buena Vista (rooms) ★★★½
12191 S. Apopka–Vineland Rd.
Lake Buena Vista, FL 32836
☎ 407-239-1115
FAX 407-239-8882
countryinns.com

LOCATION	I-4 Corridor
ROOM RATING	78
COST ($ = $50)	$+

Country Inn & Suites Orlando Lake Buena Vista (suites) ★★★½
12191 S. Apopka–Vineland Rd.
Lake Buena Vista, FL 32836
☎ 407-239-1115
FAX 407-239-8882
countryinns.com

LOCATION	I-4 Corridor
ROOM RATING	78
COST ($ = $50)	$+

Courtyard Orlando Lake Buena Vista at Vista Centre ★★★½
8501 Palm Pkwy.
Lake Buena Vista, FL 32836
☎ 407-239-6900
FAX 407-239-1287
tinyurl.com/courtyardlbv

LOCATION	I-4 Corridor
ROOM RATING	82
COST ($ = $50)	$$

Courtyard Orlando LBV in Marriott Village ★★★½
8623 Vineland Ave.
Orlando, FL 32821
☎ 407-938-9001
FAX 407-938-9002
marriottvillage.com

LOCATION	I-4 Corridor
ROOM RATING	82
COST ($ = $50)	$$−

Days Inn Clermont South ★★½
9240 W. US 192*
Kissimmee, FL 34711
☎ 863-424-6099
FAX 863-424-5779
daysinn.com

LOCATION	US 192
ROOM RATING	62
COST ($ = $50)	$−

Destiny Palms Hotel Maingate West ★★★
8536 W. US 192*
Kissimmee, FL 34747
☎ 407-396-1600
FAX 407-396-1971
destinypalmshotel.com

LOCATION	US 192
ROOM RATING	65
COST ($ = $50)	$

Disney's Old Key West Resort ★★★★½
1510 N. Cove Rd.
Lake Buena Vista, FL 32830
☎ 407-827-7700
FAX 407-827-7710
disneyworld.com

LOCATION	WDW
ROOM RATING	90
COST ($ = $50)	$$$$$

Disney's Saratoga Springs Resort & Spa ★★★★½
1960 Broadway
Lake Buena Vista, FL 32830
☎ 407-827-1100
FAX 407-827-4444
disneyworld.com

LOCATION	WDW
ROOM RATING	90
COST ($ = $50)	$$$$$

DoubleTree Resort Orlando–I-Drive (resort) ★★★★½
10100 International Dr.
Orlando, FL 32821
☎ 407-352-1100
FAX 407-354-4700
doubletreeorlandoidrive.com

LOCATION	I-Drive
ROOM RATING	92
COST ($ = $50)	$$−

DoubleTree Resort Orlando–I-Drive (tower) ★★★★½
10100 International Dr.
Orlando, FL 32821
☎ 407-352-1100
FAX 407-354-4700
doubletreeorlandoidrive.com

LOCATION	I-Drive
ROOM RATING	92
COST ($ = $50)	$$

DoubleTree Universal Orlando ★★★★
5780 Major Blvd.
Orlando, FL 32819
☎ 407-351-1000
FAX 407-363-0106
doubletreeorlando.com

LOCATION	Universal
ROOM RATING	89
COST ($ = $50)	$$+

Hotels Information Chart (continued)

Econo Lodge Inn & Suites
I-Drive ★★½
8738 International Dr.
Orlando, FL 32819
☎ 407-345-8195
FAX 407-351-9766
econolodge.com

LOCATION	I-Drive
ROOM RATING	62
COST ($ = $50)	$

Embassy Suites Orlando
I-Drive ★★★½
8978 International Dr.
Orlando, FL 32819
☎ 407-352-1400
FAX 407-363-1120
embassysuitesorlando.com

LOCATION	I-Drive
ROOM RATING	75
COST ($ = $50)	$$$$–

Embassy Suites Orlando
I-Drive/Jamaican
Court ★★★½
8250 Jamaican Ct.
Orlando, FL 32819
☎ 407-345-8250
FAX 407-352-1463
orlandoembassysuites.com

LOCATION	I-Drive
ROOM RATING	80
COST ($ = $50)	$$+

Extended Stay America
Universal ★★★½
5620 Major Blvd.
Orlando, FL 32819
☎ 407-351-1788
FAX 407-351-7899
extendedstayamerica.com

LOCATION	Universal
ROOM RATING	75
COST ($ = $50)	$

Extended Stay Deluxe
Orlando Convention Center
★★★★
6443 Westwood Blvd.
Orlando, FL 32821
☎ 407-351-1982
FAX 407-351-1719
extendedstaydeluxe.com

LOCATION	I-Drive
ROOM RATING	84
COST ($ = $50)	$$–

Extended Stay Deluxe
Pointe Orlando ★★½
8750 Universal Blvd.
Orlando, FL 32819
☎ 407-903-1500
FAX 407-903-1555
extendedstaydeluxe.com

LOCATION	I-Drive
ROOM RATING	58
COST ($ = $50)	$+

Fairfield Inn & Suites LBV in
Marriott Village ★★★½
8615 Vineland Ave.
Orlando, FL 32821
☎ 407-938-9001
FAX 407-938-9002
marriottvillage.com

LOCATION	I-4 Corridor
ROOM RATING	75
COST ($ = $50)	$$$–

Fort Wilderness Resort
(cabins) ★★★★
4510 N. Fort Wilderness Trail
Lake Buena Vista, FL 32830
☎ 407-824-2900
FAX 407-824-3508
disneyworld.com

LOCATION	WDW
ROOM RATING	86
COST ($ = $50)	$$$$$+

Four Points by Sheraton
Orlando Studio City
★★★★½
5905 International Dr.
Orlando, FL 32819
☎ 407-351-2100
FAX 407-345-5249
sheraton.com

LOCATION	I-Drive
ROOM RATING	90
COST ($ = $50)	$$

Grand Floridian
Resort & Spa ★★★★½
4401 Floridian Way
Lake Buena Vista, FL 32830
☎ 407-824-3000
FAX 407-824-3186
disneyworld.com

LOCATION	WDW
ROOM RATING	93
COST ($ = $50)	$$$$$$$$+

Grand Lake Resort ★★★½
7770 W. US 192*
Kissimmee, FL 34747
☎ 407-396-3000
FAX 407-396-1822
dailymanagementresorts.com

LOCATION	US 192
ROOM RATING	76
COST ($ = $50)	$$+

Hampton Inn I-Drive/
Convention Center
★★★
8900 Universal Blvd.
Orlando, FL 32819
☎ 407-354-4447
FAX 407-354-3031
hamptoninn.com

LOCATION	I-Drive
ROOM RATING	74
COST ($ = $50)	$$–

Hard Rock Hotel ★★★★½
5800 Universal Blvd.
Orlando, FL 32819
☎ 407-503-2000
FAX 407-503-2010
hardrockhotelorlando.com

LOCATION	Universal
ROOM RATING	93
COST ($ = $50)	$$$$$

Hawthorn Suites
Lake Buena Vista ★★★★
8303 Palm Pkwy.
Orlando, FL 32836
☎ 407-597-5000
FAX 407-597-6000
hawthorn.com

LOCATION	I-4 Corridor
ROOM RATING	87
COST ($ = $50)	$+

Hawthorn Suites Orlando
Convention Center ★★★½
6435 Westwood Blvd.
Orlando, FL 32821
☎ 407-351-6600
FAX 407-351-1977
hawthornsuitesorlando.com

LOCATION	I-Drive
ROOM RATING	80
COST ($ = $50)	$+

**Embassy Suites Orlando–
Lake Buena Vista** ★★★½
8100 Lake Ave.
Orlando, FL 32836
☎ 407-239-1144
FAX 407-239-1718
embassysuiteslbv.com

LOCATION	I-4 Corridor
ROOM RATING	81
COST ($ = $50)	$$+

Enclave Suites ★★★
6165 Carrier Dr.
Orlando, FL 32819
☎ 407-351-1155
FAX 407-351-2001
enclavesuites.com

LOCATION	I-Drive
ROOM RATING	67
COST ($ = $50)	$+

**Extended Stay America
Orlando Convention
Center** ★★★
6451 Westwood Blvd.
Orlando, FL 32821
☎ 407-352-3454
FAX 407-352-1708
extendedstayamerica.com

LOCATION	I-Drive
ROOM RATING	72
COST ($ = $50)	$+

**Extended Stay Deluxe
Orlando Lake Buena
Vista** ★★★★
8100 Palm Pkwy.
Orlando 32836
☎ 407-239-4300
FAX 407-239-4446
extendedstaydeluxe.com

LOCATION	I-4 Corridor
ROOM RATING	83
COST ($ = $50)	$$–

**Extended Stay Deluxe
Orlando Universal** ★★★½
5610 Vineland Rd.
Orlando, FL 32819
☎ 407-370-4428
FAX 407-370-9456
extendedstaydeluxe.com

LOCATION	Universal
ROOM RATING	75
COST ($ = $50)	$+

**Fairfield Inn & Suites near
Universal Orlando** ★★★
5614 Vineland Rd.
Orlando, FL 32819
☎ 407-581-5600
FAX 407-581-5601
tinyurl.com/fairfielduniversal

LOCATION	Universal
ROOM RATING	73
COST ($ = $50)	$$–

**Galleria Palms Kissimmee
Hotel** ★★★
3000 Maingate La.
Kissimmee, FL 34747
☎ 407-396-6300
FAX 407-396-8989
galleriakissimmeehotel.com

LOCATION	US 192
ROOM RATING	74
COST ($ = $50)	$+

**Gaylord Palms Hotel &
Convention Center**
★★★★½
6000 W. Osceola Pkwy.
Kissimmee, FL 34746
☎ 407-586-2000
FAX 407-586-1999
gaylordpalms.com

LOCATION	US 192
ROOM RATING	90
COST ($ = $50)	$$$$

Golden Link Resort Motel
★★
4914 W. US 192*
Kissimmee, FL 34746
☎ 407-396-0555
FAX 407-396-6531
goldenlinkmotel.com

LOCATION	US 192
ROOM RATING	54
COST ($ = $50)	$–

**Hampton Inn Kirk-
man** ★★½
7110 S. Kirkman Rd.
Orlando, FL 32819
☎ 407-345-1112
FAX 407-352-6591
hamptoninn.com

LOCATION	I-Drive
ROOM RATING	64
COST ($ = $50)	$$–

**Hampton Inn Orlando/
Lake Buena Vista** ★★★½
8150 Palm Pkwy.
Orlando, FL 32836
☎ 407-465-8150
FAX 407-465-0150
hamptoninn.com

LOCATION	I-4 Corridor
ROOM RATING	76
COST ($ = $50)	$+

Hampton Inn Universal
★★★
5621 Windhover Dr.
Orlando, FL 32819
☎ 407-351-6716
FAX 407-363-1711
hamptoninn.com

LOCATION	Universal
ROOM RATING	67
COST ($ = $50)	$$–

Hawthorn Suites Universal
★★★½
7601 Canada Ave.
Orlando, FL 32819
☎ 407-581-2151
FAX 407-581-2152
hawthornsuitesuniversal.com

LOCATION	I-Drive
ROOM RATING	82
COST ($ = $50)	$$–

**Hilton Garden Inn Orlando
at SeaWorld** ★★★½
6850 Westwood Blvd.
Orlando, FL 32821
☎ 407-354-1500
FAX 407-354-1528
tinyurl.com/hgiseaworld

LOCATION	I-Drive
ROOM RATING	82
COST ($ = $50)	$$+

**Hilton Garden Inn Orlando
I-Drive North** ★★★½
5877 American Way
Orlando, FL 32819
☎ 407-363-9332
FAX 407-363-9335
hiltongardenorlando.com

LOCATION	I-Drive
ROOM RATING	82
COST ($ = $50)	$$+

Hotels Information Chart (continued)

Hilton Grand Vacations Club at SeaWorld International ★★★★
6924 Grand Vacations Way
Orlando, FL 32821
☎ 407-239-0100
FAX 407-239-0200
hiltongrandvacations.com

LOCATION	I-Drive
ROOM RATING	89
COST ($ = $50)	$$$–

Hilton Grand Vacations Club on I-Drive ★★★★
8122 Arrezzo Way
Orlando, FL 32821
☎ 407-465-2600
FAX 407-465-2612
hiltongrandvacations.com

LOCATION	I-Drive
ROOM RATING	88
COST ($ = $50)	$$+

Hilton in the Walt Disney World Resort ★★★★
1751 Hotel Plaza Blvd.
Lake Buena Vista, FL 32830
☎ 407-827-4000
FAX 407-827-3890
hilton-wdwv.com

LOCATION	WDW
ROOM RATING	87
COST ($ = $50)	$$$

Holiday Inn in the Walt Disney World Resort ★★★★½
1805 Hotel Plaza Blvd.
Lake Buena Vista, FL 32830
☎ 407-828-8888
FAX 407-827-4263
hiorlando.com

LOCATION	WDW
ROOM RATING	90
COST ($ = $50)	$$

Holiday Inn Main Gate East ★★★★½
5711 W. US 192*
Kissimmee, FL 34746
☎ 407-396-4222
FAX 407-396-0570
holidayinn.com

LOCATION	US 192
ROOM RATING	90
COST ($ = $50)	$+

Holiday Inn Main Gate to Universal Orlando ★★★½
5905 Kirkman Rd.
Orlando, FL 32819
☎ 407-351-3333
FAX 407-351-3577
holidayinn.com

LOCATION	Universal
ROOM RATING	75
COST ($ = $50)	$$–

Homewood Suites by Hilton I-Drive ★★★½
8745 International Dr.
Orlando, FL 32819
☎ 407-248-2232
FAX 407-248-6552
homewoodsuitesorlando.com

LOCATION	I-Drive
ROOM RATING	81
COST ($ = $50)	$$+

Howard Johnson Enchanted Land Hotel ★★½
4985 W. US 192*
Kissimmee, FL 34746
☎ 407-396-4343
FAX 407-396-8998
howard-johnson-enchanted
.h-rez.com

LOCATION	US 192
ROOM RATING	59
COST ($ = $50)	$–

Howard Johnson Express Inn & Suites ★★
4836 W. US 192*
Kissimmee, FL 34746
☎ 407-396-4762
FAX 407-396-4866
hojo.com

LOCATION	US 192
ROOM RATING	50
COST ($ = $50)	$–

Hyatt Regency Grand Cypress ★★★★½
1 Grand Cypress Blvd.
Orlando, FL 32836
☎ 407-239-1234
FAX 407-239-3800
grandcypress.hyatt.com

LOCATION	I-4 Corridor
ROOM RATING	90
COST ($ = $50)	$$$$–

Imperial Swan Hotel & Suites ★★½
7050 S. Kirkman Rd.
Orlando, FL 32819
☎ 407-351-2000
FAX 407-363-1835
imperialswanhotel.com

LOCATION	I-Drive
ROOM RATING	61
COST ($ = $50)	$

The Inn at Summer Bay ★★½
9400 W. US 192*
Clermont, FL 34714
☎ 863-420-8282
FAX 352-241-2268
summerbayresort.com

LOCATION	US 192
ROOM RATING	63
COST ($ = $50)	$$–

JW Marriott Orlando Grande Lakes ★★★★½
4040 Central Florida Pkwy.
Orlando, FL 32837
☎ 407-206-2300
FAX 407-206-2301
jw-marriott.grandelakes.com

LOCATION	I-Drive
ROOM RATING	93
COST ($ = $50)	$$$$$–

Key Motel ★★
4810 W. US 192*
Kissimmee, FL 34746
☎ 407-396-6200
FAX 407-396-6987

LOCATION	US 192
ROOM RATING	51
COST ($ = $50)	$–

Knights Inn Maingate Kissimmee ★★
7475 W. US 192*
Kissimmee, FL 34746
☎ 407-396-4200
FAX 407-396-8838
knightsinn.com

LOCATION	US 192
ROOM RATING	55
COST ($ = $50)	$–

Holiday Inn Express at Summer Bay Resort ★★★
105 Summer Bay Blvd.
Clermont, FL 34711
☎ 407-239-8315
FAX 407-239-8297
hiexpress.com

LOCATION	US 192
ROOM RATING	70
COST ($ = $50)	$+

Holiday Inn Express Lake Buena Vista ★★★½
8686 Palm Pkwy.
Orlando, FL 32836
☎ 407-239-8400
FAX 407-239-8025
hiexpress.com

LOCATION	I-4 Corridor
ROOM RATING	80
COST ($ = $50)	$$–

Holiday Inn Hotel & Suites Orlando Convention Center ★★★
8214 Universal Blvd.
Orlando, FL 32819
☎ 407-581-9001
FAX 407-581-9002
holidayinn.com

LOCATION	I-Drive
ROOM RATING	74
COST ($ = $50)	$$–

Holiday Inn Resort Lake Buena Vista ★★★½
13351 FL 535
Orlando, FL 32821
☎ 407-239-4500
FAX 407-239-8463
hiresortlbv.com

LOCATION	I-4 Corridor
ROOM RATING	79
COST ($ = $50)	$+

HomeSuiteHome Eastgate ★★½
5565 W. US 192*
Kissimmee, FL 34746
☎ 407-396-0707
FAX 407-396-6644
homesuitehome.com

LOCATION	US 192
ROOM RATING	57
COST ($ = $50)	$$$

HomeSuiteHome Kissimmee Maingate ★★
7300 W. US 192*
Kissimmee, FL 34747
☎ 407-396-7300
FAX 407-396-7555
homesuitehome.com

LOCATION	US 192
ROOM RATING	48
COST ($ = $50)	$$$

Howard Johnson Inn Maingate East ★★½
6051 W. US 192*
Kissimmee, FL 34747
☎ 407-396-1748
FAX 407-396-4835
hojo.com

LOCATION	US 192
ROOM RATING	59
COST ($ = $50)	$–

Howard Johnson Inn Orlando I-Drive ★★½
6603 International Dr.
Orlando, FL 32819
☎ 407-351-2900
FAX 407-351-1327
hojo.com

LOCATION	I-Drive
ROOM RATING	59
COST ($ = $50)	$

Hyatt Place Orlando/ Universal ★★★★
5895 Caravan Ct.
Orlando, FL 32819
☎ 407-351-0627
FAX 407-351-3317
orlandouniversal.place.hyatt.com

LOCATION	Universal
ROOM RATING	84
COST ($ = $50)	$$+

Inn Nova Kissimmee ★★½
9330 W. US 192*
Clermont, FL 34714
☎ 863-424-8420
FAX 863-424-9670
magnusonhotels.com

LOCATION	US 192
ROOM RATING	64
COST ($ = $50)	$

International Palms Resort & Conference Center ★★★
6515 International Dr.
Orlando, FL 32819
☎ 407-351-3500
FAX 407-354-3491
internationalpalms.com

LOCATION	I-Drive
ROOM RATING	73
COST ($ = $50)	$$

InTown Suites Orlando Central ★½
5615 Major Blvd.
Orlando, FL 32819
☎ 407-370-3734
FAX 407-363-4650
intownsuites.com

LOCATION	I-Drive
ROOM RATING	40
COST ($ = $50)	$$$$+

La Quinta Inn Orlando I-Drive ★★★
8300 Jamaican Ct.
Orlando, FL 32819
☎ 407-351-1660
FAX 407-351-9264
lq.com

LOCATION	I-Drive
ROOM RATING	73
COST ($ = $50)	$+

La Quinta Inn Orlando I-Drive North ★★
5825 International Dr.
Orlando, FL 32819
☎ 407-351-4100
FAX 407-996-4599
lq.com

LOCATION	I-Drive
ROOM RATING	50
COST ($ = $50)	$+

La Quinta Inn Orlando– Universal Studios ★★½
5621 Major Blvd.
Orlando, FL 32819
☎ 407-313-3100
FAX 407-313-3131
lq.com

LOCATION	Universal
ROOM RATING	63
COST ($ = $50)	$+

Hotels Information Chart (continued)

Lexington Suites Orlando ★★½
7400 Canada Ave.
Orlando, FL 32819
☎ 407-363-0332
FAX 407-264-7964
lexingtonhotels.com

LOCATION	I-Drive
ROOM RATING	60
COST ($ = $50)	$+

Liki Tiki Village ★★★★½
17777 Bali Blvd.
Winter Garden, FL 34787
☎ 407-239-5000
FAX 407-239-5092
likitiki.com

LOCATION	US 192
ROOM RATING	90
COST ($ = $50)	$+

Loews Portofino Bay Hotel ★★★★½
5601 Universal Blvd.
Orlando, FL 32819
☎ 407-503-1000
FAX 407-224-7118
tinyurl.com/portofinobay

LOCATION	Universal
ROOM RATING	92
COST ($ = $50)	$$$$$$

Marriott Imperial Palm Villas ★★★★
8404 Vacation Way
Orlando, FL 32821
☎ 407-238-6200
FAX 407-238-6247
tinyurl.com/imperialpalmvillas

LOCATION	I-Drive
ROOM RATING	86
COST ($ = $50)	$$$$$$+

Marriott Residence Inn Orlando SeaWorld/ International Center ★★★★
11000 Westwood Blvd.
Orlando, FL 32821
☎ 407-313-3600
FAX 407-313-3611
tinyurl.com/residenceinnseaworld

LOCATION	I-4 Corridor
ROOM RATING	85
COST ($ = $50)	$$$+

Marriott's Grande Vista ★★★★½
5925 Avenida Vista
Orlando, FL 32821
☎ 407-238-7676
FAX 407-238-0900
tinyurl.com/marriottsgrandevista

LOCATION	I-Drive
ROOM RATING	92
COST ($ = $50)	$$$

Monumental Hotel ★★★★½
12120 International Dr.
Orlando, FL 32821
☎ 407-239-1222
FAX 407-239-1190
monumentalhotelorlandofl.com

LOCATION	I-Drive
ROOM RATING	94
COST ($ = $50)	$$–

Monumental MovieLand Hotel ★★★
6233 International Dr.
Orlando, FL 32819
☎ 407-351-3900
FAX 407-363-5119
monumentalmovielandhotel.com

LOCATION	I-Drive
ROOM RATING	68
COST ($ = $50)	$+

Motel 6 Orlando–I-Drive ★★½
5909 American Way
Orlando, FL 32819
☎ 407-351-6500
FAX 407-352-5481
motel6.com

LOCATION	I-Drive
ROOM RATING	61
COST ($ = $50)	$–

Nickelodeon Suites Resort Orlando ★★★½
14500 Continental Gateway
Orlando, FL 32821
☎ 407-387-5437
FAX 407-387-1489
nickhotel.com

LOCATION	I-Drive
ROOM RATING	82
COST ($ = $50)	$$$+

Omni Orlando Resort at ChampionsGate ★★★★★
1500 Masters Blvd.
ChampionsGate, FL 33896
☎ 407-390-6664
FAX 407-390-6600
omnihotels.com

LOCATION	I-4 Corridor
ROOM RATING	96
COST ($ = $50)	$$$

Orange Lake Resort ★★★★½
8505 W. US 192*
Kissimmee, FL 34747
☎ 407-239-0000
FAX 407-239-1039
orangelake.com

LOCATION	US 192
ROOM RATING	93
COST ($ = $50)	$$$+

Orlando Sleep Inn Hotel ★★
6301 Westwood Blvd.
Orlando, FL 32821
☎ 407-313-4100
FAX 407-313-4101
orlandosleepinn.com

LOCATION	I-Drive
ROOM RATING	54
COST ($ = $50)	$+

Orlando Vista Hotel ★★★★
12490 S. Apopka–Vineland Rd.
Orlando, FL 32836
☎ 407-239-4646
FAX 407-239-7436
orlandovistahotel.com

LOCATION	I-4 Corridor
ROOM RATING	83
COST ($ = $50)	$+

Orlando World Center Marriott Resort ★★★★
8701 World Center Dr.
Orlando, FL 32821
☎ 407-239-4200
FAX 407-238-8777
marriottworldcenter.com

LOCATION	I-4 Corridor
ROOM RATING	89
COST ($ = $50)	$$$$$+

Loews Royal Pacific Resort at Universal Orlando ★★★★½

6300 Hollywood Way
Orlando, FL 32819
☎ 407-503-3000
FAX 407-503-3010
tinyurl.com/royalpacific

LOCATION	Universal
ROOM RATING	90
COST ($ = $50)	$$$$$

Magic Castle Inn & Suites ★★

5055 W. US 192*
Kissimmee, FL 34746
☎ 407-396-2212
FAX 407-396-0253
themagiccastleinn.com

LOCATION	US 192
ROOM RATING	50
COST ($ = $50)	$–

Marriott Cypress Harbour Villas ★★★★

11251 Harbour Villa Rd.
Orlando, FL 32821
☎ 407-238-1300
FAX 407-238-1083
tinyurl.com/cypressharbourvillas

LOCATION	I-Drive
ROOM RATING	86
COST ($ = $50)	$$$$$–

Marriott's Harbour Lake ★★★★½

7102 Grand Horizons Blvd.
Orlando, FL 32821
☎ 407-465-6100
FAX 407-465-6267
tinyurl.com/harbourlake

LOCATION	I-4 Corridor
ROOM RATING	90
COST ($ = $50)	$$$–

Masters Inn Kissimmee ★★

5367 W. US 192*
Kissimmee, FL 34746
☎ 407-396-4020
FAX 407-396-5450
mastersinn.com

LOCATION	US 192
ROOM RATING	55
COST ($ = $50)	$–

Monte Carlo Motel ★★

4733 W. US 192*
Kissimmee, FL 34746
☎ 407-396-4700

LOCATION	US 192
ROOM RATING	48
COST ($ = $50)	$–

Motel 6 Kissimmee Main Gate East ★★

5731 W. US 192*
Kissimmee, FL 34746
☎ 407-396-6333
FAX 407-396-7715
motel6.com

LOCATION	US 192
ROOM RATING	47
COST ($ = $50)	$–

Motel 6 Main Gate West ★★

7455 W. US 192*
Kissimmee, FL 34747
☎ 407-396-6422
FAX 407-396-0720
motel6.com

LOCATION	US 192
ROOM RATING	52
COST ($ = $50)	$–

Mystic Dunes Resort & Golf Club ★★★★

7900 Mystic Dunes La.
Kissimmee, FL 34747
☎ 407-396-1311
mystic-dunes-resort.com

LOCATION	US 192
ROOM RATING	87
COST ($ = $50)	$$

Orlando Continental Plaza Hotel ★★

6825 Visitors Cir.
Orlando, 32819
☎ 407-352-8211
FAX 407-370-3485
orlandocontinental
plazahotel.com

LOCATION	I-Drive
ROOM RATING	47
COST ($ = $50)	$–

Orlando Metropolitan Express ★★½

6323 International Dr.
Orlando, FL 32819
☎ 407-345-4430
FAX 407-345-0742
orlandometropolitanexpress.com

LOCATION	I-Drive
ROOM RATING	63
COST ($ = $50)	$

Orlando Palm Hotel ★★★

5245 W. US 192*
Kissimmee, FL 34746
☎ 407-396-7700
FAX 407-396-0293

LOCATION	US 192
ROOM RATING	65
COST ($ = $50)	$$–

Palms Hotel & Villas ★★★½

3100 Parkway Blvd.
Kissimmee, FL 34747
☎ 407-396-2229
FAX 407-396-4833
thepalmshotelandvillas.com

LOCATION	US 192
ROOM RATING	76
COST ($ = $50)	$$+

Parkway International Resort ★★★½

6200 Safari Trail
Kissimmee, FL 34746
☎ 407-396-6600
FAX 407-396-6165
islandone.com

LOCATION	US 192
ROOM RATING	82
COST ($ = $50)	$$–

Peabody Orlando ★★★★½

9801 International Dr.
Orlando, FL 32819
☎ 407-352-4000
FAX 407-351-0073
peabodyorlando.com

LOCATION	I-Drive
ROOM RATING	90
COST ($ = $50)	$$

Hotels Information Chart (continued)

Polynesian Isles Resort
(Phase 1) ★★★★
3045 Polynesian Isles Blvd.
Kissimmee, FL 34746
☎ 407-396-1622
FAX 407-396-1744
sunterra.com

LOCATION	US 192
ROOM RATING	83
COST ($ = $50)	$$$$–

Polynesian Resort
★★★★½
1600 Seven Seas Dr.
Lake Buena Vista, FL 32830
☎ 407-824-2000
FAX 407-824-3174
disneyworld.com

LOCATION	WDW
ROOM RATING	92
COST ($ = $50)	$$$$$$$+

Pop Century Resort ★★★
1050 Century Dr.
Lake Buena Vista, FL 32830
☎ 407-938-4000
FAX 407-938-4040
disneyworld.com

LOCATION	WDW
ROOM RATING	71
COST ($ = $50)	$$–

Quality Inn & Suites Eastgate
★★
4960 W. US 192*
Kissimmee, FL 34746
☎ 407-396-1376
FAX 407-396-0716
qualityinn.com

LOCATION	US 192
ROOM RATING	55
COST ($ = $50)	$+

Quality Inn
International Drive ★★
7600 International Dr.
Orlando, FL 32819
☎ 407-996-1600
FAX 407-996-1477
orlandoqualityinn.com

LOCATION	I-Drive
ROOM RATING	50
COST ($ = $50)	$+

Quality Suites Orlando
★★★
9350 Turkey Lake Rd.
Orlando, FL 32819
☎ 407-351-5050
FAX 407-363-7953
qualitysuitesuniversalsouth.com

LOCATION	I-4 Corridor
ROOM RATING	74
COST ($ = $50)	$+

Radisson Resort Worldgate
★★★½
3011 Maingate La.
Kissimmee, FL 34747
☎ 407-396-1400
FAX 407-396-0660
radisson.com

LOCATION	US 192
ROOM RATING	77
COST ($ = $50)	$$–

Ramada Gateway Kissim-
mee (garden) ★★½
7470 W. US 192*
Kissimmee, FL 34747
☎ 407-396-4400
FAX 407-396-4320
ramada.com

LOCATION	US 192
ROOM RATING	64
COST ($ = $50)	$–

Ramada Gateway
Kissimmee (tower) ★★★
7470 W. US 192*
Kissimmee, FL 34747
☎ 407-396-4400
FAX 407-396-4320
ramada.com

LOCATION	US 192
ROOM RATING	71
COST ($ = $50)	$–

Red Roof Inn Kissimmee
★★
4970 Kyng's Heath Rd.
Kissimmee, FL 34746
☎ 407-396-0065
FAX 407-396-0245
redroof.com

LOCATION	US 192
ROOM RATING	47
COST ($ = $50)	$–

Red Roof Inn Orlando
Convention Center ★★½
9922 Hawaiian Ct.
Orlando, FL 32819
☎ 407-352-1507
FAX 407-352-5550
redroof.com

LOCATION	I-Drive
ROOM RATING	58
COST ($ = $50)	$+

Renaissance Orlando
SeaWorld ★★★★
6677 Sea Harbor Dr.
Orlando, FL 32821
☎ 407-351-5555
FAX 407-351-9991
tinyurl.com/renorlandoseaworld

LOCATION	I-Drive
ROOM RATING	89
COST ($ = $50)	$$$$–

The Ritz-Carlton Orlando,
Grande Lakes ★★★★½
4012 Central Florida Pkwy.
Orlando, FL 32837
☎ 407-206-2400
FAX 407-206-2401
grandelakes.com

LOCATION	I-Drive
ROOM RATING	94
COST ($ = $50)	$$$$$

Rodeway Inn Maingate
★★½
5995 W. US 192*
Kissimmee, FL 34747
☎ 407-396-4300
FAX 407-589-1240
rodewayinnmaingate.com

LOCATION	US 192
ROOM RATING	59
COST ($ = $50)	$–

Rosen Centre Hotel
★★★★½
9840 International Dr.
Orlando, FL 32819
☎ 407-996-9840
FAX 407-996-0865
rosencentre.com

LOCATION	I-Drive
ROOM RATING	90
COST ($ = $50)	$$$+

Port Orleans Resort
(French Quarter) ★★★★
2201 Orleans Dr.
Lake Buena Vista, FL 32830
☎ 407-934-5000
FAX 407-934-5353
disneyworld.com

LOCATION **WDW**
ROOM RATING **84**
COST ($ = $50) **$$$**

Port Orleans Resort
(Riverside) ★★★★
1251 Riverside Dr.
Lake Buena Vista, FL 32830
☎ 407-934-6000
FAX 407-934-5777
disneyworld.com

LOCATION **WDW**
ROOM RATING **83**
COST ($ = $50) **$$$**

Quality Inn & Suites ★★
2945 Entry Point Blvd.
Kissimmee, FL 34747
☎ 407-390-0204
FAX 407-390-9780
qualityinn.com

LOCATION **US 192**
ROOM RATING **55**
COST ($ = $50) **$+**

Quality Suites Orlando
Lake Buena Vista ★★★
8200 Palm Pkwy.
Orlando, FL 32836
☎ 407-465-8200
FAX 407-465-0200
qualitysuiteslbv.com

LOCATION **I-4 Corridor**
ROOM RATING **74**
COST ($ = $50) **$$**

Radisson Hotel Orlando
Lake Buena Vista ★★★½
12799 Apopka–Vineland Rd.
Orlando, FL 32836
☎ 407-597-3400
FAX 407-597-0400
radisson.com

LOCATION **I-4 Corridor**
ROOM RATING **82**
COST ($ = $50) **$$+**

Radisson Resort Orlando-
Celebration ★★★★
2900 Parkway Blvd.
Kissimmee, FL 34747
☎ 407-396-7000
FAX 407-396-6792
radisson.com

LOCATION **US 192**
ROOM RATING **86**
COST ($ = $50) **$$$–**

Ramada Inn Convention
Center I-Drive
★★★
8342 Jamaican Ct.
Orlando, FL 32819
☎ 407-363-1944
FAX 407-363-4844
ramada.com

LOCATION **I-Drive**
ROOM RATING **65**
COST ($ = $50) **$$–**

Ramada Inn Orlando I-Drive
Lakefront ★★★
6500 International Dr.
Orlando, FL 32819
☎ 407-345-5340
FAX 407-363-0976
ramada.com

LOCATION **I-Drive**
ROOM RATING **72**
COST ($ = $50) **$$$–**

Ramada Maingate West
Kissimmee ★★½
7491 W. US 192*
Kissimmee, FL 34747
☎ 407-396-6000
FAX 407-396-7393
ramada.com

LOCATION **US 192**
ROOM RATING **60**
COST ($ = $50) **$**

Residence Inn Orlando
Convention Center ★★★½
8800 Universal Blvd.
Orlando, FL 32819
☎ 407-226-0288
FAX 407-226-9979
tinyurl.com/r
esinnconventioncenter

LOCATION **I-Drive**
ROOM RATING **80**
COST ($ = $50) **$$+**

Residence Inn Orlando I-Drive
★★★½
7975 Canada Ave.
Orlando, FL 32819
☎ 407-345-0117
FAX 407-352-2689
tinyurl.com/residenceinnidrive

LOCATION **I-Drive**
ROOM RATING **75**
COST ($ = $50) **$$$$–**

Residence Inn Orlando
Lake Buena Vista ★★★½
11450 Marbella Palm Ct.
Orlando, FL 32836
☎ 407-465-0075
FAX 407-465-0050
tinyurl.com/residenceinnlbv

LOCATION **I-4 Corridor**
ROOM RATING **75**
COST ($ = $50) **$$$**

Rosen Inn at Pointe Orlando
★★★½
9000 International Dr.
Orlando, FL 32819
☎ 407-996-8585
FAX 407-996-1476
rosenhotels.com

LOCATION **I-Drive**
ROOM RATING **75**
COST ($ = $50) **$$–**

Rosen Inn at Universal ★★
6327 International Dr.
Orlando, FL 32819
☎ 407-996-4444
FAX 407-996-5806
rosenhotels.com

LOCATION **I-Drive**
ROOM RATING **51**
COST ($ = $50) **$**

Rosen Plaza Hotel
★★★★½
9700 International Dr.
Orlando, FL 32819
☎ 407-996-9700
FAX 407-354-5774
rosenplaza.com

LOCATION **I-Drive**
ROOM RATING **90**
COST ($ = $50) **$$$**

Hotels Information Chart (continued)

Rosen Shingle Creek
★★★★
9939 Universal Blvd.
Orlando, FL 32819
☎ 407-996-9939
FAX 407-996-9938
rosenshinglecreek.com

LOCATION	I-Drive
ROOM RATING	88
COST ($ = $50)	$$$$$–

Royal Celebration Inn ★★½
4944 W. US 192*
Kissimmee, FL 34746
☎ 407-396-4455
FAX 407-997-2435
royalcelebrationorlando.com

LOCATION	US 192
ROOM RATING	60
COST ($ = $50)	$+

Royale Parc Suites
★★★★½
5876 W. US 192*
Kissimmee, FL 34746
☎ 407-396-8040
FAX 407-396-6766
royaleparcsuitesorlando.com

LOCATION	US 192
ROOM RATING	95
COST ($ = $50)	$$+

**Seralago Hotel & Suites
Main Gate East** ★★★
5678 W. US 192*
Kissimmee, FL 34746
☎ 407-396-4488
FAX 407-396-8915
seralagohotel.com

LOCATION	US 192
ROOM RATING	71
COST ($ = $50)	$–

Shades of Green ★★★★½
1950 W. Magnolia Palm Dr.
Lake Buena Vista, FL 32830
☎ 407-824-3400
FAX 407-824-3665
shadesofgreen.org

LOCATION	WDW
ROOM RATING	91
COST ($ = $50)	$$–

**Sheraton Safari Hotel &
Suites Lake Buena Vista**
★★★★
12205 S. Apopka–Vineland Rd.
Orlando, FL 32836
☎ 407-239-0444
FAX 407-239-1778
sheratonsafari.com

LOCATION	I-4 Corridor
ROOM RATING	83
COST ($ = $50)	$$–

**SpringHill Suites LBV in
Marriott Village** ★★★
8601 Vineland Ave.
Orlando, FL 32821
☎ 407-938-9001
FAX 407-938-4995
marriottvillage.com

LOCATION	I-4 Corridor
ROOM RATING	71
COST ($ = $50)	$$+

Star Island Resort & Club
★★★★
5000 Avenue of the Stars
Kissimmee, FL 34746
☎ 407-997-8000
FAX 407-997-7884
star-island.com

LOCATION	US 192
ROOM RATING	84
COST ($ = $50)	$$

**Staybridge Suites
Lake Buena Vista** ★★★
8751 Suiteside Dr.
Orlando, FL 32836
☎ 407-238-0777
FAX 407-238-2640
staybridge.com

LOCATION	I-4 Corridor
ROOM RATING	72
COST ($ = $50)	$$$–

Super 8 Main Gate ★★½
1815 W. Vine St.
Kissimmee, FL 34741
☎ 407-396-8883
FAX 407-847-0728
super8maingate.com

LOCATION	US 192
ROOM RATING	60
COST ($ = $50)	$–

**Super 8 Orlando/Kissim-
mee/Lakeside** ★★½
4880 W. US 192*
Kissimmee, FL 34746
☎ 407-396-1144
FAX 407-396-4389
super8.com

LOCATION	US 192
ROOM RATING	58
COST ($ = $50)	$–

Swan ★★★★½
1200 Epcot Resorts Blvd.
Lake Buena Vista, FL 32830
☎ 407-934-4000
FAX 407-934-4499
swandolphin.com

LOCATION	WDW
ROOM RATING	90
COST ($ = $50)	$$$$+

Waldorf Astoria Orlando
★★★★½
14200 Bonnet Creek Resort La.
Lake Buena Vista, FL 32830
☎ 407-597-5500
waldorfastoriaorlando.com

LOCATION	WDW
ROOM RATING	93
COST ($ = $50)	$$$$$–

Westgate Inn & Suites
★★½
9200 W. US 192*
Kissimmee, FL 34714
☎ 863-424-2621
FAX 863-424-4630
westgateinnorlando.com

LOCATION	US 192
ROOM RATING	59
COST ($ = $50)	$–

**Westgate Lakes Resort
& Spa** ★★★★½
10000 Turkey Lake Rd.
Orlando, FL 32819
☎ 407-345-0000
FAX 407-370-3445
westgateresorts.com

LOCATION	I-4 Corridor
ROOM RATING	92
COST ($ = $50)	$+

Royal Plaza (garden) ★★★
1905 Hotel Plaza Blvd.
Lake Buena Vista, FL 32830
☎ 407-828-2828
FAX 407-827-6338
royalplaza.com

LOCATION	WDW
ROOM RATING	71
COST ($ = $50)	$$$–

Royal Plaza (tower) ★★★★
1905 Hotel Plaza Blvd.
Lake Buena Vista, FL 32830
☎ 407-828-2828
FAX 407-827-6338
royalplaza.com

LOCATION	WDW
ROOM RATING	87
COST ($ = $50)	$$$

Saratoga Resort Villas
★★★½
4787 W. US 192*
Kissimmee, FL 34746
☎ 407-397-0555
FAX 407-397-0553
saratogaresortvillas.com

LOCATION	US 192
ROOM RATING	80
COST ($ = $50)	$$+

**Sheraton Vistana
Resort Villas** ★★★★½
8800 Vistana Centre Dr.
Orlando, FL 32821
☎ 407-239-3100
FAX 407-239-3111
sheraton.com

LOCATION	I-4 Corridor
ROOM RATING	95
COST ($ = $50)	$$+

Silver Lake Resort ★★½
7751 Black Lake Rd.
Kissimmee, FL 34747
☎ 407-397-2828
FAX 407-589-8410
silverlakeresort.com

LOCATION	US 192
ROOM RATING	64
COST ($ = $50)	$$–

**SpringHill Suites Orlando
Convention Center** ★★★½
8840 Universal Blvd.
Orlando, FL 32819
☎ 407-345-9073
FAX 407-345-9075
tinyurl.com/shsconventioncenter

LOCATION	I-Drive
ROOM RATING	80
COST ($ = $50)	$$–

Staybridge Suites Orlando
★★★½
8480 International Dr.
Orlando, FL 32819
☎ 407-352-2400
FAX 407-352-4631
staybridge.com

LOCATION	I-Drive
ROOM RATING	75
COST ($ = $50)	$$+

Sun Inn & Suites ★★
5020 W. US 192*
Kissimmee, FL 34746
☎ 407-809-4594
FAX 407-809-4584
suninnandsuitesorlando.com

LOCATION	US 192
ROOM RATING	53
COST ($ = $50)	$–

**Super 8 Kissimmee/
Orlando Area** ★★★
5875 W. US 192*
Kissimmee, FL 34746
☎ 407-396-8883
FAX 407-396-8907
super8.com

LOCATION	US 192
ROOM RATING	70
COST ($ = $50)	$–

**Travelodge Suites East Gate
Orange** ★★½
5399 W. US 192*
Kissimmee, FL 34746
☎ 407-396-7666
FAX 407-396-0696
travelodge.com

LOCATION	US 192
ROOM RATING	58
COST ($ = $50)	$–

**Treehouse Villas at Disney's
Saratoga Springs Resort
& Spa** ★★★★½
1960 Broadway
Lake Buena Vista, FL 32830
☎ 407-827-1100
FAX 407-827-4444
disneyworld.com

LOCATION	WDW
ROOM RATING	90
COST ($ = $50)	$$$$$$$$$$

Vacation Village at Parkway
★★★★½
2949 Arabian Nights Blvd.
Kissimmee, FL 34747
☎ 407-396-9086
FAX 407-390-7247
dailymanagementresorts.com

LOCATION	US 192
ROOM RATING	91
COST ($ = $50)	$$–

**Westgate Palace
Resort** ★★★
6145 Carrier Dr.
Orlando, FL 32819
☎ 407-996-6000
FAX 407-355-2979
westgateresorts.com

LOCATION	I-Drive
ROOM RATING	68
COST ($ = $50)	$$+

**Westgate Vacation Villas
(towers)** ★★★½
2770 Old Lake Wilson Rd.
Kissimmee, FL 34747
☎ 407-239-0510
FAX 407-396-6517
westgateresorts.com

LOCATION	I-4 Corridor
ROOM RATING	81
COST ($ = $50)	$+

**Westgate Vacation Villas
(town center)** ★★★★½
2770 Old Lake Wilson Rd.
Kissimmee, FL 34747
☎ 407-239-0510
FAX 407-396-6517
westgateresorts.com

LOCATION	I-4 Corridor
ROOM RATING	93
COST ($ = $50)	$$–

Hotels Information Chart (continued)

Westgate Vacation Villas
(villas) ★★★★½
2770 Old Lake Wilson Rd.
Kissimmee, FL 34747
☎ 407-239-0510
FAX 407-396-6517
westgateresorts.com

LOCATION	I-4 Corridor
ROOM RATING	90
COST ($ = $50)	$$+

Westin Imagine Orlando
★★★★
9501 Universal Blvd.
Orlando, FL 32819
☎ 407-233-2200
FAX 407-233-2201
westin.com

LOCATION	I-Drive
ROOM RATING	87
COST ($ = $50)	$$$$–

Wilderness Lodge ★★★★
901 Timberline Dr.
Lake Buena Vista, FL 32830
☎ 407-824-3200
FAX 407-824-3232
disneyworld.com

LOCATION	WDW
ROOM RATING	86
COST ($ = $50)	$$$$$–

Wilderness Lodge Villas
★★★★½
901 Timberline Dr.
Lake Buena Vista, FL 32830
☎ 407-824-3200
FAX 407-824-3232
disneyworld.com

LOCATION	WDW
ROOM RATING	90
COST ($ = $50)	$$$$$$$–

Wyndham Bonnet Creek Resort ★★★★
9560 Via Encinas
Lake Buena Vista, FL 32830
☎ 407-238-3500
FAX 407-238-3501
wyndhambonnetcreek.com

LOCATION	WDW
ROOM RATING	88
COST ($ = $50)	$$$$$–

Wyndham Cypress Palms Orlando ★★★★
5324 Fairfield Lake Dr.
Orlando, FL 34746
☎ 407-397-1600
FAX 407-377-9167
cypresspalms.com

LOCATION	US 192
ROOM RATING	87
COST ($ = $50)	$$$

Wyndham Lake Buena Vista Resort ★★★½
1850 Hotel Plaza Blvd.
Lake Buena Vista, FL 32830
☎ 407-828-4444
FAX 407-828-8192
wyndhamlakebuenavista.com

LOCATION	WDW
ROOM RATING	75
COST ($ = $50)	$$–

Wyndham Orlando Resort
★★★★
8001 International Dr.
Orlando, FL 32819
☎ 407-351-2420
FAX 407-345-5611
wyndham.com

LOCATION	I-Drive
ROOM RATING	83
COST ($ = $50)	$$$–

Yacht Club Resort ★★★★
1700 Epcot Resorts Blvd.
Lake Buena Vista, FL 32830
☎ 407-934-7000
FAX 407-934-3450
disneyworld.com

LOCATION	WDW
ROOM RATING	89
COST ($ = $50)	$$$$$$$–

PART TWO

BUSCH GARDENS TAMPA BAY

SPANNING 335 ACRES, BUSCH GARDENS combines elements of a zoo and a theme park. Formerly owned by Anheuser-Busch (free beer samples were once a hallmark of the franchise), the Busch Gardens parks in Florida and Williamsburg, Virginia, along with the SeaWorld parks, were sold in 2009 to financial conglomerate The Blackstone Group. Rather symbolic of the buyout, the parks' Clydesdale horses are gone, although the Busch name has been allowed to remain.

The park is divided into nine African-themed regions (as you encounter them moving counterclockwise through the park): Morocco, Egypt, Nairobi, Timbuktu, Congo, Jungala, Stanleyville, Sesame Street Safari of Fun, and Bird Gardens. A haven for thrill-ride fanatics, several of the park's roller coasters are consistently rated among the top five in the country. Busch Gardens is more than thrill fare, however, with beautiful landscaping, excellent shows, and really wonderful children's play areas.

With the wildlife of Disney's Animal Kingdom and the thrills of Universal Studios Islands of Adventure, some may wonder, why leave Orlando for a day at Busch Gardens in Tampa? For those who love roller coasters, Busch Gardens boasts six, four in the super-coaster category. No other area attraction can top that in terms of thrills. Nor can Busch Gardens be matched in its ability to offer a balanced day of fun for all ages. Those who shy away from roller coasters will find plenty to do at the park, with its abundance of animal exhibits, children's rides, gardens, shows, and shops.

unofficial **TIP**
Busch Gardens offers proximity to Tampa, including the city's museums and other attractions.

In addition, the drive is easy and only about 90 minutes from Orlando. With Florida's fickle weather, it could be raining in Orlando but bright and sunny in Tampa, so it's a good idea to check the weather if you're rained out of O-town. Of course, this holds true in reverse, and, unlike at Disney, where most of the rides are indoors, any rain will cause the closing of most of the rides at Busch Gardens.

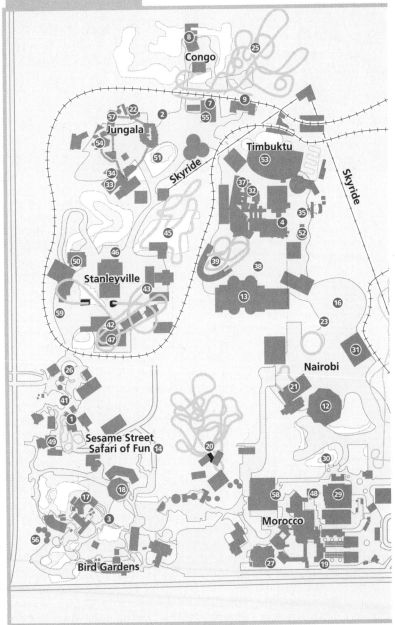

Busch Gardens

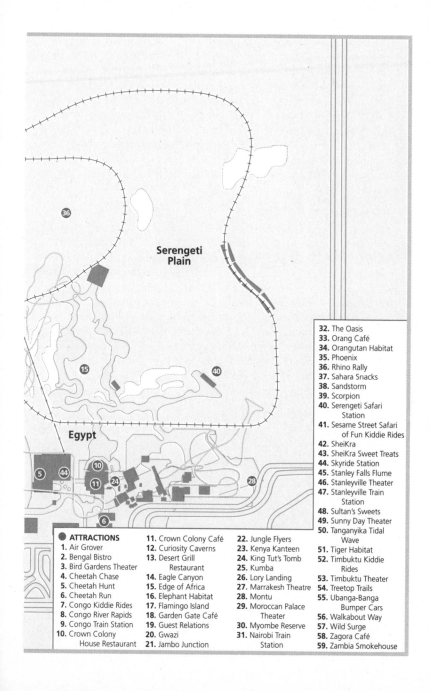

Serengeti Plain

Egypt

32. The Oasis
33. Orang Café
34. Orangutan Habitat
35. Phoenix
36. Rhino Rally
37. Sahara Snacks
38. Sandstorm
39. Scorpion
40. Serengeti Safari Station
41. Sesame Street Safari of Fun Kiddie Rides
42. SheiKra
43. SheiKra Sweet Treats
44. Skyride Station
45. Stanley Falls Flume
46. Stanleyville Theater
47. Stanleyville Train Station
48. Sultan's Sweets
49. Sunny Day Theater
50. Tanganyika Tidal Wave
51. Tiger Habitat
52. Timbuktu Kiddie Rides
53. Timbuktu Theater
54. Treetop Trails
55. Ubanga-Banga Bumper Cars
56. Walkabout Way
57. Wild Surge
58. Zagora Café
59. Zambia Smokehouse

● **ATTRACTIONS**
1. Air Grover
2. Bengal Bistro
3. Bird Gardens Theater
4. Cheetah Chase
5. Cheetah Hunt
6. Cheetah Run
7. Congo Kiddie Rides
8. Congo River Rapids
9. Congo Train Station
10. Crown Colony House Restaurant
11. Crown Colony Café
12. Curiosity Caverns
13. Desert Grill Restaurant
14. Eagle Canyon
15. Edge of Africa
16. Elephant Habitat
17. Flamingo Island
18. Garden Gate Café
19. Guest Relations
20. Gwazi
21. Jambo Junction
22. Jungle Flyers
23. Kenya Kanteen
24. King Tut's Tomb
25. Kumba
26. Lory Landing
27. Marrakesh Theatre
28. Montu
29. Moroccan Palace Theater
30. Myombe Reserve
31. Nairobi Train Station

GETTING THERE

BUSCH GARDENS IS ABOUT 70 MILES from Walt Disney World. The trip should take about an hour and a half, depending on traffic and the construction that plagues I-4. The best way to get there is via I-275. Driving west on I-4, there are signs for Busch Gardens, but ignoring them will save you a long journey through Tampa city streets. Proceed instead to the junction of I-275 and go north. Take Exit 50 onto East Busch Boulevard (FL 580), turn left, and drive a little more than 2 miles; the entrance to Busch Gardens will be on your left. Car and motorcycle parking is $13 in a lot across the street from the park (trams are provided) and $20 in a preferred lot closer to the main entrance, which fills up quickly. RV and camper parking is $15.

ADMISSION PRICES

BEFORE PURCHASING TICKETS TO BUSCH GARDENS, consider some of the choices below, which are similar to the options offered by its sister park, SeaWorld. As with SeaWorld, the best option for most visitors to Busch Gardens is a one-day pass. Busch Gardens has discontinued most of its multiday tickets in favor of package deals and annual passes. However, several options will get you a lot more time in the park for slightly more money than the cost of a one-day ticket. If you're planning to spend time at other Orlando theme parks, consider the FlexTicket, which includes admission to SeaWorld, Wet 'n Wild, Universal Studios, and Universal's Islands of Adventure. Discounts are available for AAA members, disabled visitors, senior citizens, and military personnel.

One-day Pass

Adults $77.99 + tax | *Children ages 3–9* $69.99 | *Children under age 3* Free

Busch Gardens Fun Card

This pass, for Florida residents only and only available online, is by far the best deal for admission to Busch Gardens. For the price of general admission, you can return to the park an unlimited amount of times for an entire calendar year. Fun Cards aren't valid on Memorial Day weekend or weekends between June 4 and August 7, the park's most popular times of year.

Adults $77.99 + tax | *Children ages 3–9* $69.99 | *Children under age 3* Free

Two-park Unlimited Admission Ticket

This pass is a 14-day admission ticket good for SeaWorld and Busch Gardens and includes a free shuttle between Orlando and Tampa.

Adults $114.99 + tax | *Children ages 3–9* $106.99 | *Children under age 3* Free

Annual Passports

These allow unlimited admission to either Busch Gardens alone or a combination of Busch Gardens, SeaWorld, Aquatica, or Adventure Island for one or two years and include free general parking and 10% off merchandise and food purchases in the park(s). The Platinum includes admission to nine parks across the country and also includes free preferred parking and ride-again privileges on some rides.

One Park, One Year Passport
Adults **$109.99** | Children ages 3–9 and Seniors ages 50+ **$101.99**

One Park, Two Years Passport
Adults **$169.99** | Children ages 3–9 and Seniors ages 50+ **$161.99**

Two Parks, One Year Passport
Adults **$159.99** | Children ages 3–9 and Seniors ages 50+ **$151.99**

Two Parks, Two Years Passport
Adults **$244.99** | Children ages 3–9 and Seniors ages 50+ **$236.99**

Three Parks, one Year Passport
Adults **$209.99** | Children ages 3–9 and Seniors ages 50+ **$201.99**

Three Parks, Two Years Passport
Adults **$319.99** | Children ages 3–9 and Seniors ages 50+ **$311.99**

Four Parks, one Year Passport
Adults **$249.99** | Children ages 3–9 and Seniors ages 50+ **$241.99**

Four Parks, Two Years Passport
Adults **$379.99** | Children ages 3–9 and Seniors ages 50+ **$371.99**

Platinum Passport (one year)
Adults **$299.99 + tax** |
Children ages 3–9 and Seniors ages 50+ **$291.99 + tax**

Platinum Passport (two years)
Adults **$439.99 + tax** |
Children ages 3–9 and Seniors ages 50+ **$431.99 + tax**

Orlando FlexTicket Plus

This pass is good for up to 14 consecutive days at six parks: Busch Gardens, Universal Studios Florida, Universal's Islands of Adventure, SeaWorld, Aquatica, and Wet 'n Wild. There's a version that excludes Busch Gardens, so be sure to get the one you want.

FLEXTICKET PLUS
Adults $314.95 + tax | *Children ages 3–9 and seniors ages 50+* $294.95 + tax

ARRIVING

NORMAL PARK HOURS VARY month to month and sometimes day to day but are always between 9 a.m. and 8 p.m. The park stays open until 10 p.m. mid-June through the end of July. Unlike other local attractions, Busch Gardens does not allow you through the turnstiles before the scheduled opening time. We recommend checking the website (**buschgardens.com**) for exact hours of operation. Visiting during peak season equals waiting in long lines. Busch Gardens also draws crowds of locals, so avoid visiting on weekends or holidays.

Even when crowds are low, it requires a lot of planning and hustling to see Busch Gardens in one day. In particular, expect to spend a lot of time getting oriented and consulting park maps and signage. With no central hub and few connecting walkways, it's very easy to get lost. Go slow until you have a feel for where you are in the park, or you could spend some frustrating time retracing your steps.

unofficial **TIP**
As with all the theme parks, get to the entrance at or before opening time.

Of course, group ages and personal tastes will eliminate some rides and exhibits. Groups without children, for instance, don't need to budget time for kiddie rides. However, even selective touring may not afford enough time to enjoy the park fully. Following are a few tips that may help.

PLAN AHEAD The Busch Gardens map is crammed full of rides and exhibits; the first time many visitors see it, they develop a glazed look in their eyes and begin a crazed tour. Somehow, we doubt these folks see even half of what the park offers. Instead, determine in advance what you really want to see. For many groups this involves compromise: parents may not want to spend as much time as children on rides, whereas older kids may want to steer clear of many of the zoological exhibits. If children are old enough, we recommend splitting up after determining a few meeting times and locations for checking in throughout the day. Alternately, parents may want to plan kids' rides around the live entertainment schedule, placing children safely in line and then attending a performance of a nearby show while the youngsters wait and ride. Note that bags, cameras, and other belongings are not permitted on most of the thrill rides; for $0.50, you can temporarily stow such items in lockers near the ride entrances. Thrill-ride enthusiasts should bring a roll of quarters to pay for the lockers.

ARRIVE EARLY As with other central Florida attractions, this is the single most effective strategy for efficient touring and avoiding long line waits. Leave Orlando around 7 a.m. to arrive a little before 8:30 a.m. during peak season. Give yourself an extra half hour during other times, when the park doesn't open until 9:30 a.m. Have a quick breakfast before leaving, or eat in the car to save time. Park, purchase tickets (either at windows or through the self-service kiosks), and be at the turnstile ready to roll when the gate opens at either 9 or 9:30 a.m. First thing in the morning, there should be no lines and relatively few people. Rides that require up to an hour (or more) wait later in the day can be experienced in less than 15 minutes first thing in the morning.

There are three ways to hit the four major coasters at prime times for as little waiting as possible:

Route 1: Ride Gwazi (located at the front of the park) first thing, then head to the new Cheetah Hunt, then Montu, followed by Kumba, and save SheiKra for mid- to late afternoon.

Route 2: After riding Gwazi first, continue onto Stanleyville to ride SheiKra, followed by Kumba; hit Montu and finally Cheetah Hunt late in the day.

Route 3: Head to Cheetah Hunt first, then Montu; then backtrack to Gwazi, followed by SheiKra. Because Kumba is located in the rear of the park, it will not be as crowded in the morning, and you should be able to ride all five major coasters within two hours of the park's opening. This route is only practical with very small groups on off-peak days, when the park isn't packed. Even on slower days, you will find a slight line at Gwazi, SheiKra, and Cheetah Hunt with this route, but you should still be able to check the coasters off your list first thing in the morning and free up the rest of your day for other attractions.

BE READY TO WALK AND WALK AND WALK Busch Gardens is huge and requires lots of walking. Bring strollers for little ones and consider wheelchairs for others who tire quickly. Both stroller and wheelchair rentals are available at the rentals desk, located in the fourth gift shop on the right as you enter the main gate. Reservations can be made ahead of time online or by calling ☎ 888-800-5447. Single strollers cost $15 plus tax, while double strollers cost $19 plus tax and wheelchairs are available for $15 plus tax. Four-wheel electric scooters, also known as ECV Mobility Carts, are available for $45 plus tax. Guests renting the scooters must be at least 18 years old. You can call and reserve wheelchairs or strollers 24 hours ahead of time. One reader suggests that you save money and bring your own stroller:

> [Rental] strollers at Busch Gardens really are strollers; there is very little space for bags and no cup holder. They are not like the big plastic ones they have at SeaWorld and Magic Kingdom.

Once you've secured transportation, you'll need to find your way around the park. Make sure to have all the members in your group grab a park map; show schedules are printed on the reverse side. Due to the park's confusing layout, you'll appreciate having the navigational assistance of your entire group. With all of the calories burned walking around this large park, be aware of keeping everyone fed. You might want to stop for group meals, as eateries are widely spaced and roving snack vendors are sometimes scarce.

AVOID BOTTLENECKS An early arrival will help you avoid the bottlenecks at most of the major attractions. As for smaller rides, if there's a line, don't wait. Go see a show or visit the animal exhibits that usually have no wait. Then return to the rides later in the day, when lines should subside.

CONTACTING BUSCH GARDENS

FOR MORE INFORMATION, call ☎ 888-800-5447. In addition to park information, the Busch Gardens website (**buschgardens.com**) also contains an animal information database.

▌ ATTRACTIONS

MOROCCO

Gwazi ★★★★

APPEAL BY AGE	PRESCHOOL †	GRADE SCHOOL ★★★★	TEENS ★★★★
YOUNG ADULTS ★★★★		OVER 30 ★★★★	SENIORS ★★

† *Preschoolers are generally too short to ride.*

What it is Double wooden roller coaster. **Scope and scale** Super headliner. **When to go** Before 10 a.m. or after 3 p.m. **Special comments** Riders must be at least 48" tall. **Authors' rating** Thrilling, if a little jerky; ★★★½. **Duration of ride** 2½ minutes.

DESCRIPTION AND COMMENTS Those with a nostalgic love for the wooden roller coasters of yore will be pleased with Gwazi. And fans of steel coasters shouldn't be disappointed with the 1.25 million feet of lumber, either. For a wooden ride, this coaster delivers thrills typically associated with its steel cousins. It's really two roller coasters in one, with two completely different tracks—the Gwazi Lion and the Gwazi Tiger—intertwined to create a frenzied race, including six fly-by encounters where riders pass within feet of each other. It's not as intensely confrontational as Dragon Challenge at Islands of Adventure, but it's certainly neat to see a wooden coaster use such an ultramodern gimmick. The coaster received new trains in 2011, promising a smoother and possibly faster ride.

TOURING TIPS Head here first thing in the morning to avoid long waits, or with route #3, right after Cheetah Hunt and Montu. But if you have time, try the coaster again before leaving the park, as it takes on a new feel after dark. Both of Gwazi's tracks are thrilling; the Tiger is a little wilder on the humps, whereas the Lion is a little faster. Both tracks have separate lines for the front and back cars. The front cars offer the best view, but the back cars whip around more for a little extra thrill. For little ones who don't ride, Sesame Street Safari of Fun is also nearby.

Marrakesh Theatre ★★★

APPEAL BY AGE	PRESCHOOL ★★½	GRADE SCHOOL ★★½	TEENS ★★½
YOUNG ADULTS ★★		OVER 30 ★★	SENIORS ★½

What it is Song-and-dance show. **Scope and scale** Major attraction. **When to go** Check daily entertainment schedule. **Authors' rating** Dorky but amusing; ★★★. **Duration of show** 30 minutes.

DESCRIPTION AND COMMENTS The theater holds a variety of performances, but most are of the song-and-dance nature. The show playing on our last visit was a cover-song montage of 1960s standards called *Rock-a-*

Doo Wop. As with previous years, a live band backed a group of singers-cum-dancers, with the entire ensemble decked out in time-appropriate wardrobe, hair, and make-up. The performers have fine voices, are smooth dancers, and are relentlessly cheerful.

TOURING TIPS Rows of wrought-iron patio seats fill this outdoor theater. They are not on an incline, and it is difficult to see the stage from the back. Arrive 10 minutes early to get the best seats near the front of the house. Rows to the right or left of the stage also offer great views.

Moroccan Palace Theater/
Cirque Dreams Jungle Fantasy   ★★★½

| APPEAL BY AGE | PRESCHOOL ★★½ | GRADE SCHOOL ★★★½ | TEENS ★★★★ |
| YOUNG ADULTS ★★★★½ | | OVER 30 ★★★★ | SENIORS ★★★★ |

What it is Musical stage show featuring acrobats and jugglers. **Scope and scale** Headliner. **When to go** Check daily entertainment schedule. **Authors' rating** Interesting, occasionally exciting; the show blends the skills of gymnasts, contortionists, and jugglers ; ★★★½. **Duration of show** 30 minutes.

DESCRIPTION AND COMMENTS Don't be confused by the word *cirque* in the title; this is, at best, a junior varsity version of the innovative Cirque du Soleil troupes, which are a different company. While the costumes and make-up here are dazzling—the 16 performers resemble butterflies, ostriches, frogs, and scaly things—the entertainers' activities are at the level of "You can't contort/balance/juggle like we can," rather than the sort that bring audience gasps of, "Oh my gosh—look at that!" Older viewers may be reminded of the vaudeville-style acts on Ed Sullivan's show. Still, the overall performance is entertaining.

TOURING TIPS The best time to see this show is as a break in your day of activities—it's an opportunity to get out of the Florida heat and humidity. There are no bad seats in the theater, as the entertainers stay in the center of the stage, which is rather shallow, front to back.

Myombe Reserve   ★★★

| APPEAL BY AGE | PRESCHOOL ★★★ | GRADE SCHOOL ★★★ | TEENS ★★½ |
| YOUNG ADULTS ★★½ | | OVER 30 ★★★ | SENIORS ★★★ |

What it is Gorilla habitat. **Scope and scale** Major attraction. **When to go** Anytime before 4 p.m. **Authors' rating** Great theming, informative; ★★★.

DESCRIPTION AND COMMENTS A mist-filled path through lush landscape leads you to this beautiful habitat filled with waterfalls, thick vegetation, and marshland. The first section is home to several chimpanzees that romp through the trees and greenery. The second area features large gorillas. Only one or two of the animals are regularly visible, but at least one can usually be found napping in front of the glass. Two overhead monitors play a video full of interesting information about each animal in the habitat, including how they interact with each other. Chalkboards throughout the exhibit provide facts and figures about the animals.

TOURING TIPS The animals are usually most active before 11 a.m., but check your schedule or the sign in front of the exhibit for guided tour times.

After riding Montu, you can snake through this exhibit, which exits into Nairobi, on your way to Kumba. Bronze sculptures of gorillas and chimpanzees placed throughout the exhibit provide some fun photo opportunities. Climb onto the giant gorilla at the entrance or join the train of chimpanzees combing through each other's hair for a unique snapshot.

Up Close Adventures   ★★★½

APPEAL BY AGE	PRESCHOOL ★★★	GRADE SCHOOL ★★★★	TEENS ★★★
YOUNG ADULTS ★★★★	OVER 30 ★★★½	SENIORS ★★★½	

What it is Guided tours on the plain and behind the scenes. **Scope and scale** Major attraction. **When to go** Call reservation number for a schedule. **Special comments** Must be at least 5 years old. **Authors' rating** Worthwhile for animal enthusiasts or the affluent, but can be too expensive for the average visitor; ★★★½. **Duration of tour** Varies.

DESCRIPTION AND COMMENTS Busch Gardens offers a wide variety of Adventure Tours, but many of them contain overlapping locations, so pick the one that is right for you. Although you can book all the tours listed below the day of your visit at the Adventure Touring Center near the main gate, the limited capacity of the tours makes them sell out early most of the year. During peak seasons, you should call weeks in advance. The number for reservations is ☎ 888-800-5447.

None of the tour prices include park admission, and the prices vary due to the length and capacity of each tour. Prices are the same for all participants, regardless of age. Although the tours are worthwhile for animal enthusiasts, many—if not all—are too expensive for the average visitor. All prices below are listed without tax.

SERENGETI SAFARI **$34 per person, 30 minutes.** Riding in an open-backed truck, guides drive you out into the Serengeti Plain for up-close encounters with some of the tamer animals. A zoologist accompanies the trip and doles out information on all of the animals you encounter. The highlight of the trip is feeding the antelope and giraffes. It's a treat to watch the long tongue of a giraffe remove the leaves from a prickly branch while adeptly avoiding thorns. Bring your camera! Age 5 and older.

JUNGALA INSIDER **$20 per person, 45 minutes.** The tour gives visitors an up-close look at Jungala's inhabitants, including the Bengal tigers and orangutans. Zookeepers are on hand to answer any questions. Age 5 and older. Wheelchairs cannot be accommodated.

ENDANGERED SPECIES SAFARI **$40 per person, 45 minutes.** A tour very similar to the Serengeti Safari, this is 15 minutes longer and visits the white and black rhinos. Due to their turbulent nature, you cannot feed the rhinos, only the antelope and giraffes. The park donates a portion of the proceeds ($2 per person) from this tour to the World Wildlife Fund. The tour leaves at 12:45 daily, and the tickets for this tour are nonrefundable, unless the park cancels the tour. Age 5 and older. Wheelchairs cannot be accommodated.

SUNSET SAFARI $40 per person, 45 minutes. The same sights as the Endangered Species Safari, except with beer. Guests are given a beer sample and then taken out on safari, where they are each allowed two more beers. This tour is offered only in the late afternoon for guests age 21 and older.

SERENGETI NIGHT SAFARI $60 per person, 2 hours. This lengthy tour (age 21 and older) begins with drinks and appetizers, then moves to a guided walking tour of the Edge of Africa exhibit. Afterward, visitors enter the Serengeti Plain in a truck and use night-vision goggles to view the activities of the nocturnal creatures. The trip ends with coffee, tea, and dessert.

SUNRISE SAFARI $40 per person, 45 minutes. Grab a Continental breakfast; then head out on an open-sided truck into the Serengeti to view the animals in the morning, when they are likely to be friskier than in the afternoon heat. Age 5 and older.

KEEPER FOR A DAY $250 per person, 6½ hours. If you're a zoo enthusiast ready to shell out some big cash to fulfill a personal dream, then this may be worth considering. Shadow a zookeeper for a morning with some of the herbivores on the Serengeti Plain and spend an afternoon with the Busch Gardens' avian team. If you're going to shell out this kind of money, be sure to call ahead and get a detailed itinerary for the day you're visiting.

TIGER AND ORANGUTAN KEEPER EXPERIENCE $200 per person, limited to six people, 90 minutes. Visitors go behind the scenes to see where the Bengal tigers and Bornean orangs sleep. Visitors will take part in preparing food for the animals and in an orangutan training session. A highlight: The tug of war between the humans and a tiger, pulling on a rope, inside its enclosure. Open to age 10 and older; wheelchairs cannot be accommodated.

ELEPHANT KEEPER EXPERIENCE $200 for a group of up to six guests, 90 minutes. Join the keepers for behind-the-scenes, but not inside the cages, time with the big guys and gals. Open to age 10 and older; wheelchairs cannot be accommodated.

ROLLER COASTER INSIDER $20, 45 minutes. For the coaster freak, this is a chance to go behind the scenes. You'll hear how these European-designed rides are installed and maintained. The guides focus on Montu's almost 4,000 feet of track and on the 80-foot-high braking platform. Then, it's front-of-the-line access and front-row seats on Montu. This is followed by front-of-the-line access to another coaster, to see how they compare. Open to age 14 and older; wheelchairs cannot be accommodated.

TOURING TIPS Two different half- and full-day guided tours of the park are also available, and their prices range $85–$250 plus tax and park admission. The selling point is one-time front-of-the-line access to most of the major rides and/or front seats at all of the shows and/or an Adventure Tour. Of course, if you're following the Touring Plans in the book, front-of-the-line access should not be an issue; we're here to save you those hundred bucks. If you're in the mood for the VIP treatment, call ☎ 888-800-5447 for more information.

EGYPT

Cheetah Hunt

TOO NEW TO RATE

What it is Roller coaster. **Scope and scale** Super headliner. **When to go** Immediately after park opening. **Special comments** Riders must be at least 48" tall. **Authors' rating** A super-attractive new coaster—it can't miss. **Duration of ride** 3½ minutes, including loading and unloading.

DESCRIPTION AND COMMENTS Located in the area that formerly included both the beloved Clydesdales' stables and the monorail station, this roller coaster (set to open in spring 2011) promises to be an attractive pairing of the latest in thrill rides and the eternal allure of beautiful big cats.

The park is famous for its high-speed rides. Busch officials label Cheetah Hunt a launch coaster, driven by a series of magnets—officially, a Linear Synchronous Motor propulsion system. It is the park's first coaster whose onward surge is not powered simply by gravity after the climb to the starting hill. Instead, Cheetah Hunt will feature three bursts of acceleration—up to 30 miles per hour as it starts, then farther along and at unexpected moments, suddenly up to 60 miles per hour and, after a slower stretch, back up to 40.

The riders will climb to a height of 102 feet—providing a magnificent if rapid view of the animal-filled Serengeti Plain—before plunging 130 feet as they rush through a trench. The 16-passenger trains traverse several rolling turns and a full inversion over the 4,429-foot track. Thrill seekers will undergo four g's, or four times the pull of gravity.

Five of the trains can operate simultaneously; park executives estimate that they can move 1,370 passengers per hour. The ride ends at the monorail station.

TOURING TIPS Because it is the newest sparkly thing in Busch Gardens, Cheetah Hunt is sure to be swamped when the park first opens each day. When you enter, circle to your right around the Guest Services building and check the wait time for the Cheetah Hunt.

Cheetah Run

TOO NEW TO RATE

What it is Live-animal attraction. **Scope and scale** Super headliner. **When to go** Immediately after park opening. **Authors' rating** I'll be sure to stop here both entering and leaving the park.

DESCRIPTION AND COMMENTS Located next to the Cheetah Hunt coaster and also set to open in spring 2011, the attraction highlights the cheetah, fastest of all land animals.

Visitors standing inside an African-themed, covered area (the former stables) will be able to view at least nine cheetahs through large windows. The cheetahs are trained to chase a lure, and two or three at a time will be released to pursue the lure past the windows, for just over 100 feet. This viewing arrangement is similar to the one at the Edge of Africa lion habitat.

To pass the time between the animals' runs, visitors will be able to use touchscreens to learn more about the cheetahs and the Busch Gardens/SeaWorld efforts to help their wild cousins.

TOURING TIPS Because it is the newest animal attraction in Busch Gardens, Cheetah Run is sure to be swamped when the park first opens each day. When you enter, circle to your right around the Guest Services building and you'll quickly reach the live-cheetah viewing area; check the wait time for the Cheetah Hunt. You might make this a multiple-visit area—while cheetahs naturally hunt in the daytime, they may want to rest during Florida's oppressive hot and humid summer afternoons. If you want to get out of the heat, the fine Crown Colony House Restaurant is just a few yards away.

Edge of Africa   ★★★½

APPEAL BY AGE	PRESCHOOL ★★★½	GRADE SCHOOL ★★★★	TEENS ★★★
YOUNG ADULTS ★★★		OVER 30 ★★★½	SENIORS ★★★½

What it is Walking tour of animal habitats. **Scope and scale** Headliner. **When to go** Crowds are minuscule in the afternoon, and the animals are fairly active. **Authors' rating** Good presentation; ★★★½.

DESCRIPTION AND COMMENTS This walking safari features hippopotamuses, giraffes, lions, baboons, meerkats, hyenas, and vultures in naturalistic habitats. The area was designed for up-close viewing, many times with just a pane of glass between you and the animals. Exhibits of note are the hippopotamus habitat and the hyena area. The hippopotamuses wade in 5-foot-deep water filled with colorful fish, all visible through the glass wall. In the hyena habitat, open safari vehicles are built into the glass, offering a great photo opportunity if you climb in when the animals come near.

TOURING TIPS Animals are most active during feedings and during the chats by keepers; check the park map for times of the keeper talks. Feeding times are not regularly scheduled, so the animals don't fall into a pattern that would not exist in the wild. Employees are usually willing to tell you feeding times for the day. It might be a hike to return to this area, but seeing the lions chomp into raw meat is definitely worth it.

There is a hidden entrance to this area between Tut's Tomb and the restrooms near Montu. This is useful if you ride the roller coaster before seeing the animals. There is also a recently opened entrance from Nairobi to make this area more easily accessible.

King Tut's Tomb   ★

APPEAL BY AGE	PRESCHOOL ★	GRADE SCHOOL ★	TEENS ★½
YOUNG ADULTS ★½		OVER 30 ★★	SENIORS ★★½

What it is Walking tour of a recreated tomb. **Scope and scale** Diversion. **When to go** Anytime; don't wait if there's a line. **Authors' rating** Somewhat interesting, but often not worth the time; ★. **Duration of tour** 10 minutes.

DESCRIPTION AND COMMENTS The spirit of King Tut leads you on a tour of this re-creation of his tomb. The narration features information about the tomb's artifacts and his life. Objects on display include replicas of Tut's large throne, chariot, and golden sculpted coffin, as well as urns purportedly containing his internal organs.

TOURING TIPS This air-conditioned attraction provides a break from the heat, but it should be skipped if you're in a hurry. Although a bit dull, it does work as a time killer for visitors waiting for the rest of their party to ride Montu.

Montu ★★★★★

APPEAL BY AGE	PRESCHOOL †	GRADE SCHOOL ★★★★	TEENS ★★★★★
YOUNG ADULTS ★★★★½		OVER 30 ★★★½	SENIORS ★★½

† Preschoolers are generally too short to ride.

What it is Inverted steel super roller coaster. **Scope and scale** Super headliner. **When to go** Before 10 a.m. or after 4 p.m. **Special comments** Riders must be at least 54" tall. **Authors' rating** Incredible; ★★★★★. **Duration of ride** About 3 minutes. **Loading speed** Quick.

DESCRIPTION AND COMMENTS Seats hang below the track and riders' feet dangle on this intense inverted roller coaster, which is among the top five in the country and among the best we've ever ridden. The fast-paced but extremely smooth ride begins with a 13-story drop. Riders are then hurled through a 104-foot inverted vertical loop. Speeds reach 60 miles per hour as riders are accelerated through more dizzying loops and twists, including an Immelman, an inverse loop named after German World War I fighter pilot Max Immelman.

TOURING TIPS Depending on which route you take, try to ride in the morning or later in the afternoon to avoid waits that can be as long as an hour (or even more). If lines are still long, however, don't be discouraged. As many as 32 riders can pile onto each train, so even the longest line will move quickly and steadily.

If you have time, ride twice, first near the back of the train and then in the front row. In the back, you'll glimpse a sea of dangling feet in front of you and be surprised by each twist and turn because you can't see where the track is headed, just legs swooping through the air. Riding in the front gives you a clear, unobstructed view of everything around you, including the huge trees dozens of feet below you on the first drop. If you have to choose one or the other, we definitely recommend the front row. Look for the special front-seat queue once you enter the load station. The wait for the front is usually an extra 20 minutes, but it's worth it for the thrill.

kids Skyride ★★★

APPEAL BY AGE	PRESCHOOL ★★	GRADE SCHOOL ★★½	TEENS ★★
YOUNG ADULTS ★★		OVER 30 ★★½	SENIORS ★★★

What it is Scenic transportation to Stanleyville. **Scope and scale** Minor attraction. **When to go** In the morning; lines can be long in the afternoon. **Authors'**

rating Good way to see the Rhino Rally in action; ★★★. **Duration of ride** 4 minutes.

DESCRIPTION AND COMMENTS This aerial tram travels to Stanleyville. It passes directly over the Rhino Rally attraction and offers great views of the Serengeti Plain and its wild inhabitants as well as the roller coasters. You can board here or in Stanleyville, but you cannot stay on for a round trip.

TOURING TIPS If the lines are small, you may use the Skyride as a shortcut from Montu to Kumba and SheiKra. The shortcut may only work early in the morning because if the lines are not small, this ride takes longer than walking; however, it's still faster than the train.

NAIROBI

Curiosity Caverns ★★½

| APPEAL BY AGE | PRESCHOOL ★★½ | GRADE SCHOOL ★★★½ | TEENS ★★½ |
| YOUNG ADULTS ★★★ | | OVER 30 ★★★ | SENIORS ★★½ |

What it is Walk-through exhibit of "odd" animals. **Scope and scale** Minor attraction. **When to go** Anytime. **Authors' rating** A cool break; ★★½.

DESCRIPTION AND COMMENTS This seems to be a catchall for types of animals not exhibited elsewhere in the park. You'll see snakes and other reptiles behind glass, including a Burmese python and an anaconda, though there are also a three-toed sloth, bats, and a laughing kookaburra bird (which did not appear to be in the mood for laughter on our last visit).

TOURING TIPS The cooler climate inside Curiosity Caverns makes it an ideal place for reptiles and humans to hide from the heat and the glare outside.

Elephant Habitat ★★

| APPEAL BY AGE | PRESCHOOL ★★★ | GRADE SCHOOL ★★★ | TEENS ★★ |
| YOUNG ADULTS ★★ | | OVER 30 ★★ | SENIORS ★★½ |

What it is Elephant habitat. **Scope and scale** Minor attraction. **When to go** During interaction times. **Authors' rating** ★★.

DESCRIPTION AND COMMENTS Endangered Asian elephants roam a dry dirt pen. A large pool is deep enough for these huge animals to submerge themselves and escape the Florida heat. The pen is surprisingly small; it's too bad the elephants can't roam the larger Serengeti Plain.

TOURING TIPS Visit during enrichment times, when trainers interact with the animals and speak with guests. The daily entertainment schedule doesn't list enrichment times for all the animals, so you should ask a keeper.

Jambo Junction ★★★½

| APPEAL BY AGE | PRESCHOOL ★★½ | GRADE SCHOOL ★★★½ | TEENS ★★ |
| YOUNG ADULTS ★★★ | | OVER 30 ★★½ | SENIORS ★★★ |

What it is Animals on display. **Scope and scale** Minor attraction. **When to go** Anytime. **Authors' rating** Supercute; ★★★½.

DESCRIPTION AND COMMENTS Busch Gardens is home to more than 2,700 animals, and many of the females often give birth to young. The park also rescues ill or orphaned animal infants, including a sizable number of endangered species. The animal nursery in Jambo Junction houses these infants, but other animals, such as otters, flamingos, and opossums, are also presented to the guests. No matter which animals are on display, you're sure to come down with a small case of the warm fuzzies.

TOURING TIPS The attraction was recently updated and now contains more animals in pens outside the main facility.

Rhino Rally ★★★★½

| APPEAL BY AGE | PRESCHOOL ★★★½ | GRADE SCHOOL ★★★★★ | TEENS ★★★★½ |
| YOUNG ADULTS ★★★★½ | OVER 30 ★★★★½ | | SENIORS ★★★★ |

What it is Off-road adventure through African-themed terrain. **Scope and scale** Headliner. **When to go** Before 10 a.m. or after 3:30 p.m. **Special comments** Beware if you've got back problems; the ride gets a little bumpy. **Authors' rating** Great fun, and you see a host of African wildlife; ★★★★½. **Duration of ride** About 8 minutes.

DESCRIPTION AND COMMENTS Riders board 17-passenger Land Rovers for a safari adventure across 16 acres, with one "lucky" guest riding shotgun with the wise-cracking driver. The trip gets off to a physically bumpy start, and everyone has a great view of white rhinoceroses, elephants, Cape buffaloes, Nile crocodiles, zebras, antelopes, wildebeests, and other species, with running commentary by the driver.

At one time, the Land Rover turned into a floating pontoon with an inflatable underside when a flash flood washed out the bridge. However, due to repeated problems with the ride's water portion, that part of the ride was permanently closed in 2010. The Cheetah Hunt coaster now fills part of the open space.

TOURING TIPS The 8-minute ride can board about 1,600 guests per hour, but because the attraction is popular, make it one of your early rides (either first thing, or after Gwazi and Montu if you're doing Route #1; second to last if you're doing Route #2 or #3). The queue is covered and splits into two lines near the boarding area; pick the shortest line at that point as the split is only to expedite boarding (there is no difference in the experience).

Serengeti Express ★★

| APPEAL BY AGE | PRESCHOOL ★★½ | GRADE SCHOOL ★★½ | TEENS ★★ |
| YOUNG ADULTS ★★ | OVER 30 ★★★ | | SENIORS ★★★½ |

What it is Train tour through Serengeti Plain and around the park. **Scope and scale** Minor attraction. **When to go** Afternoon. **Authors' rating** Relaxing; ★★. **Duration of ride** 12 minutes through animal area exiting at next station; 35 minutes round-trip.

DESCRIPTION AND COMMENTS Riding this train gives your feet a break and provides the best view of the animals along the Serengeti Plain. Because it's quite poky, we don't recommend it as an alternate means of transportation, but the 12-minute trip from the Nairobi station through the Serengeti Plain to the Congo station is worth the time if you're not racing to ride the coasters. On-board guides identify the animals you see and tell a little about their history and habits. The train will take you close to the ostriches, wildebeests, and white rhinos.

TOURING TIPS Since the train runs counterclockwise, sit on the left-hand side for the best view of the entire plain. If you board at the Nairobi station, get off at the Congo station for Kumba or the Congo River Rapids; get off at Stanleyville for Tanganyika Tidal Wave or the Sesame Street Safari of Fun children's area.

TIMBUKTU

Cheetah Chase ★★★

APPEAL BY AGE	PRESCHOOL ★★★	GRADE SCHOOL ★★★½	TEENS ★★
YOUNG ADULTS ★★	OVER 30 ★★★		SENIORS ★★

What it is Kiddie coaster. **Scope and scale** Minor attraction. **When to go** Line is usually relatively short compared with the big coasters, but an early stop would be wise because the line grows as the day goes on. **Special comments** Riders must be at least 6 years old and 46" tall. **Authors' rating** Fun for the little coaster lovers; ★★★. **Duration of ride** Approximately 3 minutes. **Loading speed** Moderate.

DESCRIPTION AND COMMENTS Hairpin turns and mini-drops make this a good choice for thrill seekers who aren't tall enough to take on the big coasters.

TOURING TIPS The line moves quickly here but build in the afternoon due to its proximity to other kiddie rides. This is also a good place to wait for the supercoaster-riders in your party or to burn off some time before *Pirates 4-D*.

Kiddie Rides ★★½

APPEAL BY AGE	PRESCHOOL ★★★	GRADE SCHOOL †	TEENS †
YOUNG ADULTS †	OVER 30 †		SENIORS †

† Not designed for older kids and adults.

What they are Pint-size carnival rides. **Scope and scale** Minor attraction. **When to go** Anytime. **Authors' rating** Good diversion for children; ★★½.

DESCRIPTION AND COMMENTS Nothing fancy, but these attractions help kids who aren't old enough to ride the thrillers feel that they aren't being left out. Another set of kiddie rides can be found in the Congo.

TOURING TIPS These rides are strategically placed near the adult attractions in this area (Scorpion and Phoenix), so one parent can keep the kids occupied while another rides.

Phoenix ★★

APPEAL BY AGE	PRESCHOOL †	GRADE SCHOOL ★★★	TEENS ★★★
YOUNG ADULTS ★★½	OVER 30 ★★½		SENIORS ★

† Preschoolers are generally too short to ride.

What it is Swinging pendulum ride. **Scope and scale** Minor attraction. **When to go**

Anytime. **Special comments** Riders must be at least 48" tall; not for those prone to motion sickness. **Authors' rating** Dizzying; ★★. **Duration of ride** 5 minutes.

DESCRIPTION AND COMMENTS A large wooden boat swings back and forth, starting slowly, then gaining speed before making a complete circle with passengers hanging upside down.

TOURING TIPS Remove glasses and anything in your shirt pockets to avoid losing them when the boat is suspended upside down for several seconds.

Sandstorm   ★★

APPEAL BY AGE	PRESCHOOL †	GRADE SCHOOL ★★★	TEENS ★★½
YOUNG ADULTS ★★★		OVER 30 ★★½	SENIORS ★★

† Preschoolers are generally too short to ride.

What it is Carnival ride. **Scope and scale** Minor attraction. **When to go** Anytime. **Special comments** Riders must be at least 48" tall. **Authors' rating** Amusing, but not worth a long wait; ★★. **Duration of ride** Approximately 3 minutes. **Loading speed** Slow.

DESCRIPTION AND COMMENTS This is Busch Gardens' version of a midway ride commonly known as the Scrambler. Two to three riders sit in an enclosed car. Four of the cars rotate on one of six arms that circle a central pedestal.

TOURING TIPS Although fun, this ride is nothing special. Skip it if lines are long.

Scorpion   ★★★

APPEAL BY AGE	PRESCHOOL †	GRADE SCHOOL ★★★½	TEENS ★★½
YOUNG ADULTS ★★★		OVER 30 ★★★	SENIORS ★★

† Preschoolers are generally too short to ride.

What it is Roller coaster. **Scope and scale** Headliner. **When to go** After 2 p.m. **Special comments** Riders must be at least 42" tall. **Authors' rating** Quick, but exciting; ★★★. **Duration of ride** 1½ minutes.

DESCRIPTION AND COMMENTS This coaster pales in comparison with big sisters Kumba and Montu. In spite of its small stature, with speeds of 50 miles per hour, a 360-degree vertical loop, and three 360-degree spirals, it's nothing to sneeze at.

TOURING TIPS Lines will be long for this attraction; because it doesn't have the high capacity of Kumba or Montu, they move slowly. Save it for the afternoon, when the wait is almost always shorter.

Timbuktu Theatre/*Pirates 4-D* and *Sesame Street presents Lights, Camera, Imagination!*   ★★★½

APPEAL BY AGE	PRESCHOOL ★★½	GRADE SCHOOL ★★★½	TEENS ★★★
YOUNG ADULTS ★★★		OVER 30 ★★½	SENIORS ★★½

What it is 3-D pirate- or *Sesame Street*-themed movie packed with extra punch. **Scope and scale** Headliner. **When to go** Early in the morning or after crowds diminish. **Authors' rating** Creative and a lot of fun; ★★★½. **Duration of show** 20 minutes.

DESCRIPTION AND COMMENTS *Pirates 4-D* stars Leslie Nielsen as the treacherous Captain Lucky. After abandoning his last crew on a desert island, Captain Lucky returns to retrieve his treasure. Unfortunately for him, his cabin boy is still alive and lying in wait. All ill falls on the captain and his crew of scallywags that includes Eric Idle of Monty Python fame as first mate Pierre.

The alternating film is *Sesame Street presents Lights, Camera, Imagination!* The beloved Elmo, Cookie Monster, and Big Bird try to save the Sesame Street Film Festival.

Although the antics of the cast are amusing, the 3-D and 4-D effects are underutilized. Unlike *Shrek* at Universal Studios, which was made to explode from the screen and surround the viewer, *Pirates* is more like a 20-minute short film shown in 3-D and highlighted with 4-D effects.

TOURING TIPS The show times are posted on the back of your park map, spaced around 40 minutes apart. Since the presentation is only 20 minutes, the period between shows seems a little excessive, until you realize that someone has to dry off every seat in this massive theater (yes, that does mean you will get a little wet).

Typically, one movie is shown three times in a row, followed by the other film, so you really can't hang around to see both.

Because of the sparse showings, the lines for the show can be daunting, but the size of the theater should accommodate everyone in line. Once the ropes are dropped, you will be corralled in front of the doors. Unlike *A Bug's Life* at Disney, which seats from only one side, this theater seats from both, so to get a center seat you should be near the doors when they open.

CONGO

Congo River Rapids ★★★

APPEAL BY AGE	PRESCHOOL ★★★½	GRADE SCHOOL ★★★½	TEENS ★★★½
YOUNG ADULTS ★★★		OVER 30 ★★★	SENIORS ★★½

What it is White-water raft ride. **Scope and scale** Headliner. **When to go** After 4 p.m. **Special comments** You will get soaked. **Authors' rating** A great time, but not worth more than a 45-minute wait; ★★★. **Duration of ride** 3 minutes. **Loading speed** Slow to moderate; unloading is very slow.

DESCRIPTION AND COMMENTS White-water raft rides have become somewhat of a theme-park standard, and this version is pretty much the status quo. Twelve riders sit on a circular rubber raft as they float down a jungle river, jostling and spinning in the waves and rapids. Scary signs warn of dangerous crocodiles in the "river," but no beasts (robotic or otherwise) ever show themselves. It is possible to avoid getting drenched through the sheer luck of where your boat goes, but in the end, getting very wet is almost guaranteed due to both water jets operated by mischievous onlookers on a bridge and a final gauntlet of giant water jets that soaks almost every raft that passes through. There's nothing like the helpless feeling of watching your boat drift into the path of one of these megafirehoses.

TOURING TIPS Wear a poncho, either your own or one purchased at nearby concession huts. Stow as much clothing in the lockers at the dock as you can take off and remain decent (especially socks—nobody likes squishy feet). There is no watertight center console on these rafts. Also, know that long lines are inevitable for this slow-loading and -unloading attraction. We recommend that you ride the roller coasters first, saving this attraction for later in the afternoon. The cute monkeys on display make waiting in the first third of the line fairly entertaining.

Kiddie Rides ★★½

APPEAL BY AGE	PRESCHOOL ★★★	GRADE SCHOOL †	TEENS †
YOUNG ADULTS †	OVER 30 †		SENIORS †

† Not designed for older kids and adults.

What they are Pint-size carnival rides. **Scope and scale** Minor attraction. **When to go** Anytime. **Authors' rating** Good diversion for children; ★★½.

DESCRIPTION AND COMMENTS Nothing fancy, but these attractions help kids who aren't old enough to ride the thrillers feel as if they aren't being left out. Similar to the kiddie rides in Timbuktu.

TOURING TIPS These rides are strategically placed near the adult attraction in this area (Kumba), so one parent can keep the kids occupied while another rides.

Kumba ★★★★

APPEAL BY AGE	PRESCHOOL †	GRADE SCHOOL ★★★★	TEENS ★★★★
YOUNG ADULTS ★★★★	OVER 30 ★★★★		SENIORS ★★

† Preschoolers are generally too short to ride.

What it is Steel super roller coaster. **Scope and scale** Super headliner. **When to go** Before 11 a.m. or after 2:30 p.m. **Special comments** Riders must be at least 54" tall. **Authors' rating** Excellent; ★★★★. **Duration of ride** Approximately 3 minutes.

DESCRIPTION AND COMMENTS Kumba's dramatic loops rise above the tree line in the Congo area, with a trainload of screaming riders twisting skyward. Just like sister coaster Montu, Kumba is one of the best in the country. Unlike Montu's, Kumba's trains sit on top of the track as it roars through 3,900 feet of twists and loops. Reaching speeds of 60 miles per hour, Kumba is certainly fast, but it also offers an incredibly smooth ride. This is good, because the coaster's intense corkscrews will churn your insides something fierce. Thrilling elements include a diving loop, a camelback with a 360-degree spiral, and a 108-foot vertical loop.

TOURING TIPS Kumba will be the last coaster you ride in the morning taking either route #1, #2, or #3. Following route #1, it will be after Montu; with routes #2 and #3, it will follow SheiKra. Just like Montu and SheiKra, as many as 32 riders can brave Kumba at once, so even if there is a line, the wait shouldn't be unbearable.

Ubanga-Banga Bumper Cars   ★★½

APPEAL BY AGE	PRESCHOOL ★★★	GRADE SCHOOL ★★★	TEENS ★★★
YOUNG ADULTS ★★½		OVER 30 ★★	SENIORS ★

What it is Bumper-car ride. **Scope and scale** Minor attraction. **When to go** Anytime. **Authors' rating** ★★½. **Duration of ride** Approximately 2 minutes, depending on park attendance.

DESCRIPTION AND COMMENTS Basic carnival bumper-car ride.

TOURING TIPS Don't waste time waiting in the usually very long line for this attraction if you're on the roller-coaster circuit. However, because this ride is right next to Kumba, it is a perfect place for kids and others in your group to wait for those braving the coaster.

kids JUNGALA

Jungle Flyers   ★½

APPEAL BY AGE	PRESCHOOL ★★½	GRADE SCHOOL ★★★½	TEENS ★
YOUNG ADULTS †		OVER 30 †	SENIORS †

† Not designed for older kids and adults.

What it is Zip line. **Scope and scale** Minor attraction. **When to go** Early in the morning. **Special comments** Riders must be between ages 6–13 and be at least 48" tall. Parents can ride along but the total weight cannot exceed 210 pounds. **Authors' rating** Poor call; ★. **Duration of ride** 2 minutes.

DESCRIPTION AND COMMENTS At the top of a long flight of stairs in Jungala lies Jungle Flyers. Here, six small chairs, which each seat two people, shoot back and forth across short ziplines. The chairs have hang-gliding wings attached to their tops, the only theming. Parents can ride along, but anyone over the age of 13 cannot ride without a child.

TOURING TIPS You'd think that theme parks would learn from the mistakes of their competition, but this ride proves that it's not always the case. Pteranodon Flyers is one of the biggest time wasters at Universal's Island of Adventures, yet, Busch Gardens has gone ahead and come up with a rather similar ride without the high-quality theming. The only thing Busch Gardens has managed to duplicate is the wait time. Unless there's no one here and your child meets all of the height and weight requirements, skip it.

Orangutan Habitat   ★★★

APPEAL BY AGE	PRESCHOOL ★★★½	GRADE SCHOOL ★★★½	TEENS ★★½
YOUNG ADULTS ★★★		OVER 30 ★★★	SENIORS ★★★½

What it is Zoological exhibit. **Scope and scale** Major attraction. **When to go** Anytime. **Authors' rating** Great to see the guys when they're active; ★★★.

DESCRIPTION AND COMMENTS Directly beside the Tiger Habitat, it is a place where guests can view these great apes playing in a large environ, complete with high wires and a moat. The depth of the enclosure, coupled with its many egresses, can make it difficult to spot the somewhat reclusive primates. Fortunately, Busch Gardens has provided quarter-operated telescopes, located on the enclosure's bridge, to make spotting these guys easier.

TOURING TIPS This is a good place to go if a tour group is crowding the Tiger Habitat. On occasion, you'll see the orangutans skittering along the high wires, but more often, you'll only spot a tuft of orange fur or nothing at all. The same viewing opportunities (minus the rope tricks) hold true for two other small enclosures nearby, which house the flying foxes and the gibbons.

Tiger Habitat ★★★★

APPEAL BY AGE	PRESCHOOL ★★★★½	GRADE SCHOOL ★★★★½	TEENS ★★★½
YOUNG ADULTS ★★★★		OVER 30 ★★★★	SENIORS ★★★½

What it is Zoological exhibit. Scope and scale Headliner. When to go Anytime. Authors' rating Big cats; ★★★★.

DESCRIPTION AND COMMENTS Thick glass panes separate viewers from this highly endangered species. Viewing areas surround the habitat, which makes actually seeing the inhabitants not only much more likely but also more thrilling. There's even a small ladder into a tiny glass bubble where one visitor at a time can peer up into a secluded part of the reserve.

If you're lucky enough to experience it, the tigers occasionally swim in the small stream, and the glass partition lets you see their feline feet treading the water (not a perspective you'd ever want to have in the wild).

TOURING TIPS This viewing area is a major improvement over its predecessor, where the tigers were on an island at the bottom of a pit. Actually, this is one of the best viewing areas for any species at the park. Check with trainers early in the day for the tiger tug-of-war schedule, which sets groups of visitors against the pulling power of a Bengal tiger; there is a partition in between the species, of course.

Treetop Trails ★★★½

APPEAL BY AGE	PRESCHOOL ★★★½	GRADE SCHOOL ★★★½	TEENS ★★
YOUNG ADULTS ★½		OVER 30 ★★	SENIORS ★★

What it is Climbing playground. Scope and scale Minor attraction. When to go Anytime. Authors' rating Fun escape; ★★★.

DESCRIPTION AND COMMENTS A series of cargo nets and wooden bridges link together this multistoried playground. Although not as intricate as, say, Camp Jurassic at Universal Studios, this area lets kids run free and makes a nice counterpart to Sesame Street Safari of Fun.

Its proximity to dining and benches make it a good place for weary parents to rest and kids to expend some excess energy (although they will need some of it to make it through the rest of the park).

TOURING TIPS Some of the tunnels are too small for adults to fit in without hunching over, so it's best to sit below and watch the kids from a stationary vantage. Up top, there is a good view down at the Wild Surge, where you can wave at all the folks standing in line.

Wild Surge ★★½

APPEAL BY AGE	PRESCHOOL ★★★½	GRADE SCHOOL ★★★½	TEENS ★★
YOUNG ADULTS ★½		OVER 30 ★★	SENIORS ★★

What it is Spire with two rows of seats that rise and drop. **Scope and scale** Minor attraction. **When to go** Early. **Authors' rating** Time waster; ★½. **Duration of ride** 1 minute.

DESCRIPTIONS AND COMMENTS Hidden in the center of a circle of rocks, this basic carnival ride sends up to 14 people to the top of a spire, then drops, lifts, and again drops them back down. It only freefalls part of the way, so it's fine for younger kids.

TOURING TIPS With only one low-capacity ride, wait times can exceed 45 minutes on busy days. Actual ride time is only about a minute, but load times make this a 3-minute ordeal. This is a clumsy and ill-conceived ride, and with the exception of the neighboring Jungle Flyers, it ranks up there with the worst wait-time-to-thrill ratio in the park.

kids SESAME STREET SAFARI OF FUN

Air Grover ★★★

APPEAL BY AGE	PRESCHOOL ★★★★	GRADE SCHOOL ★★★½	TEENS †
YOUNG ADULTS †		OVER 30 †	SENIORS †

† Not designed for older kids and adults.

What they are Lazy steel-track coaster. **Scope and scale** Headliner. **When to go** Before noon or after 4 p.m. **Special comments** Riders must be at least 38" tall, but if less than 41", they must be accompanied by a rider at least 14 years old. **Authors' rating** Those on the ground need to pinch themselves to stay awake while watching; ★★★. **Duration of ride** About 45 seconds.

DESCRIPTION AND COMMENTS Once the kiddies' lap bars are locked, the cars slowly take off. And they move slowly up an incline to a height of perhaps 20 feet, then slowly move down and through two 360-degree loops, before easing back to the platform.

TOURING TIPS Unlike most roller coasters, riders do NOT want to hurry to claim the front car: the view from there is blocked by a massive Grover figure.

Kiddie Rides ★★★½

APPEAL BY AGE	PRESCHOOL ★★★★	GRADE SCHOOL ★★★½	TEENS †
YOUNG ADULTS †		OVER 30 †	SENIORS †

† Not designed for older kids and adults.

What they are Playland for the stroller and trike set. **Scope and scale** Headliner. **When to go** Before your littlest ones get too pooped. **Special comments** Only those less than 56" tall can ride attractions in this area. **Authors' rating** Time to turn the teens loose while you watch the nippers; ★★★½.

DESCRIPTION AND COMMENTS Replacing the Land of the Dragons elements, this area looks like the mall on the day after Thanksgiving. Kiddie rides include a pint-size merry-go-round and tiny auto track with just two,

two-seat cars on it, plus a hard-floored splash pool that requires at least watertight diapers for the youngest.

Adults and teens can accompany little ones on the three-story-high cargo-netted playground at Elmo's Treehouse. Roped-in bridges between the higher stations lead to a central jungle gym of cargo nets. For adults not wanting to accompany children across the netting, a central staircase leads to the upper-level play area.

TOURING TIPS Height restrictions vary between 36 and 56 inches, though adults are allowed to walk in the overhead cargo netting areas with them. Adults need to study the park map to understand what is where because only the downsized Air Grover roller coaster and the theater stand out from the poorly signed entrances to some attractions.

Sunny Day Theater ★★★

APPEAL BY AGE	PRESCHOOL ★★★★		GRADE SCHOOL ★★★	TEENS †
YOUNG ADULTS †		OVER 30 †		SENIORS †

† Not designed for older kids and adults.

What they are Stage with shows featuring humans inside Sesame Street character costumes. **Scope and scale** Minor attraction. **When to go** Check daily entertainment schedule. **Special comments** Unless your kids are younger than age 8, they will likely be squirming before the end of the show. **Authors' rating** Those metal benches sure seem hard, even before the show is done; ★★½. **Duration of show** 15 minutes.

DESCRIPTION AND COMMENTS Moving about and waving their arms or paws to the soundtrack, the familiar characters offer their gentle version of education. For instance, the show *"A" Is for Africa* has the dancers holding up pictures of animals, while the prerecorded narration talks about the critters' habits and habitats and encourages the audience to imitate the animals' noises.

TOURING TIPS This small theater is the first element of the Sesame Street area if you have turned left at the park entrance and passed through Morocco. While the youngest kids may be content to sit through a show, if they glance just next door, they are liable to be drawn to Air Grover, the mini roller coaster. A better plan than stopping here first is to let the nippers enjoy the rides and active play areas, then return to the theater.

STANLEYVILLE

SheiKra ★★★★★

APPEAL BY AGE	PRESCHOOL †	GRADE SCHOOL ★★★	TEENS ★★★★½
YOUNG ADULTS ★★★★½		OVER 30 ★★★★	SENIORS ★★

† Preschoolers are generally too short to ride.

What it is Quick steel-track dive coaster. **Scope and scale** Super headliner. **When to go** Before 11 a.m. or after 4 p.m. **Special comments** Riders must be at least 54" tall. **Authors' rating** It rides like the commercial; ★★★★★. **Duration of ride** 3 minutes.

DESCRIPTION AND COMMENTS This attraction is 200 feet tall, making it the tallest coaster in the state of Florida, as well as the tallest dive coaster in the world and one of only three dive coasters that exist anywhere. (A dive coaster means the ride has a completely vertical drop.) Also incorporated are twists, swooping turns, a second huge plunge, and a tunnel of mist. The drops aren't just steep—riders hurtle down at an average of 70 miles per hour. The cars seat riders eight people across in three rows, so there are no bad seats. Any seat on SheiKra is second only to the front row of Montu, especially since the coaster's floor was removed.

TOURING TIPS You cannot take anything on this ride and must use a locker ($0.50) found across from the entrance; there are also cubbies for last-minute things you might have in shirt or blouse pockets. If you are planning on hitting any of the nearby water rides soon after, keep your gear in the locker.

If taking route #1, ride Gwazi (located at the front of the park) first thing, then retrace your steps toward the entrance but veer left of the Morocco shopping and food buildings and head to the new Cheetah Hunt. When you finish that ride, you'll be adjacent to Montu. Kumba is next, saving SheiKra for mid- to late afternoon. Leave an hour or so (just in case) to wait in line and ride before the park closes.

If you decide to take route #2, hit Gwazi when the park opens, then make SheiKra your second stop. If you opt for route #3, SheiKra will be your fourth coaster of the morning, after Cheetah Hunt, Montu, and directly after Gwazi.

Stanley Falls Flume ★★

APPEAL BY AGE	PRESCHOOL ★★★	GRADE SCHOOL ★★★	TEENS ★★
YOUNG ADULTS ★★	OVER 30 ★★½		SENIORS ★★½

What it is Water-flume ride. Scope and scale Major attraction. When to go After 3 p.m. Special comments Children not accompanied by an adult must be at least 46" tall. Authors' rating Nothing too exciting; ★★. Duration of ride 3 minutes.

DESCRIPTION AND COMMENTS Logs drift along a winding flume before plummeting down a 40-foot drop. There is almost no theming on this ride, but because the little ones can ride with an adult, it's a good way for small children (who are ready for it) to enjoy a moderate thrill. Riders are only slightly splashed on the final big drop.

TOURING TIPS This ride is exciting without being scary or jarring. During peak season, save it for the late afternoon, when lines will be shorter.

Tanganyika Tidal Wave ★★½

APPEAL BY AGE	PRESCHOOL †	GRADE SCHOOL ★★★	TEENS ★★★
YOUNG ADULTS ★★★	OVER 30 ★★★		SENIORS ★★

† Preschoolers are generally too short to ride.

What it is Quick, super water-flume ride. Scope and scale Headliner. When to go Before 11 a.m. or after 3 p.m. Special comments Riders must be at least

48" tall; you will get soaked. **Authors' rating** A long wait for a very short thrill; ★★½. **Duration of ride** 2 minutes.

DESCRIPTION AND COMMENTS The Tanganyika Tidal Wave was king before the Orlando parks realized that a super water-flume ride should entertain you as well as get you wet. Consequently, this ride pales in comparison with Splash Mountain at Walt Disney World or Jurassic Park at Islands of Adventure. It does do a spectacular job of getting you soaked, however. Riders board a 25-passenger boat and slowly float past empty stilt houses and ominous skulls before making the climb to the top of a steep drop. The cars are specifically designed to throw the water onto the passengers, guaranteeing a soggy experience.

TOURING TIPS If you didn't get enough water on the ride, stand on the bridge crossing the splash pool. An enormous wall of water shoots from each dropping car, fully drenching onlookers. If you want the visuals without the bath, a glass wall in the area blocks the water and is one of the most fun diversions in the park.

As you exit the attraction, or if you choose not to ride, visit Orchid Canyon. This gorgeous area features many varieties of orchids growing around waterfalls in artificial rocks.

BIRD GARDENS

Bird Gardens Theater/*Critter Castaways*   ★★★

APPEAL BY AGE	PRESCHOOL ★★★½	GRADE SCHOOL ★★★½	TEENS ★★
YOUNG ADULTS ★★		OVER 30 ★★½	SENIORS ★★★

What it is Show featuring exotic birds and animal tricks. **Scope and scale** Major attraction. **When to go** Check daily entertainment schedule. **Authors' rating** Beautiful birds, but a pretty ho-hum show; ★★½. **Duration of show** 30 minutes.

DESCRIPTION AND COMMENTS A group of marooned animal keepers, cruise ship refugees, dogs, cats, pigs, and a plethora of birds make up the cast of this silly theatrical number.

The set's not only a shipwreck but is also loaded with surprising gimmicks for the highly trained animals to interact with. Although some of the human actors' performances are so perky as to be nauseating, the production includes a fine showcase of creatures you won't find elsewhere in the park doing stunts you won't find anywhere.

TOURING TIPS A few birds may buzz your head as they flit around the theater, which can be upsetting to the very young.

Eagle Canyon   ★★½

APPEAL BY AGE	PRESCHOOL ★★★	GRADE SCHOOL ★★★½	TEENS ★★★
YOUNG ADULTS ★★★½		OVER 30 ★★★½	SENIORS ★★★½

What it is Small area with a few eagles. **Scope and scale** Diversion. **When to go** Anytime. **Authors' rating** ★★½.

DESCRIPTION AND COMMENTS Eagle Canyon is a small display of eagles on loan from the National Fish and Wildlife Service. All the birds have been injured and are being rehabilitated at Busch Gardens. A small moat separates you from the birds, but you are still very close, and the backdrop of rocks makes it a great photo op.

TOURING TIPS You'll have to look twice to find the path to Eagle Canyon, but it is worth a visit. Even on tethers, eagles are majestic creatures.

Lory Landing ★★★

APPEAL BY AGE	PRESCHOOL ★★★	GRADE SCHOOL ★★★	TEENS ★★★
YOUNG ADULTS ★★★	OVER 30 ★★★		SENIORS ★★★½

What it is Interactive aviary. **Scope and scale** Major attraction. **When to go** Birds are hungrier in the morning but don't mind an afternoon snack. **Authors' rating** Cute; ★★★.

DESCRIPTION AND COMMENTS Many area attractions feature aviaries, but this is by far the biggest and the best. Tropical birds from around the world dot the lush landscape, fill the air in free flight, and are displayed in habitats. Purchase a nectar cup for $5, and some of these delightful creatures will be eating right out of your hand. Many will land on your hands, arms, shoulders, or even head, making this attraction a nightmare for those with bird-in-the-hair phobia. The illustrated journal of a fictitious explorer helps differentiate the many species, including lorikeets, hornbills, parrots, and avocets.

TOURING TIPS Try to visit before lunch because the birds usually get their fill of nectar by early afternoon.

Walkabout Way ★★★½

APPEAL BY AGE	PRESCHOOL ★★★★	GRADE SCHOOL ★★★★	TEENS ★★★½
YOUNG ADULTS ★★★½	OVER 30 ★★★½		SENIORS ★★★

What it is A chance to feed kangaroos and wallabies, plus a small aviary. **Scope and scale** Minor attraction. **When to go** Anytime, but check park map for scheduled keepers' chats and feedings. **Authors' rating** ★★★½.

DESCRIPTION AND COMMENTS Redesigned in the summer of 2010, Walkabout Way is a path between the large cages holding wallabies and both red and gray kangaroos. Feed is for sale if you want to have the oddly sweet-looking creatures nuzzle your hand, or you can watch the pros do it several times a day. The Walkabout is adjacent to the smallish Aviary Walk-Thru. There are no informational handouts on the birds nor plaques to identify them, but the aviary does include kookaburras.

TOURING TIPS This far corner of the park is quiet, and you may find a bit of solace by the pond near the aviary.

DINING

BUSCH GARDENS OFFERS A SIMILAR SELECTION of food as sister park SeaWorld. Fast food should cost about $6–$10 per person, including drinks. The menu at Bengal Bistro in the Jungala area is typical: a breaded fish sandwich is $9, a grilled chicken sandwich is $8, an Italian sub filled with deli meats and cheese is $9, and a kid's hot dog with a souvenir plate is $8. All of these come with a side item such as fries. There is some variety among the dining spots. For instance, carved deli sandwiches on freshly baked bread and fajita wraps are a favorite at **Zagora Café.**

For a real treat, try a sit-down meal at **Crown Colony House** restaurant, which offers amazing views of the Serengeti Plain. The menu features chowders, salads, sandwiches, vegetable platters, pasta, and seafood. Entrees range $9–$18.

The 1,000-seat, air-conditioned **Desert Grill** restaurant is a nice break from the outside heat. Bare wooden tables surround a stage from which dancers and singers perform shows several times throughout the day, but neither the show nor the food is worth writing home about. Baby-back ribs and Italian entrees such as spaghetti and meatballs and fettuccini Alfredo, as well as sandwiches and a full kids' menu, are offered. Keeping in mind that the Desert Grill serves cafeteria-style and feeds thousands daily, the food is not bad and the prices are reasonable, with sandwiches for $7–$9, desserts for $3, and beer for about $4.

The **Zambia Smokehouse** is an indoor-outdoor restaurant, and it's positioned next to the SheiKra monster coaster, allowing great views of the screaming passengers and the ride's impressive swoops and drops. Entrees such as ribs, chicken, and brisket are smoked for several hours and are reasonably priced, ranging $8–$16

In 2010 Busch Gardens introduced the All-Day Dining Deal: parkgoers can get one entree, a side item or dessert, and a nonalcoholic drink at each of six restaurants—for $30 for adults and $15 for kids.

SHOPPING

THERE'S PLENTY OF BUSCH GARDENS–LOGO merchandise, but visitors looking for something more should be happy with the diverse selection. Find nature-themed gifts, such as wind chimes and jewelry, at **Xcursions.** African gifts and crafts, including clothing, brass urns, and leather goods, can be found throughout the park. Most have reasonable prices, although some larger, intricate items can be more expensive. For that hard-to-shop-for adult, try the **West African Trading Company,** which features handcrafted items from many countries, as well as a walk-in cigar humidor. Like SeaWorld, Busch Gardens offers a vast array of kid-pleasing stuffed animals; kids and parents should be happy with the prices.

PART THREE

LEGOLAND FLORIDA

AS THE GUIDEBOOK YOU'RE HOLDING RECOUNTS, Central Florida is thick with theme parks, amusement parks, and water parks, which are wrapped around any number of specialty topics. Each place works hard to differentiate itself from the competition.

Now, an attraction that actually comes with a different pedigree is scheduled to open in fall 2011. For unlike the massive parks that emphasize cartoon heroes, action movies, or living creatures, Legoland Florida has no similar competition: nowhere else in the Sunshine State is there a Lincoln Log Land, a Tinkertoy Town, or an Erector Set Village.

But there are four other Legolands, three in Europe and one that opened in 1999 in Carlsbad, California, north of San Diego. Another Legoland is planned for Malaysia in 2013. The original park opened in 1968, in Billund, Denmark, and the word *Lego* is a contraction of the Danish words that translate as "play well."

What filled that first 9-acre site more than 40 years ago will still be a major lure for Legoland Florida: giant models of real-life buildings, vehicles, and people, all made from the tiny plastic bricks.

But Legoland Florida has a number of rides, including four roller coasters, among its 50 attractions. However, these are not the high-speed, whipsaw attractions that draw adrenaline junkies to the larger theme parks. Instead, Legoland is designed for the chief users of the plastic blocks, kids 2–12 years old—with only a nod to the adults who bring them. While several of the pint-size rides are just for the kiddies, others are designed to accommodate adults along for the fun.

A number of the new park's elements are directly copied from their predecessors in the California attraction. And there are also elements of the new park's predecessor on this site, the legendary Cypress Gardens. Adrian Jones, Legoland's general manager, told a reporter that "75% of the [existing] infrastructure is there in terms of the buildings we're going to be reusing and redeveloping."

For instance, two of the roller coasters at Legoland are repurposed from Cypress Gardens, which closed in September 2009. A majority of the buildings in the former town area are being renovated to serve as shops and restaurants. Cypress Gardens' 700-seat theater will be converted into Fun Town Theater, which will show four different movies daily.

And in a bow to the environment and recycling, about 660 palms and oaks were moved during the new park's construction and have been replanted, some of the famed botanical gardens will be restored, and an estimated 18,000 tons of existing sidewalks and foundations were ground up by special machines that spit out tiny chunks, to be reused in Legoland.

GETTING THERE

LEGOLAND FLORIDA IS ROUGHLY 35 miles and 45 minutes west of Walt Disney World. From the Orlando area, take I-4 west and exit onto US 27 south. Continue on this road about 20 miles. Turn right at FL 540/Cypress Gardens Boulevard. The park is 4 miles away on the left. Look for green mileage signs that point the way.

ADMISSION PRICES

ONLY SPECIAL PRICING FOR THE PARK'S OPENING, called preview pricing, was available at press time. Permanent ticket pricing had not yet been determined at press time.

PREVIEW ADMISSION | Adults $65 + tax | Children ages 3–12 and Seniors age 60+ $55 + tax

Annual Passes

Annual Passes provide unlimited admission to Legoland Florida, special discounts, and invitations to events. The Plus Pass, in addition to unlimited admission to Legoland Florida, includes free parking, special discounts, invitations to events, and dining and retail discounts. The Ambassador Pass includes unlimited admission to Legoland Florida for life, free preferred parking, special discounts, invitations to events, dining and retail discounts, and an exclusive model builder session. The prices listed below are special offers during the park's preview period.

Annual Pass | All ages **$99 + tax**

Annual Plus Pass | Adults **$159 + tax** | Children ages 3–12 and Seniors age 60+ **$129 + tax**

Ambassador (lifetime) **Pass** | All ages **$2,500 + tax**

CONTACTING LEGOLAND FLORIDA

FOR MORE INFORMATION, visit the website at **legoland.com,** which has updates about the park. For general information, you may call ☎ 877-350-LEGO (5346).

ATTRACTIONS

BECAUSE LEGOLAND FLORIDA HAD NOT YET OPENED at press time, what follows are highlights of the new theme park's lands and attractions. Legoland ride minimum heights range 34–40 inches; some rides have age minimums or maximums, and some require an adult or teenager to accompany the youngest riders.

FUN TOWN

AFTER PASSING THE REQUISITE GUEST SERVICES and souvenir store, visitors will enter Fun Town, where the first attraction is the **Lego Factory.** A miniature of the real manufacturing operation, automated machinery molds, decorates, assembles, and packs Lego products.

Also here are restaurants, a carousel, and the **Fun Town Theater.** It alternates four 3-D films featuring Lego characters such as Clutch Powers and Bob the Builder. Themes range from planning before you start a project to racing cars to the dangers of living in medieval times. In addition to the usual 3-D effect, audiences experience doses of smoke, wind, snow, and water.

A few attractions from Cypress Gardens can also be found here. Island in the Sky, an observation tower, is now called **Flying Island.** Also, the **Conservatory,** which once held real butterflies, will now feature Lego flowers and butterflies. Guests, however, can make their own Lego flowers here or purchase them.

Visitors can exit Fun Town to their right, coming to Duplo Village, or go straight ahead to Miniland USA.

DUPLO VILLAGE

THIS AREA IS AIMED AT THE YOUNGEST VISITORS, down to toddlers. Here, they can pretend to fly a plane or drive a car through a mock town scaled down to their size. They can also go for a ride on a fire truck, a carryover from Cypress Gardens. To burn off some energy, kids can explore a cargo-net-style climbing and play area. And for relief from the Florida heat, they can splash around pop-up water jets.

MINILAND USA

ONE OF THE WONDERS OF ALL THE LEGOLANDS is Miniland, home of the incredible models made from the little plastic blocks. Here, a reported 20 million Legos have been used to create seven themed areas—**Washington, D.C., New York City,** and **Las Vegas,** as well as a pirate display and such **Florida** icons as Kennedy Space Center, the Daytona International Speedway, and Mallory Square in Key West.

Artisans termed master model builders create these spectacles on a 1:20 scale. Some of the specific models include animated aspects or soundtracks. For instance, at the Daytona area, visitors will be able to race tiny cars made, of course, of Legos.

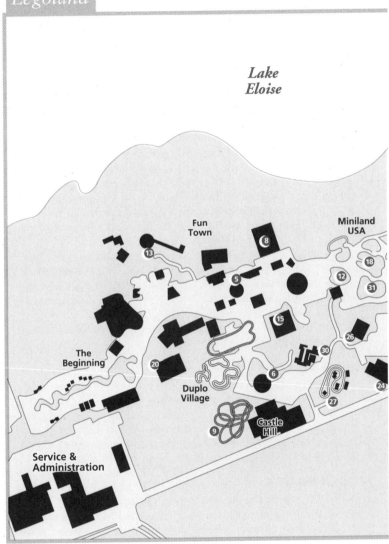

Lake Eloise

Fun Town

Miniland USA

The Beginning

Duplo Village

Castle Hill

Service & Administration

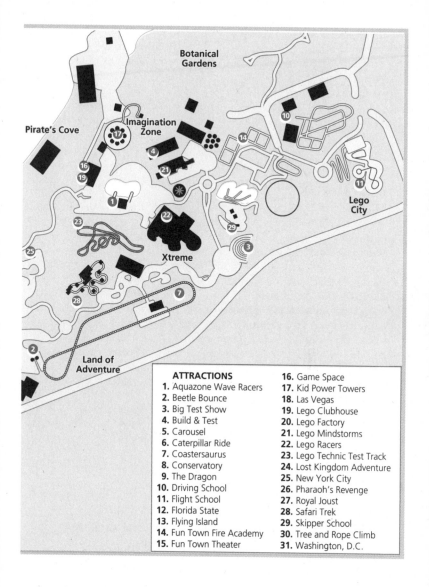

Botanical
Gardens

Pirate's Cove

Imagination
Zone

Lego
City

Xtreme

Land of
Adventure

ATTRACTIONS

1. Aquazone Wave Racers
2. Beetle Bounce
3. Big Test Show
4. Build & Test
5. Carousel
6. Caterpillar Ride
7. Coastersaurus
8. Conservatory
9. The Dragon
10. Driving School
11. Flight School
12. Florida State
13. Flying Island
14. Fun Town Fire Academy
15. Fun Town Theater
16. Game Space
17. Kid Power Towers
18. Las Vegas
19. Lego Clubhouse
20. Lego Factory
21. Lego Mindstorms
22. Lego Racers
23. Lego Technic Test Track
24. Lost Kingdom Adventure
25. New York City
26. Pharaoh's Revenge
27. Royal Joust
28. Safari Trek
29. Skipper School
30. Tree and Rope Climb
31. Washington, D.C.

The Las Vegas model includes hotels such as Luxor Las Vegas, Excalibur, Mirage, and Treasure Island, plus the Stratosphere tower and Paris Las Vegas's Eiffel Tower.

The Washington area has miniature re-creations of the White House (it measures about 5-by-4-feet), the Capitol, the Washington Monument, and the Jefferson Memorial. An animated marching band parades in front of the Capitol.

Utilizing about 2 million blocks, New York City includes Rockefeller Plaza with tiny water fountains, a fleet of yellow taxis rolling through Times Square, the Statue of Liberty, the Empire State Building (more than 10 feet tall), the Guggenheim Museum, and the Bronx Zoo. The pirate section features a battle between two opposing ships.

CASTLE HILL

THE THEME HERE IS THE WORLD OF KNIGHTS, damsels, and dragons, and the pace picks up, slightly, among the rides.

The Dragon is the name of a coaster ride that visitors board inside this area's landmark, a castle. The cars roll around within the building for a while before it ventures outside for the bigger drops and twists. It was made using Cypress Gardens' former Okeechobee Rampage family coaster.

Coaster enthusiasts will recognize this as a Vekoma "roller skater coaster," essentially, wheels in the front and back of each car. But again, the ride is aimed at young children. As park general manager Adrian Jones noted before construction began, "The least-challenging coasters are not as fast nor as steep in their hills" as the two faster coasters, Coastersaurus and Technic Test Track, which are elsewhere in Legoland.

The other major ride in Castle Hill is the **Royal Joust.** This is a procession of one-person, horse-shaped rides proceeding on a track. The horses appear to be made from large Lego blocks—as is the case throughout the park's rides.

The horses approach others as the track loops about, but despite the name of the ride, any combat takes place only in the rider's imagination—there are no weapons to wave at the oncoming rider. The height restriction for the Royal Joust is a 36-inch minimum.

The **Caterpillar Ride** quickly rotates around a central axis while moving slightly up and down, like a gentle wave.

Castle Hill includes a **Tree and Rope Climb** play area to let the little ones burn off energy on cargo nets and wooden walkways.

LAND OF ADVENTURE

AS THE NAME IMPLIES, this is another step up in the excitement factor. The chief attractions here are described below.

BEETLE BOUNCE These are two side-by-side outdoor towers, each with a seat that can hold up to four people. The seat rides as high as 15 feet, toward scarab beetles (this area has an Egyptian theme) fashioned from Legos, before the seat drops back down.

COASTERSAURUS This is the wooden roller coaster that was named the Triple Hurricane when it was purpose-built and installed for Cypress Gardens. Now it curves and dips through a prehistoric jungle of animated dinosaurs—again made from Lego bricks.

The hills—the initial one is only 40 feet up—and thrills are junior-sized, the ride now has a dinosaur theme, and for any who rode it before, they will recognize that it is mostly untouched except for a thorough cleaning and modest update. With speeds up to 21 miles per hour, the ride lasts just under 1 minute.

LOST KINGDOM ADVENTURE A 16-foot-tall Lego-brick pharaoh stands outside the entrance to this indoor ride.

Up to four people board cars for a tracked ride in the dark. Each rider has a laser gun to fire at targets at pop-up or weaving targets on each side of the car. While digital counters display the score for each passenger, there are no prizes.

PHARAOH'S REVENGE Children and parents alike can shoot foam balls at targets in this outdoor attraction. This area also has a maze for children to wander through.

SAFARI TREK An off-road vehicle takes kids through "African" plains filled with Lego wildlife, such as gorillas and elephants.

XTREME

THIS AREA HAS THE TWO RIDES designed to offer the most thrills —but again, just junior-size excitement.

AQUAZONE WAVE RACERS This ride is sort of a toned-down Jet Ski attached to a central post like spokes of a wheel. The vehicles hold two people; the driver can alter the speed of the racer and maneuver it in order to avoid blasts from the water cannon of other drivers as well as from spectators.

LEGO RACERS This 12-minute, animated 3-D movie is about car racing.

LEGO TECHNIC TEST TRACK This steel coaster, which was once the Jungle Coaster at Legoland Windsor (England) and has now been rethemed, has individual cars that seat two people each in two rows. It's what enthusiasts know as a "wild mouse" ride, meaning that it combines flat track with sharp turns and mini-dips, not just up and down hills. The ride climbs to about 52 feet at its highest and speeds up to 35 miles per hour.

PIRATE'S COVE

SANDWICHED BETWEEN XTREME AND MINILAND, along the shores of Lake Eloise, are the stands for spectators who used to thrill to a Cypress Gardens' trademark, the often-spectacular water-skiiing stunt shows. Legoland is making good use of the body of water with a **pirate water-stunt show.**

LEGO CITY

THE DESIGNERS ENVISION THIS DIVERSE AREA as a place for kids to live out their dreams, take part in a comedy stunt show, and still get in a thrill ride.

At the **Fun Town Fire Academy,** for instance, adults are encouraged to help the youngsters power one of four Lego-brick fire engines as they race to the scene of a mock fire.

One person, usually an adult, pumps a lever to propel the fire truck while someone else, usually a child, steers. Once at the pretend fire, someone pumps another lever to bring water to the hose that the other partner aims toward a hole in the mock flames. After "putting out" the fire, the first team to return to the starting line is the winner.

In a different version of playing firefighter, park comics display some acrobatic skills while pretending to be trainees in the academy. They use a much bigger fire engine, hoses, and volunteers from among the spectators to pass their own **Big Test.**

Elsewhere in this area, children ages 3–5 and 6–12 can attend two different levels of **Driving School,** steering Lego-brick shaped cars around a course. The cars, powered by onboard electric batteries, are not on a track but can't go fast enough to cause any fender benders.

At **Skipper School,** the kids can steer boats around a watercourse.

The thrill ride in Lego City is another of the former park's re-purposed roller coasters: the wonderfully named Swamp Thing. But Swamp Thing was then and the **Flight School** is now.

This ride was originally designed as an introduction—mainly for young children—to a modest roller coaster ride. It is an inverted roller coaster: two riders sit side by side in a suspended carrier that has no floor, so the extra thrill is looking down past your dangling legs.

Up to 20 can ride at a time over the 1,122 feet of track. In its previous life, Swamp Thing only went up to 26 miles per hour and rose to only 49 feet, taking just over a minute to cover the course's turns and angles.

IMAGINATION ZONE

MARKED BY A GIANT MODEL OF ALBERT EINSTEIN'S HEAD, this area essentially is the place where kids and grown-ups finally get to use both their minds and hands—and to play with the eponymous blocks. The main areas are described below.

BUILD & TEST Create your own miniature car and race against somebody else on a digitally timed track.

GAME SPACE You didn't think you could escape video games completely, did you? Here are stations for 13 G-rated games, most with a Lego tie-in but featuring such pop-culture icons as *Star Wars,* Indiana Jones, and Batman.

There is one outdoors diversion in the Imagination Zone also requiring hands and minds: the **Kid Power Towers** resemble giant stacks of—what else?—Lego blocks. Sitting in carriers that can hold two people, kids and adults pull down on ropes to hoist themselves to the top of a tower for a slightly elevated view of the park and nearby Lake Eloise, and then get an easy descent back down.

LEGO CLUBHOUSE The Clubhouse offers food, drinks, and merchandise, but children can also play a multiplayer game online, where kids from all over the world build and play together.

LEGO MINDSTORMS You can build and select simple commands to program computer-directed robots.

BOTANICAL GARDENS

LOCATED AT THE FAR END OF THE PARK, the botanical gardens were a hallmark of the former park here, Cypress Gardens. Legoland, of course, has added Lego flowers and treasure-hunt items. Stop by here when you need to take a relaxing walk.

DINING

LEGOLAND OFFERS A FEW MORE CHOICES than the standard burger and fries. **The Garden Restaurant,** formerly Aunt Julie's Country Kitchen, is the first in the park, located in the entry plaza. It offers soups, salads, and sandwiches for the health-conscious. **The Market** located nearby, serves freshly baked pastries, fruit, yogurt, soft-serve ice cream, and espresso. In Fun Town, try **Granny's Apple Fries,** which are sliced apples coated with sugar and cinnamon and served with a vanilla cream sauce. **Lego Clubhouse,** in the Imagination Zone, offers snacks and drinks. Other eateries are located throughout the park.

SHOPPING

SHOPPING HERE CONSISTS MOSTLY OF LEGO BRICKS AND KITS. **The Big Shop,** located near the entry, features a huge selection of Lego and Legoland merchandise. In Fun Town, visit the **Studio Store** for more Lego merchandise, such as Clutch Powers, Bob the Builder, and so on. **Lego Clubhouse,** in addition to hosting a multiplayer online game, offers Lego bricks and Make & Create Kits.

PART FOUR

GATORLAND

IN THESE DAYS OF GENIAL ZOOKEEPERS, it's hard to imagine a man like Florida showman Owen Godwin, who established Gatorland way back in 1949. More of a reptile-fixated P. T. Barnum than an environmental enthusiast, Godwin traveled the world collecting toothy critters for his zoo collection of gators and "jungle crocs." But the days of aggressive collecting are gone. Most of the alligators are born right in the Gatorland swamp, and Gatorland naturalists will earnestly tell you of their efforts to rehabilitate a variety of injured or displaced animals brought to them from all over Florida.

For more than 60 years, Gatorland has existed as a roadside wonder. Before the days of magic castles and studio back lots, visitors flocked to the Sunshine State for its beaches and wildlife. Sprinkled along the highways that linked the state's natural attractions were tiny outposts of tourism—must-see roadside stops meant to break up the monotony of travel. Gatorland fell brilliantly into this category. The park was ripe with tourist appeal—who can resist a park that hawks Florida's most infamous resident, the alligator?

unofficial **TIP**
For those who want variety in their sightseeing itinerary, this is the place for a real change of pace.

Today, Gatorland seems to disappear in the clutter of touristy Orlando. But rather than fall victim to its own kitsch or wither in the Disney glare, Gatorland has adapted enough to proudly call itself "Orlando's best half-day attraction." It doesn't try to be one of the highfalutin theme parks in its backyard. Although the attraction has grown to more than 100 acres, the whole place is barely big enough for a good-size Walt Disney World parking lot. But nowhere else will you see this many gators and crocs, and nowhere else are they celebrated with such abandon. In short, Gatorland is a hallmark of Old Florida made good.

The park recently added a zip line, at heights up to 56 feet above the ground. The zip line carries the brave over ponds holding crocs

Gatorland

● **ATTRACTIONS**
1. Allie's Barnyard
2. Alligator Island
3. Alligator Breeding Marsh and Bird Rookery
4. Burmese pythons
5. Cuban crocs
6. Dog Gone Gator
7. Emu enclosure
8. Flamingo Island
9. Gator Gully Splash Park
10. *Gator Jumparoo Show*
11. Gator Wrestlin' Stadium/*Gator Wrestlin' Show*
12. Gatorland Express Train Station
13. Giant tortoise
14. Jungle Crocs of the World
15. Nile crocs
16. Observation Tower
17. Parrot Playground
18. Pearl's Train Depot *(Exit Only)*
19. Saltwater crocs
20. Sandhill cranes
21. Screamin' Gator Zip Line
22. Snakes of Florida
23. Swamp Walk
24. Turkeys and fallow deer
25. *Up Close Encounters*
26. Very Merry Aviary

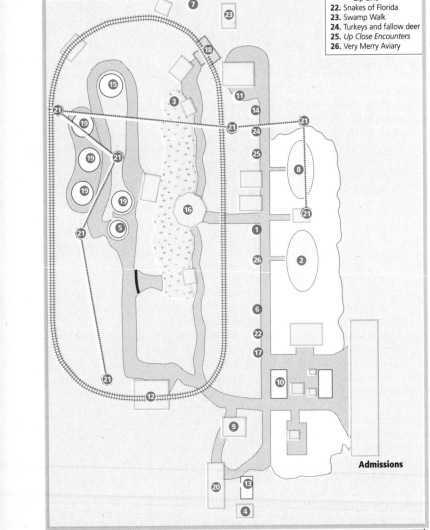

Admissions

and gators. It comes with a big ol' price tag too—more than the cost of admission.

GETTING THERE

FROM DISNEY Take FL 192 (or the Osceola Parkway, if you don't mind paying a few bucks in tolls) to FL 441 (Orange Blossom Trail). Turn left. Gatorland is on your right.

FROM ORLANDO Take I-4 to FL 528 (Beeline Highway). Exit at Consulate and turn right. Make a right on FL 441 (Orange Blossom Trail). Gatorland is about 7 miles south, between the Osceola Parkway and FL 417 (the Central Florida GreeneWay). Parking is free.

ADMISSION PRICES

FOLLOWING ARE THE FULL ADMISSION PRICES at press time. Coupons are available in Gatorland brochures (found at kiosks throughout Orlando), and discounted prices are available at **gatorland.com.** The park offers AAA, AARP, and Florida-resident discounts.

One-day Pass

Adults **$22.99 + tax** | Children ages 3–12 **$14.99 + tax**
Children under age 3 **Free**

Grunt Package (includes admission, train ticket, gator kibble, and chance to sit on a gator)

Adults **$39.15 + tax** | Children ages 3–12 **$23.55 + tax**

Annual Pass

Adults **$43.99 + tax** | Children ages 3–12 **$29.99 + tax**

ARRIVING

GATORLAND IS OPEN DAILY 9 a.m.–5 p.m. Gators don't mind rain (and most observation walkways have canopies), so the attraction is open rain or shine.

Gatorland bills itself as a half-day attraction, which makes it the perfect alternative when you don't have a full day to spend at Walt Disney World, SeaWorld, or the Kennedy Space Center Visitor Complex. Plan to spend about three to four hours to see it well. However, the park lends itself to any type of schedule. With nearby parking and the park's manageable size, it is easy to come and go. A small-gauge railroad ride traverses part of the park and passes local flora and fauna in their natural swampy habitat.

unofficial **TIP**
Colder temperatures will make the alligators sluggish and less likely to jump for food.

Shows and feeding times are scheduled throughout the day, with performances shortly after opening, after lunch, and in midafternoon. Performances are scheduled for easy back-to-back viewing.

Check the show schedule when you arrive. Because the shows are can't-miss attractions, plan your schedule around them. Plenty of diversions are near each show area. The Jungle Crocs of the World feeding "show" is the farthest away, requiring about a 12-minute walk, so keep that in mind when heading for this area of the park.

unofficial **TIP**
Plan your visit to this park around the shows.

CONTACTING GATORLAND

FOR MORE INFORMATION, contact Gatorland at ☎ 800-393-JAWS (5297) or **gatorland.com**.

▐▙ ATTRACTIONS

Alligator Breeding Marsh and Bird Sanctuary ★★★½

| APPEAL | BY | AGE | PRESCHOOL | ★★ | GRADE | SCHOOL | ★★ | TEENS | ★★ |
| YOUNG | ADULTS | ★★★ | OVER | 30 | ★★★ | | SENIORS | | ★★★ |

What it is A breeding ground for gators in a picturesque setting. **Scope and scale** Diversion. **When to go** At the warmer part of the day. **Authors' rating** The quiet heart of Gatorland; ★★★½.

DESCRIPTION AND COMMENTS The alligator breeding marsh is one of Gatorland's most unexpected attractions. Set in the middle of a park of zoolike cages and enclosures, this large body of water is home to nearly 200 alligators in their natural setting. Once you consider the somewhat grim fact that the park also doubles as an alligator farm selling meat and hides, you realize that you're looking at the real ranch behind all the wrestlin' and jumpin'. Despite this eco-unfriendly downer, a flotilla of a couple dozen gators hovering placidly by your feet is enough to make you reconsider leaning over the railing for a better photo. Try out each floor of the three-story observation tower for different (and safely distant) perspectives.

The marsh is also a haven for bird-watchers. Every year, more than 4,000 birds make their home at Gatorland, including green, blue, and tricolored herons, cattle egrets, and cormorants. At feeding time, the trees along the boardwalk marsh fill with waterbirds, including several rare and protected species.

TOURING TIPS For the best view, bring binoculars. It is truly spectacular to feed the gators here (a bag of fish is $5). There is a smaller feeding area elsewhere, but you'll get more of a show if you take the goodies here. On one visit, a family brought several loaves of bread to feed the gators. It was a fascinating sight, and it attracted what seemed like hundreds of creatures. Check the trees on your right as you walk toward the petting farm, with the marsh behind you. During summer visits, they host hundreds of nesting egrets and herons, with the accompanying chirps of their young. Because the second level of the observation tower is above the trees, it provides a rare look at these birds.

kids Gator Gully Splash Park ★★★

APPEAL BY AGE	PRESCHOOL ★★★	GRADE SCHOOL ★★★★	TEENS ★★½
YOUNG ADULTS ★★★		OVER 30 ★★	SENIORS ★

What it is A wet and dry playground for kids. **Scope and scale** Major attraction. **When to go** When the temperature kicks up a notch. **Authors' rating** A welcome way to cool down; ★★★.

DESCRIPTION AND COMMENTS Small children will go berserk when they see this Old Florida–themed water playground. Gatorland really shines here, with an attraction that rivals the children's areas located at other Orlando parks. You'll find several interactive fountains and other water-soaking games. Nearby, a dry playground is available for those who don't want to get wet.

TOURING TIPS Let the kids loose at Gator Gully *after* the shows, so they won't have to walk around wet for the rest of the day.

Gator Jumparoo Show ★★★★

APPEAL BY AGE	PRESCHOOL ★★★	GRADE SCHOOL ★★★★	TEENS ★★★½
YOUNG ADULTS ★★★		OVER 30 ★★★	SENIORS ★★★

What it is It's gators: they jump, and you watch—from a distance. **Scope and scale** Super headliner. **When to go** Check entertainment schedule. **Authors' rating** Yikes! ★★★★. **Duration of show** 15 minutes.

DESCRIPTION AND COMMENTS This is, as they say, the marrow that has kept visitors circulating through Gatorland for almost 60 years. Visitors gather around a square pond, framed by wooden boardwalks (thankfully with high railings). A trainer ventures out to a fragile-looking cupola on the water, and then the fun begins. Everyone is encouraged to stamp their feet on the boards, which lets the alligators know that supper's ready. The reptiles come gliding in from adjacent ponds, and the trainer yells and waves to attract them. Plucked chickens are strung up on wires over the water, and them gators commence to jumpin'. Trainers also dangle treats over the water and gators snatch the food right from their hands. After you see a 10-foot-long 300-pounder leap head-high out of the water to crunch some poultry, you'll spend the rest of your time at Gatorland nervously skirting the railings. Visit the nonthreatening lorikeet aviary to calm down if necessary.

TOURING TIPS There's no seating here, so be sure to arrive at least 10 minutes before show time to stake your claim along the railing.

Gator Wrestling Stadium/ *Gator Wrestlin' Show* ★★★★

APPEAL BY AGE	PRESCHOOL ★★	GRADE SCHOOL ★★★★	TEENS ★★★★
YOUNG ADULTS ★★★		OVER 30 ★★★½	SENIORS ★★★

What it is Where man (especially his head) was not meant to go. **Scope and scale** Super headliner. **When to go** Check entertainment schedule; usually three shows daily. **Authors' rating** Not to be missed; ★★★. **Duration of show** 15 minutes.

DESCRIPTION AND COMMENTS There are no bad views in the 800-seat stadium. There is one seat, however, that most audience members would rather not have. That's the perch on the back of an alligator in a sandy pit in the middle of the theater. Here, a wisecracking fool keeps the audience spellbound with his courage—or reckless disregard for bodily integrity—for 15 minutes. The show features two "crackers," the nickname for Florida ranchers who often cracked their whips to get their animals to move. Enlisting their best Foghorn Leghorn impressions, the two play off of each other while one unfortunate soul wrestles the gator, opens its mouth, and even (gulp!) places his chin under its snout.

TOURING TIPS Arrive a bit early to see the "wrestlers" warming up. Although every side offers a good view, the red bleachers typically have the best vantage.

Gatorland Express Railroad ★★

APPEAL BY AGE	PRESCHOOL ★★★		GRADE SCHOOL ★★★		TEENS ★
YOUNG ADULTS ★½		OVER 30 ★★			SENIORS ★★½

What it is A circling train. **Scope and scale** Diversion. **When to go** Anytime for a quick rest of your feet. **Authors' rating** Can a gator hijack a train? ★★. **Duration of ride** 6 minutes.

DESCRIPTION AND COMMENTS Given the park's small size, the train isn't really necessary as transportation. But it's good for a break and for getting a different view of the natural areas. Chances are that the nutty guy who narrates your ride will turn up again later in the gator-wrestling or *Jumparoo* show.

TOURING TIPS It costs an extra $2 to ride the train, but you can tack the fee onto your ticket when you arrive. The train is a good way to see the park and rest your feet but skip it if you don't need the break.

Gatorland Zoo ★★

APPEAL BY AGE	PRESCHOOL ★★★		GRADE SCHOOL ★★★		TEENS ★★
YOUNG ADULTS ★★½		OVER 30 ★★			SENIORS ★★

What it is A collection of animal displays. **Scope and scale** Diversion. **When to go** Between shows. **Authors' rating** Fun, but not as cool as gators; ★★.

DESCRIPTION AND COMMENTS Dozens of animal exhibits line the 150-foot main walkway, including Florida white-tailed deer, emus, llamas, snakes, turtles, tortoises, and birds. Allie's Barnyard petting zoo—always a favorite among young children—contains the usual collection of goats and sheep. The walk-through Very Merry Aviary is stocked with lorikeets, multicolored birds that are trained to land on visitors' shoulders in order to drink nectar from a cup (available for $2). Baby alligators are sometimes on display here, and a special Snakes of Florida exhibit highlights local serpents.

TOURING TIPS Zoo exhibits are near both main show areas and are perfect fillers between other shows. Bring a handful of quarters to buy animal food. It's a minimal cost for a big thrill.

Jungle Crocs of the World ★★★

| APPEAL BY AGE | PRESCHOOL ★★ | GRADE SCHOOL ★★★½ | TEENS ★★★ |
| YOUNG ADULTS ★★★ | | OVER 30 ★★★½ | SENIORS ★★★½ |

What it is A rare collection of international crocodiles. **Scope and scale** Headliner. **When to go** Around feeding time. **Authors' rating** Insidiously catchy theme song; ★★★. **Duration of show** 10 minutes (feeding show).

DESCRIPTION AND COMMENTS As you step onto the boardwalk leading you to Gatorland's newest animal exhibit, you'll soon notice how the park revels in its own cheese factor. Speakers lining the walkway play a song devoted entirely to founder Owen Godwin and his many adventures to claim this collection of "jungle crocs." This song, a close relative to *The Beverly Hillbillies* theme, will not leave your brain for at least an hour after departing Gatorland. But eventually, you come to the crocodile habitats. There are four total, featuring crocodiles from North and South America, Cuba, Asia, and Africa's Nile River. This exhibit features a rare collection of crocodiles, such as the Cuban crocodile. The smallest and most dangerous of breeds, Cuban crocs can leap from the water like dolphins to catch birds in flight. This area includes plenty of sight gags, including downed planes and pup tents that mysteriously lack any human beings.

TOURING TIPS Be sure to stick around for a feeding session, listed on the show schedule. On our latest visit, however, the feeding times were not listed, so you may need to ask.

Screamin' Gator Zip Line

What it is A zip line over the alligators and crocodiles. **Scope and scale** Super headliner. **Special comments** The price is relatively steep—$60—but that includes admission to Gatorland. **Authors' rating** Looks like it will be a great thrill. **Duration of experience** 45 minutes.

DESCRIPTION AND COMMENTS For the first half century or so, nothing at Gatorland caused visitors an adrenaline rush—nothing required more energy than walking about. But this new feature (which was scheduled to open in May 2011) is way different.

The zip line will whoosh the daring above ponds holding Cuban crocodiles and above the Alligator Breeding Marsh. While the crocs are noted for jumping out of the water for handouts, those zipping overhead will be harnessed to metal cables—with back-up buckles for safety.

The route covers about 1,200 feet, with four intermediate platforms to zip to. Those stations are as much as 485 feet apart, so the passengers can expect to, well, zip along as fast as 30 miles per hour. The cables are up to 56 feet above the attraction.

Including the walk through the park to reach the first tower, by the train station, and the safety orientation, experiencing the Screamin' Gator will take about 45 minutes. The final station is at Flamingo Island. Riders must weigh at least 70 pounds.

TOURING TIPS Plan ahead for this attraction; the price includes admission to the park.

Swamp Walk ★★★

APPEAL BY AGE	PRESCHOOL ★	GRADE SCHOOL ★	TEENS ★
YOUNG ADULTS ★★½		OVER 30 ★★★	SENIORS ★★★

What it is Boardwalk through undisturbed nature. **Scope and scale** Diversion.
When to go When you need some quiet time. **Authors' rating** Natural Florida;
★★★.

DESCRIPTION AND COMMENTS Cross the swinging bridge that leads to a
boardwalk trail through a beautiful natural swamp. So far removed
from the rest of the attractions that many visitors fail to discover it,
the walk is easily one of the most exotic and unusual promenades to
be found in all of Florida. The swamp is actually part of the headwaters
for the Florida Everglades, the critically important south Florida swampland hundreds of miles away. Winding gracefully with no apparent
impact on the environment, the walk, flanked by towering cypress and
draped with Spanish moss, disappears deep into the lush, green swamp.
Simultaneously tranquil and serene yet bursting with life, the swamp
radiates primeval loveliness.

TOURING TIPS Visit the Swamp Walk before sunset, when the mosquitoes
come out to feast on unsuspecting Gatorland tourists. There is no fence
underneath the railing, so keep an eye on the little ones, although the
mere idea that a gator is in this swamp should be enough to keep them
in line.

Up Close Encounters/Snake Show ★★★

APPEAL BY AGE	PRESCHOOL ★★	GRADE SCHOOL ★★★	TEENS ★★
YOUNG ADULTS ★★★		OVER 30 ★★½	SENIORS ★★

What it is Educational hands-on animal show. **Scope and scale** Minor attraction.
When to go When not at the other three shows; usually held three times a day.
Authors' rating Creepy and fun; ★★★.

DESCRIPTION AND COMMENTS This small stadium hosts a show-and-tell of
whatever creatures—mostly snakes—the keepers might have in Gatorland's bag of tricks that day. The keepers hold the venomous critters
aloft, but visitors can actually handle some of the more passive creatures,
such as birds or animals borrowed from the petting zoo. Gatorland provides a home for lots of captured or injured wildlife, including animals
confiscated from illegal pet traders. One keeper offered to let us hold
some friendly snakes and a giant emperor scorpion, creepy crawly as
can be. We respectfully declined.

TOURING TIPS Our bad example aside, the best way to enjoy the show is to
get close to the creatures and interact. Although the knowledgeable
Gatorland naturalists can tell you a lot about the snakes and other animals, the real thrill comes from holding them yourself. If you are not
selected to hold the animals during the show, you may hold most of
them afterward, including the Burmese python, for a $5 fee.

GATORLAND ADVENTURE TOURS

GATORLAND NOW OFFERS FOUR DIFFERENT up-close encounters with the alligators. The four tours are the Rookie Wrestlin' tour, in which guests can "wrestle" a gator (with the gator's mouth taped, of course), $5 for the experience, photos for an additional fee; the Adventure Hour, which allows guests behind the scenes of the breeding marsh, $15; the Gator Night Shine tour, in which guests look for gators at night, $20; and the Trainer for a Day program, which allows you to shadow a gator wrestler for a day, $125 (participants must be at least 12 years of age; program begins at 8 a.m. and lasts two hours). For more information, contact Gatorland at ☎ 800-393-JAWS or **gatorland.com.**

DINING

DINING AT GATORLAND can be either an adventure or a nonevent. Its regular menu items are nothing spectacular, but then again they are also fairly inexpensive by Orlando theme-park standards. A burger is about $3, a kids' meal, about $5. The menu is varied, however, and includes chicken breast and a fish-and-chips basket.

But who comes to Gatorland to eat a hot dog? No true adventurer can visit without trying at least a bite of gator meat. **Pearl's Patio Smokehouse** features two such items: gator nuggets and gator ribs. In humanity's never-ending quest to reduce all animals to nugget form, this is one of the less impressive examples. Yes, the

unofficial **TIP**
Ever try a gator rib? This could be your chance, and you may be pleasantly surprised.

gator nuggets *do* taste like chicken but spicier and much tougher. They come with barbecue dipping sauces to mask any unfamiliar tastes. The ribs are a bit more intimidating (large), but quite good. They contain small bones, so be careful. Try the sampler platter, which gives you a taste of both treats. If you see a nearby gator eyeing you accusingly, console yourself with the thought that he'd do the same to you—only with less barbecue sauce and a lot more screaming.

SHOPPING

IF YOU ARE LOOKING FOR A TACKY FLORIDA SOUVENIR for that prized spot on your mantel, Gatorland is the place. Similar to shops that line US 192, the park hawks everything gator-related you could ever imagine—and even a few things you would, in a sane world, never even consider. There are also several merchandise carts throughout the park and two unique photo locations.

PART FIVE

The HOLY LAND EXPERIENCE

AN ENTIRELY NEW KIND OF THEME PARK OPENED in Orlando in early 2001. The Holy Land Experience is a re-creation of biblical-era Israel by way of evangelical Christianity. Don't expect a Jehovah Coaster or Red Sea Flume, though—this park is only for thrills of the spiritual kind. The Holy Land Experience has more in common with passive attractions like Gatorland than with places like Walt Disney World or Universal Studios.

At 15 acres, this park is tiny by local standards. It's packed with a half-dozen exhibits and re-creations of structures dating from 1450 BC to the first century AD, elaborately crafted by the same company that built parts of Walt Disney World and Universal Islands of Adventure. The theming and detail are meticulous and impressive. Costumed performers roam the park and interact with guests, sometimes assembling for performances or impromptu congregations.

> **unofficial TIP**
> Not built in a day: you'll notice a similar attention to detail here as in some Disney parks.

Which brings up a big caveat: though the historical re-creations might interest period enthusiasts, straight history is not really the focus here. Some Jewish groups have expressed concern about the appropriation of Jewish history and ritual for a Christian-themed park. Because it's ministry-operated, the park is very open about its evangelical mission. Every exhibit, show, performance, and shop is geared toward the Christian faith—essentially the born-again version. No one will treat you rudely or force you to participate in anything that makes you uncomfortable, but you can no more escape Christianity at The Holy Land Experience than you could escape Mickey Mouse at Walt Disney World. If that's not your cup of tea, then this place is not for you.

> **unofficial TIP**
> Come to Holy Land only if you're interested in all things Christian.

If Christian-oriented touring suits you and your family, The Holy Land Experience is a singular attraction. Tremendous press

The Holy Land Experience

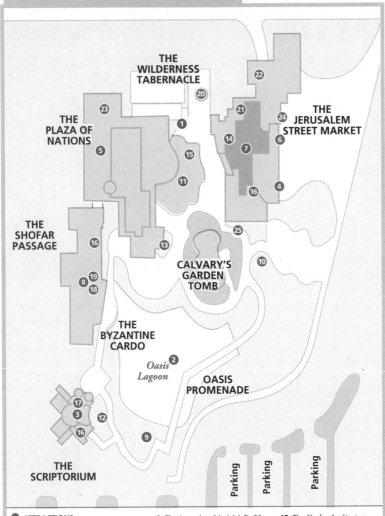

THE WILDERNESS TABERNACLE

THE PLAZA OF NATIONS

THE JERUSALEM STREET MARKET

THE SHOFAR PASSAGE

CALVARY'S GARDEN TOMB

THE BYZANTINE CARDO

Oasis Lagoon

OASIS PROMENADE

THE SCRIPTORIUM

Parking Parking Parking

● **ATTRACTIONS**

1. Church of All Nations
   Prayer Garden
2. Crystal Living Waters
3. ExLibris Book Shoppe
4. Guest Services
5. Herod's Temple
   (The Temple
   of the Great King)
6. Jerusalem City Gate
7. Jerusalem Street Market

8. The Jerusalem Model A.D. 66
9. The Jesus Boat
10. Judean Village
11. Last Supper Communion
12. Living Word Prayer Garden
13. Oasis Palms Café
14. The Old Scroll Shop
15. The Qumran Caves
16. Restrooms
17. The Scriptorium Center
    for Biblical Antiquities

18. The Shofar Auditorium
19. The Shofar Shop
20. Smile of a Child
    Adventure Land
21. Smile of a Child
    Adventure Theatre
22. The Sycamore Tree
23. Theater of Life
24. Ticket Center
25. Via Dolorosa Path

coverage and high initial attendance proved that its creators have hit on something unique. However, a general tourism slump and declining crowds led to a huge increase in ticket prices, making The Holy Land Experience less of a deal than it once was. The park's small size makes it a manageable outing, though, and the needs of the elderly, disabled, or foreign tourist get special attention here. In fact, most guests tend to be adults or seniors. Despite the often cutting-edge theming and production values, children are likely to get bored after more than a few hours here.

GETTING THERE

THE HOLY LAND EXPERIENCE is very easy to find because it's located right off I-4 near Universal Studios Florida. From Disney World or points south, take I-4 east to Exit 78 (just past Universal Studios Florida and the Florida Turnpike). The Holy Land Experience is just off the exit ramp, on the west side of I-4. From Orlando, take I-4 west for 5 miles to Exit 78.

ADMISSION PRICES

One-day Pass

Adults **$35** | Children ages 6–12 $20 | Children ages 3–5 **$7** | Children under age 3 **Free**

Multiday and Annual Passes

Jerusalem Gold annual passes cost $120 for adults and $60 for children ages 6–12. For groups of 15 or more (advance reservation and advance payment required), admission prices are discounted, so call ahead. Package deals, including a meal inside the park (lunch or dinner), are also available for groups (again, advance reservation and payment required). Parking is free.

ARRIVING

THE HOLY LAND EXPERIENCE IS OPEN DAILY, except Sunday, with special programs during holidays (call ahead for details). Hours are Monday–Saturday, 10 a.m.–6 p.m.; closed Thanksgiving, Christmas, and New Year's Day. Tickets are purchased at the Ticket Center near the front entrance. If there's a substantial line at the ticket windows, check the Guest Services desk, found through the large double doors to the left of the main entrance; tickets are sometimes sold there as well. Parking is free. If you or a family member requires transportation within the park, a single baby stroller rents for $5, a double stroller for $7, and motorized scooters are available for $20.

Most of this small park is meant to be enjoyed on a walk-through basis at your own pace, but there are several shows and presentations to see. All but the Scriptorium are less than 30 minutes long, and many repeat throughout the day. A thorough tour of The Holy Land Experience takes just over half a day, assuming you want to experience every single thing. Our advice is to check the daily schedule and make a point of seeing the featured exhibits, using the various live performances and presentations as filler. Because some of the live performances are held only once daily, be sure to arrive a few minutes before 10 a.m. if you want to catch all of the shows.

CONTACTING THE HOLY LAND EXPERIENCE

FOR INFORMATION ABOUT TICKETS, hours, or special presentations, contact the Holy Land Experience at ☎ 800-447-7235 or 407-872-2272, or **holylandexperience.com.** Ticket discounts are available online.

❗ ATTRACTIONS

Behold the Lamb ★★★

APPEAL BY AGE	PRESCHOOL ★★½	GRADE SCHOOL ★★★½	TEENS ★★★½
YOUNG ADULTS ★★★½		OVER 30 ★★★★	SENIORS ★★★★

What it is Musical interpretation of Christ's crucifixion. **Scope and scale** Super headliner. See entertainment schedule for show times. **Authors' rating ★★★.** **Duration of show** 30 minutes.

DESCRIPTION AND COMMENTS Located outside the Garden Tomb, this show lets you become witness to Christ's crucifixion and resurrection. Although at the outset of the performance you may believe that you'll need to use your imagination to see Christ—Holy Land has a tendency to employ rousing speeches over visual props—an actor does portray the King of Kings. Songs accompany the crucifixion, but all are tempered and reverent. You will not leave singing any of the tunes, but may find yourself uplifted at His sacrifice.

TOURING TIPS There are usually two showings a day: a noon show and a 5 p.m. show. The latter is bloodier and involves the entire cast of actors from around the park. Seating is taken quickly for both performances, so arrive early. A few picnic tables are available, but for the best view sit in the open-air Judean Village theater.

Calvary's Garden Tomb ★★

APPEAL BY AGE	PRESCHOOL ★	GRADE SCHOOL ★	TEENS ★
YOUNG ADULTS ★★	OVER 30 ★★		SENIORS ★★½

What it is Re-creation of Christ's empty tomb and setting for dramatic and historical presentations. **Scope and scale** Minor attraction. **When to go** During one of the presentations. **Authors' rating** Not much to see; ★★. **Duration of show** 15–20 minutes; check presentation schedule.

DESCRIPTION AND COMMENTS Visitors wind their way along a highly attenuated version of the Via Dolorosa ("way of suffering"), which Jesus walked on his way to Calvary to be crucified. Within a few paces, you end up in a garden with Jesus' tomb as its centerpiece, the door stone rolled away to reveal its emptiness. Regular dramatic and historical presentations of the life of Jesus are held in, around, and above the tomb.

TOURING TIPS This is an especially similar re-creation of the Garden Tomb in Israel—serene and poignant. Try to plan your visit during one of the presentations. The tomb closes to the public about 30 minutes before the *Behold the Lamb* show.

Crystal Living Waters ★★★

APPEAL BY AGE	PRESCHOOL ★★	GRADE SCHOOL ★★★	TEENS ★★
YOUNG ADULTS ★★½	OVER 30 ★★★		SENIORS ★★★

What it is Computer-controlled dancing waters. **Scope and scale** Diversion. **When to go** Anytime. **Authors' rating** ★★★. **Duration of show** About 15 minutes.

DESCRIPTION AND COMMENTS Located in the pond between The Scriptorium Center and the Oasis Springs Café, this brings to mind the dancing waters in front of the Bellagio hotel in that modern-day Gomorrah, Las Vegas. But this is on a much-smaller scale. Recorded religious music including hymns play, but the fountains are not synchronized to that.

TOURING TIPS Though the daily schedule lists the fountains at just twice a day, they were spurting often during a recent summer-day visit. There are no seats arranged facing the fountains, but outdoor seating at the Oasis Springs has a fair view.

The Jerusalem Model AD 66 ★★★½

APPEAL BY AGE	PRESCHOOL ★	GRADE SCHOOL ★★	TEENS ★★★
YOUNG ADULTS ★★★	OVER 30 ★★★½		SENIORS ★★★½

What it is Elaborate replica of ancient Jerusalem. **Scope and scale** Headliner. **When to go** After experiencing the Scriptorium. **Authors' rating** Very cool; ★★★½. **Duration of show** 30 minutes; check daily schedule for presentation times.

DESCRIPTION AND COMMENTS This is touted as "the world's largest indoor model of first-century Jerusalem." The 25-foot-wide model is meant to represent Jerusalem circa AD 66, including the Temple of Jerusalem as rebuilt by Herod while the Romans ruled the city. You can examine the model on your own, but a guided lecture is much more informative, since there are no plaques to reveal what is represented. The lecture covers what everything in the model is, the history of the era, where Jesus went during the last week of his life, and more.

TOURING TIPS Because this is the only headliner attraction with just a few scheduled openings (as opposed to constant, regular openings on the half hour or hour), make sure to consult the daily schedule to fit a visit into your plans. Try to make it to the first opening of the morning to ensure touring flexibility later on.

Judean Village/*The Ministries of Jesus* ★★★★

APPEAL BY AGE	PRESCHOOL ★★★	GRADE SCHOOL ★★★½	TEENS ★★★
YOUNG ADULTS ★★★½		OVER 30 ★★★★	SENIORS ★★★★

What it is Play about Christ's best-known works. **Scope and scale** Headliner. **When to go** Check daily schedule for presentation times. **Authors' rating** Greatest hits montage; ★★. **Duration of show** 20 minutes.

DESCRIPTION AND COMMENTS A well-crafted amalgamation of Jesus' miracles, this show depicts such famous stories as the restoration of sight to the blind man, the curing of leprosy, and the conversion of the tax collector Levi. The most inspirational part of the show occurs when the actor, who does a wonderful job portraying the King of Kings, breaks the fourth wall and enters the audience seating area, talking with guests and offering impromptu quotes.

The show moves quickly, and there is never a dull moment. With an enthusiastic crowd in attendance, this is easily one of the best shows in the park.

TOURING TIPS Seats are limited and fill up early, so arrive at least 15 minutes ahead of time for this short presentation. The show conflates so many stories into one that it can take a minute to recall in which book each event occurred.

Judean Village/*The Wedding of Cannae* ★★½

APPEAL BY AGE	PRESCHOOL ★	GRADE SCHOOL ★★	TEENS ★★
YOUNG ADULTS ★★		OVER 30 ★★½	SENIORS ★★★

What it is Drama about Christ's first miracle. **Scope and scale** Major attraction. **When to go** Check daily schedule for presentation times. **Authors' rating** Poorly staged; ★★. **Duration of show** 20 minutes.

DESCRIPTION AND COMMENTS An odd choice for a 20-minute show, *The Wedding of Cannae* holds almost no actual drama. The first half of the play is a reception party for the wedding. When Jesus arrives halfway through, the partygoers realize that they're out of wine, so the Savior of Man turns water into wine, and everything is fine again.

TOURING TIPS Skip this one unless you're into poor acting and dull plots. Although reading it in the New Testament is important because it depicts the first of Christ's seven miracles, the story is less than gripping when acted out.

Last Supper Communion with Jesus ★★★½

APPEAL BY AGE	PRESCHOOL –	GRADE SCHOOL ★★	TEENS ★★★
YOUNG ADULTS ★★★		OVER 30 ★★★★	SENIORS ★★★★

What it is Re-enactment of Jesus coming to the Last Supper. **Scope and scale** Major attraction. **When to go** Anytime. **Authors' rating** ★★★½. **Duration of show** 10 minutes.

DESCRIPTION AND COMMENTS Just beyond the entrance, guests can walk into a high-ceilinged room that is supposed to be the Upper Room, where

Jesus and the disciples had the Last Supper. Each guest is presented with a tiny wooden goblet holding a thimbleful of grape juice and a tiny square of unleavened bread. The only furnishing in the room is a long wooden table, and guests can sit at it or stand on one side of it.

An actor portraying John enters from the other side of the table, offers a soliloquy, and leads the assembled in a prayer. Then the actor portraying Jesus—and be aware that there is more than one portraying Jesus each day in the park—enters from the far side of the table and speaks to the assembled. At times his face is serene; at times, his voice breaks, as he forecasts what will happen to him. He leads a Communion, and as John then leads the guests in a hymn, Jesus passes among them, touching each person as he looks him or her in the eye.

As with all of the live performances in The Holy Land Experience, the young actors seem to embrace the dignity of their roles, so that this Communion is almost poignant.

TOURING TIPS Signage is not a strong point in The Holy Land Experience, so parkgoers may only *happen* upon the Quamran Caves—where the Upper Room is located—after passing through the main entrance and then through a small courtyard that includes restrooms. The Upper Room itself is spacious and the only table is quite large, so that many more than 12 can be seated. Fear not: The actor portraying Jesus moves through the room and touches or speaks briefly to every person, so have no concern if you don't get to one of the chairs.

The Scriptorium Center for Biblical Antiquities ★★★★

APPEAL BY AGE		PRESCHOOL ★	GRADE SCHOOL ★★½	TEENS ★★½
YOUNG ADULTS ★★★		OVER 30 ★★★		SENIORS ★★★½

What it is Walk-through exhibit detailing the history of the Bible itself. **Scope and scale** Super headliner. **When to go** Immediately on entering the park. **Authors' rating** World-class collection, not to be missed; ★★★. **Duration of show** 55 minutes; presentations every hour.

DESCRIPTION AND COMMENTS This museum showcases a fascinating collection of biblical antiquities, some dating from thousands of years ago. Exhibits include ancient cuneiform, scrolls, Gutenberg and Tyndale Bibles, manuscripts, and more. Narration guides visitors from room to room; spotlights shine on particular objects while the narration explains their historical and religious significance. Theming and attention to detail are the best of anywhere in the park, and The Holy Land Experience's overriding evangelism is also front and center. The walk-through ends in a modern home setting that is conspicuously Bible-free, which is meant to inspire reflection on how we can bring the Good Book back into our collective lives. (We first thought that we'd mistakenly wandered into someone's living quarters, until a man in monk's robes appeared and assured us that it was all part of the program.)

TOURING TIPS Most guests initially visit the attractions near the park entrance. Proceeding immediately to the Scriptorium will get you through it with the first batch of guests (only three people were in our group) and free you up for other attractions and shows.

Shofar Auditorium/Shows and Lectures ★★★

APPEAL BY AGE	PRESCHOOL ★★½	GRADE SCHOOL ★★★½	TEENS ★★★
YOUNG ADULTS ★★★½		OVER 30 ★★★★	SENIORS ★★★★

What it is Myriad of musicals and lectures. **Scope and scale** Minor attractions. See entertainment schedule for show times; not all shows are performed each day. **Authors' rating ★★★**.

DESCRIPTION AND COMMENTS Many different shows and a series of lectures all take place in Shofar Auditorium. The auditorium is located inside the same building as Jerusalem AD 66; the entrance is through the gift shop. The auditorium looks like the inside of many modern churches, with rows of chairs facing the stage, and is decorated in red velvet with Grecian columns. Two large screens can be found at either end of the main stage and are incorporated into the shows and presentations.

The shows that take place in the Shofar Auditorium change seasonally, but some of the long-running ones are *Praise through the Ages, Moses,* and *Centurion. Praise through the Ages* is a musical that depicts the evolution of painting and music throughout history, highlighting Western art's direct links to Christianity. To facilitate the lesson, actors dressed in period costumes sing period pieces. The songs range from the chants of Gregorian monks to upbeat modern gospel.

The show *Moses* is also a musical and relates the account of Moses' mother, Jochebed, and her struggle to save her son from the pharaoh. As told in Exodus, Jochebed places her young child into an ark of bulrushes and sends him down the river. The crux of the story rests on Jochebed's faith that the Lord will protect her child.

Centurion depicts another biblical story about heavenly protection, that of the centurion and Jesus. The story is of a centurion—a professional Roman officer—who wants to save the life of his servant. The show depicts the Matthew version of events, not the Luke version, and therefore has the centurion asking Jesus for help.

A recent addition is *The Four Ladies Who Love Jesus.* The women, three of whom know each other, gather after his arrest and help explain to a "harlot," who has also been touched by Jesus, why each of the others knows him. Typical of the teaching nature of the dialogue, each of these four recites the line, "I love you for the rest of my life."

Mood music plays almost continuously during this 25-minute show; the lighting is just right; and as Jesus, other followers, and centurions gather, as many as 11 actors occupy the rather small stage.

None of the shows dazzled us or contained significant differences in production elements. We will say that our favorite was *Praise through the Ages* for its range of costumes and toe-tapping songs. In addition to the shows, Shofar Auditorium also hosts a series of lectures that are almost always worth hearing and usually very insightful. Most of the lecturers have doctoral degrees in theology, or in a corresponding field, and although the lectures change daily, the amount of in-depth history and thorough research is more than most local clergy have time to include in their sermons.

Smile of a Child Adventure Land ★★★½

APPEAL BY AGE	PRESCHOOL ★★★½	GRADE SCHOOL ★★★★	TEENS ★★★
YOUNG ADULTS ★★		OVER 30 ★½	SENIORS ★★½

What it is Children's play area. **Scope and scale** Major attraction. **When to go** Anytime. **Authors' rating** Small but useful; ★★★.

DESCRIPTION AND COMMENTS This addition to The Holy Land Experience gives the little ones a place to get away from the more info-heavy lectures and presentations.

The play area consists of a cave meant to resemble the belly of a whale (complete with Jonah), a screening room with beanbag chairs, a small climbing wall, and a theater shaped like Noah's Ark, which occasionally hosts short plays. It's good that the area's here, but don't expect it to be on par with a Disney attraction.

TOURING TIPS The area comes off as a concession for parents whose kids grow bored in the first hour or so of touring. Unfortunately, the tiny size of the kids' area won't hold most children's attention for more than a few minutes, although the air-conditioned screening room makes a good place for exhausted youths to rest. A teen center is in the works for the Quamran Caves, but construction is slow.

Theater of Life/*The Seed of Promise* ★½

APPEAL BY AGE	PRESCHOOL ★½	GRADE SCHOOL ★★	TEENS ★½
YOUNG ADULTS ★★		OVER 30 ★★½	SENIORS ★★★

What it is Bible high points in movie form. **Scope and scale** Headliner. **When to go** After experiencing the Scriptorium and Jerusalem Model. **Authors' rating** Surprisingly chintzy; ★½. **Duration of show** 25 minutes; shows at least twice a day.

DESCRIPTION AND COMMENTS The Theater of Life is set in the behemoth Temple of the Great King, a half-scale replica of Herod's temple from first-century Jerusalem. The ornate temple is the gleaming centerpiece of The Holy Land Experience, so you can't miss it. Pass through the Corinthian columns of the Plaza of the Nations to enter the right side of the temple, where the theater is located. *The Seed of Promise* film is a sort of biblical *CliffsNotes*, covering the highlights of both the Old and the New Testament—everything from Genesis all the way to the Second Coming. Shot on location in Jerusalem, the film is projected onto a six-story-high screen. The film aims to be an "emotionally immersive" retelling of these Bible stories, with special effects.

TOURING TIPS *The Seed of Promise* is oddly disjointed and fairly boring, with historical sets and computer-generated effects that already appear dated. A lot of money was poorly spent here. Our advice: Rent *The Ten Commandments* when you get home.

The Wilderness Tabernacle ★★½

APPEAL BY AGE	PRESCHOOL ★★	GRADE SCHOOL ★★★	TEENS ★★
YOUNG ADULTS ★★		OVER 30 ★★★	SENIORS ★★★

What it is Historical demonstration of Jewish ritual. **Scope and scale** Headliner. **When to go** Later in the day, when crowds have thinned out. **Authors' rating** Interesting history; ★★½. **Duration of show** 25 minutes; shows every 30 minutes.

DESCRIPTION AND COMMENTS Visitors enter an outside preshow area where they learn about the struggles of the 12 tribes of Israel on their journey to the Promised Land. They then move into an indoor exhibition hall with bleacher seats; the lighting creates the illusion of being outdoors at dusk, and a narrator introduces himself as a Levitical priest and a descendent of Aaron, the brother of Moses. He then reenacts various rituals of the priesthood practiced during the Israelites' 40 years in the desert. Portentous rumbling, fog, and lighting effects accompany prophetic narration broadcast over loudspeakers. The details of ritual are explained plainly enough, even though part of the scenario takes place in an enclosed tent. Even with a few special effects, you are still asked to imagine quite a large amount as the actor mimes many of the rituals taking place, from animal sacrifice to the simple task of taking water from a well.

TOURING TIPS All seats have good sight lines in this small space. Moving to the far left will guarantee the best vantage to see the final portion of the presentation, as well as allowing for an easy exit.

DINING

THE ONLY RESTAURANT IS an American/Middle Eastern–themed restaurant, **Oasis Springs Café.** The menu includes fast food suited to the period and geography, such as hummus, falafel, gyros, and entire turkey legs, the latter priced at $5. American choices include the endearingly named Goliath burger. Snack stands with a limited menu—though turkey drumsticks are a staple—are also in the park.

SHOPPING

AT THE PARK'S ENTRANCE, the **Jerusalem Market** is the main shopping venue. Various costumed craftspeople hawk their wares, and a cluster of stores sell a variety of souvenirs. Typical gifts such as Bibles and crosses are available, but there are also more exotic choices such as mosaics, horn shofars, olive-wood crèches, antievolution place mats, and plush-toy camels and lambs. Another small gift shop geared toward books and the history of Bible-making can be found in the Scriptorium, and another can be found outside the Shofar Auditorium.

PART SIX

KENNEDY SPACE CENTER VISITOR COMPLEX

YOU MAY BE OLD ENOUGH TO REMEMBER the excitement and anticipation of the early days of space exploration. If not, you've probably seen the movies. Regardless, the pioneer spirit of the space program—sparked when President John F. Kennedy promised to land a man on the moon—is contagious.

Kennedy Space Center has been the training area and launch site for most major U.S. space programs, including Project Mercury's manned orbital missions, Project Apollo's voyages to the moon, and the space shuttle program. In addition, weather and communications satellites are regularly put into orbit from here.

After a $100 million expansion in 1999, the Kennedy Space Center Visitor Complex is thoroughly modern and offers many of the attractions and amenities of a contemporary theme park. The complex does a wonderful job of capturing the spirit of adventure—and the uncertainty—of the early days of America's space program. It also offers a unique glimpse into the latest NASA advancements and some interesting visions of where the future of space exploration may lead. Aware of the sometimes wide gulf of interests between the average tourist and the hard-core space junkie, the Visitor Complex is much more engaging and kid-friendly than in the past. Serious space cadets can still visit all the authentic installations and buildings they like, and others can marvel at gee-whiz exhibits, IMAX movies, and really giant rockets. Even so, be sensitive to your group's likes and dislikes, especially when it comes to the specialty tours—some of which are hours long and involve lengthy bus rides.

After the terrorist attacks of September 11, 2001, security at Kennedy Space Center increased dramatically. Some tours were drastically altered, with visits to various secure areas reduced or eliminated entirely. If you're considering a tour, we advise you to find out exactly what sights you'll be seeing and from how far away. Check out the

Kennedy Space Center Visitor Complex

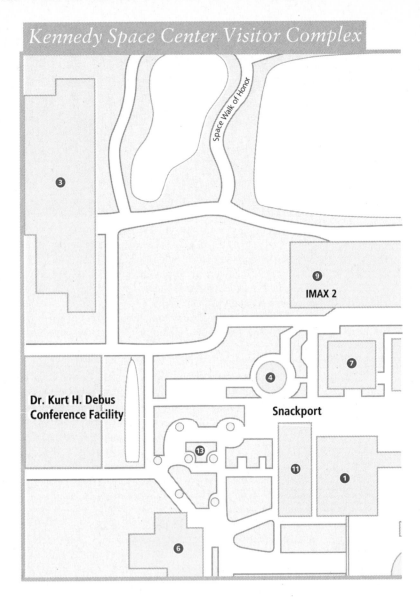

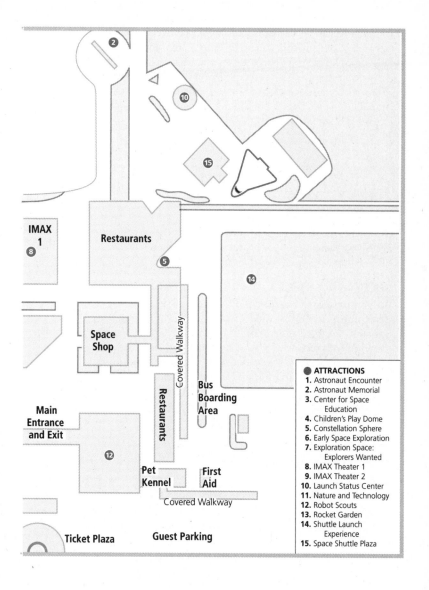

IMAX 1

Restaurants

Space Shop

Covered Walkway

Restaurants

Bus Boarding Area

Main Entrance and Exit

Pet Kennel

First Aid

Covered Walkway

Ticket Plaza

Guest Parking

● **ATTRACTIONS**
1. Astronaut Encounter
2. Astronaut Memorial
3. Center for Space Education
4. Children's Play Dome
5. Constellation Sphere
6. Early Space Exploration
7. Exploration Space: Explorers Wanted
8. IMAX Theater 1
9. IMAX Theater 2
10. Launch Status Center
11. Nature and Technology
12. Robot Scouts
13. Rocket Garden
14. Shuttle Launch Experience
15. Space Shuttle Plaza

individual tour profiles here for guidance, but be advised that all of this can change if security conditions dictate.

We can't stress enough that the tours at Kennedy Space Center are most enjoyable for those with a serious interest in the space program and a high tolerance for touring at a distance—and even then, you may not be happy. With stars quite literally in their eyes, visitors can be disappointed by security restrictions and the less-than-thrilling visual impact of bunker-style buildings seen from a mile away (or more). As a reader from Cherry Hill, New Jersey, writes:

> The tours are a waste of time (and money). In particular, the NASA Up Close tour is anything but. [Like our tour guide said,] "There's a space shuttle inside that building, over there . . . but you can't see it . . . and there's another shuttle on the launchpad over yonder . . . but you can't see that either."

If you really want to stay up close with the space stuff, it takes less time, money, and hassle to just explore the Visitor Complex proper. This is especially true for visitors with children, who would likely have little tolerance for a few hours on a bus.

GETTING THERE

KENNEDY SPACE CENTER VISITOR COMPLEX is an easy day trip from most central Florida attractions. From Orlando, visitors can take FL 528 (also called both the Beeline Highway Toll Road and the Beachline Expressway) east. (A round trip on the Beeline will cost about $5 in tolls, so have some cash handy.) Turn onto FL 407 north, then FL 405 east, and follow it to the Kennedy Space Center Visitor Complex. You can also take Colonial Drive (FL 50) and travel east to FL 405, but the Beeline is definitely the quickest and easiest route. Parking is free.

ADMISSION PRICES

Standard Admission

The Standard Admission Badge includes the Kennedy Space Center Tour, both IMAX films, and all attractions and exhibits.

Standard Admission
Adults **$41 + tax** | Children ages 3–11 **$31 + tax**
Children under age 3 **Free**

Special Interest Tours (admission not included but required)
Adults **$21 + tax** | Children ages 3–11 **$15 + tax**

Commander's Club Annual Pass
Adults **$53 + tax** | Children ages 3–11 **$43 + tax**

Astronaut Training Experience

If you're really into the astronaut thing, the Astronaut Training Experience (or ATX, as it's called) takes visitors age 14 and older and their parent or guardian through a half day of the training real astronauts use to get ready for a launch. Zero-gravity simulators, mock mission-control access, and a final simulated launch and orbit are included in the price. ATX Family allows the whole family to participate, but children must be age 7 or older. This is for true space enthusiasts only. Call ☎ 321-449-4400 for more information or to make reservations. You can also reserve a spot via the website: **kennedy spacecenter.com.**

ATX: 1 adult and 1 child ages 14–18 **$145 + tax**

ATX Family: all ages (must be age 7 or older to participate) **$145 + tax** per person

Zero-G Weightless Flight

> *un*official **TIP**
> To infinity and beyond: take kids with a real interest in becoming an astronaut on the ATX.

The Zero-G flight at the Kennedy Space Center is for the more adventurous and affluent but is only offered on certain days. An independent group, not the Space Center, takes off from the shuttle landing strip in a Boeing 727. Once airborne, the pilot takes the plane through a series of parabolic maneuvers. After a 45-degree ascent, the plane heads downward, creating a zero-gravity atmosphere for about 30 seconds, then repeats the maneuver over and over again. The price tag for the flight is out of our budget at $4,950 plus tax. Group rates are available, and tickets can be purchased online at **gozero g.com** or by phone at ☎ 800-937-6480.

ARRIVING

KENNEDY SPACE CENTER VISITOR COMPLEX is open 9 a.m.–5:30 p.m. Unlike other area attractions, the Space Center is closed on Christmas Day and may close for certain shuttle launches. Call ahead before making the drive. Also note that even though the Visitor Complex may be open during shuttle launches, the Launch Complex (LC) 39 Observation Gantry may be closed to tourists when there's "a bird on the pad." Bus tour guides will try to make it up with some other sights around the Space Center, but if you can't see LC 39, you're missing one of the highlights of the tour.

Each of the IMAX movies is about 40 minutes long, and the bus tour alone can take more than three hours. If this leaves you feeling overwhelmed, you're right—there's a lot of ground to cover here. The wrong approach is to race from attraction to attraction in one day. Instead, take it slow and soak in some of the better attractions, leaving the others behind.

> *un*official **TIP**
> This facility's tour can take an entire day, so be sure everyone in your group is truly interested in seeing everything there is to see before you board the bus.

Most visitors should start their day with some of the exhibits at the hub, which provide an informative background on space history. Then, if you've found one that really meets your interests, head for the bus tour. Buses come frequently (every 15 minutes), but if your timing is off, you can stand a full 15 minutes before boarding, then sit on the bus for a few minutes before taking off. Buses visit LC 39, the Apollo/Saturn V Center, and other locales as the tour's emphasis (or security restrictions) demand. Each of the stops involves movies and displays that are very text-heavy but usually interesting. The movies are wonderful and are of documentary quality, but after a while some may begin to grow tired of the movie-bus-movie-bus shuffle.

After the bus tour, see at least one of the IMAX movies. The five-and-a-half-story screens provide amazing views, and the sound systems are excellent. You can choose from peeking at the moon in 3-D or witnessing the thrilling sensation of spaceflight.

CONTACTING KENNEDY SPACE CENTER

FOR MORE INFORMATION about Kennedy Space Center, call ☎ 321-449-4444. You can also try ☎ 800-KSC-INFO (572-4630), but this is a quick, recorded message of basic information that doesn't allow you to transfer to an actual person. The Space Center will mail you a brochure about tours, as well as launch schedule information.

kids You can also visit **kennedyspacecenter.com,** which has a page just for kids.

ATTRACTIONS

VISITOR CENTER COMPLEX HUB

Astronaut Encounter   ★★½

APPEAL BY AGE	PRESCHOOL ★	GRADE SCHOOL ★★★	TEENS ★½
YOUNG ADULTS ★★★		OVER 30 ★★★	SENIORS ★★★½

What it is Talk with a real live astronaut. **Scope and scale** Diversion. **When to go** See daily schedule. **Authors' rating** A bit forced; ★★½.

DESCRIPTION AND COMMENTS At scheduled times throughout the day, a NASA astronaut appears in the Universal Theatre for a meet-and-greet. The astronaut's "opening act" is a Visitor Complex MC who warms up the crowd with some fun space facts and nutty science tomfoolery, assisted by a kid volunteer from the audience. The MC then introduces the astronaut, who gives a talk about his or her particular mission in space. A different astronaut will give the lecture on different days. The quality of the lecture varies on each astronaut's mission; a biologist may not excite the children as much as a shuttle pilot.

After the talk, the astronaut will take questions. The Q&A can be dull, so if you want to make it interesting, come with your own questions or have the children come up with questions during the presentation (questions about the dangers of space are good leads to more exciting stories).

Children do seem intrigued, but they don't appear to have the astronaut hero-worship more popular with preceding generations.

For an even more intimate astronaut encounter, sign up for Lunch with an Astronaut. As the name implies, this involves sharing a meal with an astronaut, who first shows a video about life on the space shuttle, then gives a personalized presentation about his or her own space experiences. A Q&A follows, as well as a chance to take photos (a signed souvenir photo is included). The meal (served at 12:30 p.m. daily) consists of rotisserie chicken, salad, sides, dessert, and beverage, with kid-friendly options available. Cost is $60.99 for adults, $43.99 for kids ages 3–11, but park admission is included in this price; call ☎ 321-449-4444 for advance reservations or purchase online at **kennedyspacecenter.com.** Tickets for Lunch with an Astronaut can also be purchased at the Visitor Complex, but same-day tickets may already be sold out.

> *unofficial* **TIP**
> To get up close and personal with an astronaut, have lunch with one—make reservations in advance.

TOURING TIPS Check the daily entertainment schedule for times. If kids get bored, the spread-out seats make it easy to tactfully get up and wander off to another attraction.

kids Astronaut Memorial ★★★

APPEAL BY AGE	PRESCHOOL ★	GRADE SCHOOL ★	TEENS ★★
YOUNG ADULTS ★★	OVER 30 ★★★		SENIORS ★★★

What it is Memorial to those who died for space exploration. **Scope and scale** Minor attraction. **When to go** At the end of the tour. **Authors' rating** Touching tribute; ★★★.

DESCRIPTION AND COMMENTS The entire memorial tilts and swivels to follow the sun, while mirrors direct the sun's rays onto glass names etched in a black marble slab. You probably won't want to spend a great deal of time here, but it's a poignant thing to see.

TOURING TIPS Visit the kiosk on the side of the Gallery Center Building. There you'll find computers that offer background information on the astronauts on the memorial.

Children's Play Dome ★★

APPEAL BY AGE	PRESCHOOL ★★★	GRADE SCHOOL ★★	TEENS †
YOUNG ADULTS †	OVER 30 †		SENIORS †

† *This attraction was not designed for older guests.*

What it is Kiddie playground. **Scope and scale** Diversion. **When to go** If your older kids are looking at the Rocket Garden, supervise the young ones here. **Authors' rating** Small but cute; ★★.

DESCRIPTION AND COMMENTS This little playground, under cover from the hot sun, is a nice diversion for kids. It's similar to kids' areas at other attractions, but a space theme prevails.

TOURING TIPS One adult can take the older kids to an IMAX movie or on a stroll through the Rocket Garden, while another supervises the little ones here.

Early Space Exploration ★★★

APPEAL BY AGE	PRESCHOOL ★	GRADE SCHOOL ★½	TEENS ★★
YOUNG ADULTS ★★★		OVER 30 ★★★½	SENIORS ★★★★

What it is Relics from the birth of spaceflight. **Scope and scale** Diversion. **When to go** While waiting for the bus or IMAX films. **Authors' rating** Very informative and nostalgic; ★★★.

DESCRIPTION AND COMMENTS This well-presented series of exhibits documents the birth and maturation of human space exploration. Space suits, lunar landers, and capsules are all on display, highlighting mostly the *Mercury* and *Gemini* programs. Newspaper clippings and other ephemera give historical context to the items on display. There's also a good deal of information on how the Russian space program evolved in competition with that of the United States, but the space race is framed as having been ultimately beneficial to both nations.

TOURING TIPS Another pleasant walk-through exhibit. Kids will have less patience with all this "old" stuff, so be prepared for some eye-rolling and heavy sighs if you tarry too long.

Exploration Space: Explorers Wanted ★★½

APPEAL BY AGE	PRESCHOOL ★	GRADE SCHOOL ★★½	TEENS ★★★
YOUNG ADULTS ★★★		OVER 30 ★★	SENIORS ★★

What it is Exhibits and brief presentation about the future of space travel. **Scope and scale** Diversion. **When to go** While waiting for the bus or IMAX films. **Authors' rating** Plea to continue the journey; ★★½.

DESCRIPTION AND COMMENTS A collection of hands-on exhibits that speculate on where our space travelers will go and how they will get there. Some exhibits are educational and straightforward, like many dealing with the various Mars landers and the Pathfinder mission (you can even sign up to send your signature to the Red Planet on the next mission). Other exhibits go on flights of fancy about how futuristic spacecraft will work and about potential colonization of other planets. For 10 minutes on the half hour, a presenter speaks in rosy terms about what space exploration has gained us on Earth, then yields to video sound bites from aerospace workers on how much more there is to learn.

TOURING TIPS An easy walk-through, with nothing too surprising. Kids will like the touching-encouraged exhibits. Hit this one as filler when needed.

IMAX Films ★★★½

APPEAL BY AGE	PRESCHOOL ★★	GRADE SCHOOL ★★★½	TEENS ★★★½
YOUNG ADULTS ★★★½		OVER 30 ★★★½	SENIORS ★★★½

What it is Large-format 3-D films projected onto huge screens with incredible sound systems. **Scope and scale** Headliner. **When to go** Check daily entertainment schedule; perfect during rain. **Authors' rating** Excellent; ★★★½. **Duration of shows** About 40 minutes.

DESCRIPTION AND COMMENTS Kennedy Space Center offers two excellent IMAX films each day:

Magnificent Desolation: Walking on the Moon 3-D. Tom Hanks narrates this 3-D feature of NASA footage mixed with quirky animation. The film focuses on the moon and the Apollo missions, a great supplement to the bus tours.

Hubble 3-D. Narrated by Leonardo diCaprio and filmed by the crews of three space shuttle missions, this film documents the demanding efforts to repair—and repair again—the Hubble Space Telescope. The scenes of astronauts delicately, or sometimes forcefully, working to replace parts of the telescope are at first interesting but become repetitive. The best images are of the stunning views, captured by Hubble, that seem to propel us inside galaxies and nebulae—the colors and shapes are breathtaking. A charming touch: The film begins and ends to the version of "Somewhere over the Rainbow" sung by the late Hawaiian Iz Kamakawiwo'ole.

TOURING TIPS Regardless of which movie you choose, we recommend sitting toward the back of the theater for the best view and to fully experience the awesome sound system. You will need to arrive early because these theaters are fairly small. Standard theater fare is sold in the lobby.

Launch Status Center ★★★★

APPEAL BY AGE	PRESCHOOL ★	GRADE SCHOOL ★½	TEENS ★★
YOUNG ADULTS ★★½	OVER 30 ★★★		SENIORS ★★★

What it is Live launch briefings and artifacts on display. **Scope and scale** Major attraction. **When to go** After visiting the Shuttle Plaza. **Authors' rating** Cool to see the real deal; ★★★★.

DESCRIPTION AND COMMENTS The artifacts are neat, but most enjoyable are the live briefings that take place on the hour 11 a.m.–5 p.m. Space Center communicators and live footage from throughout the complex give a glimpse into what is happening at the Space Center, or at the International Space Station, the day of your visit.

TOURING TIPS Visit just days before a launch and you'll catch the real action, which could include live video from the shuttle. If you visit when LC 39 is closed for a launch, this will probably be as close as you get.

Nature and Technology:
Merritt Island National Wildlife Refuge ★½

APPEAL BY AGE	PRESCHOOL ★	GRADE SCHOOL ★½	TEENS ★½
YOUNG ADULTS ★★	OVER 30 ★★		SENIORS ★★

What it is Small exhibit on the coexistence of local wildlife and high technology. **Scope and scale** Diversion. **When to go** Anytime. **Authors' rating** Unremarkable; ★½.

DESCRIPTION AND COMMENTS Even though it's harmless enough, this walk-through exhibit is largely uninspired, although the pine interior and taxidermic animals make a drastic juxtaposition to the metal shells of the Rocket Garden. Small displays catalog the lives and habits of various wild animals in the refuge as well as the Cape Canaveral National Seashore, including bald eagles, alligators, otters, sea turtles, manatees, and so on.

TOURING TIPS Skip this one unless you're killing time while someone else is on the bus or in the movie theater.

Rocket Garden ★★★

APPEAL BY AGE	PRESCHOOL ★	GRADE SCHOOL ★★	TEENS ★
YOUNG ADULTS ★		OVER 30 ★★	SENIORS ★★

What it is Outdoor rocket display. **Scope and scale** Diversion. **When to go** Before you head home. **Authors' rating** Unique; ★★★.

DESCRIPTION AND COMMENTS Rockets, spacecraft, and antennae dot a vast lawn. The big rockets take center stage and are the perfect backdrop for group photos. The Rocket Garden underwent a massive renovation and refurbishment in 2002, with new landscaping, shade, and fresh coats of paint all around, giving the attraction a much-needed face-lift. Space enthusiasts and grade schoolers may enjoy the climb-in replicas of *Mercury, Gemini,* and *Apollo* capsules.

TOURING TIPS Morning and afternoon guided tours are offered. Check the sign near the garden entrance for times.

Robot Scouts ★★

APPEAL BY AGE	PRESCHOOL ★★	GRADE SCHOOL ★★★	TEENS ★★
YOUNG ADULTS ★★		OVER 30 ★★	SENIORS ★★

What it is Walk-through exhibit featuring robots. **Scope and scale** Minor attraction. **When to go** At the end of the day, if there's time. **Authors' rating** Somewhat hokey; ★★.

DESCRIPTION AND COMMENTS Robot Starquester 2000, an animatronic robot scout, will take you through this exhibition of NASA's past, present, and future robotic space explorers. Starquester 2000 interacts with other space probes, such as the Viking Mars Lander and the Hubble Space Telescope, to explain how robotic space exploration aids human exploration.

TOURING TIPS Hit this exhibit on entering the center, before the bus tours. The tours are continuous and begin about every 5 minutes. The seating sections are small, so groups of less than ten are preferable.

Shuttle Launch Experience ★★★½

APPEAL BY AGE	PRESCHOOL ★★	GRADE SCHOOL ★★★½	TEENS ★★★½
YOUNG ADULTS ★★★		OVER 30 ★★★½	SENIORS ★★★

What it is Simulation of a space launch. **Scope and scale** Super headliner. **When to go** Make this your first stop. **Authors' rating** So close, yet, so far; ★★★½. **Duration of ride** 25 minutes.

DESCRIPTION AND COMMENTS This attraction is housed in a six-story facility in the far right corner of the park. A long gantry switchbacks to an anteroom where guests stand en masse to watch a 10-minute introduction video. It's a bit reminiscent of the scene where Dorothy first meets the Wizard of Oz. Space Shuttle commander Charlie Bolden's narration fills the room with anticipation as it warns riders of the perils of space travel; it closes with smoke machines and lights simulating the ignition of the rockets.

Riders then form a queue, and get another 5- to 10-minute talk about how this is their last chance to opt out of the ride and watch the video in a motion-free zone.

Finally riders board, strap in, and get bounced around a little bit while looking at a blue screen. They then disembark through the 2-minute experience through a large, spiraling hall filled with celestial factoids.

TOURING TIPS Bolden's continued narration during the shuttle experience does a fine job of stealing the realism and any tension that had been built up (not his fault, of course). The subpar graphics is the other major factor that contributes to this ride's truly underwhelming experience. With all the money KSC spent on both the facility and the theming, it should have invested a few more bucks for a good film instead of something that looks like an aging flight simulator. It's much closer to the jerky Wild Artic helicopter simulator at SeaWorld than the more captivating StarTours at Disney's Hollywood Studios.

Space Shuttle Plaza ★★★

APPEAL BY AGE	PRESCHOOL ★	GRADE SCHOOL ★★★	TEENS ★★
YOUNG ADULTS ★★		OVER 30 ★★	SENIORS ★★★

What it is View a space shuttle model. **Scope and scale** Minor attraction. **When to go** Immediately before or after bus tour. **Authors' rating** Impressive up close; ★★★.

DESCRIPTION AND COMMENTS The *Explorer*, a full-size replica of the space shuttle, gives you a glimpse of what it's like to be an astronaut working and living in space. You'll see the flight deck, where astronauts fly the orbiter during launch and landing, and the cramped mid-deck, where shuttle crews work on experiments, sleep, and eat.

TOURING TIPS This exhibit is easy to miss if you're racing to the bus tour because it's off the beaten path. Nevertheless, there may be a long line. We suggest trying back later in the afternoon rather than waiting for this interesting but uneventful tour.

U.S. Astronaut Hall of Fame ★★½

APPEAL BY AGE	PRESCHOOL ★★	GRADE SCHOOL ★★★	TEENS ★★½
YOUNG ADULTS ★★½		OVER 30 ★★½	SENIORS ★★★

What it is Complex of exhibits and astronaut honor roll. **Scope and scale** Major attraction. **When to go** Anytime. **Authors' rating** Worth a look if you're skipping the bus tours; ★★½.

DESCRIPTION AND COMMENTS This building, which is separate from the main Visitor Complex and set outside the guard gate, houses a collection of astronaut memorabilia and mementos, including equipment and small spacecraft, flight patches, and personal items. The Astronaut Hall of Fame itself takes up one room, listing those honored and inducted so far. Another room sports an array of simulators that will be of the most interest to kids, allowing them to land a shuttle, dock with the space station, walk on the moon, and engage in other spacely pursuits. The inevitable gift shop rounds out the proceedings.

TOURING TIPS   The Hall of Fame is situated down the road from the Visitor Complex and requires a 10-minute drive to get there. You will have to use your own vehicle because buses do not run to the Hall of Fame.

You must purchase the Maximum Access Admission to view the Hall of Fame, or purchase a ticket at the Hall of Fame for $17 for adults and $13 for children ages 3–11. This is a good last stop before heading to the hotel, as long as you do not want to ride any of the simulators. The lines at the end of the day are as tedious as any major theme park's and the rewards are not up to the wait. The Hall of Fame stays open until 6:30 p.m., an hour past the Visitor Complex, but due to the long lines, a mid-day excursion (barring IMAX presentation or bus tour) is a better plan.

KENNEDY SPACE CENTER BUS TOUR

BUSES RUN EVERY 15 MINUTES and make three stops around Kennedy Space Center. Tour at your own pace, but the entire trip, making all the stops, should average about three hours. The time spent at each exhibit is up to your discretion. The bus that drops you off will not be the same one that picks you up, so if you buy presents at the gift shops, you will have to carry them with you for the remainder of the tour. If you stay on one bus and experience none of the highlights of Kennedy Space Center—not recommended—the bus ride will still take 30–45 minutes.

In transit, there's no staring into "space." Television monitors show informative segments on space exploration to prepare you for the next destination. Think of this time as cramming for an exam. If possible, sit near the front of the bus, on the right side, for a better view of buildings in the area. Also, if you're lucky, an alert bus driver will point out signs of wildlife—which include an impressive bald eagle nest—along the way to the following stops:

Apollo/Saturn V Center   ★★★★

APPEAL BY AGE	PRESCHOOL ★★★	GRADE SCHOOL ★★★★	TEENS ★★★
YOUNG ADULTS ★★★½		OVER 30 ★★★★	SENIORS ★★★★

What it is Exhibit celebrating the race to the moon.**Scope and scale** Super headliner.**When to go** Anytime.**Authors' rating** Where else can you touch a moon rock?; ★★★★.

DESCRIPTION AND COMMENTS   The Apollo/Saturn V Center is a gigantic building (actually constructed around the enormous *Saturn V!*) with several displays. All guests enter a "holding area," where you'll see a 9-minute film on the race to the moon. This film is good, but things only get better.

The next stop is the Firing Room Theater, which catapults you back in time to December 1, 1968, for the launch of the first successful manned mission to the moon. Actual remnants of the original 1960s firing room set the mood, including countdown clocks and launch consoles. Once the show is under way, three large screens take you back to that day with original footage from the Space Center. During this 10-minute presentation, you'll sense the stress of the launch commanders and feel as though you're experiencing the actual launch through some fun special effects.

This is a pride-inducing presentation that prepares you for the real meat and potatoes of the Apollo/Saturn V Center—the actual 363-foot *Saturn V* moon rocket. When the doors of the Firing Room Theater open, guests are instantly overwhelmed by the size of the rocket. The amount of power the rocket produced on blastoff (7½ million pounds of thrust) could light up New York City for an hour and 15 minutes. In addition, this room is filled with space artifacts, including the van used to transport astronauts to the launchpad, a lunar module, and Jim Lovell's *Apollo 13* space suit. But there are more than just dusty relics here. Kennedy Space Center does a great job of telling the history of the era, with storyboards along the walls to document the highlights of each *Apollo* mission.

Another excellent exhibit at the Apollo/Saturn V Center is the Lunar Theater, where Neil Armstrong narrates a suspenseful documentary about his trip to the moon with *Apollo 11*. Younger generations may be a little shocked at how close the "eagle" came to missing its landing. The set of Lunar Theater enhances the 12-minute film with a few eccentric tricks; the whole production is short, touching, and inspired.

TOURING TIPS   If you're traveling with kids, they may well be restless by now. Check out the interactive exhibits or maybe step outside. There is a patio near the dining area where your family can get some fresh air.

International Space Station Center   ★★★½

APPEAL BY AGE	PRESCHOOL ★★★	GRADE SCHOOL ★★★	TEENS ★★★
YOUNG ADULTS ★★★½	OVER 30 ★★★½		SENIORS ★★★

What it is A bird's-eye view of ISSC components. **Scope and scale** Super headliner. **When to go** Anytime. **Authors' rating** The real thing; ★★★★.

DESCRIPTION AND COMMENTS   NASA's future missions are uncertain, but the space shuttle's last chores were to finish the International Space Station. Inside this unremarkable building, you can see walk-through replicas of all the parts. Following a catwalk to the far building, you look down into a "clean room" where the actual modules underwent final inspection before they were put in a shuttle and launched into space.

TOURING TIPS   This is usually the last stop on the bus tours. If you're not interested in seeing the sights, just stay on the bus and you'll be back to the center in 10–15 minutes.

LC 39 Observation Gantry   ★★★★

APPEAL BY AGE	PRESCHOOL ★★	GRADE SCHOOL ★★★	TEENS ★★
YOUNG ADULTS ★★★	OVER 30 ★★★★		SENIORS ★★★★

What it is Observation area that focuses on the space shuttle. **Scope and scale**

Major attraction. **When to go** Anytime. **Authors' rating** Get up close and personal with shuttle launchpads; ★★★★.

DESCRIPTION AND COMMENTS The LC 39 exhibits celebrate the space shuttle—the first spacecraft designed to be reusable. A 7-minute film at the LC 39 Theater, narrated by shuttle astronaut Marsha Ivins, explains how NASA engineers and technicians serviced the shuttle before launch. After the film, the doors open to dump you into a room with model displays. From here, head to the observation gantry, which puts you less than a mile away from Launchpads 39A and 39B, the only sites for launching the space shuttle. These are also the pads from which the *Saturn V* rockets blasted off to the moon during the Apollo program.

TOURING TIPS You'll be tempted to race to the observation gantry, but watching the film first provides for a better appreciation of the views offered there. The intricate launchpad model should be your first stop once the movie doors have opened. The model runs through a launch every few minutes, so to see the pieces move, wait for the countdown.

Once at the observation gantry, look for the Crawlerway path, a road nearly as wide as an eight-lane highway and more than 3 miles long. It was constructed to bear the weight of the Crawler-Transporter (6 million pounds) that moved the shuttle from the Vehicle Assembly Building to the launchpad.

OTHER TOURS

Cape Canaveral: Then and Now   ★★★½

APPEAL BY AGE	PRESCHOOL ★★	GRADE SCHOOL ★★½	TEENS ★★½
YOUNG ADULTS ★★★½	OVER 30 ★★★★	SENIORS ★★★★	

What it is Bus tour to Cape Canaveral. **Scope and scale** Headliner. **When to go** Check the daily schedule. **Special comments** Tour is sometimes canceled or altered due to launch activity; photo ID required. **Authors' rating** A piece of NASA history; ★★★½. **Duration of tour** About 2 hours, plus parts of the main bus tour.

DESCRIPTION AND COMMENTS Situated about 15 miles from Kennedy Space Center, Cape Canaveral Air Station is an active launch facility where unmanned rockets are sent into space on NASA, military, and commercial missions. Even more interesting, though, is Cape Canaveral's place in history as the original home of the U.S. space program. It is here that the early *Mercury* missions, as well as the first Americans, were launched into space. And unlike the main bus excursion, with its far-away viewing, this tour allows you to actually explore these historical locations firsthand. Elements of the main KSC Bus Tour are included in this tour as well.

A highlight of the tour is the Air Force Space and Mission Museum, home of the world's largest outdoor collection of missiles on display.

TOURING TIPS Unfortunately, you are not allowed to tour at your own pace and must depart with the same group on the same bus. This tour costs an extra $22 for adults and $16 extra for children ages 3–11 on top of the regular admission and is for true space aficionados only.

kids Discover KSC: Today & Tomorrow Tour ★½

APPEAL BY AGE	PRESCHOOL ★	GRADE SCHOOL ★	TEENS ★
YOUNG ADULTS ★★	OVER 30 ★★½		SENIORS ★★★

What it is Bus tour of sights not on main tour. **Scope and scale** Headliner. **When to go** Check the daily schedule. **Special comments** Tour is sometimes canceled or altered due to launch activity. **Authors' rating** Fairly tedious; ★½. **Duration of tour** About 2 hours, plus parts of the main tour.

DESCRIPTION AND COMMENTS This tour takes visitors out for photo ops at Launchpads 39A and 39B, the Vehicle Assembly Building (where the shuttle is "stacked" and loaded prior to rolling over to the pads), and likely views of the massive Crawler-Transporter, so-called because it ferries its precious payload to the launchpad at a creeping 1 mile per hour. Various other sundry sites may be visited depending on launches and the whims of your tour guide.

Fair warning: If you are not a down-to-the-bones space program maniac, this tour has the potential to bore you to tears. Despite the tour's name, many buildings are viewed at a distance.

TOURING TIPS Unfortunately, you are not allowed to tour at your own pace and must depart with the same group on the same bus. This tour costs an extra $22 for adults and $16 extra for children ages 3–11 on top of the regular admission and is for true space aficionados only.

VIEWING A LAUNCH

DOES YOUR CHILD DREAM OF BECOMING AN ASTRONAUT? Maybe you remember the exact day Neil Armstrong set foot on the moon. If so, seeing a live launch is truly awe-inspiring and will leave you with a memory that you'll never forget.

While NASA's famed space shuttles no longer operate, the government has contracted with commercial companies to stage 20 more missions to service the International Space Station, into 2016. At press time, Visitor Complex officials believe that they will still offer special passes, for a fee, for preferred viewing locations but suggest checking the website for details: **kennedyspacecenter.com.**

Launches can also be seen outside of Kennedy Space Center along US 1 in Titusville, Florida, and along US A1A in Cape Canaveral and Cocoa Beach. All of these locations can be reached from FL 528 (Beeline Highway toll road) east. You should arrive early (about three hours in advance), however, as many locals line the streets for launches.

Be aware that some of the attractions at the Kennedy Space Center Visitor Complex may be closed the day of a launch for safety reasons. Also, traffic can be unbearable after a launch, so plan to visit one of the many nearby beaches until roads are clear.

DINING

THE NEAREST RESTAURANTS TO THE VISITOR COMPLEX are almost a dozen miles away on the mainland. However, if you must eat, you'll find Italian sausage subs, hot dogs, and waffle fries with cheese or chili sauce at the **G-Force Grill** and a wider selection in a food court at **Orbit Cafe.** A sit-down restaurant, the **Countdown Café,** is generally open only on launch dates, which are infrequent now that the shuttle missions have ended. There are also many food stands throughout the entire Kennedy Space Center Visitor Complex for a quick bite, and a picnic area beside the Celestial Sphere Fountain creates a nice al fresco dining spot.

SHOPPING

GIFT SHOPS ARE AT EACH STOP on the bus tour, and a jumbo gift shop is located at the Visitor Complex hub. Don't be shy—try the freeze-dried ice-cream sandwich or strawberries. You can also find snow globes, space-shuttle gummy candy, T-shirts, and more. Prices vary from $2 for candy to $30 for T-shirts.

unofficial **TIP**
Let your kids try astronaut ice cream in the gift shop.

PART SEVEN

SEAWORLD

A WORLD-CLASS MARINE-LIFE THEME PARK, SeaWorld is the odd middle child of central Florida's megaparks—without the allure of Mickey Mouse or the glitz of the movie studio attractions. For years, this park succeeded by appealing to those who appreciated the wonder of sea creatures such as killer whales and dolphins. Walt Disney World may have cornered the market on make-believe, but Sea World offered the unique opportunity of watching people interact with live animals.

As competition for tourists' time increased and Disney ventured into the wild-animal business with its Animal Kingdom, SeaWorld created new interactive encounters that can't be found at any other area park. SeaWorld also added thrill rides, including a flight simulator, two roller coasters, and a hybrid flume-coaster.

unofficial TIP
If you and, yes, even your kids, tire of imitation animals the likes of Minnie and Mickey, try a day at SeaWorld.

Combined with the charm of the animals, these attractions and several entertaining shows have created a whole new SeaWorld that isn't just for the fish-and-whale crowd. Many *Unofficial Guide* readers consider the park to be a favorite part of an Orlando vacation.

A family from England writes:

> The best organized park [is] SeaWorld. The computer printout we got on arrival had a very useful show schedule, told us which areas were temporarily closed due to construction, and had a readily understandable map. Best of all, there was almost no queuing. We rated this day so highly that it is the park we would most like to visit again.

A woman from Alberta, Canada, gives her opinion:

> We chose SeaWorld as our fifth day at the World. What a pleasant surprise! It was every bit as good (and in some ways better) than WDW itself. Well worth the admission, an excellent entertainment

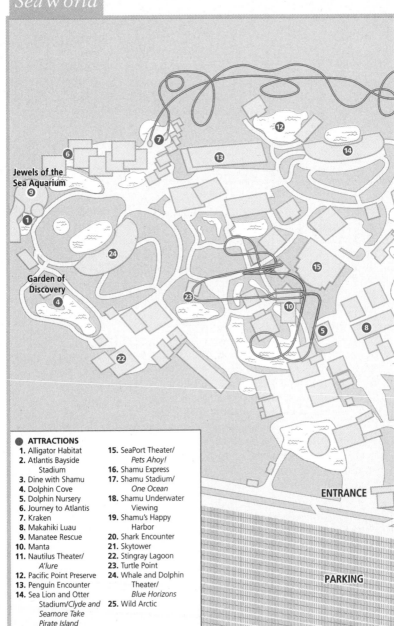

SeaWorld

Jewels of the
Sea Aquarium

Garden of
Discovery

ENTRANCE

PARKING

● **ATTRACTIONS**
1. Alligator Habitat
2. Atlantis Bayside Stadium
3. Dine with Shamu
4. Dolphin Cove
5. Dolphin Nursery
6. Journey to Atlantis
7. Kraken
8. Makahiki Luau
9. Manatee Rescue
10. Manta
11. Nautilus Theater/ *A'lure*
12. Pacific Point Preserve
13. Penguin Encounter
14. Sea Lion and Otter Stadium/*Clyde and Seamore Take Pirate Island*
15. SeaPort Theater/ *Pets Ahoy!*
16. Shamu Express
17. Shamu Stadium/ *One Ocean*
18. Shamu Underwater Viewing
19. Shamu's Happy Harbor
20. Shark Encounter
21. Skytower
22. Stingray Lagoon
23. Turtle Point
24. Whale and Dolphin Theater/ *Blue Horizons*
25. Wild Arctic

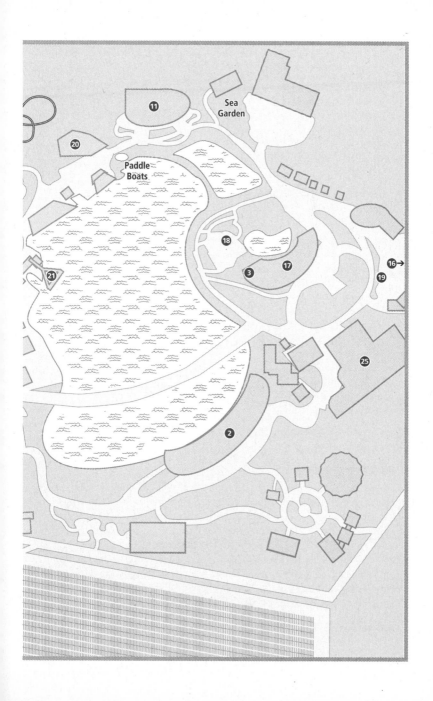

value, educational, well run, and better value for the dollar in food services. Perhaps expand your coverage to give them their due!

A father of two from Manitoba, Canada, gives SeaWorld's night-time laser show top marks, commenting:

But the absolute topper is the closing laser show, which beats out IllumiNations at Epcot for extravaganza. The SeaWorld show combines fireworks, lasers, and moving holographic images back-projected on a curtain of water. In the word of our older daughter: awesome! And you watch the whole thing seated in the lakeside arena, instead of jostling for a standing view around the Epcot lagoon.

A reader from Sylvania, Georgia, believes Disney could learn a thing or two from SeaWorld:

Disney ought to take a look at how well this place is run. I know they don't have the same crowds or the exciting rides, but there is still a lot of entertainment here and never a wait. This allows you to set your pace without worrying about what you'll have to miss. You'll see it all no matter how you do it, you'll come away feeling you got better value for your dollars, you won't feel as tired as a Disney day, and you will probably learn more too. Only downside is you'll probably be hungry. Food is not one of the park's assets.

unofficial **TIP**
There's more than just marine life at this well-organized park to keep everyone entertained.

On top of its accumulated charms, SeaWorld also boasts its aquatic subpark, Discovery Cove. Here, you can swim with live dolphins—an attraction offered nowhere else in central Florida. All of this makes SeaWorld a great way to shift gears from the Mouse race, while still enjoying the big production values of a major theme-park destination.

GETTING THERE

SEAWORLD IS ABOUT 10 MILES EAST of Walt Disney World. Take I-4 to FL 528 (Beeline Highway east). Exit at the first ramp, which is International Drive. Turn left off the exit ramp. Turn right at Central Florida Parkway. The entrance to SeaWorld is on the right just prior to a large SeaWorld sculpture. Car and motorcycle parking is $14, and preferred parking is available for $20 in a lot closer to the main entrance that fills up quickly. RV and camper parking is $15. Discovery Cove is directly across the Central Florida Parkway from SeaWorld. Parking at the Discovery Cove lot is free.

ADMISSION PRICES

EXCEPT UNDER THE MOST CROWDED CONDITIONS, a typical visitor can see most (if not all) of SeaWorld in one solid day of touring, so a standard One-day Pass makes sense. However, several options will get you a lot more time in the park for slightly more money than a one-day ticket. If you're planning to spend time at other local theme parks, consider the money-saving Orlando FlexTicket, good for admission to six parks. Several deals are also available combining SeaWorld admission with tickets for Busch Gardens and the water park Adventure Island, both in Tampa. Discounts are available for AAA members, disabled visitors, senior citizens, and military personnel. All tickets, even the FlexTicket, can be purchased on the park's website, usually for less (**seaworld.com**). Purchasing tickets online, from an authorized vendor, or from any of the authorized ticket agents in Orlando will save you from the logjam at the park ticket kiosks, and purchasing online will also save you a few dollars. If you fail to obtain tickets in advance, try the electronic ticket machines located outside SeaWorld's main gate and to the right of the ticket kiosks. To use the machines, bring your credit card and your patience. The touch-screen interface is temperamental at best and the purchase process more complicated than necessary. Select your language choice and then follow the instructions as you would with an ATM. When you are finished—it will take about 3–5 minutes per purchase—the machine will print out your tickets.

One-day Pass

Adults **$79.99 + tax** | Children ages 3–9 **$71.99 + tax** | Children under age 3 **Free**

SeaWorld Fun Card

This pass is good only for residents of Florida and is by far the best deal for admission to SeaWorld, but there are a few catches. For $4 less than the One-day Pass, you get unlimited admission to SeaWorld for one calendar year, except blackout dates of Easter weekend and December 27–31. There's also a Fun Card that allows admission to Busch Gardens (with the same restrictions).

unofficial **TIP**
It's a major time-saver to pay admission before heading to the park.

Fun Card

Adults **$79.99 + tax** | Children ages 3–9 **$71.99 + tax** | Children under age 3 **Free**

Fun Card plus Aquatica *(after 2 p.m.)*

Adults **$129.99 + tax** | Children ages 3–9 **$121.99 + tax** | Children under age 3 **Free**

Two-park Unlimited Admission Ticket

This pass is a 14-day admission ticket good for both SeaWorld and Busch Gardens (includes a free shuttle between Orlando and Tampa) or Aquatica.

Adults **$114.99 + tax** | Children ages 3–9 **$106.99 + tax**

Three-park Unlimited Admission Ticket

This pass is a 14-day admission ticket good for SeaWorld, Busch Gardens (includes a free shuttle between Orlando and Tampa), and Aquatica. | Adults **$129.99 + tax** | Children ages 3–9 **$121.99 + tax**

Annual Passports

These allow unlimited admission to either SeaWorld alone or a combination of SeaWorld, Aquatica, Adventure Island, or Busch Gardens for one or two years and include free general parking and 10% off merchandise and food purchases in the park(s). The Platinum includes admission to nine parks across the country and also includes free preferred parking and ride-again privileges on some rides.

One Park, One Year Passport
Adults **$109.99** | Children ages 3–9 and Seniors ages 50+ **$101.99**

One Park, Two Years Passport
Adults **$169.99** | Children ages 3–9 and Seniors ages 50+ **$161.99**

Two Parks, One Year Passport
Adults **$159.99** | Children ages 3–9 and Seniors ages 50+ **$151.99**

Two Parks, Two Years Passport
Adults **$244.99** | Children ages 3–9 and Seniors ages 50+ **$236.99**

Three Parks, one Year Passport
Adults **$209.99** | Children ages 3–9 and Seniors ages 50+ **$201.99**

Three Parks, Two Years Passport
Adults **$319.99** | Children ages 3–9 and Seniors ages 50+ **$311.99**

Four Parks, One Year Passport
Adults **$249.99** | Children ages 3–9 and Seniors ages 50+ **$241.99**

Four Parks, Two Years Passport
Adults **$379.99** | Children ages 3–9 and Seniors ages 50+ **$371.99**

Platinum Passport (*one year*)
Adults **$299.99 + tax** | Children ages 3–9 and Seniors ages 50+ **$291.99 + tax**

Platinum Passport (*two years*)
Adults **$439.99 + tax** | Children ages 3–9 and Seniors ages 50+ **$431.99 + tax**

Orlando FlexTicket

This pass is good for up to 14 consecutive days at six parks: Busch Gardens, Universal Studios Florida, Universal Islands of Adventure, SeaWorld, Aquatica, and Wet 'n Wild. There's also a version that excludes Busch Gardens, so be sure to get the one you want.

FlexTicket | Adults **$274.95 + tax** | Children ages 3–9 **$254.95 + tax**

FlexTicket PLUS | Adults **$314.95 + tax** | Children ages 3–9 **$294.95 + tax**

ARRIVING

SEAWORLD OFFICIALLY OPENS AT 9 A.M. Ropes to a smaller section on the north side drop at 10 a.m., except during the busiest times of year, when the entire park opens all at once. Closing time fluctuates from 6 or 7 p.m. in late fall and winter to 10 p.m. in summer and on holidays.

Exploring SeaWorld takes a full day. Because the majority of attractions are shows, it won't be a mad rush to avoid lines like at other theme parks. However, avoiding the rare long wait and large crowds requires getting there early during busy times of the year. Like other area parks, SeaWorld opens its turnstiles at either 8:30 a.m. or 8:45 a.m. depending on the season, which means you can enter the park before the scheduled 9 a.m. opening. You can only wander around a limited area with a bakery and a few shops, however. Nonetheless, during peak season, we suggest that you arrive no later than 8:20 a.m., allowing time to park and purchase tickets. At other times, arriving at 8:40 a.m. should give you a jump on the crowds.

While a member of your party purchases tickets, have another track down a SeaWorld map. Map-toting employees are usually positioned in front of the ticket booth. While waiting for the park to open, plan your attack.

During peak season, if you're a fan of water thrill rides, locate the quickest route to Journey to Atlantis, which combines elements of a water ride and dry roller coaster. When the ropes drop, head straight there. You'll be tempted to stop at animal exhibits along the route, but save those for later. The line for Journey to Atlantis will be most manageable early in the day.

If roller coasters are your thing, head for the Manta coaster first. The coaster is clearly visible from the main entrance. After Manta, hustle over to Kraken, located at the back of the park between Journey to Atlantis and the Penguin Encounter.

When attendance isn't at its highest, lines for Journey to Atlantis and Kraken can be quite short. Because Manta is fairly new and located close to the park entrance, its lines are only short immediately after park opening regardless of season. At those slower times of the year, or if you don't like water rides or coasters, plan to hurry to Dolphin Cove in the Key West area when the park opens. In addition to beating the bulk of the crowd, you'll get to see the animals at their most active time in the morning. You can stand along the edge of this gorgeous 2-acre pool teeming with dolphins to get a close-up view. But if the dolphins are one of your main reasons for visiting SeaWorld, use your morning visit to get

unofficial **TIP**
Animals at SeaWorld and other parks are most active early in the morning.

the feeding schedule for the day, which is posted at the mint-green fish house on the left side of the pool. A feeding is usually scheduled at 9:15 a.m., and you can get in line to purchase fish right away.

Arrange the remainder of your day around the show schedule. Attractions encircle a large lagoon, and the best strategy to see it all is to travel clockwise, especially because the opposite side does not open until 10 a.m. This tactic depends on the entertainment schedule, of course, but at the very least, allow time to see the attractions in the area surrounding each show. You will save time and energy by not roaming aimlessly, and there's not much point in rushing—the entertainment schedule is not designed for immediate back-to-back viewing of shows.

Walt Disney World might be known for its friendly, informative cast members, but they certainly haven't cornered the market. At each animal exhibit in SeaWorld, you can find pleasant and extremely knowledgeable employees who will share interesting information and answer any questions.

SeaWorld also allows visitors to view training sessions that occur at many of the show stadiums. A schedule for these sessions isn't published, but if you're near any of the stadiums between shows, pop in. You can also hang out a bit after a show to possibly catch some unscripted action.

CONTACTING SEAWORLD

  FOR MORE INFORMATION, call ☎ 888-800-5447 or visit the SeaWorld website at **seaworld.com.** If you or your children are interested in learning more about the park's animals before visiting, SeaWorld also maintains a website designed for students and teachers at **seaworld.org.**

ATTRACTIONS

Alligator Habitat ★★

APPEAL BY AGE	PRESCHOOL ★★½	GRADE SCHOOL ★★½	TEENS ★★★
YOUNG ADULTS ★		OVER 30 ★½	SENIORS ★★

What it is Outdoor alligator viewing. **Scope and scale** Distraction. **When to go** Anytime. **Authors' rating** Easy to miss; ★½.

DESCRIPTION AND COMMENTS How a Florida theme park that focuses on aquatic creatures went without alligators for so long is a mystery. The relatively new exhibit is located on the walkway directly beside the entrance to the manatee exhibit. The docile gators don't move much except at feeding times, which occur at random throughout the day, but asking a nearby attendant may get you the schedule for your visit.

TOURING TIPS This is not Gatorland, and the guys in the habitat are small, but for those who've never seen Florida's most famous residents, it's worth a peek.

A'lure: The Call of the Ocean/Nautilus Theater ★★★

APPEAL BY AGE	PRESCHOOL ★★★½	GRADE SCHOOL ★★★★	TEENS ★★
YOUNG ADULTS ★★★		OVER 30 ★★★	SENIORS ★★★

What it is Acrobatics show. **Scope and scale** Major attraction. **When to go**

Check daily entertainment schedule. **Authors' rating** Interesting showcase; ★★★. **Duration of show** 20 minutes.

DESCRIPTION AND COMMENTS   A dancing fisherman, a prancing queen, undulating sea horses, and gymnast nymphs make up the ensemble of the park's latest theatrical mainstay. It's the age-old story of a fisherman sinking to the bottom of the sea and discovering a city of exotic sea creatures. The creatures' queen, clad from head to toe in purple crinoline, grows jealous when the fisherman falls in love with a nymph who climbs out of an oyster shell—the odds of her name being Pearl?—and sets her minions of evil sea horses upon the couple, who run around the stage while acrobats climb up poles.

If the plot seems weak, let us assure you: it is. Thankfully, the choreographer opted to not include any speaking parts, so there's no bad dialogue with which to contend. The show is really an excuse to showcase some excellent acrobatics, and in that respect it is a serious success.

TOURING TIPS   The aluminum bench–style seating fills up quickly, so it's best to arrive about 20 minutes beforehand to snag seats in the center of the auditorium. The show contains both strobe lights and loud effects that may startle some audience members.

Blue Horizons/**Whale and Dolphin Theater**   ★★★

APPEAL BY AGE	PRESCHOOL ★★★½	GRADE SCHOOL ★★★★	TEENS ★★½
YOUNG ADULTS ★★★½		OVER 30 ★★★½	SENIORS ★★★½

What it is Killer whale show. **Scope and scale** Headliner. **When to go** Check daily entertainment schedule. **Authors' rating** This remake needs a remake; ★★★. **Duration of show** 30 minutes.

DESCRIPTION AND COMMENTS   The *Blue Horizons* show—which includes whales, dolphins, birds, acrobats, spraying water, a huge set with an enormous truss, and a full symphonic score—is one of the premiere attractions at SeaWorld. With all of these elements, the show should succeed. Unfortunately, it contains critical flaws. The plot is incoherent, and the show contains many lulls in action; the only way to grasp the plot is to watch the making-of-*Blue Horizons* DVD. Even after the video, you'll still be a little baffled. The show opens with a young girl named Marina opening a door into a fantasy world, and after that, the plot goes to pot. Without some foreknowledge—and even with it—the appearance of a lady in bird costume with her minions of birdman-acrobats is both disconcerting and confusing. This lady is *supposed* to represent the Spirit of the Sky while her male counterpart in the water is supposed to represent the Spirit of the Sea. Instead, he comes across as the young girl's creepy love interest, partly because of his blue costume that counters the young girl's pink costume, but more because too much frolicking.

The title—*Blue Horizons*—derives from the horizon line where sky and sea meet. The young girl wants to be part of the sky and the sea, and so does the set. The set's scale is impressive but the look is less so; the large orbs attached to the backdrop are meant to simultaneously represent clouds and bubbles but look like poorly painted globs of glue.

kids Even with the flaws, the show's animal stunts are impressive. The cetaceans leap in the air and spin underwater while the macaws fly about accompanied by a memorable symphonic score. If a coherent plot can be added, the lulls in action removed, and the human acrobatics integrated with the animal acrobatics, then the show will be spectacular. At the moment, it is only a spectacle whose appeal is for children under age 10.

TOURING TIPS Due to crowd flow into the *Blue Horizons'* stadium, the best entrance to the stadium is located near the Journey to Atlantis attraction. This entrance will place you in front of the stadium, and as long as you arrive 45 minutes to an hour before show time, you should be able to claim a seat up front.

Clyde and Seamore Take Pirate Island/   ★★★½
Sea Lion and Otter Stadium

APPEAL BY AGE PRESCHOOL ★★★★   GRADE SCHOOL ★★★★   TEENS ★★★
YOUNG ADULTS ★★★½   OVER 30 ★★★   SENIORS ★★★

What it is Show featuring sea lions, otters, and a walrus. **Scope and scale** Headliner. **When to go** Check daily entertainment schedule. **Authors' rating** Unabashed cornball comedy; ★★★½. **Duration of show** 30 minutes.

DESCRIPTION AND COMMENTS One of the three headlining shows at SeaWorld, this attraction draws a crowd, so attempt to arrive up to 45 minutes to an hour ahead of show time. Fortunately for early entries, unlike other attractions at SeaWorld, the Clyde and Seamore show has a preshow performer. This pirate-mime warms up the seated audience by mocking the individuals from the incoming crowd. The clown is completely irreverent, so if you are extremely self-conscious, you had better enter from the rear of the stadium.

The irreverence continues onward with the start of the show. The sea lion stars are named Clyde and Seamore; Clyde plays alongside the protagonist Robin Plunder, who has been shipwrecked on the island, while Seamore plays the first mate of the pirate ship under the villainous Captain Squid, who is seeking a hidden treasure. The show takes a self-aware and self-deprecating stance as Robin Plunder talks directly to the audience, points out any mistakes made by the sea lions, and even slights Captain Squid on her horrific acting. Due to the great ensemble work between trainers and animals—including the supporting cast members Opie the Otter and Sir Winston Walrus—as well as the coherent plot that showcases the animals' talents, this show is the funniest and most well-rounded performance at SeaWorld.

TOURING TIPS Arrive early and from the rear of the stadium to avoid the mime.

Dolphin Cove   ★★★★

APPEAL BY AGE PRESCHOOL ★★★   GRADE SCHOOL ★★★★   TEENS ★★★★
YOUNG ADULTS ★★★★   OVER 30 ★★★★   SENIORS ★★★★

What it is Outdoor dolphin habitat. **Scope and scale** Major attraction. **When to go** In the morning; for scheduled feedings. **Authors' rating** Impressive; ★★★★.

DESCRIPTION AND COMMENTS This sprawling, 2-acre habitat is filled with a community of swimming and leaping dolphins. You can stand along one side of the pool and touch or feed the dolphins. A path along the opposite side of the pool leads to an overlook area with excellent views and a great photo location. If you can live without touching the dolphins, this area is also much less crowded. Next to the overlook is a walkway to an underwater viewing area that provides the best glimpse of these delightful mammals in action. The interior walkway is air-conditioned and one of the most memorable sights at SeaWorld.

TOURING TIPS Feedings take place at scheduled times throughout the day, usually immediately following the dolphin show at nearby Whale and Dolphin Theater. Feedings provide the best opportunity to interact with the dolphins but also generate large crowds. Check the schedule at the fish house to the left of the pool to see if the feeding times fit into your schedule to view the park. A tray of fish costs $7.

There is a chance to touch the dolphins at other times. SeaWorld employees say the key is simply to keep your hands still under the water and patiently wait for the animals to brush against you. You may see SeaWorld trainers slapping the water to get the dolphins' attention, but this doesn't seem to work for guests. Apparently, the dolphins know and trust the trainers, but they are frightened by strange hands hitting the water.

With the opening of Discovery Cove, SeaWorld's swim-with-the-dolphins subpark, the pool of available dolphins has been stretched a little thin. Some of the park's dolphins might be away at Discovery Cove when you visit, although SeaWorld claims all bases are covered.

Dolphin Nursery ★★

APPEAL BY AGE	PRESCHOOL ★	GRADE SCHOOL ★★	TEENS ★
YOUNG ADULTS ★★		OVER 30 ★★	SENIORS ★★

What it is Outdoor pool for expectant dolphins or mothers and calves. **Scope and scale** Diversion. **When to go** Anytime. **Authors' rating** Only worth a quick glimpse unless a baby is present; ★★.

DESCRIPTION AND COMMENTS Seeing this tiny pool that used to be the sole dolphin experience at SeaWorld should make you appreciate Dolphin Cove and Discovery Cove all the more. But the small size is perfect for its current purpose—providing a separate area for pregnant dolphins and new moms and calves. Stop by for a quick glance if it's an expectant dolphin. Stay longer if there's a baby in the pool.

TOURING TIPS This area will be roped off and guests understandably kept away when a dolphin goes into labor. Because it's near the park entrance, swing by on your way out to see if the area has reopened, and you might be able to view mom and baby.

Hiding next to the Dolphin Nursery is one of the most beautiful and secluded areas of SeaWorld. Find the path next to the nursery and enter a lush tropical rain forest. A large banyan tree and 30-foot-tall bamboo trees shade the entire area. Large fish swim in a small pond, and two beautiful macaws perch on a branch.

There is also an aviary featuring blue dacnis and red-legged honey-creepers, both adorably tiny birds. There are no formal benches, but a few stone ledges provide the perfect place to get away from the sun and the theme park hustle and bustle.

kids Journey to Atlantis ★★½

APPEAL BY AGE PRESCHOOL †	GRADE SCHOOL ★★★	TEENS ★★★
YOUNG ADULTS ★★½	OVER 30 ★★	SENIORS ★★

† Preschoolers are generally too short to ride.

What it is Water ride and roller coaster combo. **Scope and scale** Headliner. **When to go** Before 10 a.m. or after 4 p.m. during peak season; avoid visiting immediately after a Whale and Dolphin Theater show. **Special comments** Riders must be 42" tall; pregnant women or people with heart, back, or neck problems should not ride. **Authors' rating** Fun, if not cheesy; ★★½. **Duration of ride** 6 minutes. **Loading speed** Moderate.

DESCRIPTION AND COMMENTS Riders board eight-passenger boats and plunge down a nearly vertical 60-foot waterfall before careening through a mini–roller coaster. Although this ride is housed in a truly impressive edifice that spouts fire and water, the payoff inside is pretty meager. The attraction supposedly takes guests on a voyage through Atlantis as they try to avoid an evil spirit, but even after several trips, we still didn't have a good grasp on this story line (what's up with that goldfish, or sea horse, or whatever it was?). For that reason, and because of an "it's over before you know it" feeling, we have to give the ride lower marks than those of Disney's Splash Mountain. However, Journey to Atlantis definitely provides the bigger thrill.

TOURING TIPS Closer to sunset, the special effects in this attraction are more intense because the darker evening sky helps keep light from leaking into the ride when the boats travel outdoors. However, during peak seasons the wait in line can be an hour or longer, and we don't think Journey to Atlantis is worth that much of your time. For best results, arrive early and dash to this attraction when the park opens at 9 a.m. to minimize the wait. Then stop by in the evening and ride again if the line isn't too long.

Journey to Atlantis will get you wet, especially in the front seats. If you want to minimize the drenching, bring a poncho or purchase one at the gift shop at the attraction. Place any items that you don't want to get soaked, such as cameras, in the pay lockers near the entrance to the queue. Free bins are available at the loading dock, but they are not secured.

Kraken ★★★★

APPEAL BY AGE PRESCHOOL †	GRADE SCHOOL ★★★★	TEENS ★★★★
YOUNG ADULTS ★★★½	OVER 30 ★★★	SENIORS ★

† Preschoolers are generally too short to ride.

What it is Roller coaster. **Scope and scale** Super headliner. **When to go**

Immediately following a ride on Manta. **Special comments** Riders must be 42" tall; pregnant women or people with heart, back, or neck problems should not ride. **Authors' rating** A real brain rattler; ★★★★. **Duration of ride** 3 minutes. **Loading speed** Moderate.

DESCRIPTION AND COMMENTS   The roller coaster war has reached epic propor-
tions in central Florida. SeaWorld enters the battle with Kraken, named
after the mythological underwater beast. At a top speed of 65 miles per
hour, a length of more than 4,000 feet, and with a first drop of 144 feet,
it is Orlando's fastest, longest, and tallest roller coaster. How long will it
reign? If history is any indication, it's only a matter of time before
Disney or Universal ups the ante yet again.

This "floorless" coaster puts riders in 32 open-sided seats, in eight
rows, riding on a pedestal above the track. It's a sort of combination of
the newer inverted coasters (where riders dangle in seats, rather than
sit in cars) with the open ceiling of a traditional coaster. The net effect
is that nothing up, down, or sideways blocks your view, an especially
amazing effect on that first big drop—when it seems like you're about
to plunge right into a lake.

Despite its overall great fun, be warned that this coaster does not
offer the smoothest ride. You will be jerked around a bit, and repeated
rides may lead to woozy crab-walking.

TOURING TIPS   This extremely popular coaster draws the crowds, but it can
move them too. Even large lines will move at a good clip, but you can still
cut down your wait by riding before 10 a.m. or after 4 p.m. During peak
season, we suggest you arrive when the park opens, ride Manta, and
immediately head to Kraken. You must put your items in a pay locker.

Manatee Rescue   ★★★

APPEAL BY AGE	PRESCHOOL ★★½	GRADE SCHOOL ★★½	TEENS ★★★
YOUNG ADULTS ★★★	OVER 30 ★★★		SENIORS ★★★

What it is Outdoor manatee habitat and underwater viewing. **Scope and scale**
Minor attraction. **When to go** Anytime. **Authors' rating** Remarkable animals in
a creative habitat; ★★★.

DESCRIPTION AND COMMENTS   Manatees, which are on the endangered species list, are still disappearing at a rapid rate. All of the docile creatures
in this exhibit were injured in the wild and have been rescued by
SeaWorld. The area resembles an inland canal, a favorite spot of these
gentle giants. For most of the rescued animals, this is the last part
of their rehabilitation, and many will be returned to their natural
environment.

TOURING TIPS   Be sure to visit the underwater viewing area. It offers an excellent view of the huge creatures. Along the way, you'll see a short video
about the plight of these endangered giants.

On occasion, SeaWorld rescues orphaned baby manatees. Check with
an educator in the area to find out if any are in the exhibit, if they might
be bottle-fed, and at what time. It's pure, distilled cuteness.

Manta ★★★★★

† *Preschoolers are generally too short to ride.*

What it is Inverted steel super roller coaster. **Scope and scale** Super headliner. **When to go** Before 10 a.m. or after 4 p.m. **Special comments** Riders must be 54" or taller. **Authors' rating** So much action that it's hard to take it in on just one ride; ★★★★★. **Duration of ride** 2½ minutes. **Loading speed** Moderate.

DESCRIPTION AND COMMENTS The new king of SeaWorld rides, Manta is a steel coaster on which riders are arranged four across lying facedown beneath the expanse of a giant manta ray–shaped carriage. The coaster soars and swoops through a pretzel loop, a 360-degree in-line roll, and two corkscrews—not to mention a first drop of 113 feet. There are four inversions while Manta reaches a height of 140 feet and speeds of over 55 miles per hour. But don't worry—lying facedown puts you in the perfect position to throw up. Actually, the ride is relatively smooth, though the action seems nonstop. If you get sick, it will be from the bugs you pick out of your teeth (keep you mouth closed at all times—you're supposed to be a ray, not a bat). The queuing area passes aquarium windows displaying rays and vividly colored fish.

TOURING TIPS Riders are not allowed to carry backpack or shoulder bags on Manta; they must be left with nonriders or in nearby lockers that rent for 50 cents. Before climbing into the Manta seats, riders with nonlacing shoes must leave them in wire baskets hanging at the exit fence. On busy days, two carriers operate; on slower days, only one, so riders who have finished the course may hang, facing down, for another minute and a half while the carrier in front of theirs is loaded.

Children too short for Manta or those parkgoers who don't want to accompany others on the ride can pass the time viewing a bevy of rays, a large Pacific octopus, darling sea horses, and more in the adjacent Manta Aquarium, which occupies what formerly was the tropical reef section of Stingray Lagoon.

One Ocean/Shamu Stadium

What it is Killer whale show. **Scope and scale** Super-headliner. **When to go** Check daily entertainment schedule. **Authors' rating** Designed to be the premier live-animal event at SeaWorld. **Duration of show** 30 minutes.

DESCRIPTION AND COMMENTS Following the shocking death of a trainer working with one of the killer whales just after a performance in February 2010, SeaWorld withdrew its orca trainers from the tanks at all of its parks. But just three weeks before the one-year anniversary of the trainer's death, SeaWorld announced a major new killer whale show that would replace the long-running *Believe,* which had been the park's major live-animal presentation for five years. (It was not during *Believe* that the death occurred.)

No trainers will be in the water with the whales during any performances—at any SeaWorld park—for the foreseeable future. Yet the theme of the new show, *One Ocean,* which debuted in April 2011, is that humans and animals are "connected," a word used repeatedly by SeaWorld staff in describing the new show. The show will focus on conservation and what viewers can do to help the environment.

One Ocean has as many as three orcas in the giant Shamu Stadium pool simultaneously, where they swim and leap past newly installed fountains. Also new are the backdrops, lighting, and color schemes.

The production elements are, of course, only a filler for the real wonder at *One Ocean:* the highly trained family of orcas, commonly known as killer whales. Like most celebrities, they're known by stage names—most notably, Shamu and Baby Shamu.

Always the icon of SeaWorld, the killer whales now come closer to the huge glass-window walls of the tank. Members of the audience are brought down to the glass during the performances for some interaction, and the audience can observe the older whales teaching the younger ones.

One thing that won't change: the famous Splash Zone—the dozen-plus rows of seats at tank side—is still a gonna'-get-wet area for the guests sitting there. Gallons and gallons of 55°F salt water are flung into the first 14 rows by the flukes of a large whale. The audience is warned, but most folks must not realize how much water will head their way or how cold it really is. Nevertheless, some, especially the under-age-12 set, make it a point to be in the water's path.

kids TOURING TIPS We're not kidding when we say gallons of chilly salt water. You will get soaked in the first few rows. If you or the kids think you're up for it, you might want to bring some extra clothes to change into after the cold shower. You should leave your cameras with someone out of the range of the corrosive salt water.

Although this is a large stadium, you must arrive early to get a seat.

kids Pacific Point Preserve ★★★

APPEAL BY AGE	PRESCHOOL ★★★½	GRADE SCHOOL ★★★½	TEENS ★★★
YOUNG ADULTS ★★★		OVER 30 ★★★	SENIORS ★★★

What it is Outdoor sea lion habitat. **Scope and scale** Major attraction. **When to go** Feeding times (scattered throughout the day). **Authors' rating** Fun and startling; ★★★.

DESCRIPTION AND COMMENTS Let the sound of more than 50 barking sea lions and harbor seals lead you to this nifty area tucked behind Sea Lion and Otter Stadium. An elevated walkway behind a glass partition surrounds the sunken habitat. The animals can be found sunning themselves on the rocky terrain or lounging in the shallow waves. More often, though, they'll be barking impatiently—perhaps very impatiently—for a snack. Although these animals aren't trained, a few of the sea lions will improvise cute antics for food, such as mimicking you sticking out your tongue. Sometimes, they get so excited about a possible meal that their barking reaches amazing, earsplitting levels.

TOURING TIPS If you participate in a feeding, which costs $3 for one tray of fish (or $5 for two), watch out for the large, aggressive birds that lurk in this area. They are poised to steal the fish right out of your hand, snatch one in midair as you toss it to the sea lions, or even land on your head or shoulders to make a grab for the goods (we saw this happen twice).

Look closely at the animals, and you might spot some adorable sea lion or harbor seal pups—especially if you visit during spring or summer.

Penguin Encounter ★★★

APPEAL BY AGE	PRESCHOOL ★★★½	GRADE SCHOOL ★★★	TEENS ★★★
YOUNG ADULTS ★★★		OVER 30 ★★★	SENIORS ★★★

What it is Indoor penguin habitat. **Scope and scale** Major attraction. **When to go** Anytime. **Authors' rating** Adorable tuxedo models; ★★★.

DESCRIPTION AND COMMENTS The first section of this exhibit features an icy habitat behind a glass wall, providing an excellent view of about 280 penguins' antics in several feet of water. Step on the people-mover to the right for a close-up view of these critters as they congregate, waddle, and dive into the frigid water. Then circle back behind the people-mover to an elevated section where you can take a longer look at the large emperor penguins. A learning area is just past the habitat, where interactive kiosks provide information about the animals and their environment. The walkway then leads to a smaller exhibit, which is home to puffins and other species that prefer a warmer climate.

TOURING TIPS The pungent penguin odor will hit you before you step through the door, but after a couple of minutes, you'll get used to it. During summer, SeaWorld darkens the exhibit to simulate the Antarctic environment, where it is actually winter. The birds are still active and visible, but you may need to spend more time on the stationary upper level to get a good look. During this season, you will not be allowed to shoot any photos of the habitat because the flash negates the effect of the darkened room for the animals.

There is a way, albeit astoundingly finicky, to enter the environment via the Penguin Encounter Program. The program is not listed on the park map, so stop by the exhibit to get the daily schedule. Bone up on your penguin facts beforehand; one guest who answers all of the keeper's questions is allowed to enter the environment.

Pets Ahoy!/SeaPort Theater ★★★

APPEAL BY AGE	PRESCHOOL ★★★	GRADE SCHOOL ★★★	TEENS ★★½
YOUNG ADULTS ★★★		OVER 30 ★★★	SENIORS ★★★

What it is Show featuring trained pets. **Scope and scale** Major attraction. **When to go** Check daily entertainment schedule. **Authors' rating** The truth about cats and dogs?; ★★★. **Duration of show** 25 minutes.

DESCRIPTION AND COMMENTS Despite its cornball name—SeaWorld's need to uphold its nautical theme seems to exceed its need to reel in a crowd—the show remains a draw due to the elaborate integration of the beach-town set with the animals who inhabit it. The show is a series of skits that each imitate a Rube Goldberg machine: a dog pulls a lever that signals a cat to run across the stage that, in turn, signals a different cat to climb a rope onto a roof, and so on. The skits are accented with sound effects and music, as well as a basic plot that always ends with a humorous, if predictable, twist. The only low points in the show are the appearance of the trainers who demonstrate an animal performing one stunt with neither plot nor set-ploys, and the 5-minute shill for the Humane Society, from where most of the animals were rescued. At the end of the show, you can talk to the trainers and get close to the animals. Keep your eyes open, kids; you might spot a few creatures Mom has *never even considered* for pets.

TOURING TIPS The Pets Ahoy Pavilion is located on The Waterfront between the Skytower and the southern bridge that leads to Shamu Stadium. The theater is small but, because the show is not a headliner, seats are usually available.

Shamu Express   ★★

APPEAL BY AGE PRESCHOOL ★★★		GRADE SCHOOL ★★★½		TEENS ★★
YOUNG ADULTS ★½		OVER 30 ★★		SENIORS ★★

What it is Children's roller coaster. **Scope and scale** Minor attraction. **When to go** Avoid visiting after a Shamu show. **Special comments** Open from 10 a.m. until an hour before the park closes. **Authors' rating** Thrill ride for kids; ★★.

DESCRIPTION AND COMMENTS With Kraken towering over the park, riders under 42" tall may feel left out of the roller coaster market. SeaWorld consoles its younger riders with the Shamu Express, located in Shamu's Happy Harbor. The coaster is very small, with only 800 feet of track, but the ride is smooth and makes a great starter coaster. Besides, who can resist cars shaped like the park's biggest star?

TOURING TIPS The roller coaster holds only 28 guests at a time, but the short track keeps the lines from piling up. Still, avoid the Shamu Express, and all of Happy Harbor, directly before and after performances at Shamu Stadium.

Shamu Underwater Viewing   ★★★

APPEAL BY AGE PRESCHOOL ★★		GRADE SCHOOL ★★★		TEENS ★★½
YOUNG ADULTS ★★★		OVER 30 ★★★		SENIORS ★★★

What it is Whale viewing area. **Scope and scale** Minor attraction. **When to go** Avoid visiting immediately before or after a Shamu show. **Authors' rating** Good look at these incredible animals; ★★★.

DESCRIPTION AND COMMENTS Go behind the scenes at Shamu Stadium for a peek at the stars of the show in their 1.5 million–gallon pool. Check the above-water viewing area for a training session or a veterinary visit. When standing "next to" these animals in the underwater viewing area, be prepared to be awestruck by their enormous size.

TOURING TIPS When the animals are not active, or not even present, this area is not worth visiting. Check with the SeaWorld employee usually stationed nearby for the best times to visit on a particular day.

Have your camera ready at the underwater viewing area. The whales usually slowly circle the pool, offering an amazing backdrop for a group photo.

Shamu's Happy Harbor ★★★½

APPEAL BY AGE	PRESCHOOL ★★★	GRADE SCHOOL ★★★	TEENS ★
YOUNG ADULTS ★		OVER 30 ★	SENIORS ★★

What it is Children's play area. **Scope and scale** Minor attraction. **When to go** Avoid visiting after a Shamu show. **Special comments** Open from 10 a.m. until an hour before the park closes. **Authors' rating** A nice oversize playground; ★★★½.

DESCRIPTION AND COMMENTS Four stories of net span this 3-acre children's play area. Children and brave adults can climb, crawl, and weave through this net jungle. Other activities include an air bubble where kids under 54" tall can bounce and play and an interactive submarine with several water cannons and fountains. There is also an area for smaller kids (they must be under 42" tall) with a standard ball-filled room and several playground contraptions. Standard carnival rides with aquatic theming are also located here.

TOURING TIPS Parents can grab a cool drink and relax at Coconut Cove while watching their children play. Most adults should stay clear of the patience-testing, headache-causing, steel-drum area, where kids are allowed to bang to their hearts' content.

Shark Encounter ★★★½

APPEAL BY AGE	PRESCHOOL ★★★	GRADE SCHOOL ★★★½	TEENS ★★★★
YOUNG ADULTS ★★★½		OVER 30 ★★★½	SENIORS ★★★½

What it is Exhibit of sharks, eels, and other dangerous sea creatures. **Scope and scale** Major attraction. **When to go** Anytime. **Authors' rating** Pleasantly creepy; ★★★½.

DESCRIPTION AND COMMENTS This walk-through exhibit immerses you (almost literally) in the frightening world of dangerous marine life. First, you are surrounded by moray eels as you walk through an acrylic tube at the bottom of a large aquarium. These eels peer out from lairs in an artificial tropical reef or undulate through the water. Next are several large aquariums housing poisonous fish, including the beautiful but lethal scorpion fish and the puffer fish, one of the world's most deadly. Then get ready for the grand finale—a 600,000-gallon tank filled with six species of sharks, including bull sharks, nurse sharks, and lemon sharks, as well as dozens of enormous grouper and other smaller fish. An entire wall of a large room gives a comprehensive view of this beautifully lit tank. Its amazing creatures will glide next to you and directly overhead as you pass through an acrylic tunnel. As you exit the tunnel, you'll learn that it supports 500 tons of salt water, but if necessary, it could handle nearly five times that weight—the equivalent of more than 370 elephants. A reassuring thought.

TOURING TIPS The crowd usually bottlenecks at the eel habitat. If possible, worm your way through the initial backup. The tube is fairly long, and you'll find the same great view with a smaller crowd near the other end.

If you visit SeaWorld on a Tuesday or Thursday, don't miss the feeding frenzy when the sharks in the main habitat feast at 11 a.m. (call beforehand to verify the schedule).

You can get in on the feeding yourself on select days at a small pool at the entrance to the exhibit. Purchase a tray of fish for $3 (two for $5) and toss them cheerfully to small hammerhead and nurse sharks. If that's still not enough all-shark action for you, consider the Sharks Deep Dive, in which guests don scuba or snorkel gear and plunge directly into the shark tank (in a shark cage). Cost is $99–$149 per person plus tax; participants must be at least 10 years of age; children under the age of 14 must be ccompanied by a paying adult. Call ☎ 888-800-5447 for reservations and information.

Skytower ★★

APPEAL BY AGE	PRESCHOOL ★★		GRADE SCHOOL ★★	TEENS ★★
YOUNG ADULTS ★★½		OVER 30 ★★½		SENIORS ★★★

What it is Scenic aerial ride. **Scope and scale** Minor attraction. **When to go** Anytime, although it's quite beautiful at night. **Special comments** Costs $4. **Authors' rating** ★★. **Duration of ride** Nearly 7 minutes. **Loading speed** Slow.

DESCRIPTION AND COMMENTS This attraction forces visitors to make a philosophical decision. Should a theme park charge an additional fee for one of its rides? Although the answer is probably no, a ride to the top of the tower is somewhat calming. The tower has two levels of enclosed seats that rotate as they rise to the top for great views of the park. It's amazing how serene the park looks—and how tiny the killer whales appear—from the top. On a clear day, you can see many other interesting sites, including downtown Orlando, the top of Spaceship Earth at Epcot, and the unmistakable toaster shape of Disney's Contemporary Resort.

TOURING TIPS This attraction closes if lightning or high winds pop up, and both are frequent in central Florida. It also doesn't run during the peak season's nighttime fireworks display. The Sandbar Lounge at the bottom of the tower serves a variety of refreshments.

Stingray Lagoon ★★★

APPEAL BY AGE	PRESCHOOL ★★		GRADE SCHOOL ★★★½	TEENS ★★★
YOUNG ADULTS ★★★		OVER 30 ★★★		SENIORS ★★½

What it is Stingray pool. **Scope and scale** Minor attraction. **When to go** Feeding times. **Authors' rating** Ray-riffic; ★★★.

DESCRIPTION AND COMMENTS The shallow water in this waist-high pool is filled with dozens of undulating stingrays. After the death of world-renowned zoologist Steve Irwin (the "Croc Hunter") in 2006 due to a stingray attack, these creatures seem even more menacing than before.

However, all of the stingrays at SeaWorld continue to have their barbs removed so they are not a threat to visitors. They may seem ominous, but they are actually quite mellow, and you shouldn't be afraid to stick your fingers into the tank and feel their silky skin.

TOURING TIPS   Although a small tray of fish costs $3, don't miss feeding these graceful creatures. (Feedings are scheduled throughout the day.) The fish are slimy, and the tail end must be carefully placed between two fingers, but even the most squeamish in our group enjoyed the stingrays swimming over their hands and lightly sucking the food into their mouths.

kids Turtle Point ★★

APPEAL BY AGE	PRESCHOOL ★★	GRADE SCHOOL ★★★	TEENS ★★
YOUNG ADULTS ★★		OVER 30 ★★	SENIORS ★★

What it is   Outdoor turtle habitat. Scope and scale   Diversion. When to go   Anytime; most informative when an educator is present. Authors' rating   Just turtles; ★★.

DESCRIPTION AND COMMENTS   A white-sand beach and palm trees surround a small pool at this exhibit. Several large turtles can be seen swimming or sunning themselves. Most of them have been rescued by SeaWorld, and many of their injuries are evident, such as missing flippers (caused by discarded fishing line or shark attacks) or cracked shells (from boat propellers).

TOURING TIPS   Because the turtles are not terribly active, this attraction is worth only a quick peek. A visit becomes more interesting if an educator is present to talk about the animals and the ways humans can help protect them in the wild.

Wild Arctic ★★★½

APPEAL BY AGE	PRESCHOOL ★★★	GRADE SCHOOL ★★★★	TEENS ★★★
YOUNG ADULTS ★★★		OVER 30 ★★½	SENIORS ★★

What it is   Simulator ride and animal exhibit. Scope and scale   Major attraction. When to go   Avoid going immediately following a Shamu show; wait will be shorter before 11 a.m. and after 4 p.m. Authors' rating   Animal exhibit is better than the simulator; ★★★½. Duration of ride   5 minutes for simulator; at your own pace for exhibit. Loading speed   Moderate.

DESCRIPTION AND COMMENTS   Wild Arctic combines a mediocre simulator ride with a spectacular animal habitat, featuring huge polar bears, blubbery walruses, and sweet-faced beluga whales. The usually long line gives you the option of not riding the simulator—a great idea if you're prone to motion sickness, or have experienced the superior simulators at Disney and Universal. Unfortunately, skipping the simulator will not allow you to enter Wild Artic any sooner; you will still have to watch the simulator's movie before entering.

The simulator provides a bumpy ride aboard a specially designed 59-passenger "helicopter." Once passengers are safely strapped in, the ride ostensibly takes visitors to a remote Arctic research station (the wildlife habitat). On the way, riders fly over polar bears and walruses, but, of course, Things Go Horribly Wrong. A storm blows through, the engine inconveniently fails during an avalanche, and there is much wailing and gnashing of teeth. The loud hullabaloo and dated effects amount to nothing in particular, and in the end you make it to the station unscathed.

As you step off the simulator, or if you bypass it, you'll enter a cavernous, fog-filled room. A walkway on the far side overlooks a large pool that is home to a few beluga whales and, if you're lucky, some cute harbor seals. This room establishes the Arctic theme, but unless it's feeding time, the animals rarely surface here.

Proceed down a wooden ramp and you may come face to face with an enormous polar bear. The most famous inhabitants of this exhibit are twins, Klondike and Snow. The duo received tons of media coverage after they were abandoned by their mother and hand-raised at the Denver Zoo. SeaWorld uses toys and enrichment devices to keep the bears occupied. Variations in their schedule help keep them on their toes, so feeding times change frequently. Next to the bears are the gigantic walruses, often lounging near the glass or swimming lazily by.

As you descend farther into the exhibit, you'll discover a deep, underwater viewing area. Swarms of fish circle in the polar bear exhibit. If you're lucky, you'll spot a bear diving for fish. In addition, the underwater view gives you a real sense of the walruses' immense size. If it's quiet, you can also hear the deep, reverberating vocalizations of these large beasts. This is also the best location to catch a glimpse of the beluga whales. Looking like puffy, bulbous dolphins, these gentle creatures glide through the water. On occasion, a few playful harbor seals will join them. These crazy critters will come right up to the glass for a staring match with you.

TOURING TIPS Wild Arctic has two queues: "By Air," which is for the simulator, and "By Land," which still makes you watch the simulator movie, but without all the jarring effects of the ride. Given the so-so quality of the simulator ride, we recommend skipping it if there's a significant line. The animals are definitely worth seeing, though. As in all animal exhibits, several SeaWorld educators are scattered around to answer any questions. Here, they are easy to spot in bright red parkas.

The simulator holds nearly 60 riders, who flood the animal area after each trip. Hang back behind the crowd for a few minutes when the simulator offloads and wait for the masses to clear. Then you can have the area next to the beluga whales mostly to yourself until the ride dumps off the next group.

If this isn't close enough to the whales for you, try the Beluga Interaction Program, where you can swim with, feed, and even attempt to signal to these sub-Arctic mammoths. The price for this program is not cheap, but if you are a beluga enthusiast willing to drop $99–149, you can make reservations online or by calling ☎ 888-800-5447. Participants must be at least 10 years of age; children under the age of 14 must be ccompanied by a paying adult.

Behind-the-Scenes Tours　★★★★

What it is Get up close and personal with, even touch, the critters. **Scope and scale** Major attraction. **When to go** Advance reservations are a must, but there's a catch: times for the four briefest tours (60–90 minutes) are not available in advance of booking. You call or go online to make the reservation, and then are told to arrive as early as possible on the day of the visit and to report to the reservations desk, where you are told the time of your tour. Departures for the four longer (4–7 hours) and far-more-expensive tours are decided at the time of booking. **Special comments** Prices for the shorter tours range $30–$50 for adults, $10–$30 for children; for the longer tours, $75–$275 for adults and $55–$275 for children. **Authors' rating** A wonderful experience; ★★★★.

DESCRIPTION AND COMMENTS　Park staff lead groups, usually with a maximum of 16, behind the scenes to speak with the animals' caretakers, hear about the differences and peculiarities between animals of the same species, and, if these are performers, learn how they are trained.

The educational side may be too much for youngsters, but everyone loves the big event of each of the eight tours: getting to touch and be photographed with a penguin, shark, or dolphin, or to feed stingrays, seals, and sea lions.

Three briefer tours each focus on one animal—penguins, sea lions, or dolphins; another shorter tour is broader. All of them walk you into the backstage areas for the animals. The other, longer tours include the backstage visits, a lunch, front-of-the-line access to three major rides, and reserved seats at the animal shows.

Another type of meet-the-critter tour is called the Animal Connection Program. Two of these $149 tours involve donning wet suits to get personal with beluga whales and sharks. The third such tour is the Marine Mammal Keeper Experience.

TOURING TIPS　You must stop by the guided-tour counter at the front of the park on the day of your visit or reserve a spot on the park's website (**seaworld.com**). If you want to take one of the tours, make a reservation online because spots fill quickly and it's first-come, first-served.

Taking an hour out of your SeaWorld visit for these tours will require careful planning, but for sea-life enthusiasts, it's a neat experience. Longer tours are also available, and the price increases with each of these tours, but places such as the Dolphin Nursery may be worth a few extra dollars.

Marine Mammal Keeper Experience　★★★

† Preschoolers and grade-school kids are not old enough.

What it is Chance to shadow a SeaWorld trainer for a day. **Scope and scale** Major attraction. **When to go** Program begins at 7 a.m. **Special comments** Costs $299–$399 plus tax (admission is included); participants must be at least 13 years old and 52" tall. **Authors' rating** Extremely expensive, but worth it for enthusiasts; ★★★.

DESCRIPTION AND COMMENTS Shadow a SeaWorld trainer during this 8-hour program. Learn through hands-on experience how SeaWorld staff members care for and train their animals, from stuffing vitamins into a slimy fish to positive-reinforcement training techniques. The fee includes lunch, a T-shirt, souvenir photo, and a 7-day pass to SeaWorld.

TOURING TIPS Attendance for this program is limited to four people per day. Calling up to 6 months ahead is best, but cancellations do occur. For information and reservations, call ☎ 888-800-5447. Participants must be in good physical condition and at least 13 years old.

DINING

SEAWORLD OFFERS MUCH MORE than the usual theme-park fare of burgers and fries. The food for the most part is very good, and prices are a bit lower than at Disney World.

Your feasting can begin at **Cypress Bakery,** which opens at 8:30 a.m. during the busy season and 8:45 a.m. otherwise. Choose from an array of wonderful pastries, cakes, and muffins to enjoy while you plan your day.

Also offered in the morning is a SeaWorld character breakfast, held 8:45–10 a.m. at the **Seafire Inn** in the Waterfront area. A buffet with classic offerings such as scrambled eggs, pancakes, muffins, and fruit is served for $14.95

unofficial **TIP**
Cypress Bakery opens early and offers fantastic breakfast breads and pastries.

(adults) and $9.95 (children ages 3–9); children under age 3 eat free with reservations. Speaking of reservations, they are recommended, though walk-ups will be seated on availability. Reservations can be made by calling ☎ 800-327-2420. Usually only one character is present, often Shamu.

For a more toothsome experience, try **Sharks Underwater Grill** at the Shark Encounter attraction, which offers "Floribbean" cuisine served next to floor-to-ceiling windows on the shark tank. A typical meal will run $20 per person at this ostensibly upscale eatery.

For quick service, try **Mango Joe's Café** for fajitas, salads, and sandwiches. Along the Waterfront there are several options, including the **Spice Mill,** a walk-up café with selections such as grilled chicken Caesar salads, steak burgers, and low-fat vegetable chili. There's also **Voyagers Smokehouse,** offering barbecued meats and kids' meals of chicken tenders, hot dogs, or mac and cheese—with the option of substituting carrots for the standard side of fries.

The **Antarctic Market,** near the Penguin Encounter, is a sit-down place where the sandwiches include buffalo chicken, roast beef, turkey, pulled barbecue pork, and a veggie wrap. The chili con carne comes in a bowl of bread. Across from the SeaPort Theater is **Seaport Pizza,** with four kinds of personal pie ranging $6–$7.

Beyond Shamu Stadium and the Nautilus Theater, and worth the walk, the pleasant **Terrace Café** has seating indoors and out. The menu boasts thick sandwiches of turkey, bratwurst, or beef, plus a club of ham, turkey, salami, and Monterey jack on multigrain bread. There's also a grilled chicken Caesar salad—and for that rare cool Florida day, beef stew.

Parkgoers can also buy an All-Day Dining Option—$30 for adults, $15 for children—and get an entrée, side or dessert, and drink from one of six restaurants, as well as snacks and beverages.

SHOPPING

UNLIKE AT DISNEY, shopping at SeaWorld isn't an attraction in and of itself. There is, of course, a huge selection of SeaWorld merchandise. Some of it is unique, and prices are relatively reasonable. Fans of ocean wildlife can find a vast array of marine merchandise, ranging from high-quality, expensive sculptures to T-shirts, beach towels, and knickknacks. Children will be overwhelmed by the huge selection of stuffed animals, and parents will be pleased by their low prices—many small- to medium-size toys are priced under $10.

Along the Waterfront area, there are more shopping selections, such as the **Tropica Trading Shop** with goods from Africa, Bali, and Indonesia, among other origins, and do-it-yourself shops such as a bead store and a doll factory.

DISCOVERY COVE

INSPIRED BY A LARGE NUMBER OF REQUESTS for dolphin swims as well as the success of the original Dolphin Interaction Program, SeaWorld created Discovery Cove in 2000. This intimate subpark is a welcome departure from the hustle and bustle of other Orlando parks; the relaxed pace here could be the overstimulated family's ticket back to mental health. With a focus on personal service and one-on-one animal encounters, Discovery Cove admits only 1,000 guests per day. The park is also an all-inclusive experience so once you enter, you don't need to open your wallet; provided are all meals, snacks, and beverages plus all animal interactions and swim gear, even parking and a pass to your choice of either SeaWorld or Busch Gardens. The tranquil setting and unobtrusive theming make this park unique for central Florida. Why, there are only two gift shops! And you don't even have to walk through them to get out!

The main draw at Discovery Cove is the chance to swim with an Atlantic bottlenose dolphin, from among the 30 here. The 30-minute dolphin swim experience is open to visitors age 6 and up who are comfortable in the water. The experience begins with an orientation

Discovery Cove

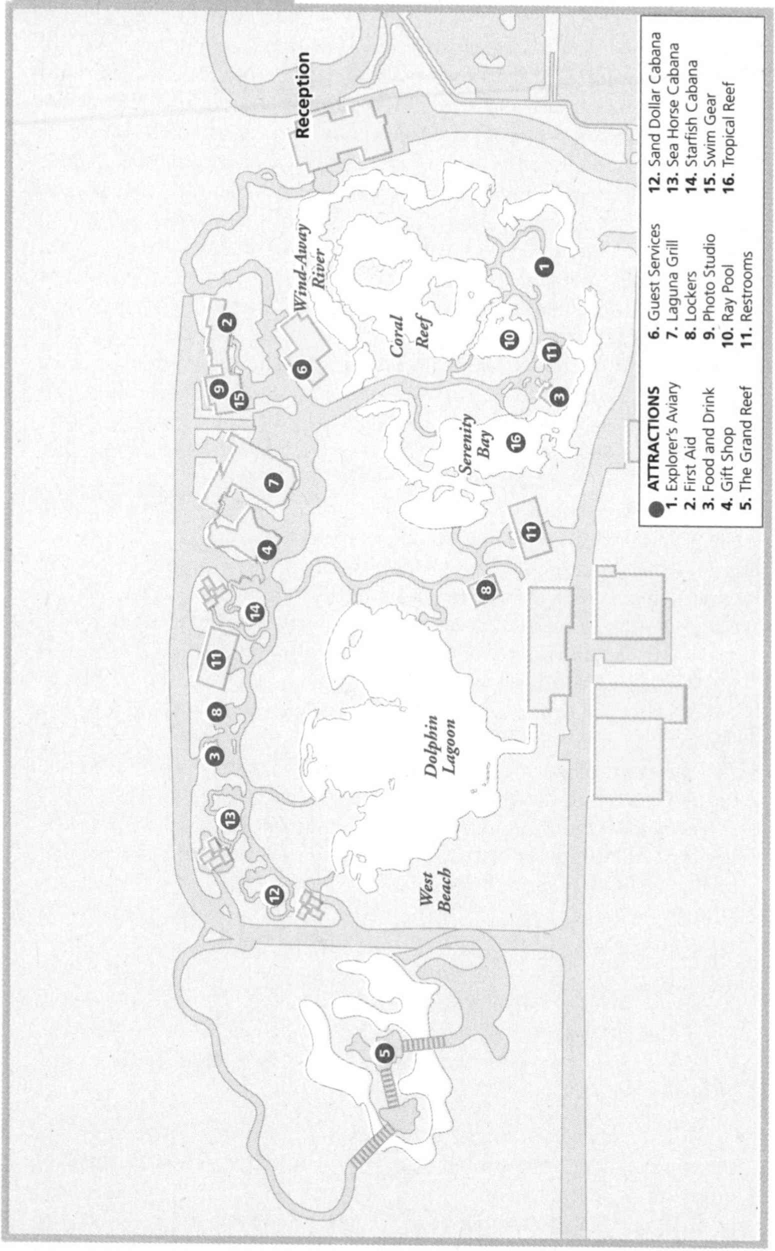

Reception

Wind-Away River

Coral Reef

Serenity Bay

Dolphin Lagoon

West Beach

led by trainers and an opportunity for participants to ask questions before entering the dolphin lagoon. Next, groups of six to eight guests wade into shallow water for an introduction to one of the dolphins in its habitat; this includes touching and even hugging the dolphin. The experience culminates when the group enters deeper water and each person is towed back by holding onto the dolphin's dorsal fin. Although this is not an inexpensive endeavor, the singular nature of the experience cannot be overstated. The dolphins are playful, friendly, and frankly amazing to be around. This is as hands-on as it gets. Be aware that you're dealing with a powerful mischievous animal in its element, so don't be surprised if you get splashed, squirted, or even affectionately bonked with a flipper or fluke. The trainers are always in control, though, so there is nothing to fear. Overall, if this is to your taste at all, it's not to be missed. Author's rating? Five stars.

SeaWorld opened a major new addition, The Grand Reef, in June 2011. The Grand Reef is a new pool—holding almost a million gallons of salt water—and surrounding sandy beaches covering nearly 2.5 acres. In the water are about 10,000 animals, including roughly 125 species of fish, rays, and sharks.

Grand Reef guests can wander over bridges to tiny islands, relax on the beach, and simply wade around to observe the fish and 90 pieces of coral from above the surface. Or visitors can pay $59 for the SeaVenture experience: don a diving helmet to walk below the water, get up close views of sharks and venomous lionfish—through a window— and hand-feed the tamer species. Fresh air is pumped through a hose— no SCUBA certification is required. The helmeted guests, in groups limited to six, descend a ladder to play aquanaut and walk among the fish and rays. The SeaVenture lasts about 1 hour.

The Tropical Reef, on the other side of the park, is also scheduled to undergo a renovation and open as a new experience in 2012.

Be careful about planning who does what at Discovery Cove. The perils of being left out are illustrated by this letter sent in by a mother of three from Croydon, England:

> Only two of the five [in our group] swam with the dolphins because that is the only booking we could get. We would recommend that all people in the party swim with the dolphins to avoid the awful, sad feeling of being left out that three of us had. The two children refused to look at their brother, and Dad just wanted to go home. Dad felt guilty, and what was supposed to be the highlight of the trip turned into a downer.

Not an ideal situation. If you're visiting Discovery Cove as a group, try to time your visit so everyone who wants to swim with the dolphins can.

Other exhibit areas at Discovery Cove include the Tropical Reef, the Explorer's Aviary, the Ray Pool, and the Freshwater Lagoon. You can snorkel or swim in the Tropical Reef, which houses thousands of exotic fish and dozens of rays as well as an underwater shipwreck and hidden grottoes. In the Aviary, you can touch and feed gorgeous tropical birds. Stingrays occupy the small Ray Pool next to the Tropical Reef; you can wade in among them, under the guidance of a lifeguard. The Freshwater Lagoon is just a salt-free rocky pond, empty of aquatic life. The park is threaded by the freshwater Wind-Away River, in which you can float or swim to all these areas. Pleasant beaches, with hammocks, lounges, and chairs, serve as pathways connecting the attractions.

Guests at Discovery Cove need not be exceptional swimmers—the water is shallow and so heavily salted that it's very difficult not to float. Watchful lifeguards are omnipresent. You'll need to wear your bathing suit and pool shoes as well as a cover-up. On rare days when it's too cold to swim in Orlando, guests are provided with wet suits. The park also supplies masks and snorkels, and you get to keep the snorkel (after all, nobody wants to reuse those). Discovery Cove provides "fish"-friendly sunscreen: guests may not use their own sunscreen. You must also remove all watches and jewelry (except wedding bands), as they might end up getting swallowed by the animals if you lose them. Free lockers enable you to stow everything you need to put away, all day. Comfortable, clean, well-appointed bathrooms and showers are also provided.

GETTING THERE

DISCOVERY COVE IS LOCATED DIRECTLY across the Central Florida Parkway from SeaWorld. Parking is free.

PRICES AND RESERVATIONS

DISCOVERY COVE IS OPEN 9 a.m.–5:30 p.m. daily year-round. Because admission is limited to 1,000 guests per day, you should purchase tickets in advance by calling ☎ 877-4-DISCOVERY (877-434-7268) or visiting **discoverycove.com.** There are two admission options. The all-inclusive package, depending on month and day of the week, is $212–$319, tax included, per person and includes the dolphin swim; breakfast, lunch, snacks, and beverages; unlimited access to the Tropical Reef, Explorer's Aviary, and Wind-Away River; and the use of beach umbrellas, lounge chairs, towels, lockers, and swim and snorkel gear.

If you're not interested in the dolphin swim, the Non-Dolphin Package is $138–$180 (depending on season), tax included, per person for the day and includes everything but the dolphin encounter. Discovery Cove admission includes parking at Discovery Cove as well as a seven-day, unlimited-use pass to either SeaWorld Orlando or Busch Gardens Tampa Bay, making the high price tag a bit easier to swallow. The Trainer for a Day package includes everything the all-inclusive dolphin package does, along with a second enhanced dolphin experience and backstage tours of the dolphin and shark areas. Admission to participate is $398–$488, plus tax (depending on season).

ARRIVING

ALTHOUGH THE PARK PROPER DOESN'T OPEN UNTIL 9 A.M., the entrance hall usually opens about 8 a.m. (during peak seasons the park does open at 7:30 a.m.) It's not a bad idea to get there a little early, because if you do, you can be among the first guests to register for your dolphin interaction. Guests are assigned time slots for the dolphin swims throughout the day, but you're not assigned your time slot until you show up on the day of your reservation (unless you request it in advance). The later you register, the later in the day your dolphin swim will be. Dolphins are generally more active in the morning, and once you do the interaction, you can spend the rest of your day lazily snorkeling or snoozing on the beach (without worrying about missing your appointment with Flipper).

On registering, you'll be asked to provide a credit card number. You'll then be issued a lanyard card with your picture on it. This card corresponds to the credit card you just gave, so it can be used for purchases anywhere in Discovery Cove. This means you can stow your wallet or purse in a locker for your whole stay. The locker key is also on a lanyard, so it's very easy to keep up with everything.

You'll be assigned one of three cabanas as your meeting place for the dolphin interaction. These are easy to find because Discovery Cove is really not that large. Show up about 5 minutes before your assigned time. A trainer will give a short orientation, and then it's off to the dolphin swim. Enjoy.

PART EIGHT

UNIVERSAL ORLANDO

DISNEY'S HOLLYWOOD STUDIOS *versus* UNIVERSAL STUDIOS FLORIDA

DISNEY'S HOLLYWOOD STUDIOS (DHS) and Universal Studios Florida are direct competitors. Because both are large and expensive and require at least one day to see, some guests must choose one park over the other. To help you decide, we present a head-to-head comparison of the two parks, followed by a description of Universal. In the summer of 1999, Universal launched its second major theme park, **Universal's Islands of Adventure,** which competes directly with Disney's Magic Kingdom. (**Universal Studios Florida** theme park, Islands of Adventure, the three Universal hotels, and the **CityWalk** complex are collectively known as **Universal Orlando.**)

Both DHS and Universal Studios draw their inspiration from film and TV. Both offer movie- and TV-themed rides and shows, some of which are just for fun, while others provide an educational, behind-the-scenes introduction to the cinematic arts.

Unlike DHS's open area, Universal Studios' includes the entire back lot, where guests can walk at leisure among movie sets. Universal Studios is about twice as large as DHS, and because almost all of it is open to the public, the crowding and congestion so familiar at DHS are eliminated. Also, hardly any actual TV or movie production goes on at DHS anymore, but on any day at Universal, production crews will be shooting on its back lot in full view of guests who care to watch.

> *unofficial* **TIP**
> Half of Disney's Hollywood Studios is off-limits to guests—except by guided tour—while most of Universal Studios Florida is open to exploration.

Attractions at both parks are excellent, though DHS's are on average engineered to move people more efficiently. Each park offers stellar attractions that break new ground, transcending in power, originality, and technology any prior standard for theme park entertainment. Though Universal Studios must be credited with pioneering a number of innovative and technologically advanced rides, we must also point out that Universal's attractions break down more often than DHS's.

Amazingly, and to the visitor's advantage, each park offers a completely different product mix, so there's little or no redundancy for those who visit both. DHS and Universal Studios Florida each provide good exposure to the cinematic arts. DHS over the years has turned several of its better tours into infomercials for Disney films. At Universal, you can still learn about postproduction, soundstages, set creation, and special effects without being bludgeoned by promotional hype.

We recommend you try one of the studios. If you enjoy one, you probably will enjoy the other. If you have to choose, consider:

1. TOURING TIME If you tour efficiently, it takes about 8–10 hours to see DHS (including a lunch break). Because Universal Studios Florida is larger and contains more rides and shows, touring, including one meal, takes about 9–11 hours. One reader laments:

> There's a lot more "standing" at Universal Studios, and it isn't as organized as DHS. Many of the attractions don't open until 10 a.m., and many shows seem to be going at the same time. We were not able to see nearly as many attractions at Universal as we were at DHS during the same amount of time. The one plus at Universal Studios is that there seems to be more property, and things are spaced out better so you have more elbow room.

As the reader observes, many Universal Studios attractions don't open until 10 a.m. or later. During one research visit, only a third of the major attractions were up and running when the park opened, and most theater attractions didn't schedule performances until 11 a.m. or after. This means that early in the day all park guests are concentrated among the relatively few attractions in operation. DHS also has attractions that open late and shows that schedule no performances until late morning. The number of attractions operating at opening time varies according to season, at both parks.

2. CONVENIENCE If you're lodging along International Drive, I-4's northeast corridor, or Orange Blossom Trail (US 441), or in Orlando, Universal Studios Florida is closer. If you're lodging along US 27 or US 192 or in Kissimmee or Disney World, DHS is more convenient.

3. ENDURANCE Universal Studios Florida is larger and requires more walking than DHS, but it's also much less congested, so the walking is easier. Both parks offer wheelchairs and disabled access.

4. COST Universal's standard one-day, one-park admissions are less expensive than similar ones at Disney parks. In fact, for the price of a one-day, one-park pass to a Disney park, you can buy a Universal admission that includes park-hopping privileges and no expiration date. When Disney instituted the multiday Magic Your Way admission system, in which you pay extra for park-hopping and No Expiration options, Universal was quick to move in the opposite direction. With Universal passes, all these extras are included at no additional charge. What's more, unlike Disney, Universal offers modest discounts when you purchase passes online and is always running specials on admissions. Not long ago, Universal offered a free two-day, two-park park-hopping ticket for kids (ages 3–9) for every adult two-day, two-park ticket purchased online at **universalorlando.com.** Total cost was $212 for the whole family, tax included. For the same family to spend two days with park-hopping privileges at Walt Disney World, the cost was more than three times that amount.

5. BEST DAYS TO GO In order, Tuesdays, Fridays, and Saturdays are best to visit Universal Studios. Tuesdays, Mondays, and Saturdays are best for IOA. For DHS, see the Crowd Calendar at **touringplans.com.**

6. WHEN TO ARRIVE For DHS, arrive with your ticket in hand 30–40 minutes before official opening time. For Universal Studios, arrive with your admission already purchased about 25–35 minutes before official opening time.

7. YOUNG CHILDREN Both DHS and Universal Studios Florida are relatively adult entertainment offerings. By our reckoning, half the rides and shows at DHS and about two-thirds at Universal Studios have a significant potential for frightening young children.

8. FOOD For counter-service food, Universal Studios has a decided edge. DHS full-service restaurants are marginally better.

9. FASTPASS VERSUS UNIVERSAL EXPRESS Until recently, Disney's Fastpass and Universal Express were roughly comparable. They both offered a system whereby any guest could schedule an appointment to experience an attraction later in the day with little or no waiting. Universal was the first to monkey with the status quo by making unlimited Universal Express passes available to guests in Universal-owned resorts. This meant that resort guests could go to the front of the line anytime. Next, Universal cooked up an enhanced Express pass, called Universal Express Plus, available to anyone—for an extra charge. Then they got really greedy. In the last installment, Universal terminated Express privileges for all day guests unless they were willing to cough up the extra bucks for Universal Express Plus. This relegates day guests (guests not staying at Universal-owned resorts) without Express Plus to long lines all day.

Fastpass and the old Universal Express system worked because setting appointment times to experience attractions helped to more equally distribute crowds throughout the day. Without appointments, Universal will return to the same recurring bottlenecks as before Universal Express was introduced. Disney, by way of contrast, has maintained an egalitarian philosophy with regard to Fastpass. Though they're considering some Fastpass perks for resort guests, the basic program will continue to be available for every Bubba, Bob, and Betty who passes through the turnstiles.

Universal Orlando

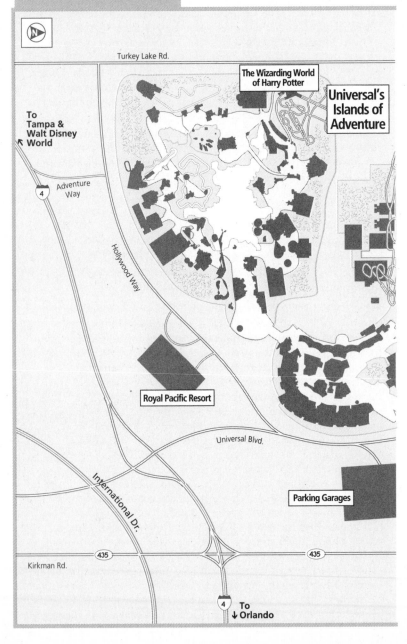

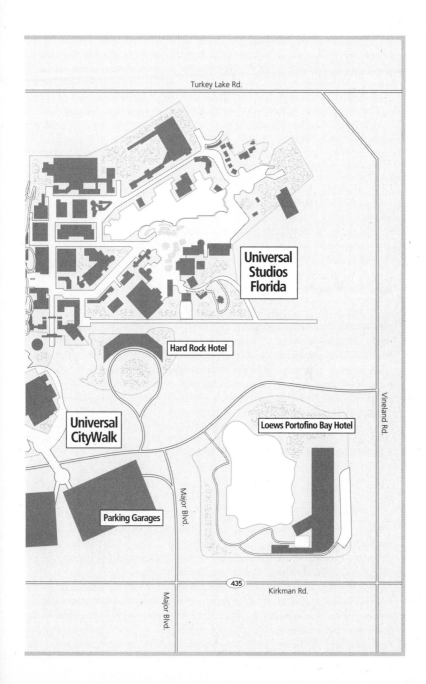

Turkey Lake Rd.

Universal
Studios
Florida

Hard Rock Hotel

Universal
CityWalk

Loews Portofino Bay Hotel

Vineland Rd.

Major Blvd.

Parking Garages

Major Blvd.

435 · Kirkman Rd.

For the moment at least, here is how the current Universal Express program works. Guests at Universal hotels can access the Universal Express lines all day long simply by flashing their hotel keys. This can be especially valuable during peak season. With Universal Express Plus, for an extra $20–$50 (depending on the season) you can buy a pass that provides line-cutting privileges at each Universal Express attraction at a given park. The Plus feature is good for only one day at one park (in other words, no park-hopping), and for one ride only on each participating attraction. More than 90% of rides and shows are included in the Universal Express program, a much higher percentage than those included in the Fastpass program at the Disney parks.

When we tested Express Plus one recent summer, we discovered that Universal employees very rarely scrutinize the Express Plus card, and that we could use the card several times on most attractions as long as we waited 15 minutes or so between attempts. Although there's a bar code on the pass, it was never scanned, nor did we see any scanning devices at the entrances of the attractions.

UNIVERSAL ORLANDO

UNIVERSAL ORLANDO HAS TRANSFORMED into a complete destination resort, with two theme parks, three hotels, and a shopping, dining, and entertainment complex. The second theme park, **Universal's Islands of Adventure,** opened in 1999 with five themed areas.

A system of roads and two multistory parking facilities are connected by moving sidewalks to **CityWalk,** a shopping, dining, and nighttime-entertainment complex that is also a gateway to the **Universal Studios Florida** and Islands of Adventure parks. (For more on CityWalk dining, see page 327; for CityWalk entertainment, see page 309.)

LODGING AT UNIVERSAL ORLANDO

UNIVERSAL CURRENTLY HAS THREE OPERATING resort hotels. The 750-room **Loews Portofino Bay Hotel** is set on an artificial bay and themed like an Italian coastal town. The 650-room **Hard Rock Hotel** is an ultracool "Hotel California" replica, with slick contemporary design and a hip, friendly attitude. The 1,000-room, Polynesian-themed **Loews Royal Pacific Resort** is sumptuously decorated and richly appointed. All three are excellent hotels; the Portofino and the Hard Rock are on the pricey side, and the Royal Pacific ain't exactly cheap.

Universal offers a number of incentives for visitors to stay at its hotels. Perks available include free parking, delivery to your room of purchases made in the parks, tickets and reservation information from hotel concierges, priority dining reservations at Universal restaurants, and the ability to charge purchases to your room account.

In addition, Universal offers complimentary transportation by bus or water taxi to Universal Studios, Islands of Adventure, CityWalk,

SeaWorld, Aquatica (SeaWorld's water park), and Wet 'n Wild. Hotel guests may use the Universal Express program and are also eligible for "next available" table privileges at CityWalk restaurants and similar priority admission to Universal Orlando theme park shows.

ARRIVING AT UNIVERSAL ORLANDO

THE UNIVERSAL ORLANDO COMPLEX can be accessed directly from I-4. Once on-site, you'll be directed to park in one of two multi-tiered parking garages. Parking runs $15 for cars ($3 after 6 p.m.) and $20 for RVs ($8 after 6 p.m.). Be sure to write down the location of your car before heading for the parks. From the garages, moving sidewalks deliver you to the CityWalk dining, shopping, and entertainment venue. From CityWalk, you can access the main entrances of both Universal Studios Florida and Islands of Adventure theme parks. Even with the moving walkways, it takes about 10–12 minutes to commute from the garages to the entrances of the theme parks. If you're staying at Disney World and don't have a car, Mears Transportation (☎ 407-423-5566) will shuttle you from your hotel to Universal and back for $18. Pickup and return times are at your convenience.

Universal offers One-day, Two-day, Three-day, Four-day, and Seven-day Park-to-Park Access passes that allow you to visit both Universal Studios and Islands of Adventure on the same day. Also available are One-day, Two-day, Three-day, and Four-day One-Park Access Passes. With these passes you are limited to visiting your choice of one park per day. Prices listed below are what you'd pay at the gate and include tax.

There is a $10 per pass discount on the multiday tickets when you buy in advance at **universalorlando.com.** Passes purchased online are printable and can be used at the turnstiles. Undercover Tourist, a ticket discounter at **undercover tourist.com,** offers the most deeply discounted tickets we're aware of to subscribers of **mousesavers .com.** Note that admission prices listed on the Universal website or at the park ticket kiosks do not include a 6.5% sales tax. Tickets purchased via the *MouseSavers Newsletter,* on the other hand, include tax and free shipping.

unofficial **TIP**
The Two-park Ultimate Flexibility Admission Pass allows you to visit both Universal theme parks on the same day; it's good for seven consecutive days of admission.

If you want to visit more than one park on a given day, have your park pass and hand stamped when exiting your first park. At your second park, use the readmission turnstile, showing your stamped pass and hand.

The five-park, 14-day **Orlando Flex Ticket** allows unlimited entry to Universal Studios, Universal's Islands of Adventure, SeaWorld, Aquatica, and Wet 'n Wild and costs $293 for adults and $272 for children ages 3–9, tax included. The six-park, 14-day **Orlando Flex Ticket Plus** provides unlimited entry to Universal Studios, Universal's Islands of Adventure, SeaWorld, Wet 'n Wild, and Busch Gardens and costs $335 for adults and $314 for children. All Orlando Flex Tickets can be purchased online at the websites of the participating parks or at discount from Visit Orlando at **orlandoticketsales.com/oi/orlando_flexticket_c329.cfm.** Flex Tickets are a good deal only if you visit each of the included parks.

The main Universal Orlando information number is ☎ 407-363-8000. Reach Guest Relations at ☎ 407-224-4233, and order tickets by mail at ☎ 877-247-5561. The numbers for Lost and Found are ☎ 407-224-4244 (Universal Studios) and 407-224-4245 (Islands of Adventure).

	ADULTS	CHILDREN (ages 3–9)
One-day, One-park Pass	$87.33	$78.81
One-day, Two-park Pass	$119.28	$110.76
Two-day, One-park Pass	$133.11	$119.27
Two-day, Two-park Pass	$154.41	$140.57
Three-day, One-park Pass	$149.09	$133.11
Three-day, Two-park Pass	$165.06	$149.09
Four-day, One-park Pass	$159.74	$141.63
Four-day, Two-park Pass	$170.39	$152.28
Seven-day, Two-park Pass	$197.01	$175.71
Power Annual Pass	$149.09	$149.09
Preferred Annual Pass	$234.29	$234.29
Premier Annual Pass	$308.84	$308.84

EARLY ENTRY AND UNIVERSAL EXPRESS

WITH ONE EXCEPTION (discussed following), Universal no longer operates an early-entry program. Universal Express is for Universal hotel guests, and Universal Express Plus is available to everyone for an additional fee.

This discontinuation of the old Universal Express has enraged many readers. This comment from a Manchester, England, dad is typical:

Imagine my shock when I arrived to find Universal has done away with its free version of Fastpass. Although I can afford to pay for Express Plus, I will not. Why pay for something Disney gives you for free?

In 2010 Universal initiated a new early-entry program in conjunction with its Wizarding World of Harry Potter Exclusive Vacation Package. Purchasers can enter the Wizarding World section of Islands of Adventure theme park 1 hour before the general public.

Universal Express Plus

If you're willing to pay extra, you can upgrade your regular ticket to Universal Express Plus, which allows you to use the Express entrance one time only at each designated Universal Express attraction (although we've found that the one-time use policy is loose and is enforced only for major attractions on crowded days). Universal Express Plus is good only for the date of purchase *at one park* (though there's a more expensive two-park option) and can be used only by one person.

Universal Express Plus prices vary $21–$64 with tax; they're cheaper in the off-seasons and more expensive during peak seasons and holidays. You can purchase Universal Express Plus online or at the theme park's ticket windows, just outside the front gates. Once in the Universal Studios theme park, Universal Express Plus is available at Nickstuff. Inside Islands of Adventure, you can buy Universal Express Plus at Jurassic Outfitters, Toon Extra, and the Marvel Alterniverse Store. Universal Express Plus is available online for up to eight months in advance. You must also know what date you plan on using Universal Express Plus, because different dates have different prices.

A father of four from Watford, England, reports on his experience using Universal Express:

The Universal parks' attractions were better than I expected; however, crowd management is poorer than at Disney, and it gets very busy around the middle of the day. I bought Universal Express Plus in advance. It was expensive ($40 per person extra per day) but, I think, worth it—we never waited more than 10 minutes for anything, as not many people have these passes. As we also arrived early at the parks, we could get on the main attractions without waiting or using the Express passes. Then later we went back a second or third time to our favorites using the passes and completely avoided the queues, which were up to 2 hours long at that point. My son went on the Hulk coaster four times without any wait as a result of using Express Plus.

A New York mom had a similarly trouble-free experience but questions the value of the investment:

We bought Universal's Express Plus, but it was both less necessary and less consistently effective. Arriving at park opening, we were able to see many attractions right away without the passes. They helped on about three attractions between the two parks—a poor return for an investment of $156, but it was a good thing to have just in case. On Dudley Do-Right, we still had to wait 30 minutes even with Express Plus, whereas with Disney's free Fastpass we never waited more than 5 minutes for an attraction. The only aspect of UEP that was better than FP is that touring order was unaffected: UEP could be used whenever you first approached an attraction instead of having to come back later.

IS UNIVERSAL EXPRESS PLUS WORTH IT? The answer depends on the season you visit, hours of park operation, and crowd levels. Because of the new Wizarding World of Harry Potter, crowd levels are expected to increase dramatically at Islands of Adventure while remaining steady or declining slightly at Universal Studios. In the Studios, only one attraction, Hollywood Rip Ride Rockit, might be hard to ride without your waiting an inordinate amount of time. But if you arrive 30 minutes before park opening and use our touring plan (page 196), you should experience "The Triple R" with a minimal wait. For the Studios, therefore, you shouldn't need Universal Express Plus.

Islands of Adventure is a different story. Because of all the hoopla surrounding Harry Potter and the lack of high-capacity theater shows at IOA to siphon off crowds (one show at IOA compared with six at the Studios), rides here are sure to be inundated. Using our touring plan (page 223) will cut your waiting to a minimum, so we encourage you to try it first. The beauty of Universal Express Plus is that you can purchase it in the park if waits for the rides become intolerable.

UNIVERSAL EXPRESS PROGRAM AVAILABLE TO UNIVERSAL RESORT GUESTS The Universal Express program for Universal resort guests allows guests to bypass the regular line anytime and as often as desired by simply showing their room key.

How Universal Express Affects Crowd Conditions at the Attractions

This system dramatically affects crowd movement (and touring plans) in the Universal parks. A woman from Yorktown, Virginia, writes:

> People in the Express line were let in at a rate of about 10 to 1 over the regular-line folks. This created bottlenecks and long waits for people who didn't have the Express privilege at the very times when it's supposed to be easier to get around!

SINGLES LINES

AND THERE'S YET ANOTHER OPTION: the singles line. Several attractions have this special line for guests riding alone. As Universal employees will tell you, this line is often even faster than the Express line. We strongly recommend using it whenever possible, as it will decrease your overall wait and leave more time for repeat rides.

LOCKERS

UNIVERSAL HAS INSTITUTED a mandatory locker system at its big thrill rides. Lockers outside these attractions are free for the first 30 minutes, then $3 for the next 1½ hours and $1 for each half hour after that, with a $20 maximum.

The locker banks are easy to find; each bank has a small computer in the center. When the sun is bright, the screen is almost impossible to read, so have someone block the sun or use a different computer. After selecting your language, press your thumb onto the keypad to have your fingerprint scanned. We've seen people walk off cursing at this step, having repeated it over and over with no success. Most patrons simply press their thumb down too hard.

After your thumb scans, you'll receive a locker number. Write it down! When you return from your ride, go to the same kiosk machine, enter your locker number, and scan your thumb again. At Guest Relations, family-sized lockers are available for $10 for the entire day, but remember that only the person who used his or her thumb to get the locker can retrieve anything from it.

UNIVERSAL, KIDS, AND SCARY STUFF

ALTHOUGH THERE'S PLENTY FOR YOUNGER CHILDREN to enjoy at the Universal parks, the majority of the major attractions have the potential for wigging out kids under 8 years of age. At Universal Studios Florida, forget Revenge of the Mummy, Hollywood Rip Ride Rockit, *TWISTER . . . Ride It Out, Disaster!,* JAWS, Men in Black Alien Attack, The Simpsons Ride, and *Terminator 2: 3-D.* The first part of the E.T. ride is a little intense for a few preschoolers, but the end is all happiness and harmony. Interestingly, very few families report problems with *Beetlejuice's Graveyard Revue* or *Universal Orlando's Horror Make-Up Show.* Anything not listed is pretty benign.

At Universal's Islands of Adventure, watch out for The Incredible Hulk Coaster, Doctor Doom's Fearfall, The Amazing Adventures of Spider-Man, the Jurassic Park River Adventure, Dragon Challenge, Harry Potter and the Forbidden Journey, and *Poseidon's Fury.* Popeye & Bluto's Bilge-Rat Barges is wet and wild, but most younger children handle it well. Dudley Do-Right's Rip Saw Falls is a toss-up, to be considered only if your kids like water-flume rides. The *Eighth Voyage of Sindbad Stunt Show* includes some explosions and startling special effects, but once again, children tolerate it well. Nothing else should pose a problem.

unofficial **TIP**
If you have tots age 7 or younger, consider that many of Universal's attractions can be frightening for little ones.

QUITTING TIME

BECAUSE THE PARKING FOR BOTH UNIVERSAL theme parks and the CityWalk shopping, dining, and entertainment complex is consolidated in the same parking structure, chaos ensues when the parks close. An Orlando woman, obviously very perturbed, comments thusly:

> *Universal needs to change the hours when each park closes! Both Universal Studios and Islands of Adventure share the same parking lot. IT MAKES NO SENSE for the two theme parks to close at the same time (especially since Islands has no night finale). I cannot even explain the amount of people. It was insane at closing (and other people were coming IN to go to CityWalk so it was SUCH a big mess)! There was less of a crowd coming out of Epcot on July 4! I think they really need to rethink their hours, especially on weekends in the summer!*

TNA WRESTLING AND BLUE MAN GROUP

UNIVERSAL ORLANDO OFFERS TWO theater productions. At Soundstage 21, guests can sit in on the taping of Spike TV's **TNA iMPACT!** professional-wrestling program (no admission fee), while Sharp Aquos Theatre, near CityWalk, is home to **Blue Man Group.** Tickets for the latter can be purchased online or at the Universal Box Office.

TNA iMPACT!

About five TNA (Total Nonstop Action) shows are filmed each month, usually with audience seating at 5 p.m. and taping starting at 6 p.m. For the uninitiated, TNA, like any good pro-wrestling show, is more brawl than sporting event; whether you consider it good theater is a matter of taste. Abandoning the usual square ring for a six-sided rumpus room, TNA features "concept matches" like Ultimate X, King of the Mountain, and Six Sides of Steel, accompanied by the usual out-of-ring histrionics you see on TV. Wrestlers include Kurt Angle, Hulk Hogan, Jeff Jarrett, Samoa Joe, Sting, AJ Styles, and Team 3D, among others. If you go, you can pretty much depend on witnessing great athleticism, terrible acting, horrifying staged brutality, and a down-to-earth introduction to chaos theory. It's as American as bluegrass banjo, and a perfect show to see on a first date. The taping calendar and directions to Soundstage 21 (from both inside and outside of Universal Studios) can be found at **universalorlando.com/shows/tna-wrestling.html.** Arrive an hour early to score the best seats. Minimum age is 14.

Blue Man Group

Blue Man Group gives Orlando its first large-scale introduction to that nebulous genre called "performance art." If the term confuses you, relax—it won't hurt a bit. Blue Man Group serves up a stunning show that can be appreciated by folks of all ages.

The three blue men are just that—blue—and bald and mute. Wearing black clothing and skull caps slathered with bright-blue grease paint, they deliver a fast-paced show that uses music (mostly percussion) and multimedia effects to make light of contemporary art and life in the information age. The Universal act is just one expression of a franchise that started with three friends in New York's East Village. Now you can catch their zany, wacky, smart stuff in New York, Las Vegas, Boston, Chicago, and Berlin, among other places.

Funny, sometimes poignant, and always compelling, Blue Man Group pounds out visceral tribal rhythms on complex instruments (made of PVC pipes) and makes seemingly spontaneous eruptions of visual art rendered with marshmallows and a mysterious goo. The weekly supplies include 25½ pounds of Cap'n Crunch, 60 Twinkies, 75 gallons of Jell-O, 996 marshmallows, 9½ gallons of paint, and 185 miles of rolled recycled paper. It's strangely thought-provoking and deals with topics such as the value of modern art, DNA, the persistence of vision, the way rock music moves you, and how we're all connected.

A live percussion band backs Blue Man Group with a relentless and totally engrossing industrial dance riff. The band resides in long, dark alcoves above the stage. At just the right moments, the lofts are lit to reveal a group of pulsating neon-colored skeletons.

The blue men often move into the audience to bring audience members on stage. At the end of the show, the entire audience is involved in an effort to move a sea of paper across the theater.

This show is decidedly different and requires an open mind to be appreciated. It also helps to be a little loose, because, like it or not, everybody gets sucked into the production and leaves the theater a little bit lighter in spirit. If you don't want to be pulled onstage to become a part of the improvisation, don't sit in the first half-dozen or so rows.

The Universal Box Office (☎ 888-340-5476 or 407-224-3200) is open 7 a.m.–7 p.m. EST, or you can purchase tickets online at **universal orlando.com.** Advance tickets at the Universal Orlando website run $64–$74, $49–$64 for children; tickets purchased at the box office are $10 higher. The show is staged in the Sharp Aquos Theatre, which can be accessed from inside or outside Universal Studios theme park. We recommend seats at least 15 rows back from the stage.

UNIVERSAL STUDIOS FLORIDA

UNIVERSAL CITY STUDIOS INC. HAS RUN a studios tour and movie-themed tourist attraction for more than 30 years, predating all Disney parks except Disneyland. In the early 1980s, Universal announced plans to build a new theme park complex in Florida. But while Universal labored over its new project, Disney jumped into high gear and rushed its own studios and theme park into the market, beating Universal by more than a year.

Universal Studios Florida opened in June 1990. At the time, it was almost four times the size of Disney's Hollywood Studios (which has since expanded), and much more of the facility was accesible to visitors. Like its sister park in Hollywood, Universal Studios Florida is spacious and delightfully varied in its entertainment. Rides are exciting and innovative and, as with many Disney rides, focus on familiar and/or beloved movie characters or situations.

While these rides incorporate state-of-the-art technology and live up to their billing in terms of excitement, creativity, uniqueness, and special effects, some lack the capacity to handle the number of guests who frequent major Florida tourist destinations. If a ride has great appeal but can accommodate only a small number of guests per ride or per hour, long lines form. It isn't unusual for the wait to exceed an hour and a quarter for the E.T. ride.

Like the Disney parks, Universal posts expected wait times at most attractions. However, as this reader from Oxford, United Kingdom, comments, the estimates are often far from accurate:

The day we visited Islands of Adventure, the queues were awful. Universal is not as accurate as Disney at predicting queue times. A 45-minute wait for Dudley Do-Right's Rip Saw Falls (which we felt was reasonable) was actually 90 minutes—we wouldn't have even considered this ride had we known. This meant that when we saw the queues for Spider-Man at no less than 2 hours during the day— we daren't risk it! Presumably with people paying a fortune for express passes they have to keep those lines short!

Universal Studios Florida

1. *Animal Actors on Location*
2. *Beetlejuice's Graveyard Revue*
3. *A Day in the Park with Barney*
4. *Disaster!*
5. E.T. Adventure
6. *Fear Factor Live* (open seasonally)
7. Fievel's Playland
8. Hollywood Rip Ride Rockit
9. JAWS
10. Jimmy Neutron's Nicktoon Blast
11. *Lucy—A Tribute*
12. Men in Black Alien Attack
13. Revenge of the Mummy
14. *Shrek 4-D*
15. The Simpsons Ride
16. *Terminator 2: 3-D*
17. *TWISTER . . . Ride It Out*
18. *Universal 360: A Cinesphere Spectacular* (summer only)
19. *Universal Orlando's Horror Make-Up Show*
20. Woody Woodpecker's Nuthouse Coaster, Curious George Goes to Town

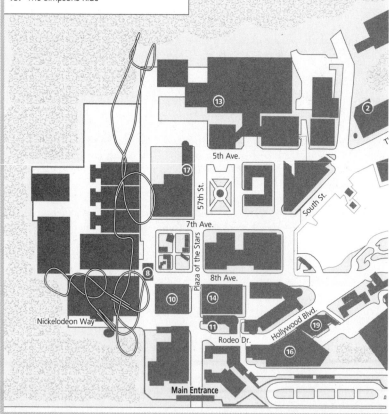

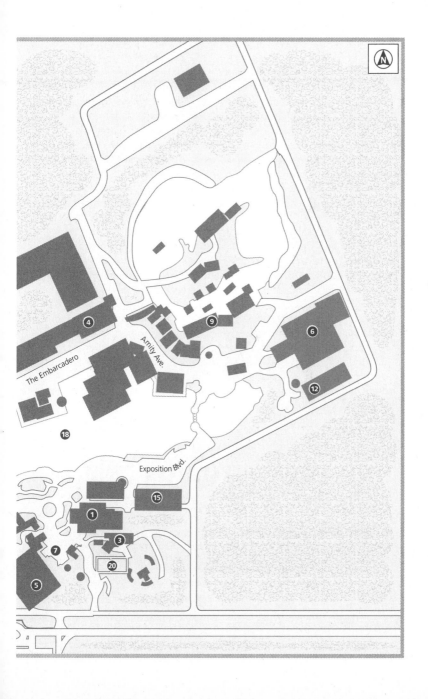

Happily, most shows and theater performances at Universal Studios Florida are in theaters that accommodate large numbers of people. Since many shows run continuously, waits usually don't exceed twice the show's performance time (15–30 minutes).

Universal Studios Florida is laid out in an upside-down-*L* configuration. Beyond the main entrance, a wide boulevard stretches past several shows and rides to the park's New York section. Branching off this pedestrian thoroughfare to the right are four streets that access other areas of the park and intersect a promenade circling a large lake.

The park is divided into six sections: **Hollywood, New York, Production Central, San Francisco–Amity, Woody Woodpecker's KidZone,** and **World Expo.** Where one section begins and another ends is blurry, but no matter. Guests orient themselves by the major rides, sets, and landmarks and refer, for instance, to "New York," "the waterfront," "over by E.T.," or "by Mel's Diner." The area of Universal Studios Florida open to visitors is about the size of Epcot.

Dining at Universal Studios is on par with Disney's Hollywood Studios. Our favorites include **Finnegan's Bar & Grill,** with a fun setting and good burgers and fish-and-chips, and **Lombard's Seafood Grille,** the park's premier restaurant (but not in the same league as DHS's Hollywood Brown Derby). For something quick and satisfying, there's usually a **Nathan's Famous Hot Dogs** stand at Central Park in the New York section of the studios. For milk shakes made the old-fashioned way, try **Schwab's Pharmacy** on Hollywood Boulevard.

The park offers all standard services and amenities, including stroller and wheelchair rental, lockers, diaper-changing and infant-nursing facilities, car assistance, and foreign-language assistance. Most of the park is accessible to disabled guests, and TDDs are available for the hearing impaired. Almost all services are in the Front Lot, just inside the main entrance.

UNIVERSAL STUDIOS FLORIDA ATTRACTIONS

Animal Actors on Location (Universal Express)   ★ ★ ★

APPEAL BY AGE	PRESCHOOL ★ ★ ★ ★	GRADE SCHOOL ★ ★ ★ ★	TEENS ★ ★ ★
YOUNG ADULTS ★ ★ ★		OVER 30 ★ ★ ★	SENIORS ★ ★ ★ ★

What it is Animal-tricks and comedy show. **Scope and scale** Major attraction. **When to go** After you have experienced all rides. **Authors' rating** Cute li'l critters; ★ ★ ★. **Duration of presentation** 20 minutes. **Probable waiting time** 25 minutes.

DESCRIPTION AND COMMENTS This show integrates video segments with live sketches, jokes, and animal tricks performed onstage. The idea is to create eco-friendly family entertainment. Several of the animal thespians are veterans of TV and movies; many were rescued from shelters.

Audience members can participate as well—where else will you get the chance to hold an 8-foot albino reticulated python in your lap?

TOURING TIPS Check the daily entertainment schedule for showtimes. You shouldn't have any trouble getting in to this show.

Beetlejuice's Graveyard Revue (Universal Express) ★★★½

APPEAL BY AGE	PRESCHOOL ★★★★	GRADE SCHOOL ★★★★	TEENS ★★★★
YOUNG ADULTS ★★★★		OVER 30 ★★★★	SENIORS ★★★★

What it is Rock-and-roll stage show. **Scope and scale** Almost major attraction. **When to go** At your convenience. **Authors' rating** Capable of waking the dead; ★★★½. **Duration of presentation** 18 minutes.

DESCRIPTION AND COMMENTS Revamped in 2006, this high-powered rock-and-roll stage show stars Beetlejuice, Frankenstein, the Bride of Frankenstein, Wolfman, Dracula, and a pair of fly girls called Hip and Hop. The show features contemporary dance and pop songs rather than classic rock. The show is high-energy, silly, bawdy, and generally funnier than it has any right to be.

TOURING TIPS Mercifully, this attraction is under cover.

The Blues Brothers ★★★½

APPEAL BY AGE	PRESCHOOL ★★★	GRADE SCHOOL ★★★½	TEENS ★★★½
YOUNG ADULTS ★★★½		OVER 30 ★★★★	SENIORS ★★★★

What it is Blues concert. **Scope and scale** Diversion. **When to go** Scheduled showtimes. **Special comments** A party in the street. **Authors' rating** High energy; ★★★½. **Duration of presentation** 15 minutes.

DESCRIPTION AND COMMENTS An impromptu concert featuring live singing and saxophone playing with a background track. The show takes place on a stoop in the street scene, across from Revenge of the Mummy. The show is one of the more unconventional diversions we've found. Jake and Elwood pull up in the infamous police cruiser from the *Blues Brothers* movie and hop on stage. Interacting with the audience, they begin conga lines in the audience, turning the city set into a scene from a musical—people are literally dancing together in the streets.

TOURING TIPS The concert is a great pick-me-up, and the short running time keeps the energy high. Don't miss this little bit of magic. If you arrive early, you might be able to find a seat on a stoop across the street, but why would you want to sit?

A Day in the Park with Barney (Universal Express) ★★★★

APPEAL BY AGE	PRESCHOOL ★★★★★		GRADE SCHOOL ★★★		TEENS ★★
YOUNG ADULTS ★★★		OVER 30 ★★★			SENIORS ★★★

What it is Live character stage show. **Scope and scale** Major children's attraction. **When to go** Anytime. **Authors' rating** A great hit with preschoolers; ★★★★. **Duration of presentation** 20 minutes, plus 5-minute preshow and character greeting after the show. **Probable waiting time** 15 minutes.

DESCRIPTION AND COMMENTS Barney, the purple dinosaur of public-television fame, leads a sing-along with the help of the audience and sidekicks Baby Bop and BJ. A short preshow gets the kids lathered up before they enter Barney's Park (the theater). Interesting theatrical effects include wind, falling leaves, clouds and stars in the simulated sky, and snow. After the show, parents and children gather along the stage. Barney then moves from child to child, hugging each and posing for photos.

TOURING TIPS If your child likes Barney, this show is a must. It's happy and upbeat, and the character greeting that follows is the best organized we've seen in any theme park. There's no line and no fighting for Barney's attention. Just relax by the rail and await your hug. There's also a great indoor play area nearby, designed especially for wee tykes.

Disaster! (Universal Express) ★★★★

APPEAL BY AGE	PRESCHOOL ★★★	GRADE SCHOOL ★★★★		TEENS ★★★★
YOUNG ADULTS ★★★★		OVER 30 ★★★★		SENIORS ★★★★

What it is Combo theater presentation and adventure ride. **Scope and scale** Major attraction. **When to go** In the morning or late afternoon. **Special comments** May frighten young children. **Authors' rating** Shaken, not stirred; not to be missed; ★★★★. **Duration of presentation** 20 minutes. **Loading speed** Moderate.

DESCRIPTION AND COMMENTS *Disaster!* is a retooled and modernized version of *Earthquake—The Big One,* one of Universal Studios' charter attractions. In this version, guests are recruited for roles in a film called *Mutha Nature,* directed by the overbearing and conceited Frank Kincaid (Christopher Walken) and starring an unnamed actor you'll recognize as Dwayne "The Rock" Johnson. After the recruiting, the audience enters a sound stage where scenes are filmed starring the guests-cum-volunteers. The filming demonstrates various techniques for integrating sets, blue screens, and matte painting with live-action stunts. Next, guests board a faux subway where they experience a simulated earthquake. Following the quake, while the subway returns to the station, guests view a finished cut of *Mutha Nature* that incorporates all the sound-stage shots.

TOURING TIPS Experience *Disaster!* after tackling the park's other rides.

E.T. Adventure (Universal Express) ★★★½

APPEAL BY AGE	PRESCHOOL ★★★★	GRADE SCHOOL ★★★★		TEENS ★★★
YOUNG ADULTS ★★★		OVER 30 ★★★★		SENIORS ★★★★

What it is Indoor adventure ride based on the E.T. movie. **Scope and scale** Major attraction. **When to go** During the first 90 minutes the park is open. **Authors'**

rating A happy reunion; ★★★½. **Duration of ride** 4½ minutes. **Loading speed** Moderate.

DESCRIPTION AND COMMENTS Guests aboard a bicycle-like conveyance escape with E.T. from earthly law enforcement officials and journey to E.T.'s home planet. The attraction is similar to Peter Pan's Flight at the Magic Kingdom but longer, with more elaborate special effects and a wilder ride.

TOURING TIPS Most preschoolers and grade-school children love E.T. We think it worth a 20- to 30-minute wait, but nothing longer. Lines build quickly after 10:30 a.m., and waits can be more than 2 hours on busy days. Ride in the morning or late afternoon. Guests who balk at sitting on the bicycle can ride in a comfortable gondola.

A mother from Columbus, Ohio, writes about horrendous lines at E.T.:

The line for E.T. took 2 hours! The rest of the family waiting outside thought that we had gone to E.T.'s planet for real.

A woman from Richmond, Virginia, objects to how Universal represents the waiting time:

We got into E.T. without much wait, but the line is very deceptive. When you see a lot of people waiting outside and the sign says "10-minute wait from this point," it means 10 minutes until you're inside the building. But there's a very long wait inside before you get to the moving vehicles.

Fear Factor Live (Universal Express) ★★★★
(open seasonally)

APPEAL BY AGE	PRESCHOOL ½	GRADE SCHOOL ★★	TEENS ★★★★
YOUNG ADULTS ★★★		OVER 30 ★★★	SENIORS ★½

What it is Live version of the gross-out-stunt television show on NBC. **Scope and scale** Headliner. **When to go** 6–8 shows daily; crowds are smallest at the first and second-to-last shows. **Authors' rating** Engrossing; ★★★★. **Duration of presentation** 30 minutes. **Probable waiting time** 25 minutes.

DESCRIPTION AND COMMENTS *Fear Factor* is a live stage show in which up to six volunteers compete for one prize; this varies but is always a package that contains at least $400 worth of Universal goodies ranging from park tickets to T-shirts. Contestants must be 18 years or older (with a photo ID to prove it) and weigh at least 110 pounds. Those demented enough to volunteer should arrive at least 75 minutes before showtime to sign papers and complete some obligatory training for the specific competitive events. Anyone who doesn't wish to compete in the stage show itself can sign up for the Critter Challenge or the Food Challenge. With an adult's permission, volunteers as young as age 16 can compete in the latter.

The stage show is performed in a covered theater and consists of three different challenges. In the first, all six contestants are suspended two and a half stories in the air and try to hang on to a bar as long as possible. The difficulty is compounded by heavy-duty fans blasting the contestants' faces while they hold on for dear life (are we having fun yet?). Only four people go on to the next round, and the person who hangs on to the bar the longest gets to choose his or her partner for the next event.

Once the first two contestants are eliminated, it's time for a brief intermission called the Desert Hat Ordeal. This involves a brave audience member who has signed up for the Critter Challenge. Prepared with eye goggles and a mouthpiece, the volunteer is put in a chair with a glass case over his or her head. A wheel is spun to determine what will be crawling over the volunteer's head; the creepy-crawly choices include spiders, snakes, roaches, and scorpions. The only incentive to participate is a free photo of the ordeal for contestants to take to their therapists.

Back at the main competition, the four remaining contestants are split into two teams to compete in the Eel Tank Relay. This consists of one team member grabbing beanbags out of a tank full of eels and throwing them to his or her partner to catch in a bucket. Audience members drench the contestants with high-powered water guns. The team that buckets the most beanbags wins, with the winning team members going on to compete against each other in the final round for the $400 prize.

As the stage is prepared for the finale, the folks who volunteered for the Food Challenge steel themselves for the Guess What's Crawling to Dinner event. Here four contestants are split into two teams and invited to drink a mixture of sour milk, mystery meat, and various live bugs that are all blended together on stage. The team that drinks the most of the mixture within the time limit wins a glamorous plastic mug that says, "I Ate a Bug." The winners (?) are asked to refrain from upchucking all over the audience as they return to their seats to watch the final challenge.

The last event has the two last contestants scramble up a wall to retrieve flags, jump into a car that is lifted in the air, then jump out of the car to retrieve more flags. The first to remove a rocket launcher from the car's backseat and hit a target on the stage wall wins. Whether you participate or simply watch, this show will keep your innards in an uproar.

TOURING TIPS *Fear Factor Live* is a seasonal attraction, meaning that it operates only during the busiest times of the year. Frequently when Universal relegates an attraction to seasonal status, that foreshadows a permanent closing. If it's open, however, and if you've ever wanted a chance to test your mettle (sanity?), this theme park show may be your big chance. Participants for the physical stunts are chosen early in the morning and between performances outside the theater, so be sure to head there first thing if you want to be a contestant. Although there are usually female contestants in every show, the game is weighted against women. The first challenge, hanging from the bar, requires exceptional upper-body strength. In the several performances we observed, the first two contestants eliminated were almost always women. In fact, the only way women usually make it to the second round is when there are three or four (very rare) female contestants to start with. The contestants for the ick-factor stunts, like the bug-smoothie drinking, are chosen directly from the audience. Sit close to the front and wave your hands like crazy when it comes time for selection. Finally (and seriously), this show is too intense and too gross for children age 8 and under.

An extremely relevant query from two University of Iowa students:

We're thinking about volunteering to drink the bug smoothie and want to know if it's better to chew the bugs or just chug the smoothie and hope they die after crawling around for a while in your stomach. Also, do you recommend holding your nose?

We recommend practicing both options at home, preferably while heavily medicated and under the supervision of a psychiatrist.

Fievel's Playland ★★★★

APPEAL BY AGE	PRESCHOOL ★★★★	GRADE SCHOOL ★★★★	TEENS –
YOUNG ADULTS –		OVER 30 –	SENIORS –

What it is Children's play area with waterslide. **Scope and scale** Minor attraction. **When to go** Anytime. **Authors' rating** A much-needed attraction for preschoolers; ★★★★. **Probable waiting time** 20–30 minutes for the waterslide; otherwise, no waiting.

DESCRIPTION AND COMMENTS Imaginative playground features ordinary household items reproduced on a giant scale, as a mouse would experience them. Preschoolers and grade-schoolers can climb nets, walk through a huge boot, splash in a sardine-can fountain, seesaw on huge spoons, and climb onto a cow skull. Most of the playground is reserved for preschoolers, but a combo waterslide and raft ride is open to all ages.

TOURING TIPS Walk in without waiting, and stay as long as you want. Younger kids love the oversize items, and there's enough to keep teens and adults busy while little ones let off steam. The waterslide–raft ride is open to everyone but is extremely slow-loading and carries only 300 riders per hour. With an average wait of 20–30 minutes, we don't think the 16-second ride is worth the trouble. Lack of shade is a major shortcoming of the entire attraction.

Hollywood Rip Ride Rockit ★ ★★★

APPEAL BY AGE	PRESCHOOL –	GRADE SCHOOL ★★★★	TEENS ★★★★½
YOUNG ADULTS ★★★★½		OVER 30 ★★★★½	SENIORS ★★★½

What it is High-tech roller coaster. **Scope and scale** Headliner. **When to go** Immediately after park opening. **Special comments** 51" minimum height requirement; expect *long* waits in line. **Authors' rating** *Woo-hoo!* Not to be missed; ★★★★. **Duration of ride** 2½ minutes. **Probable waiting time per 100 people ahead of you** 6–8 minutes.

Motion Sickness

DESCRIPTION AND COMMENTS Opened in the summer of 2009, Hollywood Rip Ride Rockit is Universal Studios' candidate for the most technologically advanced coaster in the world. Well, we know how long that distinction will last, but for sure this ride has some features we've never seen before. Let's start with the basics: Rip Ride Rockit is a sit-down X-Car coaster that runs on a 3,800-foot steel track, with a maximum height of 167 feet and a top speed of 65 miles an hour. Manufactured by German coaster maker Maurer Söhne, X-Car vehicles are more maneuverable than most other kinds and use less restrictive restraints, making for an exhilarating ride.

You ascend—vertically—at 11 feet per second to crest the 17-story-tall first hill, the highest point reached by any coaster in Orlando. The drop is almost vertical, too, and launches you into Double Take, a loop inversion in which you begin on the inside of the loop, twist to the outside at the top (so you're upright), and then twist back inside the loop for the descent. Double Take stands 136 feet tall, and its loop is 103 feet in diameter at its widest point. You next hurl (not that hurl—it comes later) into a stretch of track shaped like a musical treble clef. As on Double Take, the track configuration on Treble Clef is a first. Another innovation is Jump Cut, a spiraling negative-gravity maneuver. Usually on coasters, you experience negative gravity on long, steep vertical drops; with Jump Cut you feel like you're in a corkscrew inversion, but you never actually go upside down. Other high points include a 95-degree turn, a downhill into an "underground chasm," and a final incline loop banked at 150 degrees.

The ride starts in the Production Central area; weaves into the New York area near *TWISTER*, popping out over guests in the square below; and then storms over the lagoon separating Studios from IOA.

Each train consists of two cars, with riders arranged two across in three rows per car. Each row is outfitted with color-changing LEDs and high-end audio and video technology for each seat. Like the Rock 'n' Roller Coaster at DHS, this coaster features a musical soundtrack. With Rip Ride Rockit, however, you can choose the genre of music you want to hear as you ride: classic rock, country, disco, pop, or rap. After the ride, Universal flogs a digital-video "rip" of your ride, complete with the soundtrack you chose, that you can upload to websites such as YouTube.

From a Whalton, England, mom:

A fabulous, gut-wrenching coaster that thrilled the socks off my 8- and 9-year-olds. (Mum found it a bit too brutal to repeat.) At the end of the ride you'll be offered a video and photo package for about $50. You get the impression that your whole terrifying, toe-curling experience on the ride will be videoed; in fact, it's only a few seconds at the beginning, which is a bit disappointing. The rest of the video is padded out with video graphics and, of course, your chosen soundtrack, which from now on will get your heart beating that bit faster each time you hear it!

A perhaps-jaded Easton, Connecticut, coaster aficionado offers this:

The loud music blasting in our ears cancelled out the sound of the coaster. If only they had a "None of the Above: Silence" button as a selection.

Theme park attractions are subjected to incredible stresses and strains all day long. When Hollywood Rip Ride Rockit premiered in 2009, it was pretty smooth. Alas, the wheels on the coaster cars haven't held up well in the hot Florida sun. While perfectly safe, Rip Ride Rockit now subjects you to a lot of side-to-side jarring. To crib a phrase from Ike and Tina Turner's version of "Proud Mary," some folks like it easy . . . and some folks like it *rough*.

TOURING TIPS Hollywood Rip Ride Rockit can put more trains on the tracks simultaneously than any other coaster in Florida, which means on paper that the ride should be able to handle about 1,850 riders per hour. In practice, you'll wait about 6–8 minutes for every 100 people in the queue ahead of you, indicating an hourly capacity of 1,500 riders. Because the ride is so close to the Universal Studios entrance, it's a crowd magnet and creates bottlenecks from park opening on. Your only chance to ride without a long wait is to be one of the first to enter the park when it opens.

JAWS (Universal Express) ★★★★

APPEAL BY AGE   PRESCHOOL ★★★   GRADE SCHOOL ★★★★   TEENS ★★★★
YOUNG ADULTS ★★★★   OVER 30 ★★★★   SENIORS ★★★★

What it is Adventure boat ride. **Scope and scale** Headliner. **When to go** Before 11 a.m. or after 5 p.m. **Special comments** Frightens young children; 51" minimum height requirement. **Authors' rating** World's largest bathtub toy—not to be missed; ★★★★. **Duration of ride** 5 minutes. **Loading speed** Fast. **Probable waiting time per 100 people ahead of you** 3 minutes; assumes all 8 boats are running.

DESCRIPTION AND COMMENTS JAWS delivers 5 minutes of nonstop action, with the huge shark repeatedly attacking. A West Virginia woman, fresh from the Magic Kingdom, told us the shark is "about as pesky as that witch in Snow White." While the story is entirely predictable, the shark is fairly realistic and as big as a boxcar; but what makes the ride unique is an amazing degree of suspense. It isn't just a cruise into the middle of a pond where a rubber fish assaults the boat interminably. Add inventive sets and powerful special effects, and you have a first-rate attraction.

A variable at JAWS is the enthusiasm and acting ability of your boat guide. Throughout the ride, the guide must set the tone, elaborate the plot, drive the boat, as well as fight the shark. Most guides are quite good. They may overact, but you can't fault them for lack of enthusiasm. Consider also that each guide repeats this wrenching ordeal every 8 minutes.

TOURING TIPS JAWS is well designed to handle crowds. People on the boat's left side tend to get splashed more. If you have young children, consider switching off (the entire family waits in line together and then the adults take turns riding).

A mother of two from Williamsville, New York who believes our warning about getting wet should be more strongly emphasized says this:

Your warning about the JAWS attraction . . . is woefully understated. Please warn your readers—we were seated on the first row of the boat. My 9-year-old sat at the end of the boat (first person on the far left), and I was seated next to him. We were wary of these seats as I had read your warning, but I felt prepared. NOT! At "that" moment the water came flooding over the left front side of the boat, thoroughly drenching the two of us and filling our sneakers with water.

A dad from Seattle suggests that getting wet takes a backseat to being terrified:

Our 8-year-old was so frightened by JAWS that we scrapped the rest of the Universal tour and went back to E.T. An employee said she wouldn't recommend it to anyone under age 10. Maybe you should change "may frighten small children" to "definitely will scare the pants off most children."

Jimmy Neutron's Nicktoon Blast ★★★
(Universal Express)

APPEAL BY AGE	PRESCHOOL ★★★	GRADE SCHOOL ★★★★	TEENS ★★★
YOUNG ADULTS ★★★		OVER 30 ★★★	SENIORS ★★

What it is Cartoon science demonstration and simulation ride. **Scope and scale** Major attraction. **When to go** The first hour after park opening or after 5 p.m. **Authors' rating** Incomprehensible but fun; ★★★. **Duration of ride** A little over 4 minutes. **Loading speed** Moderate–slow. **Probable waiting time per 100 people ahead of you** 5 minutes; assumes all 8 simulators in use.

DESCRIPTION AND COMMENTS This ride features motion simulators that move and react in sync with a cartoon projected onto a huge screen. Based on the Nickelodeon movie *Jimmy Neutron: Boy Genius,* this attraction features a mob of other characters (besides Jimmy) from Nickelodeon, including SpongeBob SquarePants, the Rugrats, the Fairly OddParents, and the Wild Thornberrys. The story, inasmuch as Universal explains it, takes place in two parts. First, guests are invited to participate in a demonstration of Jimmy's newest invention, which is stolen before the demo can proceed. After that, an alien plot is revealed, and guests are strapped into motion-simulator vehicles to help Jimmy rescue his invention and defend the Earth. In practice, the plot is incomprehensible (at least to an adult). All we can report after riding about a dozen times is that there's a frenetic high-speed chase punctuated by an abundance of screaming in piercing, very high-pitched, cartoony voices.

TOURING TIPS This attraction draws sizable crowds primarily because it's just inside the entrance and is next door to the *Shrek 4-D* attraction. We think Jimmy Neutron is at best a so-so effort. Except for avid *Jimmy Neutron* cartoon fans, in other words, it's expendable. If you can't live without it, ride during the first hour the park is open or after 5 p.m. Be aware that a very small percentage of riders suffer motion sickness. Stationary seating is available and is mandated for persons less than 40 inches tall.

Lucy—A Tribute ★★★

APPEAL BY AGE	PRESCHOOL ★	GRADE SCHOOL ★★	TEENS ★★
YOUNG ADULTS ★★★		OVER 30 ★★★	SENIORS ★★★

What it is Walk-through tribute to Lucille Ball. **Scope and scale** Diversion. **When to go** Anytime. **Authors' rating** A touching remembrance; ★★★. **Probable waiting time** None.

DESCRIPTION AND COMMENTS The life and career of comedienne Lucille Ball are spotlighted, with emphasis on her role as Lucy Ricardo in the long-running television series *I Love Lucy.* Well designed and informative, the exhibit succeeds admirably in recalling the talent and temperament of the beloved redhead.

TOURING TIPS See Lucy during the hot, crowded midafternoon. Adults could easily stay 15–30 minutes. Children get restless after a few minutes.

Men in Black Alien Attack (Universal Express) ★★★★½

APPEAL BY AGE	PRESCHOOL†	GRADE SCHOOL ★★★★★	TEENS ★★★★★
YOUNG ADULTS ★★★★★		OVER 30 ★★★★★	SENIORS ★★★★

†Due to height requirement, sample size is too small for an accurate rating.

What it is Interactive dark thrill ride. **Scope and scale** Super-headliner. **When to go** During the first 90 minutes the park is open. **Special comments** May induce motion sickness. 42" minimum height requirement. **Authors' rating** Buzz Lightyear on steroids; not to be missed; ★★★★½. **Duration of ride** 2½ minutes. **Loading speed** Moderate–fast.

DESCRIPTION AND COMMENTS   Based on the movie of the same name, Men in Black brings together actors Will Smith and Rip Torn (as Agent J and MIB director Zed) for an interactive sequel to the hit film. The story line has you volunteering as a Men in Black (MIB) trainee. After an introduction warning that aliens "live among us" and articulating MIB's mission to round them up, Zed expands on the finer points of alien spotting and familiarizes you with your training vehicle and an alien "zapper." Following this, you load up and are dispatched on an innocuous training mission that immediately deteriorates into a situation where only you are in a position to prevent aliens from taking over the universe. Now, if you saw the movie, you understand that the aliens are mostly giant exotic bugs and that zapping the aliens involves exploding them into myriad gooey body parts. Thus, the ride consists of careening around Manhattan in your MIB vehicle and shooting aliens. The technology at work is similar to that used in the Spider-Man attraction at Islands of Adventure, which is to say that it's both a wild ride and one where movies, sets, robotics, and your vehicle are all integrated into a fairly seamless package.

Men in Black is interactive in that your marksmanship and ability to blast yourself out of some tricky situations will determine how the story ends. Also, you're awarded a personal score (as at the Magic Kingdom's Buzz Lightyear's Space Ranger Spin) and a score for your car. There are about three dozen possible outcomes and literally thousands of different ride experiences determined by your pluck, performance, and, in the final challenge, your intestinal fortitude.

TOURING TIPS   Each of the 120 or so aliens has sensors that activate special effects and respond to your zapper. Aim for the eyes and keep shooting until the aliens' eyes turn red. Also, many of the aliens shoot back, causing your vehicle to veer or spin. In the mayhem, you might fail to notice that another vehicle of guests runs along beside you on a dual track. This was included to instill a spirit of competition for anyone who finds blowing up bugs and saving the universe less than stimulating. Note that at a certain point, you can shoot the flashing "vent" on top of the other car and make it spin around. Of course, they can do the same to you.

Although there are many possible endings, the long lines at this headliner attraction will probably dissuade you from experiencing all but one or two. To avoid a long wait, ride during the first 90 minutes the park is open.

Revenge of the Mummy (Universal Express)   ★★★★½

What it is Combination dark ride and roller coaster. **Scope and scale** Super-headliner. **When to go** The first hour the park is open or after 6 p.m. **Special comments** 48" minimum height requirement. **Authors' rating** Killer! Not to be missed; ★★★★½. **Duration of ride** 3 minutes. **Probable waiting time per 100 people ahead of you** 7 minutes. **Loading speed** Moderate.

DESCRIPTION AND COMMENTS It's hard to wrap your mind around the attraction, but trust us when we say you're in for a very strange experience. Here, quoting Universal, are some of the things you can look forward to:

- Authentic Egyptian catacombs
- High-velocity show-immersion system (something to do with fast baptism?)
- Magnet-propulsion launch wave system
- A "Brain Fire" (!) that hovers [over guests] with temperatures soaring to 2,000°F
- Canoptic jars containing grisly remains

When you read between the lines, Revenge of the Mummy is an indoor dark ride based on the *Mummy* flicks, where guests fight off "deadly curses and vengeful creatures" while flying through Egyptian tombs and other spooky places on a high-tech roller coaster. The special effects are cutting-edge with groundbreaking visuals. It's way cool.

The queuing area serves to establish the story line: you're in a group touring a set from the *Mummy* films when you enter a tomb where the fantasy world of film gives way to the real thing. Along the way, you're warned about a possible curse. The visuals are rich and compelling as the queue makes its way to the loading area where you board a clunky, jeep-like vehicle. The ride begins as a slow, very elaborate dark ride, passing through various chambers, including one where flesh-eating scarab beetles descend on you. Suddenly your vehicle stops, then drops backward and rotates. Here's where you're shot at high speed up the first hill of the roller coaster part of the ride. We don't want to ruin your experience by divulging too much, but the coaster part of the ride offers its own panoply of surprises. We will tell you this, however: there are no barrel rolls or upside-down stuff. And though it's a wild ride by anyone's definition, the emphasis remains as much on the visuals, robotics, and special effects as on the ride itself.

TOURING TIPS The newer Hollywood Rip Ride Rockit and The Simpsons Ride have diminished the early-morning crowds. Nevertheless, try to ride during the first hour the park is open. One fallback is to use the singles line. This is often more expedient than Universal Express. Concerning motion sickness, if you can ride Space Mountain without ill effect, you should be fine on Revenge of the Mummy. Switching off is available (the entire family waits in line together and then the adults take turns riding).

Shrek 4-D (Universal Express)   ★★★★½

APPEAL BY AGE   PRESCHOOL ★★★★   GRADE SCHOOL ★★★★★   TEENS ★★★★★
YOUNG ADULTS ★★★★★   OVER 30 ★★★★★   SENIORS ★★★★★

What it is 3-D movie. **Scope and scale** Headliner. **When to go** The first hour the park is open or after 4 p.m. **Authors' rating** Warm, fuzzy, sometimes smelly mayhem; not to be missed; ★★★★½. **Duration of presentation** 20 minutes.

DESCRIPTION AND COMMENTS   Based on characters from the hit movie *Shrek*, the preshow presents the villain from the movie, Lord Farquaad, as he appears on various screens to describe his posthumous plan to reclaim his lost bride, Princess Fiona, who married *Shrek*. The plan is posthumous since Lord Farquaad ostensibly died in the movie, and it's his ghost making the plans, but never mind. Guests then move into the main theater, don their 3-D glasses, and recline in seats equipped with "tactile transducers" and "pneumatic air propulsion and water spray nodules capable of both vertical and horizontal motion." As the 3-D film plays, guests are also subjected to smells relevant to the on-screen action (oh boy).

Technicalities aside, *Shrek 4-D* is a real winner. It's irreverent, frantic, laugh-out-loud funny, and iconoclastic. Concerning the latter, the film takes a good poke at Disney with Pinocchio, the Three Little Pigs, and Tinker Bell (among others) all sucked into the mayhem. The film quality and 3-D effects are great, and like the feature film, it's sweet without being sappy. Plus, *Shrek 4-D* doesn't generally frighten children under age 7.

TOURING TIPS   Universal claims it can move 2,400 guests an hour through *Shrek 4-D*. However, the show's popularity means that waits in line may exceed an hour. Bear that in mind when scheduling your day.

The Simpsons Ride (Universal Express)   ★★★★

APPEAL BY AGE   PRESCHOOL –   GRADE SCHOOL ★★★★   TEENS ★★★★
YOUNG ADULTS ★★★★   OVER 30 ★★★★   SENIORS ★★★½

What it is Mega–simulator ride. **Scope and scale** Super-headliner. **When to go** During the first hour the park is open. **Special comments** 40" minimum height requirement; not recommended for pregnant women or people prone to motion sickness. Switching off available (the entire family waits in line together and then the adults take turns riding). **Authors' rating** Jimmy Neutron with attitude; not to be missed; ★★★★. **Duration of ride** 4 minutes and 20 seconds, plus preshow. **Probable waiting time per 100 people ahead of you** 5 minutes. **Loading speed** Moderate.

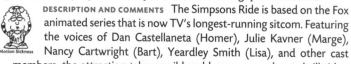

DESCRIPTION AND COMMENTS   The Simpsons Ride is based on the Fox animated series that is now TV's longest-running sitcom. Featuring the voices of Dan Castellaneta (Homer), Julie Kavner (Marge), Nancy Cartwright (Bart), Yeardley Smith (Lisa), and other cast members, the attraction takes a wild and humorous poke at thrill rides, dark rides, and live shows "that make up a fantasy amusement park dreamed up by the show's cantankerous Krusty the Clown."

Two preshows involve Simpsons characters speaking sequentially on different video screens around the line area. Their comments help define the characters for guests who are unfamiliar with the TV show. The attraction is a simulator ride similar to Star Tours at DHS and

Jimmy Neutron's Nicktoon Blast at Universal, but with a larger screen more like that of Soarin' at Epcot. The visuals aren't as sharp as Soarin's, but they're sharp enough.

The story line has the conniving Sideshow Bob secretly arriving at Krustyland, the aforementioned amusement park, and plotting his revenge on Krusty and Bart, who, in a past *Simpsons* episode, revealed that Sideshow Bob had committed a crime for which he'd framed Krusty. Sideshow Bob gets even by making things go wrong with the attractions that the Simpsons (and you) are riding.

Like the show, The Simpsons Ride definitely has an edge, and more than a few wild hairs. There will be jokes and visuals that you'll get but will fly over your kid's heads—and most assuredly vice versa.

A mom from Huntington, New York, had this to say:

The ride is lots of fun and suitable for all guests. I'm not a fan of wild motion simulators, but I was fine on this ride. The field of vision makes it very engrossing, like Soarin'. However, our family still rates Star Tours higher than The Simpsons Ride or Jimmy Neutron, as participating in the Star Tours simulation was most like actually being a character in the original Star Wars *movie!*

TOURING TIPS Because The Simpsons Ride is relatively new, you can expect large crowds all day. We recommend arriving at the park before opening and making the ride your third stop after riding Hollywood Rip Ride Rockit and Revenge of the Mummy. Though not as rough and jerky as *Back to the Future—The Ride*, it's a long way from being tame. Skip it if you're an expectant mom or prone to motion sickness. Several families we interviewed found the humor a little too adult for their younger kids.

Street Scenes ★★★★★

| APPEAL BY AGE | PRESCHOOL ★★★ | GRADE SCHOOL ★★★★★ | TEENS ★★★★★ |
| YOUNG ADULTS ★★★★★ | OVER 30 ★★★★★ | SENIORS ★★★★★ |

What it is Elaborate outdoor sets for making films. **Scope and scale** Diversion. **When to go** Anytime. **Special comments** You'll see most sets without special effort as you tour the park. **Authors' rating** One of the park's great assets; ★★★★★. **Probable waiting time** No waiting.

DESCRIPTION AND COMMENTS Unlike at DHS, all Universal Studios Florida's back-lot sets are accessible for guest inspection. They include a New York City street, San Francisco's waterfront, a New England coastal town, Rodeo Drive, and Hollywood Boulevard.

TOURING TIPS You'll see most as you walk through the park.

Terminator 2: 3-D (Universal Express) ★★★★

| APPEAL BY AGE | PRESCHOOL ★★★ | GRADE SCHOOL ★★★★ | TEENS ★★★★ |
| YOUNG ADULTS ★★★★★ | OVER 30 ★★★★★ | SENIORS ★★★★ |

What it is 3-D thriller mixed-media presentation. **Scope and scale** Super-headliner. **When to go** After 3:30 p.m. **Special comments** The nation's best theme park theater attraction; very intense for some preschoolers and grade-schoolers. **Authors' rating** Furiously paced high-tech experience; not to be missed; ★★★★.

Duration of presentation 20 minutes, including an 8-minute preshow. **Probable waiting time** 20–40 minutes.

DESCRIPTION AND COMMENTS The evil "cop" from *Terminator 2* morphs to life and battles Arnold Schwarzenegger's T-100 cyborg character. In case you missed the *Terminator* flicks, here's the plot: A bad robot arrives from the future to kill a nice boy. Another bad robot (who has been reprogrammed to be good) pops up at the same time to save the boy. The bad robot chases the boy and the rehabilitated robot, menacing the audience in the process.

The attraction, like the films, is all action, and you really don't need to understand much. What's interesting is that it uses 3-D film and a theater full of sophisticated technology to integrate the real with the imaginary. Images seem to move in and out of the film, not only in the manner of traditional 3-D, but also in actuality. Remove your 3-D glasses momentarily and you'll see that the guy on the motorcycle is actually onstage.

Terminator 2: 3-D, however, goes way beyond lasers, with moving theater seats, blasts of hot air, and spraying mist. It creates a multidimensional space that blurs the boundary between entertainment and reality. Is it seamless? Not quite, but it's close. We rank *Terminator 2: 3-D* as not to be missed.

TOURING TIPS The 700-seat theater changes audiences about every 19 minutes. Even so, because the show is popular, expect to wait about 30 minutes. *Terminator 2: 3-D* has been eclipsed somewhat by newer attractions like Hollywood Rip Ride Rockit, The Simpsons Ride, and Revenge of the Mummy. We suggest that you save *Terminator* and other theater presentations until you've experienced all the rides. Families with young children should know that the violence characteristic of the *Terminator* movies is largely absent from the attraction. There's suspense and action but not much blood and guts.

TWISTER . . . Ride It Out (Universal Express)   ★ ★ ★ ½

APPEAL BY AGE	PRESCHOOL ★ ★	GRADE SCHOOL ★ ★ ★ ★	TEENS ★ ★ ★ ★
YOUNG ADULTS ★ ★ ★ ★		OVER 30 ★ ★ ★ ★	SENIORS ★ ★ ★

What it is Theater presentation featuring special effects from the movie *Twister*. **Scope and scale** Major attraction. **When to go** Should be your first show after experiencing all rides. **Special comments** High potential for frightening young children. **Authors' rating** Gusty; ★ ★ ★ ½. **Duration of presentation** 15 minutes. **Probable waiting time** 26 minutes.

DESCRIPTION AND COMMENTS *TWISTER* combines an elaborate set and special effects, climaxing with a five-story-tall simulated tornado created by circulating more than 2 million cubic feet of air per minute.

TOURING TIPS The wind, pounding rain, and freight-train sound of the tornado are deafening, and the entire presentation is exceptionally intense. Schoolchildren are mightily impressed, while younger children are terrified and overwhelmed. Unless you want the kids hopping in your bed whenever they hear thunder, try this attraction yourself before taking your kids.

Universal Orlando's Horror Make-Up Show ★★★½ (Universal Express)

APPEAL BY AGE	PRESCHOOL ★★★	GRADE SCHOOL ★★★★	TEENS ★★★★
YOUNG ADULTS ★★★★		OVER 30 ★★★★	SENIORS ★★★★

What it is Theater presentation on the art of makeup. **Scope and scale** Major attraction. **When to go** After you've experienced all rides. **Special comments** May frighten young children. **Authors' rating** A gory knee-slapper; ★★★½. **Duration of presentation** 25 minutes. **Probable waiting time** 20 minutes.

DESCRIPTION AND COMMENTS Lively, well-paced look at how makeup artists create film monsters, realistic wounds, severed limbs, and other unmentionables. Funnier and more upbeat than many other Universal Studios presentations, the show also presents a wealth of fascinating information. It's excellent and enlightening, if somewhat gory.

TOURING TIPS Exceeding most guests' expectations, the *Horror Make-Up Show* is the sleeper attraction at Universal. Its humor and tongue-in-cheek style transcend the gruesome effects, and most folks (including preschoolers) take the blood and guts in stride.

It's the exception that proves the rule, as this reader relates:

My 7- and 9-year-olds had no problem with Jurassic Park, Terminator, Spider-Man, *or the like but were scared by the* Horror Make-Up Show *(despite my telling them the guy really was not cutting anyone's arm off!).*

Universal 360: A Cinesphere Spectacular ★★★½ (summer only)

APPEAL BY AGE	PRESCHOOL ★★★	GRADE SCHOOL ★★★★	TEENS ★★★½
YOUNG ADULTS ★★★★		OVER 30 ★★★★	SENIORS ★★★★

What it is Fireworks, lasers, and movies. **Scope and scale** Major attraction. **When to go** 1 show a day, usually 10 minutes before park closes. **Authors' rating** Good effort; ★★★½. **Special comments** Movie trailers galore. **Duration of presentation** 10 minutes.

DESCRIPTION AND COMMENTS *Universal 360* is a nighttime summer spectacular presented at the Universal Studios lagoon in the middle of the park. The presentation, a celebration of hit movies, is built around four 360-degree projection cinespheres, each 36 feet tall and 30 feet wide. The cinespheres project images relating to the chosen films, augmented by lasers and fireworks; 300 speakers positioned around the lagoon broadcast the shows' original scores. You'll be surprised to see the number of films the studio has released over its 95-year existence. *Universal 360* is presented during the summer and holiday periods.

A season-pass holder was a bit disappointed with *Universal 360:*

Universal's nighttime fireworks were a bit of a letdown. The whole 360 thing would work great if you could actually see the movies on these balls in the water. I stood directly in front of one of the balls, and I could only see half of the projection—guests have to be at an angle to see the whole movie screen. The show really didn't flow at all. The only theme seemed to be showing a bunch of movies and putting fireworks in the air every now and then. **TOUR-ING TIPS** The 360-degree projections are split rather awkwardly, since the movies weren't shot to be projected on a sphere. The ends of the lagoon are not recommended for viewing. The best spot is directly across the lagoon from Richter's Burger Co., where the sidewalk makes a small protrusion into the water. This side of the lagoon also offers the best view of the projections on the buildings. Acquiring a place here can be very difficult. We recommend arriving at least 45 minutes ahead of time and taking turns holding the spot while the rest of your crew rides JAWS.

Before the show begins, realize that not all of the movie clips may be suitable for young viewers. During the horror-movie montage, which includes scenes from *An American Werewolf in London,* parents may want to cover some eyes. The action movie montage is also stuffed with gunplay and gore.

Woody Woodpecker's Nuthouse Coaster and ★ ★ ★ Curious George Goes to Town

APPEAL BY AGE	PRESCHOOL ★ ★ ★ ★	GRADE SCHOOL –	TEENS –
YOUNG ADULTS –	OVER 30 –		SENIORS –

What it is Interactive playground and kids' roller coaster. **Scope and scale** Minor attraction. **When to go** Anytime. **Authors' rating** *The* place for rambunctious kids; ★ ★ ★.

DESCRIPTION AND COMMENTS Rounding out the selection of other nearby child-friendly attractions, this offering at Woody Woodpecker's Kid-Zone includes Woody Woodpecker's Nuthouse Coaster, Fievel's Playland, and an interactive playground called Curious George Goes to Town. The child-sized roller coaster is small enough for kids to enjoy but sturdy enough for adults, though its moderate speed might unnerve some smaller children (the minimum height to ride is 36 inches). The Curious George playground exemplifies the Universal obsession with wet stuff; in addition to innumerable spigots, pipes, and spray guns, two giant roof-mounted buckets periodically dump 1,000 gallons of water on unsuspecting visitors below. Kids who want to stay dry can mess around in the foam-ball playground, also equipped with chutes, tubes, and ball-blasters.

TOURING TIPS Visit after you've experienced all the major attractions.

LIVE ENTERTAINMENT *at* UNIVERSAL STUDIOS

IN ADDITION TO THE SHOWS PROFILED PREVIOUSLY, Universal offers a wide range of street entertainment. Costumed comic book and cartoon characters (Shrek, Donkey, SpongeBob SquarePants, Woody

Woodpecker) roam the park for photo ops supplemented by look-alikes of movie stars, both living and deceased, plus the Frankenstein monster, who can be said to be neither. Musical acts also pop up.

UNIVERSAL STUDIOS FLORIDA TOURING PLAN

BUYING ADMISSION TO UNIVERSAL STUDIOS FLORIDA

ONE OF OUR BIG GRIPES ABOUT UNIVERSAL STUDIOS is that there are never enough ticket windows open in the morning to accommodate the crowds. You can arrive 30 minutes before official opening time and still be in line to buy your admission when the park opens. Therefore, we strongly recommend that you buy your admission in advance. Passes are available online or by mail from Universal Studios at ☎ 800-711-0080. They're also sold at the concierge desk or attractions box office of many Orlando-area hotels. If your hotel doesn't offer tickets, try Guest Services at the DoubleTree Universal Hotel (☎ 407-351-1000), at the intersection of Major Boulevard and Kirkman Road.

Many hotels that sell Universal admissions don't issue actual passes. Instead, the purchaser gets a voucher that can be redeemed for a pass at the theme park. Fortunately, the voucher-redemption window is separate from the park's ticket-sales operation.

UNIVERSAL STUDIOS FLORIDA ONE-DAY TOURING PLAN

THIS PLAN IS FOR ALL VISITORS. If a ride or show is listed that you don't want to experience, skip that step and proceed to the next. Move quickly from attraction to attraction and, if possible, don't stop for lunch until after Step 9. Minor street shows occur at various times and places throughout the day; check the daily schedule for details.

1. Call ☎ 407-363-8000 the day before you visit for the official opening time.

2. Arrive 50 minutes before opening, and pick up a map and entertainment schedule.

3. Line up at the turnstile. Ask any attendant whether any rides or shows are closed that day. Adjust the touring plan accordingly.

4. Ride Hollywood Rip Ride Rockit roller coaster.

5. After Hollywood Rip Ride Rockit, exit left toward the New York area of the park, and ride Revenge of the Mummy.

6. After the Mummy, head across the park to the World Expo section and experience The Simpsons Ride.

7. After The Simpsons, turn left to the Hollywood area to try E.T. Adventure.

8. Exit to the right and follow the lake to Men in Black Alien Attack.

9. Continue around the lake counterclockwise and ride Jaws.

10. Exit right and head to the San Francisco area. Experience *Disaster!*

11. Backtrack past Mummy and, on the far side of the square, see *Twister.*

12. Exit right after *Twister* toward the park entrance. See *Shrek 4-D.*

13. If you haven't already eaten, take a break for lunch.

14. See *Animal Actors on Location, Beetlejuice's Graveyard Revue, Universal Orlando's Horror Make-Up Show,* and *Fear Factor Live* as convenient according to the daily entertainment schedule. See *Terminator 2: 3-D* after 3:30 p.m.

15. Take preschoolers to see Barney after riding E.T., and then head for Woody Woodpecker's KidZone.

16. Revisit favorite rides and shows. See any live performances you may have missed.

UNIVERSAL'S ISLANDS *of* ADVENTURE

WHEN UNIVERSAL'S ISLANDS OF ADVENTURE theme park opened in 1999, it provided Universal with enough critical mass to actually compete with Disney. Universal finally has on-site hotels, a shopping and entertainment complex, and two major theme parks. Doubly interesting is that the second Universal park is pretty much just for fun—in other words, a direct competitor to Disney's Magic Kingdom, the most-visited theme park in the world. How direct a competitor is it? Check out the box below for a comparison.

And though it may take Central Florida tourists a while to make the connection, here's what will dawn on them when they finally do: Universal's Islands of Adventure is a state-of-the-art park competing with a Disney park that is more than 35 years old and has not added a new super-headliner attraction for many years.

Of course, that's only how it looks on paper. The Magic Kingdom, after all, is graceful in its maturity and much loved. Thus, the clash

ISLANDS OF ADVENTURE VERSUS THE MAGIC KINGDOM	
ISLANDS OF ADVENTURE	**MAGIC KINGDOM**
Seven "islands" (includes Port of Entry)	Seven "lands" (includes Main Street)
Two adult roller-coaster attractions	Two adult roller-coaster attractions
A Dumbo-type ride	Dumbo
One flume ride	One flume ride
Toon Lagoon character area	Main Street, U.S.A. character greeting

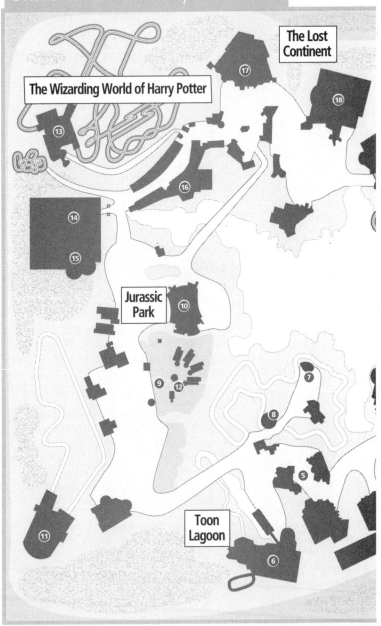

Universal's Islands of Adventure

The Lost Continent

The Wizarding World of Harry Potter

Jurassic Park

Toon Lagoon

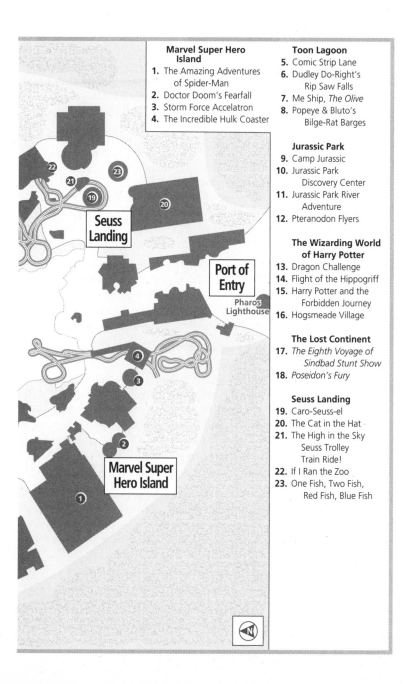

Marvel Super Hero Island
1. The Amazing Adventures of Spider-Man
2. Doctor Doom's Fearfall
3. Storm Force Accelatron
4. The Incredible Hulk Coaster

Toon Lagoon
5. Comic Strip Lane
6. Dudley Do-Right's Rip Saw Falls
7. Me Ship, *The Olive*
8. Popeye & Bluto's Bilge-Rat Barges

Jurassic Park
9. Camp Jurassic
10. Jurassic Park Discovery Center
11. Jurassic Park River Adventure
12. Pteranodon Flyers

The Wizarding World of Harry Potter
13. Dragon Challenge
14. Flight of the Hippogriff
15. Harry Potter and the Forbidden Journey
16. Hogsmeade Village

The Lost Continent
17. *The Eighth Voyage of Sindbad Stunt Show*
18. *Poseidon's Fury*

Seuss Landing
19. Caro-Seuss-el
20. The Cat in the Hat
21. The High in the Sky Seuss Trolley Train Ride!
22. If I Ran the Zoo
23. One Fish, Two Fish, Red Fish, Blue Fish

of the titans is still hot. Universal is coming on strong with the potential of sucking up three days of a tourist's week. And that's more time than anyone has spent off the Disney campus for a long, long time.

In one of the greatest seismic shifts in theme park history, Universal secured the rights to build a Harry Potter–themed area within the park. Harry P. is possibly the only character extant capable of trumping Mickey Mouse, and Universal has gone all-out, under J. K. Rowling's watchful and exacting eye, to create a setting and attractions designed to be the envy of the industry.

If you're having trouble sizing up how big a deal The Wizarding World of Harry Potter is, you need only check the discussion boards of any website associated with Orlando, theme parks, Harry Potter, Daniel Radcliffe, J. K. Rowling, or dozens of other tenuously related topics. What you're likely to see is a billion or so postings like this:

> OMG I CAN'T WAIT!!!!!!!!! I wuz just lking 4 Harry Potter stuff &
> I saw a link 2 this!! SQUEEEEEEE!!!!

Disney and Universal officially downplay their fierce competition, pointing out that any new theme park or attraction makes Central Florida a more marketable destination. Behind closed doors, however, the two companies share a Pepsi versus Coke–type rivalry that will keep both working hard to gain a competitive edge. The good news, of course, is that all this translates into better attractions for you to enjoy.

BEWARE OF THE WET AND WILD

ALTHOUGH WE HAVE DESCRIBED Universal's Islands of Adventure as a direct competitor to the Magic Kingdom, you should be aware of one major qualification: whereas most Magic Kingdom attractions are designed to be enjoyed by guests of any age, attractions at IOA are largely created for an under-40 population. The coasters at Universal are serious with a capital *S*, making Space Mountain and Big Thunder Mountain look about as frightening as Dumbo. Seven out of the nine top attractions at IOA are thrill rides, and of these, three will not only scare the bejeepers out of you but also drench you with water.

For families, there are three interactive playgrounds as well as six rides that young children will enjoy. Of the thrill rides, only the two in Toon Lagoon (described later) are marginally appropriate for young children, and even on these rides your child needs to be fairly stalwart.

GETTING ORIENTED AT ISLANDS OF ADVENTURE

BOTH UNIVERSAL THEME PARKS are accessed via the Universal CityWalk entertainment complex. Crossing CityWalk from the parking garages, you can bear right to Universal Studios Florida or left to Universal's Islands of Adventure.

Islands of Adventure is arranged much like Epcot's World Showcase, in a large circle surrounding a lagoon, but it evidences the sort of thematic continuity present in the Magic Kingdom. Each land, or island in this case, is self-contained and visually consistent in its theme.

You first encounter the Moroccan-style Port of Entry, where you'll find Guest Services, lockers, stroller and wheelchair rentals, ATM banking, lost and found, and shopping. From the Port of Entry, moving clockwise around the lagoon, you can access Marvel Super Hero Island, Toon Lagoon, Jurassic Park, The Wizarding World of Harry Potter, The Lost Continent, and Seuss Landing. You can crisscross the lagoon on small boats, but there's no in-park transportation.

DECISIONS, DECISIONS

WHEN IT COMES TO TOURING IOA efficiently, you have two basic choices, and as you might expect, there are trade-offs. The Wizarding World of Harry Potter sucks up guests like a Hoover. If you're keen to experience Harry Potter and the Forbidden Journey without suffering 1–2 hours in line, you need to be at the turnstiles waiting to be admitted at least 30 minutes before the park opens. Once admitted, move as swiftly as possible to The Wizarding World and then ride Forbidden Journey and Dragon Challenge, in that order. If you can get them out of the way in about an hour, you'll find much of the remainder of the park sparsely populated. Come back to The Wizarding World later in the day to explore Hogsmeade and the shops.

If you can't be at the park when it opens, you're better off enjoying other attractions in IOA at first. You'll still be able to visit The Wizarding World later in the day, but you probably won't be able to experience the attractions there without exceedingly long waits.

UNIVERSAL'S ISLANDS *of* ADVENTURE ATTRACTIONS

MARVEL SUPER HERO ISLAND

THIS ISLAND, WITH ITS FUTURISTIC AND RETRO-FUTURE design and comic book signage, offers shopping and attractions based on Marvel Comics characters.

The Amazing Adventures of Spider-Man ★★★★★ (Universal Express)

APPEAL BY AGE	PRESCHOOL ★★★	GRADE SCHOOL ★★★★★	TEENS ★★★★★
YOUNG ADULTS ★★★★★		OVER 30 ★★★★★	SENIORS ★★★★

What it is Indoor adventure simulator ride based on Spider-Man. **Scope and scale** Super-headliner. **When to go** During the first 40 minutes the park is open. **Special comments** 40" minimum height requirement. **Authors' rating** One of the best attractions anywhere; not to be missed; ★★★★★. **Duration of ride** 4½ minutes. **Loading speed** Fast.

DESCRIPTION AND COMMENTS Covering 1.5 acres and combining moving ride vehicles, 3-D film, and live action, Spider-Man is frenetic, fluid, and astounding. The visuals are rich, and the ride is wild but not jerky. Although the attractions are not directly comparable, Spider-Man is technologically on a par with DHS's Tower of Terror, which is to say that it will leave you in awe.

The story line is that you're a reporter for the *Daily Bugle* newspaper (where Peter Parker, also known as Spider-Man, works as a mild-mannered photographer), when it's discovered that evil villains have stolen (we promise we're not making this up) the Statue of Liberty. You're drafted on the spot by your cantankerous editor to get the story. After speeding around and being thrust into "a battle between good and evil," you experience a 400-foot "sensory drop" from a skyscraper roof all the way to the pavement. Because the ride is so wild and the action so continuous, it's hard to understand the plot, but you're so thoroughly entertained that you don't really care. Plus, you'll want to ride again and again. Eventually, with repetition, the story line will begin to make sense.

TOURING TIPS If you were on hand at park opening, ride after experiencing the Forbidden Journey, Dragon Challenge, and The Incredible Hulk. If you elect to bypass the crowds at Forbidden Journey, ride after Dragon Challenge and the Hulk. If you arrived more than 15 minutes after park opening, skip Wizarding World attractions and ride Spider-Man after the Hulk.

Doctor Doom's Fearfall (Universal Express) ★★★

APPEAL BY AGE	**PRESCHOOL** –	**GRADE SCHOOL** ★★★	**TEENS** ★★★★
YOUNG ADULTS ★★★★		**OVER 30** ★★★	**SENIORS** –

What it is Lunch liberator. **Scope and scale** Headliner. **When to go** During the first 40 minutes the park is open. **Special comments** 52" minimum height requirement. **Authors' rating** More bark than bite; ★★★. **Duration of ride** 40 seconds. **Loading speed** Slow.

DESCRIPTION AND COMMENTS Here you are strapped in a seat with your feet dangling and blasted 200 feet up in the air, then allowed to partially free-fall down. If you have trouble forming a mental image of this, picture the game where someone swings a sledgehammer, propelling a metal sphere up a vertical shaft. At the top is a bell. If the person drives the sphere high enough to ring the bell, he or she wins a prize. On this ride you're the sphere.

The scariest part by far is the apprehension that builds as you sit, strapped in, waiting for the thing to launch. The blasting up and free-falling down parts are really very pleasant.

TOURING TIPS We've seen glaciers that move faster than the line for Doctor Doom. If you want to ride without investing half a day, be one of the first in the park to ride. Fortunately, if you're on hand at opening time, being among the first isn't too difficult (mainly because the nearby Wizarding World, Hulk, and Spider-Man attractions are bigger draws).

The Incredible Hulk Coaster ★★★★½
(Universal Express)

APPEAL BY AGE   PRESCHOOL ★   GRADE SCHOOL ★★★★★   TEENS ★★★★★
YOUNG ADULTS ★★★★   OVER 30 ★★★★   SENIORS ★★★

What it is Roller coaster. **Scope and scale** Super-headliner. **When to go** During the first 40 minutes the park is open. **Special comments** 54" minimum height requirement. **Authors' rating** A coaster-lover's coaster; not to be missed; ★★★★½. **Duration of ride** 2¼ minutes. **Loading speed** Moderate.

DESCRIPTION AND COMMENTS There is, as always, a story line, but for this attraction it's of no importance whatsoever. What you need to know about this attraction is simple. You'll be shot like a cannonball 0–40 mph in 2 seconds, and then you'll be flung upside down 100 feet off the ground, which will, of course, induce weightlessness. From there it's a mere six rollovers punctuated by two plunges into holes in the ground before you're allowed to get out and throw up.

Seriously, the Hulk is a great roller coaster, perhaps the best in Florida, with an accelerated launch (instead of the more typical uphill crank). Plus, this coaster has a smooth ride.

TOURING TIPS Arrive before park opening and ride after experiencing Harry Potter and and Dragon Challenge. If you want to stay clear of the crowds at Forbidden Journey, ride after Dragon Challenge. If you arrived more than 15 minutes after park opening, skip the Wizarding World attractions and ride the Hulk first. Use lockers near the entrance of the Hulk to deposit any items that might depart your person during the ride. The locker is free if you use it for a short time. If you leave things in the locker for a couple of hours, however, you'll have to pay a rental charge. Hulk has a separate line for those who want to ride in the first row.

> *unofficial* **TIP**
> Roller coasters at Islands of Adventure are the real deal—not for the faint of heart or for little ones.

Storm Force Accelatron (Universal Express)   ★★★

APPEAL BY AGE   PRESCHOOL ★★★★   GRADE SCHOOL ★★★   TEENS ★★★
YOUNG ADULTS ★★★   OVER 30 ★★★   SENIORS ★★★

What it is Indoor spinning ride. **Scope and scale** Minor attraction. **Special comments** May induce motion sickness. **When to go** During the first hour the park is open. **Authors' rating** Teacups in the dark; ★★★. **Duration of ride** 1½ minutes. **Loading speed** Slow.

DESCRIPTION AND COMMENTS Storm Force is a spiffed-up indoor version of Disney's nausea-inducing Mad Tea Party. Here you spin to the accompaniment of a simulated thunderstorm and swirling sound and light. A story line loosely ties this midway-type ride to the Marvel Super Hero Island area, but it's largely irrelevant and offers no advice on keeping your lunch down.

TOURING TIPS   Ride early or late to avoid long lines. If you're prone to motion sickness, keep your distance.

TOON LAGOON

TOON LAGOON IS CARTOON ART TRANSLATED into real settings. Whimsical and gaily colored, with rounded and exaggerated lines, Toon Lagoon is Universal's answer to the old Mickey's Toontown Fair in the Magic Kingdom. The main difference between the two is that you have about a 60% chance of drowning at Universal's version.

Comic Strip Lane

What it is Walk-through exhibit and shopping and dining venue. **Scope and scale** Diversion. **When to go** Anytime.

DESCRIPTION AND COMMENTS   This is the main street of Toon Lagoon. Here you can visit the domains of Beetle Bailey, Hagar the Horrible, Krazy Kat, the Family Circus, and Blondie and Dagwood, among others. Shops and eateries tie into the funny-papers theme.

TOURING TIPS   This is a great place for photo ops with cartoon characters in their own environment. It's also a great place to drop a few bucks in the diners and shops, but you probably already figured that out.

Dudley Do-Right's Rip Saw Falls ★★★½ (Universal Express)

APPEAL BY AGE	PRESCHOOL ★★★	GRADE SCHOOL ★★★★		TEENS ★★★★
YOUNG ADULTS ★★★		OVER 30 ★★★★	SENIORS ★★★	

What it is Flume ride. **Scope and scale** Major attraction. **When to go** Before 11 a.m. **Special comments** 44" minimum height requirement. **Authors' rating** A minimalist Splash Mountain; ★★★½. **Duration of ride** 5 minutes. **Loading speed** Moderate.

DESCRIPTION AND COMMENTS   Inspired by the *Rocky and Bullwinkle* cartoons, this ride features Canadian Mountie Dudley Do-Right as he attempts to save Nell from evil Snidely Whiplash. Story line aside, it's a flume ride, with the inevitable big drop at the end. Universal claims this is the first flume ride to "send riders plummeting 15 feet below the surface of the water." In reality, though, you're just plummeting into a tunnel.

   The only problem with this attraction is that everyone inevitably compares it to Splash Mountain at the Magic Kingdom. The flume is as good as Splash Mountain's, and the final drop is a whopper, but the theming and the visuals aren't even in the same league. The art, sets, audio, and jokes at Dudley Do-Right are minimalist at best; it's Dudley Do-Right's two-dimensional approach versus Splash Mountain's three-dimensional presentation. Taken on its own terms, however, Dudley Do-Right is a darn good flume ride.

TOURING TIPS   This ride will get you wet, but on average not as wet as you might expect. If you want to stay dry, however, arrive prepared with a poncho or at least a big garbage bag with holes cut out for your head and arms. After riding, take a moment to gauge the timing of the water cannons that go off along the exit walk, where you can really get drenched. While younger kids are often intimidated by the big drop, those who ride generally enjoy themselves. Ride after experiencing the Marvel Super Hero rides.

Me Ship, *The Olive* ★★★

APPEAL BY AGE   PRESCHOOL ★★★★   GRADE SCHOOL ★★★★   TEENS ½
YOUNG   ADULTS   ½   OVER   30   ½   SENIORS   –

What it is Interactive playground. **Scope and scale** Minor attraction. **When to go** Anytime. **Authors' rating** Colorful and appealing for kids; ★★★.

DESCRIPTION AND COMMENTS *The Olive* is Popeye's three-story boat come to life as an interactive playground. Younger children can scramble around in Swee'Pea's Playpen, while older sibs shoot water cannons at riders trying to survive the adjacent Bilge-Rat raft ride.

TOURING TIPS If you're into the big rides, save this for later in the day.

Popeye & Bluto's Bilge-Rat Barges ★★★★ (Universal Express)

APPEAL BY AGE   PRESCHOOL ★★★   GRADE SCHOOL ★★★★★   TEENS ★★★★
YOUNG   ADULTS ★★★★   OVER 30 ★★★★   SENIORS ★★★

What it is White-water raft ride. **Scope and scale** Major attraction. **When to go** Before 11 a.m. **Special comments** 42" minimum height requirement. **Authors' rating** Bring your own soap; ★★★★. **Duration of ride** 4½ minutes. **Loading speed** Moderate.

DESCRIPTION AND COMMENTS This sweetly named attraction is a white-water raft ride that includes an encounter with an 18-foot-tall octopus. Engineered to ensure that everyone gets drenched, the ride even provides water cannons for highly intelligent nonparticipants ashore to fire at those aboard. The rapids are rougher and more interesting, and the ride longer, than Animal Kingdom's Kali River Rapids. But nobody surpasses Disney for visuals and theming, though the settings of these two attractions (cartoon set and Asian jungle river, respectively) are hardly comparable.

TOURING TIPS If you didn't drown on Dudley Do-Right, here's a second chance. You'll get a lot wetter from the knees down on this ride, so use your poncho or garbage bag and ride barefoot with your britches rolled up. In terms of beating the crowds, ride the barges in the morning after experiencing the Marvel Super Hero attractions and Dudley Do-Right. If you lack foul-weather gear or you've forgotten your trash bag, you might want to put off riding until last thing before leaving the park. Most preschoolers enjoy the raft ride. Those who are frightened react more to the way the rapids look as opposed to the roughness of the ride.

JURASSIC PARK

JURASSIC PARK (for anyone who's been asleep for 20 years) is a Steven Spielberg film franchise about a theme park with real dinosaurs. Jurassic Park at Universal's Islands of Adventure is a real theme park (or at least a section of one) with fictitious dinosaurs.

Camp Jurassic ★★★

APPEAL BY AGE	PRESCHOOL ★★★		GRADE SCHOOL ★★★		TEENS –
YOUNG ADULTS	–		OVER 30	–	SENIORS –

What it is Interactive play area. **Scope and scale** Minor attraction. **When to go** Anytime. **Authors' rating** Creative playground, confusing layout; ★★★.

DESCRIPTION AND COMMENTS   Camp Jurassic is a great place for children to cut loose. Sort of a Jurassic version of Tom Sawyer Island, it allows kids to explore lava pits, caves, mines, and a rain forest.

TOURING TIPS   Camp Jurassic will fire the imaginations of the under-13 set. If you don't impose a time limit on the exploration, you could be here a while. The layout of the play area is confusing and intersects the queuing area for Pteranodon Flyers.

Jurassic Park Discovery Center   ★★★

APPEAL BY AGE	PRESCHOOL ★★★	GRADE SCHOOL ★★★★	TEENS ★★★
YOUNG ADULTS ★★★		OVER 30 ★★★	SENIORS ★★★

What it is Interactive natural history exhibit. **Scope and scale** Minor attraction. **When to go** Anytime. **Authors' rating** Definitely worth checking out; ★★★.

DESCRIPTION AND COMMENTS   The Discovery Center is an interactive educational exhibit that mixes fiction from the movie *Jurassic Park,* such as using fossil DNA to bring dinosaurs to life, with various skeletal remains and other paleontological displays. One exhibit allows you to watch an animatronic raptor being hatched. Another allows you to digitally "fuse" your DNA with a dinosaur's to see what the resultant creature would look like. Other exhibits include dinosaur-egg scanning and identification.

TOURING TIPS   Cycle back after experiencing all the rides or on a second day. Most folks can digest this exhibit in 10–15 minutes.

Jurassic Park River Adventure   ★★★★
(Universal Express)

APPEAL BY AGE	PRESCHOOL ★★★	GRADE SCHOOL ★★★★★	TEENS ★★★★★
YOUNG ADULTS ★★★★		OVER 30 ★★★★	SENIORS ★★★★

What it is Indoor-outdoor adventure river-raft ride based on the *Jurassic Park* movies. **Scope and scale** Super-headliner. **When to go** Before 11 a.m. **Special comments** 42" minimum height requirement. **Authors' rating** Better than its Hollywood cousin; not to be missed; ★★★★. **Duration of ride** 6½ minutes. **Loading speed** Fast.

DESCRIPTION AND COMMENTS   Guests board boats for a water tour of Jurassic Park. Everything is tranquil as the tour begins, and the boat floats among brontosauruses and stegosauruses. Then, as word is received that some of the carnivores have escaped their enclosure, the boat is accidentally diverted into Jurassic Park's maintenance facilities. Here, the boat and its riders are menaced by an assortment of hungry meat-eaters led by T-Rex. At the climactic moment, the boat and its passengers escape by plummeting over an 85-foot drop, which at the time of its construction was the longest, fastest, steepest theme park water descent yet built.

TOURING TIPS Once you're under way, there's a little splashing but nothing major until the big drop at the end of the ride. Fortunately, not all that much water lands in the boat.

Young children must endure a double whammy on this ride. First, they're stalked by giant, salivating (sometimes spitting) reptiles, and then they're sent catapulting over the falls. Unless your children are fairly stalwart, wait a year or two before you spring the River Adventure on them.

Because the Jurassic Park section of IOA is situated next to the Wizarding World of Harry Potter, the boat will experience heavy crowds earlier in the day. Try to ride before 11 a.m.

Pteranodon Flyers ½

APPEAL BY AGE	PRESCHOOL ★★★		GRADE SCHOOL ★★★	TEENS ★
YOUNG ADULTS ★★		OVER 30 ★		SENIORS ★★

What it is Slow as Christmas. **Scope and scale** Minor attraction. **When to go** When there's no line. **Authors' rating** All sizzle, no steak. ½. **Duration of ride** 1¼ minutes. **Loading speed** Slower than a hog in quicksand.

DESCRIPTION AND COMMENTS This is Islands of Adventure's biggest blunder. Engineered to accommodate only 170 persons per hour—about half the hourly capacity of Dumbo!—the ride dangles you on a swing below a track that passes over a small part of Jurassic Park. We recommend skipping this one. Why? Because the Jurassic period will probably end before you reach the front of the line! And your reward for all that waiting? A 1-minute-and-15-second ride.

TOURING TIPS Photograph the pteranodon as it flies overhead. You're probably looking at something that will someday be extinct.

Triceratops Encounter ★★★½

What it is Prehistoric petting zoo. **Scope and scale** Minor attraction. **When to go** After experiencing all the rides. **Special comments** Expect *long* waits in line. **Authors' rating** Clever and different; ★★★½. **Duration of experience** 5 minutes. **Probable waiting time per 100 people ahead of you** 30 minutes.

DESCRIPTION AND COMMENTS Triceratops Encounter was one of the original Islands of Adventure attractions. Presumably because of its low capacity and staffing requirements, it was taken out of operation several years ago. In 2010 it was revived but who knows for how long. Guests are ushered in groups into a feed and control station, where they can view and pet a 24-foor-long, animatronic triceratops dinosaur. While the trainer lectures about the creature's behaviors, habits, and lifestyle, the triceratops breathes, blinks, chews, and flinches at the touch of the guests.

TOURING TIPS Nothing is certain, but this is one of only a couple of IOA attractions where you won't get wet. Just to be sure, though, we suggest that you stand along the side of the beast rather than near the head or tail. Though not a major attraction, Triceratops Encounter is well executed and quite worthwhile. Make it your first show/exhibit after experiencing the rides.

THE WIZARDING WORLD OF HARRY POTTER

IN WHAT MAY PROVE TO BE the competitive coup of all time between theme park archrivals Disney and Universal, the latter inked a deal with Warner Brothers Entertainment to create a "fully immersive" Harry Potter–themed environment based on the bestselling books by J. K. Rowling and the companion blockbuster movies from Warner Brothers. The books have been translated into 68 languages, with more than 400 million copies sold. The movies have grossed more than $5.4 billion worldwide, the largest-grossing film franchise in history.

The project was blessed by Rowling, who is known for tenaciously protecting the integrity of her work. In the case of the films, she demanded that Warner Brothers be true, to an almost unprecedented degree, to the books on which the films were based.

The 20-acre Wizarding World is an amalgamation of landmarks, sights, creatures, and themes that are faithful to the films and books. You access the area through an imposing gate that opens onto **Hogsmeade Village,** depicted in winter and covered in snow. This section is The Wizarding World's primary shopping and dining venue. Exiting Hogsmeade, you first glimpse towering **Hogwarts Castle,** flanked by the **Forbidden Forest** and **Hagrid's Hut.** The grounds and interior of the castle house part of the queue for the super-headliner **Harry Potter and the Forbidden Journey.** Universal has gone all-out on the castle, with the intention of creating an icon even more beloved and powerful than Cinderella Castle at Disney's Magic Kingdom.

"What a Long Strange Trip It's Been"

That Grateful Dead lyric is appropriate when recounting the evolution of The Wizarding World. A Harry Potter theme park (or themed area) has been the dream of the amusement industry for a decade. First, of course, there were the books. Next came the movies. In securing the film rights, Warner Brothers, along with several unsuccessful suitors, learned the most important thing about exploiting the Harry Potter phenomenon: that J. K. Rowling is boss. She put her stamp on the films, making sure that every detail was painstakingly true to her novels.

As the Potter books, films, and characters took the world by storm, entertainment conglomerates began approaching Rowling about theme park rights. When she spurned a Universal Studios concept for a show based on the Potter characters, industry observers were certain that she had struck a deal with Disney. In fact, Disney was in talks with Rowling about a stand-alone Harry Potter theme park and had a team to develop concepts for Rowling's inspection. For her part, Rowling had no problem visualizing what she wanted in a theme park, but, to paraphrase another song, when an irresistible force such as Rowling meets an immovable object like Disney, something's gotta give. And give it did: from Disney's point of view, what Rowling wanted was operationally problematic, if not altogether impossible. Never an entity to concede control, Disney walked.

Universal caught Rowling on the rebound and brought her to Orlando to tour Islands of Adventure. Among other things, they squired her around the Lost Continent section of the park, impressing her with its detailed theme execution and showing her how with a little imagination it could be rethemed. Rowling saw the potential but wasn't much more flexible with Universal than she was with Disney. She insisted that Stuart Craig, her trusted production designer for the films, be responsible for faithfully re-creating sets from the movies. Universal, on fire to land Harry Potter, became convinced that the collaboration could work.

But theme parks and movies are two very different things. With a film, a set has to look good only for a few moments and then it's on to something else. With a theme park, a set has to look good 12–16 hours a day, in all manner of weather, and with tens of thousands of tourists rambling through it in need of food, restrooms, protection from rain, and places to rest. A narrow trail to Hagrid's Hut is perfect for a movie set but is totally inadequate in a theme park when half the population of Vermont is treading it at any given moment. In developing The Wizarding World, Rowling's insistence on authenticity occasioned conundrums not anticipated by the park designers, who, for example, logically assumed that guests would like to see the interior of Hagrid's Hut. No problem—a walk-through attraction will serve nicely. Of course, there's the Americans with Disabilities Act, so we'll need ramps both in and out of the hut. No way, say the movie people: Hagrid's Hut in the films had steps, so the theme park version must have them, too.

Universal executed a masterful promotional campaign, including events, TV commercials, magazine ads, high-tech Web previews, even a traveling Harry Potter exhibit. It teasingly parceled out one tidbit of information after another, each of which promptly went viral in the hands of information-hungry fans.

One salient piece of information that Universal *didn't* get across well, however, is that The Wizarding World is not a stand-alone park but part of a bigger one. Drawing conclusions to the contrary were many Potterphiles who had been exposed to the relentless marketing blitz. So as opening day approached, Universal braced itself for blowback from guests who expected Harry Potter and nothing but.

Bone Up

It's beyond the scope of this guide to explain all the Potter references, situations, and icons incorporated into The Wizarding World. Because they so accurately replicate scenes from the books and films, it helps immeasurably to be well versed in all things Harry. Elements that seem like nice decorative touches to the uninitiated will be familiar and laden with meaning for the Potter aficionado. If it's been a while since you've seen one of the movies or read one of the novels, you can brush up by watching the first four flicks in the series, in particular *Harry Potter and the Sorcerer's Stone* (*Harry Potter and the Philosopher's Stone* outside the United States) and *Harry Potter and the Goblet of Fire*. For an easy memory jog, check out the films' trailers at YouTube. If you know nothing at all about Harry Potter, you'll still have fun, but to truly appreciate the nuance and detail, we suggest you hit the books.

Getting In

Unless you're a Universal resort guest, expect a goodly wait in line to enter The Wizarding World. Crowds will certainly be larger during summer and holidays, but because The Wizarding World is new and proving popular beyond all expectations, you'll encounter lines even at slower times of year.

Going into the Wizarding World's second year, Universal is still experimenting with how to handle the crowds. During less crowded times of year, the norm is to open both the park and the Wizarding World at 8 a.m. for Universal hotel guests and to the general public at about 8:50 a.m. All guests are allowed to proceed directly to the Wizarding World main entrance via Seuss Landing. During holiday periods and the summer high season, hotel guests are admitted an hour early and can go directly to Potterland. Day guests are given a choice. They can either queue up in a standby line to enter Wizarding World via Jurassic Park or they can queue up to obtain a return ticket stamped with a time to visit the Wizarding World later in the day. If you enter the park during the first 30 minutes it's open, the standby line is fine. If you arrive later, pick up one of the time-stamped return tickets.

The standby line can be hours long and does not allow you to leave the line at any time. The return-ticket line allows each member of your party to get a ticket with a printed time stating when to come back to the Wizarding World. The return time is predicated on where you are in line and how many people are in your party. The best suggestion is to get into the return-ticket line as soon as you enter the park. The sooner you receive your ticket, the sooner you can gain entry to Potterland. For example, if you are in line at 10 a.m., the return time on the ticket will most likely be before 1 p.m. The longer you wait to get a return ticket, however, the longer the time frame to return will be. Once all slots for the day have been filled, return ticket distribution is discontinued. It is not uncommon for all return tickets for the day to be distributed by 2 p.m. If you want to enter the Wizarding World and all return tickets have been distributed, you must wait in the standby line. After receiving a return ticket, you can plan your day around your assigned time to drop in on Harry. This arrangement allows you to experience other attractions in the park while waiting for your return time. When the time designated to enter the Wizarding World comes around, go to the designated return area, which is usually on the Jurassic Park side of the bridge to Potterland. A cast member will take your return ticket and you can now enter the Wizarding World. Once inside there will still be waits for all rides, stores, and the one restaurant.

On busy days, because Universal continues to screw around with all this, there are no signs posted directing you to the two lines or indicating which line is which. Lines can form up almost anywhere on a particular day at the whim of management. Given the confusion, your best bet is to collar a Universal cast member as you pass through the Port of Entry. If you're lucky, the cast member should be able to clue you in on the crowd control plan of the day, differentiate the lines, and direct you to the one you need.

If you opt for the time-stamped return ticket, arrive before 11 a.m. Sometimes the return-ticket line terminates at a set place where the tickets are distributed. On other occasions a cast member will work his or her way along the line, distributing return tickets as they go.

The best strategy during the busier times of year is to arrive at the park, admission in hand, 30–40 minutes before park opening time. When you're admitted, take a moment to get the skinny from a cast member and then follow his instructions. Whatever time you burn getting directions is nothing compared to the time you'll squander by getting in the wrong line or looking for the line in the wrong place.

If you go with the standby line, how fast the line moves depends on crowd conditions and how many Universal resort guests are in The Wizarding World before the park opens to the general public. During a research trip, we saw 400–500 day guests admitted on a Sunday morning at 9 a.m. because there weren't enough hotel guests to fill The Wizarding World.

As a precaution, always keep at least one of your group in line. If you're waiting in Jurassic Park, none of your party should leave the queue from about 8:40 a.m. on. If you're farther back—in Toon Lagoon, Marvel Super Hero Island, Port of Entry, or Seuss Landing—you can leave the line without worrying too much. Some individuals in your group can even hold your place in line while you break away to enjoy attractions in the rest of IOA.

Another factor that will affect your wait is how well Harry Potter and the Forbidden Journey is operating, since this is what most of those in line are waiting for. If the ride comes up on schedule and runs trouble-free, the queue to The Wizarding World will advance in timely fashion. If Forbidden Journey experiences problems, though, especially first thing in the morning, the line will back up halfway to Tampa and not unjam until late afternoon. When the attraction behaves, and when IOA manages the queue properly, it's not unusual for the line to disappear entirely by around 11:30 a.m. to 1 p.m.—no guarantees, though. In any case, slather on the sunscreen and stay hydrated. Vendors work their way up and down the queue all day selling bottled water and other drinks.

Usually the main entrance at Hogsmeade becomes a dedicated exit after the park opens. If you leave The Wizarding World after opening, the only way back in is via the end of the standby or stamped-ticket line; this is true for hotel guests as well as day guests. When there is no queue, both hotel guests and day guests can enter The Wizarding World at will through the Jurassic Park gateway.

Crowds finally dissipate between 7 and 8 p.m. At night you won't have the place to yourself exactly, but it will seem almost empty compared with earlier in the day. An extra bonus for visiting late is enjoying the exquisite lighting and magical nighttime personality of The Wizarding World. Forbidden Journey will accommodate anyone already in line at park closing, and many of the Hogsmeade shops remain open awhile after the park closes. If you have a two-park pass, you can spend the day at Universal Studios, eat dinner at CityWalk, and visit Harry and friends in the relative tranquility and cool of the evening.

Gentlemen, Start Your Broomsticks

The Wizarding World is in the northwest corner of Islands of Adventure, between The Lost Continent and Jurassic Park. From the IOA entrance, the most direct route there is through Port of Entry then right, through Seuss Landing and The Lost Continent, to the Hogsmeade main gate. As we've mentioned, this entrance usually becomes an exit once the park is open, but if you cross the bridge connecting The Lost Continent with Jurassic Park, then turn right after entering the latter area, the path will take you directly to The Wizarding World's Jurassic Park entrance. This is the fastest route when there's no queue or when the queue is relatively short. Otherwise, you'll find the end of the queue faster by walking clockwise around the lagoon.

For the moment, however, let's begin our exploration at The Wizarding World's main entrance, on the Lost Continent side of the themed area. Passing beneath a stone archway, you enter the village of **Hogsmeade.** The **Hogwarts Express** locomotive sits belching steam on your right, and the village stretches before you, following the contours of a gently curving street. The setting is rendered in exquisite detail: stone cottages and shops have steeply pitched slate roofs, bowed multipaned windows, gables, and tall, crooked chimneys accented by cobblestone streets and gas street lamps.

On your left, opposite the locomotive and station, is **Zonko's,** a novelty shop specializing in such necessities as Shrunken Heads, Extendable Ears, and Screaming Yo-yos. If your sweet tooth is on a rampage, the shop also sells sweets such as Nosebleed Nougat, U-No-Poo, and our personal favorite, Puking Pastilles. (By the way, not only the attractions but all the merchandise and food had to meet with the approval of the redoubtable Ms. Rowling.)

Connected to Zonko's through an interior passage is **Honey-dukes.** For those whose appetites have recovered from disgorging their Puking Pastilles, Honeydukes offers another opportunity to expand your midriff, specializing in Acid Pops (no flashbacks, guaranteed), Tooth Splintering Strong Mints, and Fizzing Whizzbees. Across the street from Honeydukes, next to the train station, is the entrance to the **Dragon Challenge** dueling roller coasters (see page 219).

Next door to Honeydukes and set back from the main street is **Three Broomsticks,** a rustic tavern serving English staples such as fish-and-chips, shepherd's pie, Cornish pasties, and turkey legs. Kids' fare includes the obligatory mac-and-cheese and chicken fingers. Three Broomsticks is also a good, albeit expensive, venue for ice cream and other sweet treats. To the rear of the tavern is the **Hog's Head** pub, which serves a nice selection of beer as well as The Wizarding World's signature nonalcoholic brew, Butterbeer. Three Broomsticks and the Hog's Head were carved out of The Lost Continent's popular Enchanted Oak Tavern, which was Potterfied pretty effectively in its reincarnation, although a good deal of seating capacity was sacrificed—the restaurant and pub combined seat only 123. To dine at Three Broomsticks anytime from its opening until roughly 8 p.m., you'll have to wait in a long queue during busier times of year. In the summer of 2010, waiting times for Three Broomsticks were upwards of 90 minutes most of the day. This, coupled with the facts that (1) one usually can't reenter The Wizarding World without starting over in the queue leading to the Jurassic Park gateway and (2) no other food is available in the themed area save some meager snacks from vendor carts, meant that many guests were left without a practical alternative for getting something to eat. What's more, Three Broomsticks doesn't participate in any of Universal's meal plans.

Down the street from the Hog's Head are restrooms. Roughly across the street from the pub, you'll find benches in the shade at the **Owlery,** where animatronic owls ruffle and hoot from the rafters. Next to the Owlery is the **Owl Post,** a functioning post office where any postcards you mail will be delivered with a Hogsmeade postmark. The Owl Post also sells stationery, toy owls, and the like. Here, once again, a nice selection of owls preens on the timbers overhead. You access the Owl Post in either of two ways: through an interior door following the wand-choosing demonstration at Ollivanders (see next page), or through **Dervish and Banges,** a magical-supplies shop that's interconnected with the Owl Post. You *can't* enter through the Owl Post front door, which serves exclusively as an exit. Because it's so difficult to get into the Owl Post, IOA sometimes stations a team member outside to stamp your postcards with the Wizarding World postmark.

Next to the Owl Post is the previously mentioned **Ollivanders,** a musty little shop stacked to the ceiling with boxes of magic wands. Here, following a script from the Potter books, you can pick out a wand or, in an interactive experience, let it pick you. This is one of the most truly imaginative elements of The Wizarding World: a Wandkeeper sizes you up and presents a wand, inviting you to try it out; your attempted spells produce unintended, unwanted, and highly amusing consequences. Ultimately, a wand chooses you, with all the attendant special effects. The experience is delightful, but the tiny shop can accommodate only about 24 guests at a time. Usually just one person in each group gets to be chosen by a wand, and then the whole group is dispatched to the Owl Post and Dervish and Banges to make purchases. Wands run upwards of $19, with most in the $28–$38 range. The wand experience is second in popularity only to Harry Potter and the Forbidden Journey—lines build quickly after opening, and there's little to no shade. If Ollivanders is a priority, experience it first thing in the morning or after 7:30 p.m. The average wait time during summer and other busy periods is 45–85 minutes between 9:30 a.m. and 7:30 p.m.

At the far end of the village, the massive **Hogwarts Castle** comes into view, set atop a rock face and towering over Hogsmeade and the entire Wizarding World. Follow the path through the castle's massive gates to the entrance of Harry Potter and the Forbidden Journey. Below the castle and to the right, at the base of the cliff, are the **Forbidden Forest, Hagrid's Hut,** and the **Flight of the Hippogriff** children's roller coaster. In the village, near the gate to Hogwarts Castle, is **Filch's Emporium of Confiscated Goods,** which offers all manner of Potter-themed gifts and apparel, including Quidditch clothing, magical-creature toys, film-inspired chess sets, and, of course, Death Eater masks (breath mints extra).

In keeping with the stores depicted in the Potter films, the shopping venues in The Wizarding World are small and intimate—so intimate, in fact, that they feel congested when they're serving only 12–20 shoppers. With so many avid Potter fans, lines for the shops develop most days by 9:30 or 10 a.m., creating a phenomenon we've never seen in our 27 years of covering theme parks: the lines for the shops are longer than the lines for Dragon Challenge and Flight of the Hippogriff—at 11 a.m. on a Sunday morning, there was a 30- to 40-minute wait to get into the shops, compared with a less-than-10-minute wait to ride the coasters. Filch's Emporium is the only shop in The Wizarding World that you can enter during high season without waiting in line; problem is, it doubles as the exit for Forbidden Journey. Because the stores are so jammed, IOA sells some Potter merchandise, including wands, through street vendors and in Port of Entry shops.

At the end of the village and to the left is the walkway to **Jurassic Park,** the themed area contiguous to The Wizarding World.

The Butterbeer Craze

Butterbeer is a nonalcoholic, cream-soda-like beverage served from a tap, with a butterscotch-y head that's added after the drink is poured. There's also a frozen version that's sort of like a slushie. Both were invented for The Wizarding World and had to meet J. K. Rowling's stringent specifications, which, among other things, required natural sugar (don't ask for Butterbeer Lite). We didn't expect to like it but were pleasantly surprised: it's tasty and refreshing, though some of us found it too sweet. Twelve ounces in a plastic cup goes for $2.50; the same pour in a Harry Potter souvenir cup sells for $9.50.

It seems everyone in the park is dead-set on trying Butterbeer. Unfortunately, it's sold only at Three Brooksticks, the Hog's Head pub, and a single street vendor—and that means, once again, long lines. Most folks buy from the street vendor, many waiting over 30 minutes or more to be served. One Butterbeer queue, totally out of sight from the street, forms on the patio behind the Hog's Head: to find the patio, go down the alley between the restrooms and the Dogweed & Death Cap Exotic Plants Shop. The wait here is usually only about 10 minutes, with most of your time spent in the quaint air-conditioned pub. Once served, you can relax with your drink at a table in the pub or out on the patio. In addition to Butterbeer, there's a pumpkin-juice drink that comes in a bottle with a pumpkin cap; it's sold by several street vendors and is much more easily obtained, though not as well received. At Rowling's behest, no brand-name soft drinks are available in The Wizarding World—if you want a Coke, you have to go to The Lost Continent or Jurassic Park.

Wizarding World Entertainment

Nearly every retail space sports some sort of animatronic or special-effects surprise. At Dervish and Banges, the fearsome *Monster Book of Monsters* rattles around and snarls at you as Nimbus 2000 brooms strain at their tethers overhead. At the Hog's Head pub, the titular porcine part, mounted behind the bar, similarly thrashes and growls. Street entertainment at the Forbidden Journey end of Hogsmeade includes the **Hogwarts Choir,** accompanied by frogs sitting on pillows, and the **Triwizard Spirit Rally,** featuring dancing and acrobatics. Performances run about 15 minutes—which, given the absolute lack of shade, is about all that anybody can stand.

Harry Potter and the Forbidden Journey ★★★★½

APPEAL BY AGE	PRESCHOOL –	GRADE SCHOOL ★★★★★	TEENS ★★★★★
YOUNG ADULTS ★★★★★		OVER 30 ★★★★★	SENIORS ★★★★★

What it is Motion-simulator dark ride. **Scope and scale** Super-headliner. **When to go** Immediately after park opening. **Special comments** Expect *long* waits in line; 48" minimum height requirement. **Authors' rating** Marvelous for muggles; not to be missed; ★★★★½. **Duration of ride** 4¼ minutes. **Probable waiting time per 100 people ahead of you** 4 minutes.

Motion Sickness

DESCRIPTION AND COMMENTS This ride provides the only opportunity to actually come in contact with the Harry Potter characters. Half the attraction is a series of preshows that set the stage for the main event, a dark ride. The shows are incorporated into the queue and serve as an integral element of the overall experience—not merely something to keep you occupied while you wait for the main event. You can get on the ride in only 10–20 minutes using the singles line, but everyone should go through the main queue at least once. Everything is so clever and well executed that you are thoroughly entertained while you wait.

To its credit, the Universal creative team has never been reluctant to embrace bleeding-edge technology. But it's equally true that incorporating a number of new scientific innovations into a single attraction means that lots can go wrong. The Wizarding World's main (and only original) attraction, Harry Potter and the Forbidden Journey is loaded to the gills with stuff that will astonish you provided the creative team can keep it all working at the same time. It looks like the science experiment that is the Forbidden Journey will be a while getting the bugs worked out. Fresh off the blocks, however, the attraction has been more dependable than most (including us) anticipated.

From Hogsmeade you reach the attraction through the imposing Winged Boar gates and progress along a winding path. Entering the castle on a lower level, you walk through a sort of dungeon festooned with various icons and prop replicas from the Potter flicks, including the Mirror of Erised from *Harry Potter and the Sorcerer's Stone.* You later emerge back outside and into the Hogwarts greenhouses. Cleverly conceived and executed, with some strategically placed mandrakes to amuse you, the greenhouses compose the larger part of the Forbidden Journey's queuing area. If you're among the first in the park and you hustle to the attraction, you'll move through this area pretty quickly. Otherwise . . . well, we hope you like plants. The greenhouses are not air-conditioned, but fans move the (hot) air around. Blessedly, there are water fountains in the greenhouses, but, alas, no restrooms—you'll need to take care of business before you get in line.

Having finally escaped horticulture purgatory, you reenter the castle, moving along its halls and passageways. One chamber you'll probably remember from the films is a multistory gallery of portraits, many of whose subjects come alive when they take a notion. You'll recognize the Fat Lady but will see for the first time the four founders of Hogwarts: Helga Hufflepuff holding her famous cup, Godric Gryffindor and Rowena Ravenclaw nearby, and the tall, moving portrait of Salazar Slytherin straight ahead. The founders argue about Quidditch and Dumbledore's controversial decision to host an open house at Hogwarts for muggles (garden-variety humans without special powers). Don't rush through the gallery—the effects are very cool, and the conversation among the portraits is essential to understanding the rest of the attraction.

Next up, after you've navigated some more passages, is Dumbledore's office, where the chief wizard appears on a balcony and welcomes you to Hogwarts. The headmaster's appearance is your introduction to Musion Eyeliner technology, a high-definition video-projection system that produces breathtakingly realistic, three-dimensional, life-size moving holograms. The technology uses a special foil that reflects images from HD video projectors producing holographic images of variable sizes and incredible clarity. After his welcoming remarks, Dumbledore dispatches you to the Defense Against the Dark Arts classroom to hear a presentation on the history of Hogwarts. The classroom is recognizable from the Potter films, although in this version there are no desks.

As you gather to await the lecturer, Harry, Ron Weasley, and Hermione Granger pop out from beneath an invisibility cloak. They suggest you ditch the lecture in favor of joining them for a proper tour of Hogwarts, including a Quidditch match. After some repartee among the characters and a couple of special-effects surprises, you're off to receive instructions presented by animated portraits, including an etiquette teacher. Later on, even the famed Sorting Hat gets into the act. All this leads to the Requirement Room, where hundreds of candles float overhead. This is where you board the ride.

After all the high-tech stuff in your queuing odyssey, you'll naturally expect to be wowed by your ride vehicle. Surely it's a Nimbus 3000 turbo-broom, a Phoenix, a Hippogriff, or at least the Weasleys' flying car. But no, what you'll ride on the most technologically advanced theme park attraction in America is . . . a *bench*? Yep, a bench. Not that there's anything wrong with a bench. We're just saying that maybe the well ran a little dry in the imagination department.

As benches go, though, it's a doozy, mounted on a Kuka robotic arm. When not engaged in Quidditch matches, a Kuka arm is a computer-controlled robotic arm similar to the kind used in heavy manufacturing. If you think about pictures you've seen of automotive assembly plants, Kuka arms are like those long metal appendages that come in to complete welds, move heavy stuff around, or fasten things. With the right programming the arms can handle just about any repetitive industrial tasks thrown at them (see **kuka-robotics.com** for more info).

Bear with us for a moment; you know how we *Unofficials* like technical stuff. When you put a Kuka arm on a ride platform, it provides six axes—six degrees of freedom, with synchronized motion that can be programmed to replicate all the sensations of flying, including broad swoops, steep dives, sharp turns, sudden stops, and fast acceleration. Here's where it gets really good: Up to now, when Kuka arms and similar robotic systems have been employed in theme park rides, the arm has been anchored to a stationary platform. In Forbidden Journey, the arm is mounted on a ride vehicle that moves you through a series of action scenes projected all around you. The movement of the arm is synchronized to create the motion that corresponds to what's happening in the film. When everything works right, it's mind-blowing.

When the ride was being designed, it was assumed that Kuka's robotic programming could easily produce the various movements called for in each scene. What nobody considered, however, is that the program was designed for maximum industrial efficiency. If, to correspond to the action in a given scene, the Kuka arm had to simulate 22 different motions, the software, not knowing a theme park ride from a diesel plant, would think, "OK, let's knock these 22 movements down to 13 and save half a minute." Because this would throw the timing of everything out of whack, Universal ended up having to create a program that would behave as it was told. For you, the practical implication of all this is an extraordinary attraction with more gremlins than inhabit the dark-arts lab. If all goes well, however, you'll soar over Hogwarts Castle, get tossed into a Quidditch match, spar with the Whomping Willow, narrowly evade an attacking dragon, and fight off Dementors.

Having experienced Forbidden Journey for ourselves, we have two primary bones to pick. First, Islands of Adventure team members rush you through the queue. To understand the story line and get the most out of the attraction, you really need to see and hear the entire presentation in each of the preshow rooms. This won't happen unless, contrary to the admonishments of the team members, you just park yourself and watch a full run-through of each preshow. Try to find a place to stop where you can let those behind you pass and where you're as far away from any team members as possible. If you're not creating a logjam, the team members will leave you alone as often as not.

Secondly, the dialogue in the preshows is delivered in English accents of varying degrees of intelligibility, and at a very brisk pace. Add an echo effect owing to the cavernous nature of the preshow rooms, and it can be quite difficult for Yanks to understand what's being said.

TOURING TIPS Harry Potter and the Forbidden Journey has quickly become the most popular attraction at Islands of Adventure, and arguably the most in-demand theme park attraction in America. The only way to experience the ride without a prohibitive wait is to be one of the first through the turnstiles in the morning or to visit after 7:30 or 8 in the evening.

If you see a complete iteration of each preshow in the queue and then experience the ride, you'll invest 25–35 minutes even if you don't have to wait. If you elect to skip the preshows (the Gryffindor Common Room, where you receive safety and loading directions, is mandatory) and use the singles line, you can get on in about 10–25 minutes at any time of day. At a time when the posted wait in the regular line was 2 hours, we rode and were out the door in 15 minutes using the singles line.

Many riders experience some degree of motion sickness on Forbidden Journey. It's possible that Universal will tone down the ride or introduce a tamer version, but don't count on it. The best defense against motion sickness is not to ride on an empty stomach. If you feel yourself becoming queasy, don't close your eyes. Instead, fix your gaze on your feet and try exclude as much from your peripheral vision as possible.

If you have a child who doesn't meet the minimum height requirement of 48 inches, a child-swapping option is provided at the loading area. If you ride with a child who meets the minimum height, be advised that the seats on each bench are compartmentalized—your child will not be able to see you or hold your hand.

The seats on Forbidden Journey are designed for certain body types. If you are a chesty woman or you have a waist of 38 inches or more, you may very possibly be prohibited from riding. There are sample seats at the beginning of the queue that you can try on for size, but they don't have a locking mechanism for the over-the-shoulder restraints. Just before the boarding area, however, is a bench with four fully functional seats. IOA team members select guests of all sizes to plop in the seats, but they're just being politically correct: they're really looking for large people or those who have a certain body shape. Team members handle the situation as delicately and politely as possible, but if they suspect you're not the right size, you'll be asked to sit down for a test. This is the time to suck it in to the maximum extent possible. To ride, the overhead restraint has to click three times. If you don't pass muster, you'll be escorted quietly to a boarding area to await new benches designed to accommodate larger people. Once again, it's body shape rather than weight (unless you're over 300 pounds) that is determinant. Most team members will let you try a second time if you don't achieve three clicks on the first go.

Forbidden Journey has a Universal Express–Express Plus line, but for the time being it's not being used, and the attraction is not on the Universal Express roster. We think this is a fair way to accord all guests equal access, but we don't know how long it will last. With The Wizarding World and especially Forbidden Journey soaking up so many guests in IOA, the waits for attractions in the other themed areas are minimal up to around 11 a.m.–noon (providing Forbidden Journey doesn't break down)—so there's no reason to pay the big extra bucks for Universal Express. The Wizarding World even sucks people out of Universal Studios next door, making Universal Express nonessential there as well.

Dragon Challenge (Universal Express) ★★★★½

APPEAL BY AGE	PRESCHOOL –	GRADE SCHOOL ★★★★	TEENS ★★★★
YOUNG ADULTS ★★★★		OVER 30 ★★★★	SENIORS ★★

What it is Roller coaster. **Scope and scale** Headliner. **When to go** Immediately after Harry Potter and the Forbidden Journey. **Special comments** 54" minimum height requirement. **Authors' rating** As good as the Hulk coaster; not to be missed; ★★★★½. **Duration of ride** 2½ minutes. **Loading speed** Moderate.

DESCRIPTION AND COMMENTS This high-tech coaster launches two trains, Chinese Fireball and Hungarian Horntail, at the same time on tracks that are closely intertwined. Each track is differently configured so that you get a different experience on each. A collision with the other train sometimes seems imminent—a catastrophe that seems all the more real because the coasters are suspended from above, so that you sit with your feet dangling. At times the two trains and their passengers are separated by a mere 12 inches.

Because this is an inverted coaster, your view of the action is limited unless you're sitting in the front row. This means most passengers miss seeing all these near-collisions. But don't worry; regardless of where you sit, there's plenty to keep you busy. Dragon Challenge is the highest coaster in the park and also claims the longest drop at 115 feet, plus five inversions. And as on the Hulk, it's a smooth ride all the way.

Coaster cadets argue about which seat on which train provides the wildest ride. We prefer the front row on either train, but some hype the front row of Chinese Fireball and the last row of Hungarian Horntail.

Dragon Challenge, formerly Dueling Dragons and part of The Lost Continent, was renamed and incorporated into The Wizarding World in 2010. The story line is that you are preparing to compete in the Triwizard Tournament from *Harry Potter and the Goblet of Fire*. As you wind through the long, long queue, you pass through tournament tents and dark passages that are supposed to be under the stadium. You'll see the Goblet of Fire on display and hear the distant roar of the crowd in the supposed stadium above you.

TOURING TIPS The queuing area for Dragon Challenge is the longest, most convoluted affair we've ever seen, winding endlessly through a maze of subterranean passages. After what feels like a comprehensive tour of Mammoth Cave, you finally emerge at the loading area, where you must choose between Chinese Fireball or Hungarian Horntail. Of course, at this critical juncture, you're as blind as a mole rat from being in the dark so long. Just follow the person in front of you until your eyes adjust.

Waits for Dragon Challenge, which is one of the best coasters in the country, rarely exceed 30 minutes all day long. Even so, to avoid backtracking, ride after experiencing Harry Potter and the Forbidden Journey. Warn anyone waiting for you that you might be a while. Even if there's no line to speak of, it takes 10–12 minutes just to navigate the passages and not much less time to exit the attraction after riding. If lines are short, however, park employees will open special doors marked REENTRY TO CHINESE FIREBALL or REENTRY TO HUNGARIAN HORNTAIL (depending on what coaster you just rode) that allow you to get right back to the head of the queue and ride again. Finally, if you don't have time to ride both coasters, the *Unofficial* crew unanimously prefers Hungarian Horntail.

Flight of the Hippogriff (Universal Express) ★★½

APPEAL BY AGE	PRESCHOOL ★★★★	GRADE SCHOOL ★★★★	TEENS ★★
YOUNG ADULTS ★★		OVER 30 ★	SENIORS ★

What it is Kiddie roller coaster. **Scope and scale** Minor attraction. **When to go** First 90 minutes the park is open. **Special comments** 36" minimum height requirement. **Authors' rating** A good beginner coaster; ★★½. **Duration of ride** 1 minute. **Loading speed** Slow.

DESCRIPTION AND COMMENTS Previously called the Flying Unicorn, this coaster underwent a name and theme change when it was incorporated into The Wizarding World. Below and to the right of Hogwarts Castle, next to Hagrid's Hut, the Hippogriff is short and sweet but not worth much of a wait. Fortunately, waits usually don't exceed 20 minutes, even in the non-Express line.

TOURING TIPS Have your kids ride soon after the park opens while older sibs enjoy Dragon Challenge. Even if you don't ride, it's worth a stroll to see Hogwarts Castle from the cliff bottom and to check out Hagrid's Hut, above the path for the regular line.

THE LOST CONTINENT

The Eighth Voyage of Sindbad Stunt Show (Universal Express) ★★

APPEAL BY AGE	PRESCHOOL ★★★	GRADE SCHOOL ★★★★	TEENS ★★★
YOUNG ADULTS ★★★		OVER 30 ★★★	SENIORS ★★★

What it is Theater stunt show. **Scope and scale** Major attraction. **When to go** Any time on the daily entertainment schedule. **Authors' rating** Vapid; ★★. **Duration of presentation** 17 minutes. **Probable waiting time** 15 minutes.

DESCRIPTION AND COMMENTS   A story about Sindbad the Sailor is the glue that (loosely) binds this stunt show featuring water explosions, 10-foot-tall circles of flame, and various other daunting eruptions and perturbations. The show reminds us of those action movies that substitute a mind-numbing succession of explosions, crashes, and special effects for plot. The production is so vacuous and redundant that it's hard to get into the action.

TOURING TIPS   See *The Eighth Voyage* after you've experienced the rides and the better-rated shows.

Poseidon's Fury (Universal Express)   ★★★★

| APPEAL BY AGE | PRESCHOOL ★★ | GRADE SCHOOL ★★★★ | TEENS ★★★★ |
| YOUNG ADULTS ★★★★ | | OVER 30 ★★★★ | SENIORS ★★★★ |

What it is High-tech theater attraction. **Scope and scale** Headliner. **When to go** After experiencing all the rides. **Special comments** Audience stands throughout. **Authors' rating** Not to be missed; ★★★★. **Duration of presentation** 17 minutes, including preshow. **Probable waiting time** 25 minutes.

DESCRIPTION AND COMMENTS   In the first incarnation of this story, the Greek gods Poseidon and Zeus duked it out, with Poseidon as the heavy. Poseidon fought with water, and Zeus fought with fire, though both sometimes resorted to laser beams and smoke machines. In the new version, the rehabilitated Poseidon now tussles with an evil wizardish guy, and everybody uses fire, water, lasers, and smoke machines. As you might have inferred, the new story is somewhat incoherent, but the special effects are still amazing, and the theming of the preshow area is quite imposing. The plot unfolds in installments as you pass through a couple of these areas and finally into the main theater. Though the production is a little slow and plodding at first, it wraps up with quite an impressive flourish. There's some great technology at work here. *Poseidon* is far and away the best of the Islands of Adventure theater attractions.

TOURING TIPS   If you're still wet from Dudley Do-Right, the Bilge-Rat Barges, and the Jurassic Park River Adventure, you might be tempted to cheer the evil wizard's flame jets in hopes of finally drying out. Our money, however, is on Poseidon. It's legal in Florida for theme parks to get you wet, but setting you on fire is frowned on.

Frequent explosions and noise may frighten younger children, so exercise caution with preschoolers. Shows run continuously if the technology isn't on the blink. We recommend catching *Poseidon* after experiencing your fill of the rides.

SEUSS LANDING

A 10-ACRE THEMED AREA BASED ON Dr. Seuss's famous children's books. As at the old Mickey's Toontown Fair in the Magic Kingdom, the buildings and attractions replicate a whimsical, brightly colored cartoon style with exaggerated features and rounded lines. Seuss Landing has four rides (described following) and an interactive play area, **If I Ran the Zoo,** populated by Seuss creatures.

Caro-Seuss-el (Universal Express) ★★★½

APPEAL BY AGE	PRESCHOOL ★★★★	GRADE SCHOOL ★★★★	TEENS –
YOUNG ADULTS –		OVER 30 –	SENIORS –

What it is Merry-go-round. **Scope and scale** Minor attraction. **When to go** Before 11 a.m. **Authors' rating** Wonderfully unique; ★★★½. **Duration of ride** 2 minutes. **Loading speed** Slow.

DESCRIPTION AND COMMENTS Totally outrageous, Caro-Seuss-el is a full-scale, 56-mount merry-go-round made up exclusively of Dr. Seuss characters.

TOURING TIPS Even if you're too old or you don't want to ride, this attraction is worth an inspection. Whatever your age, chances are good you'll see some old friends.

The Cat in the Hat (Universal Express) ★★★½

APPEAL BY AGE	PRESCHOOL ★★★★	GRADE SCHOOL ★★★★	TEENS ★★★
YOUNG ADULTS ★★★★		OVER 30 ★★★★	SENIORS ★★★★

What it is Indoor adventure ride. **Scope and scale** Major attraction. **When to go** Before 11:30 a.m. **Authors' rating** Seuss would be proud; ★★★½. **Duration of ride** 3½ minutes. **Loading speed** Moderate.

DESCRIPTION AND COMMENTS Guests ride on "couches" through 18 different sets inhabited by animatronic Seuss characters, including The Cat in the Hat, Thing 1, Thing 2, and the beleaguered goldfish who tries to maintain order in the midst of bedlam. Well done overall, with nothing that should frighten younger children.

TOURING TIPS This is fun for all ages. Try to ride early.

A father of three from Natick, Massachusetts, thinks we're off-base when we say that nothing should frighten younger children:

I think you need to revise the Cat in the Hat ride review by saying that it has quite the fright potential. My fairly advanced 3½-year-old was terrified on the ride. Besides all the things popping out at you, it whips you around very wildly. My wife took her on the ride, and she was screaming her head off. I did a switch-off and rode it just to see; it was pretty intense, and I nearly got whiplash! Nearly two years later, she still reminds me of the scary Cat in the Hat ride (it hasn't affected her love for the books, though!).

The High in the Sky Seuss Trolley Train Ride! ★★★½ (Universal Express)

APPEAL BY AGE	PRESCHOOL ★★★★	GRADE SCHOOL ★★★½	TEENS ★
YOUNG ADULTS ★★½		OVER 30 ★★½	SENIORS ★★★

What it is Elevated train. **Scope and scale** Major attraction. **When to go** Before 11:30 a.m. **Special comments** A relaxed look at the park; 34" minimum height requirement. **Authors' rating** ★★★½. **Duration of ride** 3½ minutes. **Loading speed** Molasses.

DESCRIPTION AND COMMENTS Trains putter along elevated tracks while a voice reads a Dr. Seuss story over the train's speakers. As each train makes its way through Seuss Landing, it passes a series of animatronic characters in scenes that are part of the story being told. Little tunnels and a few mild turns make this a charming ride.

There are two tracks at the station. As you face the platform, to your left is the Beech track, which is aquamarine; to your right is the Star track, which is purple. Each track offers a different story.

TOURING TIPS The line for this ride is much less charming than the attraction. The trains are small, fitting about 20 people, and the loading speed is glacial. Save High in the Sky for the end of the day or ride first thing in the morning.

One Fish, Two Fish, Red Fish, Blue Fish ★★★½ (Universal Express)

APPEAL BY AGE	PRESCHOOL ★★★★	GRADE SCHOOL ★★★★	TEENS ★★★
YOUNG ADULTS ★★★	OVER 30 ★★★		SENIORS ★★★

What it is Wet version of Dumbo the Flying Elephant. **Scope and scale** Minor attraction. **When to go** Before 10 a.m. **Authors' rating** Who says you can't teach an old ride new tricks?; ★★★½. **Duration of ride** 2 minutes. **Loading speed** Slow.

DESCRIPTION AND COMMENTS Imagine Dumbo with Seuss-style fish instead of elephants and you've got half the story. The other half of the story involves yet another opportunity to drown. Guests steer their fish up or down 15 feet in the air while traveling in circles. At the same time, they try to avoid streams of water projected from "squirt posts." A catchy song provides clues for avoiding the squirting.

Though the ride is ostensibly for children, the song and the challenge of steering your fish away from the water make this attraction fun for all ages.

TOURING TIPS We don't know what it is about this theme park and water, but you'll get wetter than at a full-immersion baptism.

UNIVERSAL'S ISLANDS *of* ADVENTURE TOURING PLAN

ROLLING THE DICE WITH HARRY POTTER

THE WIZARDING WORLD, and Harry Potter and the Forbidden Journey in particular, create some real challenges when trying to develop an optimum touring plan for IOA. Some of this will sort itself out over time, but for The Wizarding World's first couple of years:

- The 20-acre section of the park will be completely overrun by crowds.
- The science and innovation behind Forbidden Journey are remarkable, but the ride is subject to malfunctions both large and small.
- Because of Forbidden Journey's several preshows, it takes about 30–35 minutes to experience, even if you don't have to wait.

After Forbidden Journey works out the bugs, we'll probably recommend unequivocally that you experience it first thing. The first few years, however, you're really rolling the dice. If you try to enjoy Forbidden Journey first thing after the park opens, and if the ride operates as designed, you're golden. You'll be off to other must-see attractions before the park gets crowded. On the other hand, if the ride suffers technical difficulties, you may be stuck there a long while, during which time the crowds will have spread to other areas of IOA. By the time you exit the Forbidden Journey, there will be long lines for all of the park's other popular attractions. Even if everything goes perfectly, experiencing Forbidden Journey will consume more prime morning touring time than Dragon Challenge, the Incredible Hulk, and Spider-Man put together.

If, like many, you have The Wizarding World as your top priority, your best bet is to experience it early in the morning and take your chances with crowds in the other parts of the parks later on. If you're an IOA first-timer, or if The Wizarding World isn't such a hot button, skip Forbidden Journey and enjoy short waits at the park's other top attractions.

UNIVERSAL'S ISLANDS OF ADVENTURE ONE-DAY TOURING PLAN

BE AWARE THAT IN THIS PARK there are an inordinate number of attractions that will get you wet. If you want to experience them, come armed with ponchos, large plastic garbage bags, or some other protective covering. Failure to follow this prescription will make for a squishy, sodden day.

When it comes to dining, the best restaurant in Islands of Adventure is the exotic **Mythos** in The Lost Continent, serving pizza, pasta, burgers, sandwiches, and Asian specialties.

The IOA touring plan is for groups of all sizes and ages and includes thrill rides that may induce motion sickness or get you wet. If the plan calls for you to experience an attraction that doesn't interest you, simply skip that attraction and proceed to the next step. Be aware that the plan calls for some backtracking. If you have young children in your party, customize the plan to fit their needs and take advantage of switching off (the entire family waits in line together and then the adults take turns riding) at thrill rides.

1. Call ☎ 407-363-8000 the day before you visit for the official opening time.

2. Arrive 1 hour before opening, and pick up a map and entertainment schedule.

3. Line up at the turnstile. Ask any attendant whether any rides or shows are closed that day. Adjust the touring plan accordingly.

4. Hurry to Harry Potter and the Forbidden Journey as soon as you clear

the turnstiles and ride. Be warned that even without much waiting, you'll invest at least 35–40 minutes here.

5. Ride Dragon Challenge if the wait is 30 minutes or less. Otherwise, skip to Step 6.

6. At Marvel Super Hero Island, ride The Incredible Hulk Coaster.

7. Exit left and experience The Adventures of Spider-Man.

8. On exiting Spider-Man, backtrack right and ride Dr. Doom's Fearfall. Skip it if the wait exceeds 20 minutes.

9. Depart Super Hero Island and cross into Toon Lagoon. On your right, ride Popeye & Bluto's Bilge-Rat Barges.

10. Continue yor clockwise circuit of the park. Ride Dudley Do-Right's Ripsaw Falls.

11. Continue around the lagoon to Jurassic Park. Ride Jurassic Park River Adventure.

12. Pass through The Wizarding World to The Lost Continent. Experience *Poseidon's Fury*.

13. Continue clockwise to Seuss Landing and ride The Cat in the Hat.

14. Check the daily entertainment schedule for performances of *The Eighth Voyage of Sindbad Stunt Show* in The Lost Continent. See the show when convenient.

15. Return to The Wizarding World and explore Hogsmeade Village.

16. Revisit favorite rides and check out attractions you may have missed.

PART NINE

The *WATER PARKS* *and* WATER SPORTS

WET 'N WILD, AQUATICA, *and* ADVENTURE ISLAND *versus* DISNEY WATER PARKS

DISNEY'S WATER PARKS, and to a somewhat lesser extent SeaWorld Aquatica, are distinguished more by their genius for creating an integrated adventure environment than by their slides and individual attractions. At the Disney and SeaWorld water parks, both eye and body are deluged with the strange, exotic, humorous, and beautiful. Both Disney water parks are stunningly landscaped. Parking lots, street traffic, and so on are far removed from the swimming areas and out of sight. Also, each park has its own story to tell, a whimsical tale that forms the background for your swimming experience. Once you've passed through the turnstile, you're enveloped in a fantasy setting that excludes the outside world. This holds true for SeaWorld Aquatica as well, albeit on a more modest scale, and with an aquatic theme rather than a background story.

For many, however, the novelty of the theme is quickly forgotten once they hit the water, and the appreciation of being in an exotic setting gives way to enjoying specific attractions and activities. In other words, your focus narrows from the general atmosphere of the park to the next slide you want to ride. Once this occurs, the most important consideration becomes the quality and number of attractions and activities available and their accessibility relative to crowd conditions. Viewed from this perspective, the non-Disney water parks, especially Universal's Wet 'n Wild, give Disney more than a run for the money. Wet 'n Wild and SeaWorld Aquatica

unofficial **TIP**
Water parks are one area where the heightened thrills of the non-Disney water rides may outweigh the decor of the Disney water parks.

are located in the bustling International Drive tourist area, while Adventure Island is located in Tampa. On its own merits, Adventure Island isn't worth a special trip from the Orlando area. But it's a fine way to pass the morning if you've spent the night in Tampa after a visit to Busch Gardens. Plus, the tamer rides and lighter crowds than at the Orlando parks are a nice break for the younger members of your family.

A FLUME-TO-FLUME COMPARISON

THE FOLLOWING CHART PROVIDES a sense of what each water park offers, inside and outside Walt Disney World. In standard theme-park jargon, the water parks refer to their various features, including slides, as attractions. Some individual attractions consist of several slides. If each slide at a specific attraction is different, we count them separately. Runoff Rapids at Blizzard Beach, for example, offers three corkscrew slides, each somewhat different. Because most guests want to experience all three, we count each individually. At the Toboggan Racers attraction (also at Blizzard Beach), there are eight identical slides, side by side. There's no reason to ride all eight, so we count the whole attraction as one slide.

Do the numbers tell the story? In the case of Wet 'n Wild, they certainly do. If you can live without the Disney and SeaWorld parks' theme setting or story line, Wet 'n Wild offers more attractions and more variety than any of the other parks. Plus, throughout the summer, Wet 'n Wild is open until 11 p.m., offering live bands and dancing nightly. Even if you don't care about the bands or dancing, summer nights are more comfortable, lines for the slides are shorter, and you don't have to worry about sunburn.

Did we mention the giant toilet bowl? Wet 'n Wild has an attraction dubbed The Storm. The ride actually looks like a lot of fun, but in all honesty it strongly resembles a huge commode. Riders wash down a chute to gain speed, then circle around a huge bowl before dropping into a pool below. This must be how that goldfish you flushed in third grade felt.

Generally speaking, during the day, you'll find Adventure Island in Tampa the least crowded of the parks, followed by Wet 'n Wild. The Disney and SeaWorld parks quite often sell out by about 11 a.m. This is followed by long waits for all the slides.

Although not approaching Disney's or Sea World's standard for aesthetic appeal and landscaping, both Wet 'n Wild and Adventure Island are clean and attractive. In the surf and wave pool department, SeaWorld Aquatica's side-by-side wave and surf pools edge out Disney's Typhoon Lagoon. Whereas its surf pools produce 6-foot waves that you can actually body surf, the wave pools at the other parks offer only bobbing action. All of the parks have

unofficial **TIP**
Wet 'n Wild's later summer hours may mean shorter lines for the slides in the evenings.

SLIDES	BLIZZARD BEACH	TYPHOON LAGOON	WET 'N WILD	ADVENTURE ISLAND	AQUATICA
Vertical Speed Body Slide	1	1	2	1	–
Vertical Speed Tube Slide	1	–	–	–	–
Twisting Body Slide	–	–	1	4	–
Camel Hump Body Slide	1	–	1	–	–
Camel Hump Mat Slide	1	–	–	–	–
Camel Hump Tube Slide	–	–	1	2	–
Corkscrew Mat Slide	–	–	1	1	1
Corkscrew Body Slide	–	3	1	–	1
Open Corkscrew Tube Slide	3	4	2	3	–
Dark Corkscrew Tube Slide	1	–	2	1	2
FLUMES	**BLIZZARD BEACH**	**TYPHOON LAGOON**	**WET 'N WILD**	**ADVENTURE ISLAND**	**AQUATICA**
1- to 3-person Raft Flume	3	2	3	1	2
4- to 5-person Raft Flume	1	1	3	–	–
Total Slides	**12**	**11**	**17**	**13**	**6**
OTHER ATTRACTIONS					
Interactive Water Ride	1	1	1	1	–
Wave Pool	1	1	1	1	1
Surf Pool	–	1	1	1	1
Snorkeling Pool	–	1	–	–	–
Floating River	1	1	1	1	2
Isolated Children's Area	2	2	2	2	2
Other Attractions Total	**5**	**7**	**6**	**6**	**6**
Total Slides and Attractions	**17**	**18**	**23**	**19**	**12**

outstanding water-activity areas for younger children, and each park features at least one unique attraction: Wet 'n Wild has an interactive ride where you control your speed and movements with water blasts; Blizzard Beach has a 1,200-foot water bobsled; Adventure Island has a multistage slide broken up with pools of water; SeaWorld Aquatica's Loggerhead Lane float-stream passes through a fish grotto with hundreds of exotic fish to view. Typhoon Lagoon takes fish-watching a step further with its Shark Reef, where you can snorkel among live fish.

Prices for one-day admission are about the same at Blizzard Beach, Typhoon Lagoon, SeaWorld Aquatica, Wet 'n Wild, and Adventure Island. Discount coupons are often available in free local visitor magazines for Wet 'n Wild.

WET *'n* WILD

WET 'N WILD (on International Drive in Orlando, one block east of I-4 at exit 75A; ☎ 800-992-WILD (9453) or 407-351-1800; **wetnwild orlando.com**) is a non-Disney water-park option. Unlike Typhoon Lagoon and Blizzard Beach, in which scenic man-made mountains and integrated themes create a colorful atmosphere, Wet 'n Wild's only themes appear to be concrete, plastic, and water. Fortunately, the thrill, scope, and diversity of its rides make Wet 'n Wild an excellent alternative to the Disney swimming parks. Besides, contrary to what some Disney execs might believe, their water isn't any wetter.

Mears Transportation operates a shuttle to Wet 'n Wild that stops three times a day at Disney hotels. It's the same shuttle that commutes between Walt Disney World and Universal Orlando. Cost is $18 round-trip for guests age 3 and older. There is no transportation to Wet 'n Wild from Disney property. If you are staying in Walt Disney World, in Lake Buena Vista, or along US 192, you will need a car. If you're staying on International Drive, you can take the **International Drive trolley** (visit **iridetrolley.com** for schedules and fees). If you drive, there is a large Wet 'n Wild parking lot that charges $10 per day for cars and $12 for vans and RVs. Parking is ample; just be sure to hold the kids' hands when crossing the street.

> *un*official **TIP**
> Wet 'n Wild, though clean, is cluttered and not very appealing to the eye.

You can buy your Wet 'n Wild tickets at the main gate. Prices are $48 for adults and $42 for children, and weekday season passes are $50 (or $70 with parking), but call beforehand for special deals and discounts for those in the military, AAA members, Florida residents, and groups. For the same price as a single-day ticket, Wet 'n Wild offers a Length of Stay pass on its website that is good for 14 consecutive days. Ticket prices are similar to those of the Disney parks, but if you attend during the summer, the park is open late (hours vary, from 9 a.m. until 11 p.m. at the latest; call or visit the website for details), allowing visitors to hit the slides in the morning, go back to their hotels for lunch and a nap, and then return for a dip at night. Disney water parks typically close by 6 or 7 p.m.

When you get hungry, the main food pavilions are the centrally located **All You Can Eat BBQ, Wild Tiki Lounge, Bubba's BBQ, Manny's Pizza,** and **Surf Grill,** together offering such staples as burgers, pizza, and barbecued-pork sandwiches as well as more-nutritious (and non-traditional) items such as veggie burgers and tabbouleh. Wait times are long—Wild Tiki has flat-panel TVs to keep you occupied—and prices are high but not outrageous. For guests whose budgets and impatience thresholds are less flexible, feel free to bring in a cooler of lunch fixings (remember, glass containers and alcoholic beverages are prohibited, but you can purchase beer inside).

All the slides outside the **Kids' Park** have a 48-inch height requirement except for multipassenger slides, for which the minimum height is 36 inches if an adult accompanies the short rider; the only exceptions to this are the rides at the **WakeZone,** for which the height requirements are 51 inches (The Wild One) and 56 inches (KneeSki and Wake Skating).

BODY AND MAT SLIDES

SLIDES AT WET 'N WILD INCLUDE **Mach 5, Bomb Bay, Der Stuka,** and **The Storm.** The Mach 5 tower, located to the left of the park entrance, consists of three mat slides. The mats increase your speed and eliminate the chafing often experienced on body slides. To go even faster, try to get a newer mat with a smoother bottom. They are easily distinguishable: the new mats have white handles, while the old mats have blue ones.

unofficial **TIP**
Although ride attendants say that all three of the Mach 5 slides are equal, the center slide appears to be the zippiest route to the bottom.

Among the body slides (those without mats or rafts) are Bomb Bay and Der Stuka, twin speed flumes with pitches up to 79 degrees that descend from the top of a six-story tower. On Bomb Bay you stand on a pair of doors that open, dropping you into the chute. You have to work up the nerve to launch yourself on Der Stuka. The lack of a fully enclosed tube (such as the one on the Humunga Kowabunga speed slide at Typhoon Lagoon) adds the (perhaps justifiable) fear of falling off the 250-foot slides, but their ability to float your stomach somewhere near your teeth is a pretty unforgettable thrill.

The Storm body slide, located near Bomb Bay and Der Stuka, is a hybrid ride: half slide, half toilet bowl. The steep slide creates enough momentum to launch riders into a few laps around the bowl below before they begin slipping toward the hole in the center, eventually falling into a 6-foot-deep pool. The ride is exhilarating and disorienting; when the lifeguard at the ending pool begins hollering, just stumble toward his voice and give him a thumbs-up.

RAFT AND TUBE RIDES

THE HEADLINERS AT WET 'N WILD are the raft and tube rides, including **Brain Wash, Disco H2O, The Surge, Black Hole,** the **Bubba Tub, The Flyer,** and **The Blast.** Brain Wash is an extreme six-story tube ride with a 53-foot vertical drop into a 65-foot funnel; tubes hold two or four riders. Disco H2O holds up to four people in one raft, ushering them down a long tube into a 1970s-era nightclub complete with lights, music, and a disco ball. The basic design of the ride is similar to that of The Storm (a long tube into a bowl), only not as frantic and disorienting; the disco theme, coupled with the fluidity of the ride, makes it a main draw.

The Surge launches from the same tower as Disco H2O and uses the same four-person rafts. Riders spin down the open-air course, drifting high onto the walls on each banked corner. To reach the top of the walls, try to go with a full raft—as with all raft rides, the more riders squeezed in, the faster you'll all go. Directly across from The Surge's splashdown pool is the entrance for Black Hole. Bring a partner for this one; Black Hole requires two riders on each raft, and honestly, who wants to embark into endless murk without some company? As impressive as the ride seems from afar, the anxiety created by the gaping entrance is the most exciting part of the ride. Yes, it's dark—there is track lighting down the entire course—but besides the darkness, the ride lacks the dips and turns found on the other slides. If you're claustrophobic and scared of the dark, this isn't the ride for you; if tight spaces and inky blackness don't give you a rush, then this isn't the ride for you either.

The three gentler raft rides are The Flyer, The Blast, and the Bubba Tub. The first two launch from the same tower as the Mach 5, but their entrance is accessible through the Kids' Park. At the base of the entrance are one- and two-person rafts; these are only for The Blast, so don't carry them up to the tower to the Flyer entrance. The Flyer is a calmer, toboggan-style ride in which riders sit one behind the other; it's suitable for families with smaller children. The Blast is a themed ride, like Disco H20, and is the wettest you can get without swimming. The theme of The Blast appears to be a broken waterworks, complete with spinning dials and broken pipes, all painted in comic-book red and yellow. From mist to falling water to spraying pipes, this is the best way to cool off at Wet 'n Wild. The Bubba Tub, located across the park from The Flyer and The Blast, is a long, straight track with three hummocks to impede momentum, but with a full tube of four people, you hit the "tub" at a good clip.

OTHER ATTRACTIONS

THE CENTRAL FIXTURE AT WET 'N WILD, the **Wave Pool Surf Lagoon,** is on par with Blizzard Beach's. Unlike at Typhoon Lagoon, there's no surfing in this wave pool, but you can rent tubes at the main rental stand or go bobbing with your body. The wave-making machine takes long breaks every day, so when you walk by and see waves, be sure to wade in.

Another any-time-of-day option is the **Lazy River.** Unlike the Lazy River at Typhoon Lagoon, the Lazy River at Wet 'n Wild is misnamed: the circuit is short, the current fast. Don't even bother trying to walk upstream to catch a tube—it's better to swim down the river or wait patiently until one passes within reach.

Wet 'n Wild's 3,200-square-foot **Kids' Park** is a smaller-scale version of the adult menu. It's located to the left of the main gate; look for the oversize sand castle capped off with a big blue bucket. The bucket actually fills with water and tips over, soaking the people in front of the castle, while the castle has two slides that leave from its porticos and one small wet ramp for toddlers located on the castle's left side. There are three longer slides in back of the castle: two body slides and one tube slide. The kids' area also contains a mini–wave pool, a kid-sized climbing net, a junior river ride, and two very short zip lines. If keeping your towels in a rented locker is too much of a hassle, the kids' area is a good safe place to keep your towels.

WAKEZONE

THE MOST DISTINCTIVE OFFERING AT WET 'N WILD is the WakeZone, situated on a lake that's roughly the same size as the rest of the park and offering three different activities: wakeboarding, kneeboarding, and tubing. The lines can be considerable, especially since the attraction only runs from noon to dusk, May–September. Be sure to call before going to Wet 'n Wild to see if the area is open that day. To avoid lines, wander over to the WakeZone at least 20 minutes before noon.

At the boarding area, you can choose either a wakeboard or a kneeboard. Helmets and life jackets, provided free at the entrance, are required; there is also a height requirement of 56 inches. The ride is basically a cable with hanging towlines that, like a T-bar at a ski resort, pull riders along the half-mile loop. You board from a slightly submerged dock where you grab the towline as it passes overhead. Brace yourself— towlines have a tendency to jerk. Keep your arms rigid and the nose of the board up. There are no instructors, so watch the other riders and chat up the good ones for tips while you're in line. If you fall down while riding, get out of the cable's path and swim to shore. If you fall where there is no nearby dock, a Jet Ski will come and pick you up.

The name of the tubing ride is **The Wild One.** For an extra fee ($6 per person), a Jet Ski will pull you around the lake while you sit in an inner tube. The ride lasts five minutes, but it's worth the money if you've never been tubing before.

AQUATICA *by* SEAWORLD

ORLANDO'S FIRST NEW SWIMMING PARK to open in more than a decade, Aquatica is across International Drive from the back side of SeaWorld. From Kissimmee, Walt Disney World, and Lake Buena Vista, take I-4 east, exiting onto the Central Florida Parkway and then bearing left on International Drive. From Universal Studios, take I-4 west to FL 528 and from there exit onto International Drive. Admission costs about the same as at the Disney water parks and a couple of bucks less than Wet 'n Wild. If you don't want to wait in a queue to purchase tickets, buy them in advance at **aquaticabyseaworld .com** or use the credit-card ticket machines to the left of Aquatica's main entrance.

As at the other water parks, there are lockers, towels, wheelchairs, and strollers to rent, gift shops to browse, and places to eat. The three restaurants are **WaterStone Grill,** offering specialty sandwiches, fried fish, wraps, and salads; **Banana Beach Cookout,** an all-you-can eat venue dishing up burgers, hot dogs, and chicken; and **Mango Market,** a diminutive eatery serving pizza, wraps, and salads. WaterStone Grill and Mango Market serve beer.

Aquatica is comparable in size to the other water theme parks in the area. Attractively landscaped with palms, ferns, and tropical flowers, it's far less themed than Disney's Typhoon Lagoon and Blizzard Beach but much greener and more aesthetically appealing than Wet 'n Wild. Promotional material suggests that Aquatica is unique in its combination of SeaWorld's signature marine-animal exhibits with the expected water-park assortment of wave pools, slides, and creek floats. Marine exhibits, however, stop and end with a float-through tank of tropical fish and a pool of black-and-white Commerson's dolphins. Ads for the park show guests viewing the dolphins as they descend through a clear tube at the end of the **Dolphin Plunge** body slide. The reality is that you are flushed through the clear tube so fast, with so much water splashing around your face, that it's pretty much impossible to see anything. At Aquatica, the best option by far is to view the dolphins from the walkway surrounding the exhibit or from the subsurface viewing windows.

RAFT AND TUBE RIDES

REGARDING THE DOLPHIN PLUNGE SLIDE, it's a corkscrewing romp through a totally dark tube until you blast through the clear tube at the end. SeaWorld's promotion hype, coupled with the location of the Plunge just inside the park entrance and the slide's low carrying capacity (approximately 280 persons per hour), ensures that the slide stays mobbed all day. To experience the slide without a long wait, be on hand at park opening and ride first thing.

Other slides include **Tassie's Twisters,** in which an enclosed tube slide spits you into an open bowl where you careen around the bowl's edge much in the manner of the ball in a roulette wheel. Located close to Dolphin Plunge, Tassie's Twisters should be your second early-morning stop. Next, head over to **Walhalla Wave** and **HooRoo Run,** both on the park's far right side. Both slides use circular rafts that can accommodate up to three people. Walhalla Wave splashes down an enclosed twisting tube, while HooRoo Run is an open-air run down a steep, straight, undulating slide. The same entrance serves both slides. Line up for Walhalla (vastly more popular) on the right, for HooRoo on the left. Make Walhalla your third slide of the day, followed by HooRoo.

Then pass along the right side of the children's adventure area, **Walkabout Waters,** to **Taumata Racer,** the park's highest-capacity slide with eight enclosed corkscrewing tubes.

The remaining slides are **Whanau Way** and **Omaka Rocka,** all the way across the park to the left of the entrance. Sporting one corkscrew and a few twists, Whanau Way employs tubes that can carry one or two people. Because it's hard to see from the park entrance, Whanau Way doesn't attract long lines until midmorning.

Just next door is Aquatica's newest slide, the twin tubes of Omaka Rocka. Riders haul the single-person rafts up the stairs and select either the purple or aqua tube, then whoosh on down through one 360-degree turn and lots of others during a 50-second ride.

The side-by-side tubes mirror each other, with each including open, or half-pipe, sections and passing through curtains of water during the plunge. Including the hike to the top, figure on spending 3 minutes for each climb and descent here.

Taken as a whole, the slides at Aquatica are not nearly as interesting, thrilling, or imaginative as those of its competitors, and aside from whisking you through a dolphin tank, they don't break any new ground. Also, all the slides except HooRoo Run and Omaka Rocka have you launching yourself down a black hole, making every ride seem like the one before it. Dark slides are an essential part of every water-park lineup, but to have all slides dark save two makes for a very homogenized experience.

OTHER ATTRACTIONS

IN ADDITION TO THE SLIDES, Aquatica offers side-by-side wave pools, **Cutback Cove** and **Big Surf Shores.** This arrangement allows one cove to serve up body-surfing waves while the other puts out gently bobbing floating waves. A spacious beach arrayed around the coves is the park's primary sunning venue. Shady spots, courtesy of beach umbrellas, ring the perimeter of the area for the sun-sensitive.

Loggerhead Lane and **Roa's Rapids** are the two floating streams. The former is a slow and gentle tube journey that circumnavigates the Tassie's Twisters slide. Its claim to fame is a section of the float where a Plexiglas tunnel passes through the Fish Grotto, a tank populated by hundreds of exotic tropical fish. Unique to Aquatica, Roa's Rapids is a much longer course with a very swift current. (The other water parks have floating creeks, but they're leisurely affairs where you can fall asleep in your tube.) Buoyancy vests are available, but most adults float or swim the stream. The name notwithstanding, there are no rapids, but the flow is constricted from time to time, considerably increasing the already fast speed of the current. There's only one place to get in and out, so if you miss the takeout, you're in for another lap.

When it comes to children's water attractions, Aquatica more than equals the other area parks. In the back of the park, to the left of the wave pools, is **Kata's Kookaburra Cove,** featuring a wading pool and slides for the preschool crowd. But the real pièce de résistance is Walkabout Waters. If you have children under age 10, this alone may be worth the price of admission. Located in a calf-deep 15,000-square-foot pool, it's an immense three-story interactive playground set with slides, stairs, rope bridges, landings, and more. Water sprays, spritzes, pulsates, and plops at you from every conceivable angle. Randomly placed plastic squirting devices allow kids to take aim at unsuspecting adults, but the kids disperse quickly when either of two huge buckets dumps hundreds of gallons of water down on the entire structure. It's impossible not to get wet. It's also impossible not to have fun.

ADVENTURE ISLAND

ADMISSION PRICES

A SINGLE-DAY ADMISSION TO ADVENTURE ISLAND is $42 plus tax for adults, $38 plus tax for children age 3 and older, free for children under age 3. A one-year passport to Adventure Island is $99.95 for adults; a two-year passport is $149.95 for adults. Child and senior rates are $8 less. Adventure Island also offers combination passports with up to three other parks—neighboring Busch Gardens, SeaWorld, and Aquatica—for one and two years, ranging $149.95–$239.95 for one year, $224.95–$359.95 for two years. Again, child and senior rates are $8 less.

ARRIVING

ADVENTURE ISLAND HAS DIFFERENT opening and closing times depending on the day of your visit. It may open as early as 9 a.m. and close as late as 9 p.m., with it longest days being on summer weekends. The park is closed November–February, and open only on select days and weekends during March and October. Call ahead for park hours the day of your visit. You should arrive at the park at least 30 minutes before it opens, as the parking lot fills quickly, and during peak season it reaches capacity before noon. By arriving early, you'll be able to park directly in front of the main entrance and should be able to both purchase tickets and visit all of the attractions before any crowds begin to form.

Besides affording quick access to the ticket booth, parking close to the entrance is also helpful if you bring a picnic. Large coolers are permitted in the park, but glass containers, alcoholic beverages, and knives are prohibited. Although the theming at Adventure Island is light, there are some wonderful shaded picnic areas. All of the picnic areas are to the left of the park entrance. We recommend the picnic tables under the live oaks between the Everglides and the Riptide. Quieter picnic spots, also in the shade, can be found behind the Riptide, and a gazebo—first come, first served—is located near the run-out pool for the Caribbean Corkscrew.

To purchase food within the park, stop by the **Surfside Cafe** at the park's entrance, or **Mango Joe's** in the rear of the park near the Volleyball Spike Zone. Surfside Cafe offers traditional grill food and pizza, but healthy choices such as a turkey wrap are available. Unfortunately, seating here is all outside without any shade. Mango Joe's has a more diverse menu, including burger platters, PB&Js, and chicken fajitas. The park also offers an All-Day Dining Deal, providing an entrée, side item or dessert, and a drink, for $25 for adults, $15 for kids. The deal is honored at both the Surfside Cafe and Mango Joe's and can be used repeatedly on that day.

When you want to buy food, you may find your money is soaked. Adventure Island's solution to wet money is a scannable armband. Using a credit card or cash, you may preload an armband with the amount of money you would like to spend. When purchasing food or merchandise, swipe your armband and the money is deducted from your account. The program, available at Guest Services, is free, and any leftover money on the armband is fully refunded. The armband, cash, or credit card can be used at any of the snack bars and at the gift shop where you can purchase sunscreen, swim equipment, or any other forgotten items (for a severe markup).

If you want to store any gear that you have purchased or brought, small lockers are available for $8 each, $3 of which is refunded to you on the return of your key, but only as a gift certificate to the gift shop. The locker keys come with a safety pin to clip to your clothing, and there is no fee for lost keys. Be aware, if you receive a key numbered between 1 and 650, your locker will be on an elevated wooden platform above a small lake. The slats in the platform are far apart, so be very careful about dropping anything as you open and close your locker; there's no way to get it back without persuading an employee to let you go swimming.

Although you may be able to coax an employee to let you into restricted areas, there is no finagling your way onto the rides if you don't meet the height requirements.

For all of the major body slides or raft rides, you must be at least 42 inches tall, although a few require that you be at least 48 inches tall to ride. There are slides and other attractions that have no height requirement. If we do not mention a height requirement for an attraction, you may assume that the height requirement is 42 inches.

GETTING THERE

TO GET TO ADVENTURE ISLAND, follow the directions to Busch Gardens in Tampa in the Busch Gardens chapter. Once you have arrived on East Busch Boulevard, continue to Busch Gardens. Turn left onto McKinley Drive, the first road past Busch Gardens, and you will find Adventure Island on your right. The park is set back from the road, and there is ample parking, which costs $12 for both cars and campers.

CONTACTING ADVENTURE ISLAND

FOR MORE INFORMATION, contact Adventure Island at ☎ 888-800-5447 or 813-987-5600, or visit **adventureisland.com.**

RAFT RIDES

ADVENTURE ISLAND HOSTS FIVE RAFT RIDES, and in clockwise order from the entrance, they are **The Everglides, Calypso Coaster,**

Aruba Tuba, Key West Rapids, and the **Wahoo Run.** All of the raft rides are tame, but the Wahoo Run is as good a ride as any found at Wet 'n Wild.

The Everglides is the first ride you come to when you take a left at the entrance. At the bottom of the run-out pool, pick up a yellow sled. The sleds are rather heavy, but even children should have no problem carrying them up to the top of the 72-foot tower. To get down from the top, you can choose either of the two identical slides. Once you're settled in your sled, signal to the lifeguard that you are ready and then hold onto the side handles. A hydraulic ram lifts the back of your sled and pitches you forward down the slide. Although the drop is exhilarating, skipping across a 60-foot run-out pool is the high point of the ride. You can steer your sled by lightly pulling on the handles and leaning in the direction you want to go.

Across from the Everglides is the tower for the Aruba Tuba and the Calypso Coaster. Each ride requires different rafts and tubes, so check to make sure you have the transportation you want before you schlep it to the top of the tower (if you get confused as to which tube goes on which slide, pick up your tube from the run-out pool at the base of the slide that you want to ride). The Aruba Tuba is green and requires either a single-person tube or a two-person raft. The slide has both open and enclosed portions, and as you spin around backward, the pitch-dark patches will take you by surprise. The Aruba Tuba's curves are both plentiful and evenly spaced, creating a more docile and rhythmic run than Calypso Coaster's. The Calypso Coaster tube is white, and you may use either single-person blue tubes or double-person rafts. The slide is faster than the Aruba Tuba and sends you high onto the walls. There are no steep pitches common on other raft rides, just a steady side-to-side motion.

The Adventure Island ride with the greatest lack of pitch is the Key West Rapids, located in the back, left-hand corner of the park. You may ride in single-person tubes or in two-person rafts, but the combined weight of the raft cannot exceed 900 pounds—according to the sign at the base of the ride. Children under 42 inches tall may ride if they wear a life vest, available at stations around the park. From the top of the tower, you can see into Busch Gardens and down toward the Greater Tampa area. Although the height exceeds that of almost all of the other attractions (except for the Wahoo Run), the trip down Key West Rapids, interrupted with three small pools, is equivalent to a green trail on a ski mountain. The pools in the middle of the slide are unique, but there appears to have been a mild miscalculation in the strength of the pools' water jets that are supposed to push you across each pool to the next portion of the slide. Instead of being pushed via jets, you get tugged from one portion to the next by a lifeguard waiting in each pool. Although the ride down is meandering and slow, the final drop is steep, waking you up just in time to make your way to the next attraction.

In the opposite corner of the park from Key West Rapids is Wahoo Run, tucked away behind the Runaway Rapids. Our favorite ride in the park, Wahoo Run seats up to five people with a combined weight of 800 pounds. Children under 42 inches tall may ride as long as they wear a life vest. There is no lap riding, so little guys must be able to sit up on their own. After everyone is on board, the raft is sent spinning as it descends through both open and enclosed sections of slide. Unlike other enclosed slides, Wahoo Run has a wide enough diameter on its enclosed sections to keep claustrophobia at bay. Small waterfalls splash down on you as you enter and exit each of the enclosed sections. Even though these portions are pitch-black, there are no steep drops, so breathe easy. The ride is fast enough to keep thrill junkies entertained, but smooth enough for the entire family to enjoy.

BODY AND MAT SLIDES

THE BODY AND MAT SLIDES AT ADVENTURE ISLAND are, for the most part, tamer than those at Wet 'n Wild. The calmer rides are on par with Disney's Typhoon Lagoon, although the slides are generally shorter than Disney's. These calmer, shorter slides allow younger guests moderate thrills without forcing them to ride through a whitewash of water that may frighten them. There are five attractions at Adventure Island that contain body or mat slides, and only two of them are moderately frantic. The five attractions are, in clockwise order beginning at the park's entrance, the **Gulf Scream,** the **Riptide,** the **Caribbean Corkscrew,** the **Water Moccasin,** and the **Runaway Rapids.**

The Gulf Scream is across from the Everglides and is one of the two body-slide attractions built for older kids. Riders must be 48 inches tall to take the plunge from the top of the 210-foot tower. The slide is a straight descent, allowing riders to gain speeds of up to 25 miles per hour before dumping them into the run-out pool. Even though it is a moderately thrilling straight slide, we can't count it as a speed flume because there is no major drop at the beginning, like that found on the Der Stuka slide at Wet 'n Wild. Still, the ride is the fastest your body will go at Adventure Island without the aid of a tube, and it should meet or exceed your expectations.

The only mat slide in the park, Riptide is not as fast or entertaining as Wet 'n Wild's Mach 5 mat slide, in part because all the mats at Riptide have corrugated bottoms, making them slower. The Riptide slide is also shorter than the Mach 5, and although we would usually just write this off as a ride for younger kids, there is a 48-inch height requirement to ride. The attraction consists of two pink and two blue enclosed tubes that descend from the 55-foot tower. Four riders begin at the same time and race one another to the bottom. To get the most out of these mats, keep your feet off the slide, and move your body weight as far forward as comfortable while keeping your center of gravity pressed low. Take the turns high and stay in the center of the slide for the straightaways. Other than that, the slides nearest the lifeguard stand toward the inside are a bit shorter than the outer slides.

Another enclosed slide is the Caribbean Corkscrew body slide. Eerily similar to the Blue Niagara slide at Wet 'n Wild, these two intertwined cylinders are twisted together like Twizzler candy and are just as likely to cause tooth loss. The ride is not as violent as the Blue Niagara, but you will still be unceremoniously ground and mashed about in the dark until you are finally spat out into the run-out pool.

A more amenable attraction is the Water Moccasin, located near the Key West Rapids. The Water Moccasin consists of three slides. The slides are set up like a mouth harp, with two slides curving around to each side of the pool and one flume dropping into the center. All of the slides are short, a benefit since the seams between each section of tubing have mild ridges that may sting your back as you pass over them. The truncated flume has the fewest seams and is also the fastest. There are no height requirements for the Water Moccasin.

If you enjoy mellow, shorter slides, five such slides are located in the Runaway Rapids, located in the rock formation to the right of the park's entrance. None of these slides has a height requirement. The rocks, which each slide weaves through, make up the best theming in the park. As you climb up the path through the rocks, it diverges in two directions. The path to the left takes you to the kiddie slide, numbered and named #1-Corkscrew Canal and #2-Little Squirt. The Corkscrew Canal wraps around a central post, while the Little Squirt takes you straight down. Children may wear life vests if they sit in the laps of adults. The path to the right winds through a crag in the rocks that contains a stream and a bench, and then rises up to the slides, numbered and named #3–Corkscrew Falls, #4–River of No Returns, and #5–Barracuda Run. Although all three slides are very similar, the ride is anything but. Corkscrew Falls is the fastest, River of No Returns is the rowdiest with plenty of sharp turns, and Barracuda Run is the most scenic, with bamboo and palm leaves overhead. Although there is no height requirement, there is no lap riding or life vests allowed on these three slides.

OTHER ATTRACTIONS

ADVENTURE ISLAND HAS A FEW OTHER ATTRACTIONS that merit note. They are, again in clockwise order, the **Ramblin' Bayou, Splash Attack, Fabian's Funport,** the **Endless Surf Wavepool,** and the **Paradise Lagoon.** Ramblin' Bayou is a stream that encircles the left side of the park. Much larger than Wet 'n Wild's Lazy River, Ramblin' Bayou is more akin to the stream at Typhoon Lagoon. Although the theming isn't Disney-grade, palm trees and flower beds line the Ramblin' Bayou, giving you something to look at as you float around on your inner tube. The stream splits at one point; the left-hand channel takes you back around immediately toward the Riptide, while going right extends your ride, taking you through a greenhouse coated in Spanish moss. Be advised that there are sprinklers in the greenhouse and the water is noticeably cooler than that of the stream. There are no height requirements for Ramblin' Bayou, but children under 42 inches tall must wear a life vest. There are no lines here, and when the other attractions are crowded, wade into the stream, grab a tube, and wait till the crowds thin out for lunch.

Ramblin' Bayou will take you next to Splash Attack, a wet jungle gym. Splash Attack has no water underneath, but plenty above. Perched atop the four slides, cargo nets, water cannons, treehouse, and other contraptions is a 1,000-gallon bucket that dumps water onto its victims underneath every 7 minutes. Parents who want to watch their kids will be able to see them from a dry vantage point, but very little shade is available, so it's best to bring an umbrella or a bottle of sunscreen.

Fabian's Funport is another wet jungle gym located between the Spike Zone and the Endless Surf Wavepool. Fabian's Funport caters to a 50-inch-tall-and-under crowd, and although its play area is not as large as Wet 'n Wild's kids' zone, Fabian's miniature wave pool, water mushrooms, wet tunnels, and mini-aqueducts serve their purpose of keeping the little ones cool. The maximum water depth is 12 inches and swim diapers are required.

Behind Fabian's Funport and Mango Joe's cafe is the **Spike Zone Volleyball Court.** The area does not see much activity unless a tournament is under way, but volleyballs are available at Mango Joe's for a refundable deposit. Sunbathers who want to savor the illusion of being at the beach should head here to lie out on the secluded sands.

For those interested in regular bathing, the Endless Surf Wavepool is the place to head. Located in the center of the park, it's impossible to miss. The wave pool is about the same size as Wet 'n Wild's wave pool, but at the head of the pool, replacing the big Wet 'n Wild sign, is a countdown clock that clicks off the time until the waves begin again. Unlike other wave pools, the Endless Surf Wavepool makes choppy waves only up to 5 feet high.

Paradise Lagoon is another large pool, sans the waves. Although swimming about is fun, the draw here is the three "cliff"-jumping platforms and two small slides, located at the back of the lagoon. Jumpers wait until a lifeguard sets the streetlight signal to green, and then jump the 10 feet—feet first only—into the pool. There are two staging areas, and facing the water from above, the left-hand area contains both slides and one jumping platform. (Be sure to hold your nose when you go through the slides, or you'll come up spitting water.) The right-hand area contains no slides but two cliff-jumping platforms. Although the 10-foot jump into the water is the same from both left and right, many jumpers will wait in line on the left for the platform next to the slides, while the other two platforms go unused. Skip the line and go to the right-hand area, wait for the green light, and jump in.

WATER SPORTS

BUENA VISTA WATERSPORTS

Getting There

FROM DISNEY Take World Center Parkway to FL 535 (also called Kissimmee Vineland Road) and turn left. Just before you cross under I-4, you will see a small sign on your right for Buena Vista WaterSports. If you miss the sign, do not pass under I-4. Instead, take a right onto Vineland Avenue and pull into the parking lot. The parking lot is connected to Lake Bryan Drive. Buena Vista WaterSports is at 13245 Lake Bryan Drive, Orlando.

FROM ORLANDO Take I-4 to Exit 68 and go south on FL 535. You should be able to see the sign for Buena Vista WaterSports on your left almost immediately after you start south.

Admission Prices

Buena Vista WaterSports rents out Seadoo GTI Jet Skis that fit two to three people. The fee for a **Jet Ski** is $98 per hour. To drive, you need to be at least 17 years of age.

Buena Vista will also tow you behind their competition ski boats on a **tube,** a **kneeboard, water skis,** or a **wakeboard.** The cost, including equipment rental, is $50 for 15 minutes, $85 for 30 minutes, or $145 for a full hour. Although it's not stated, a "tips for tips" gratuity policy for personal instruction is the standard for most vacation activities.

Arriving

Located in an old lakeside mansion, Buena Vista WaterSports is only a 10-minute drive from Walt Disney World. Buena Vista is open year-round, weather permitting, 10 a.m.–5 p.m. daily.

Once you've gotten off of the stress-filled freeways and byways of Greater Orlando, you'll welcome the laid-back surfer atmosphere lakeside. The wicker chairs on the antebellum mansion's large wooden deck face the lake, and although we could tide ourselves over with a game of volleyball and a cooler filled with snacks, the action's on the water, so don't forget to bring a swimsuit, sunscreen, and a towel.

Be sure to call ahead before you come to Buena Vista WaterSports. The lakefront site holds many competitions throughout the summer. When these are under way, you will not be able to rent certain vehicles or obtain lessons. The entire facility is also rented out for occasional parties, which will preclude you from using the site.

Contacting Buena Vista WaterSports

For information, call ☎ 407-239-6939 or **bvwatersports.com.**

ORLANDO WATERSPORTS COMPLEX

Admission Prices

All prices are listed without tax or equipment rental.

1 Hour **$22** for adults and **$20** for children age 16 and under

2 Hours **$28** for adults and **$25** for children age 16 and under

4 Hours **$34** for adults and **$30** for children age 16 and under

All-day Pass **$40** for adults and **$36** for children age 16 and under

Weekly Pass **$185.50**

Basic Equipment Rental $3 for a basic wakeboard, $2 for a life vest, $4 for both; $5 for 1-hour helmet or wet-suit rental, $10 for 2 hours, $15 for one day. Other types of water transportation (skis, kneeboards, and the like) are available at the Pro Shop for $10–$30.

Lessons

Cable Lessons Children age 10 and under must take a lesson before being allowed to use the cable; 45-minute cable lessons are $65. Children age 10 and under receive an additional 2-hour pass with the lesson.

Boat Lessons 30 minutes, $50; 1 hour, $95.

All-you-can-ride Pass includes three sets with the boat and an all-day cable pass: $185.

Getting There

Getting to the Orlando Watersports Complex can be rather difficult, although it is visible off of the Beachline Expressway (also called the Beachline Toll Road or FL 528). From I-4, take Exit 72 east. Take the Beachline east from Orlando toward Kennedy Space Center to Exit 4. (You will have to bring $2.50 for round-trip tolls.) Exit onto Orange Blossom Trail/FL 441/Consulate Drive. Follow the signs to Orange Blossom Trail/441, then take a left on South Orange Blossom Trail. After a half mile, turn right onto Landstreet Road and follow it for 2 miles to the large yellow sign for the Orlando Watersports Complex at 8615 Florida Rock Road. Follow the road, cross the railroad tracks, and stick to the right. Within a few hundred yards you will be at the blue gates of the complex.

Arriving

Orlando Watersports is open Monday–Friday, 11 a.m.–sunset, and Saturday–Sunday, 10 a.m.–sunset, May–September. October–February, it is open daily, 11 a.m.–sunset.

The 50-acre complex features **two tow-cable courses for wakeboarding, water-skiing, kneeboarding,** and **wake-skating** (similar to wakeboarding except that your feet are not attached to the board). The novice park is larger and contains one small jump that you can ride over if you choose, but only if you wear a helmet. The advanced park is smaller and features large ramps, tabletops, and rails to slide on. The advanced park requires a helmet. In order to ride in the advanced park, you must first show your competence by completing at least one lap in the novice park.

The tow-cable system is moderately complex, so here is how it works. A single, thick elevated cable, like those found on ski resort chairlifts, moves around the perimeter of the pond at a constant speed. Permanently attached to the thick cable are a series of evenly spaced cable carriers (for explanation purposes, envision the cable carriers as large hooks). The last components of the system are the thin cables that dangle from the cable carriers. At the dangling end of the thin cables is the handle that the riders hold.

The departure area is a long dock that slopes down to the water. Riders wait their turn in a queue. When their turn is approaching, riders put on their boards and stand in ankle-deep water. Riders then take hold of the handle to a thin cable and stand by for the next cable carrier. As the cable carrier passes overhead, it unhooks the thin cable used by the previous rider and then hooks into the thin cable held by the awaiting rider. Riders, if they hold on while being jerked forward, are now off the dock and skimming around the pond.

The novice pond has nine cable carriers and the advanced pond has four; this means that only nine people can be on the novice pond at one time and only four on the advanced pond at one time. When the park is crowded, each rider is allowed one lap around the pond before he or she has to let go of the handle. To avoid crowds, arrive when the park opens. Within 2 hours after opening, the lines can become excessive. During the off-season or on slow days, riders are allowed as many as five laps around the pond before they have to let go. When your turn is up, or if you fall, let go of the handle and swim out of the way of other riders. Detach your board and finish swimming to the shoreline, then walk back around to the queue for another go.

Riders under the age of 18 need a release form signed by their parent or guardian for any activity at the Orlando Watersports Complex. Forms can be signed on-site or can be faxed to ☎ 407-816-9070.

Before you get in the water, you can store your gear in lockers on land. Lockers cost $3, but require an additional $5 deposit that is repaid when you return the key. There are also adequate changing facilities on-site (bring your towel, sunscreen, and swimsuit), and food is available at the concession stand. Among other items, a cheeseburger is $4, a slice of cheese pizza is $2.75, and bottled sodas are $1.75.

Contacting Orlando Watersports Complex

For more information about site availability, contact Orlando Watersports Complex at ☎ 407-251-3100 or **orlandowatersports. com.**

PART TEN

MINIATURE GOLF

ORLANDO WOULDN'T BE A VACATION TOWN without miniature golf. Almost as abundant as fast-food chains, miniature-golf courses dot the landscape on US 192, International Drive, FL 535, and inside Walt Disney World. Because courses have different themes, quality of play, costs, and such, the golf course profiles that follow offer comparisons as well as short reviews focusing on what makes each course unique, plus course location and contact information.

Most of the miniature golf in the Greater Orlando area features long greens with few obstacles. You won't find ball-eating clowns or obnoxious windmills on any of the courses in town—the only places offering this ilk of in-course obstacles are the Disney courses. What you will find are 18 holes on clean grounds, trick shots, lots of cascading water, and a myriad of different themes.

The rules for miniature golf do differ from course to course, but the basics are fairly standard. A group consists of a maximum of four to five players. To tee off, all players in a group hit their shot. The player whose shot is farthest from the cup shoots first, then the next player, and so on. The maximum amount of strokes per hole is six. When you hit the ball out of bounds or into a water trap, retrieve the ball and place it back on the course as close to the trap as possible; you will incur a one-stroke penalty. When you lose your ball in the water and you can't recover it, you can get another ball from the main booth, but you will incur a two-stroke penalty. There is no running at any of the courses, and all of the establishments are very wary about injury. By purchasing a ticket, you waive your right to sue if you fall or stumble, or get hit with a club or a ball. If you swing the putter back too far—as if making a slap shot in hockey—you will be asked to leave. The odds of injury are much greater crossing International Drive, so don't let that rule dissuade you from one of the best family games around.

Bonanza Golf   ★★½
7761 W US 192 (Irlo Bronson Memorial Highway), Kissimmee;
☎ **407-396-7536**

Hours Daily, 9 a.m.–midnight. **Cost** $9.95 per person; children age 3 and under are free.

DESCRIPTION AND COMMENTS At the far end of US 192, you will find Bonanza Golf. There are two courses here, but the play on both is the same. Bonanza Golf has the longest greens of any of the courses (excluding Disney's Fantasia Fairway), but most are flat with a dogleg left or right. The long greens make the holes fairly easy, if not a bit bland.

The theming is supposedly a mining town, but is light at best. We don't expect animatronics, but one prospector or a few pieces of mining equipment would animate this rather dull and uninspired course. Even the waterfall, which should add some charisma to the holes, faces out toward the parking lot. Still, the grounds are very clean and all the greens are in fine condition.

Congo River Kissimmee   ★★★★½
4777 W. US 192, Kissimmee; ☎ **407 396-6900; congoriver.com**

Hours Sunday–Thursday, 10 a.m.–11 p.m.; Friday–Saturday, 10 a.m.–midnight. **Cost** $10.99 + tax for adults; $8.99 + tax for children ages 5–9; and free for children age 4 and under. Unlimited play is $17.95 per person.

DESCRIPTION AND COMMENTS A member of the Congo River family, the Kissimmee location is very similar to the other courses in theming and play, but it is by far the largest. There are two courses at the Kissimmee location, dubbed Stanley and Livingston. Stanley is less difficult than Livingston by six shots. Although we prefer the play on the Livingston course, the Stanley course is more scenic with one hole on a boat and a path that takes you next to the crashed zebra-striped plane. The Kissimmee location is mountainous, filled with thin paths that make backtracking to the entrance difficult and can also make finding the next hole slightly confusing. The entire complex, including the air-conditioned bathrooms, is clean, and the greens are all in great condition. The staff is accommodating and very friendly. There is also a small arcade.

Congo River Orlando   ★★★★
6312 International Dr., Orlando; ☎ **407-352-0042; congoriver.com**

Hours Sunday–Thursday, 10 a.m.–11 p.m.; Friday–Saturday, 10 a.m.–midnight. **Cost** $10.99 + tax for adults; $8.99 + tax for children ages 5–9; and free for children age 4 and under.

DESCRIPTION AND COMMENTS Next to Wet 'n Wild is another of the three Congo River courses. This is the smallest of the courses, but the play is equally as enjoyable as the others. The two courses are the Livingston, with a par of 41, and the Stanley, with a par of 43. The challenges at Congo River Orlando are the long uphill shots, which are plentiful. As with the other Congo Rivers, the grounds are clean, the African-themed course is in great condition, and the staff is friendly. However, due to its location next to Wet 'n Wild on I-Drive, this course is more crowded during the day than the other Congo River courses and can be packed at night. Although we enjoyed this course, you might be better off proceeding up I-Drive a few more blocks until you reach Congo River Orlando North.

Congo River Orlando North ★★★★
5901 International Dr,, Orlando; ☎ 407-248-9181; congoriver.com

Hours Sunday–Thursday, 10 a.m.–11 p.m.; Friday–Saturday, 10 a.m.–midnight. **Cost** $10.99 + tax for adults; $8.99 + tax for children ages 5–9; and free for children age 4 and under.

DESCRIPTION AND COMMENTS Congo River Universal is just a short drive up from Wet 'n Wild. The grounds are superbly clean, and the lies of the greens put the ball where you aim it. There is only one course and the first nine holes are relatively level, making them handicapped accessible, but not as challenging as holes at the other Congo River locations.

What sets this apart from its kin is the quality of theming. All the Congo River golf courses have African themes, but the execution here surpasses the others. To start with, the course is built both around and within a large red-rock mountain. On the mountain, you will find a Land Rover stuck in a waterfall, a zebra-striped airplane sticking out of a slope, and caverns with skeletons. A great baobab tree caps off this I-Drive landmark. Even some of the holes are themed: hole #7 is played on a dilapidated ship.

Congo River Universal also contains a few nongolf attractions. Like the two other Congo River courses, the Universal course has a baby alligator pit with pieces of meat to feed the gators, available for $3.15 including tax, but it also contains a pond filled with koi you can feed for $0.25, a gift shop, a small arcade, and a game called Ubanki Hoops that consists of 18 basketball hoops slung in unorthodox ways. There are also some larger alligators in the back for a seasonal wrestling match; call ahead for show times.

Fantasia Gardens ★★★★½
1205 Epcot Resorts Blvd., Lake Buena Vista; ☎ 407-560-4870; disneyworld.disney.go.com

Hours Daily, 10 a.m.–11 p.m. **Cost** $12 + tax for adults; $10 + tax for children ages 3–9; repeat rounds within 24 hours of playing are half-price with receipt.

DESCRIPTION AND COMMENTS Disney creativity is uncanny. A short walk from the Dolphin Hotel, Fantasia Gardens has two courses, one called Fantasia Gardens and the other called Fantasia Fairway. Although the greens have been bleached out by the sun and trodden down by tourists, Fantasia Gardens is one of the best courses in Orlando. What Disney excels at is not making difficult holes (they aren't), or making big rocky mountains to play on (none of those either), but instead making each hole unique. Each hole is themed after a different character from the *Fantasia* movies, including Cupid, the flamingos, and the ballerina hippos. From holes that sound trumpets when you sink a putt to fountains on motion sensors that squirt water at you as you walk along, Disney has set the bar for creative design.

The Fantasia Fairway is, literally, a miniature golf course. There are grass greens and sand traps. The holes are long, some in excess of 100 feet. You can't use any irons, but you will have to putt farther than you ever have before. Both of these courses are open to non-Disney guests.

Hawaiian Rumble Adventure Golf, Buena Vista ★★½
13529 S. Apopka-Vineland Rd., Orlando; ☎ 407-239-8300; hawaiianrumbleorlando.com

Hours Sunday–Thursday, 10 a.m.–11 p.m.; Friday–Saturday, 10 a.m.–11:30 p.m. **Cost** $9.95 + tax for adults; $7.95 + tax for children ages 4–10; free for children age 3 and under. The 36-hole special is $14.95.

DESCRIPTION AND COMMENTS Like the Hawaiian Rumble course on I-Drive, the course on FL 535 in Buena Vista has two courses named the Lani and the Kahuna. Although the Lani is supposed to be the more difficult, we didn't notice a significant difference between them. What is obvious is that Hawaiian Rumble Buena Vista pales next to the I-Drive locale. The greens at Buena Vista have been redone, but the play is relatively flat. There is a large volcano in the middle and a few flowers, but the theming ends there. Other attractions include an air-hockey table and an original Ms. Pacman machine.

Hawaiian Rumble Adventure Golf, I-Drive ★★★½
8969 International Dr., Orlando; ☎ 407-351-7733; hawaiianrumbleorlando.com

Hours Sunday–Thursday, 9 a.m.–11:30 p.m.; Friday–Saturday, 9 a.m.–midnight. **Cost** $9.95 + tax for adults; $7.95 + tax for children ages 4–10; free for children age 3 and under.

DESCRIPTION AND COMMENTS Located next to WonderWorks on I-Drive. Parking is available just behind the course, but you will have to walk around the front to enter. One of the busiest courses in Orlando, Hawaiian Rumble features a 40-foot volcano, plenty of flora, fountains, and a series of streams. Unlike the heavily rock-themed Pirate's Cove locales or Congo Rivers, Hawaiian Rumble is a very flat course; you can play through the volcano but not on it.

There are two courses, the Kahuna and the Lani. Kahuna is easier and takes players through the volcano. Lani is very challenging. Hole #5 has a long uphill green ending in a jump over the stream. The 17th hole, where players hit the ball through a series of logs, is one of the more creative, and difficult, holes around.

There is a concession stand at the entrance as well as a Ben & Jerry's ice-cream parlor.

Pirate's Cove International Drive ★★★½
8501 International Dr., Orlando; ☎ 407-352-7378;
piratescove.net

Hours Daily, 9 a.m.–11:30 p.m. **Cost** $10.95 + tax for adults; $9.95 + tax for children ages 4–12; free for children age 3 and under. The 36-Hole Special is $16.50 + tax for adults and $14.95 + tax for children ages 4–12.

DESCRIPTION AND COMMENTS Pirate's Cove on I-Drive is almost impossible to miss: it's located beside the Castle Hotel. Just keep an eye out for the pirate marooned in the middle of a lake. Pirate's Cove has two courses. The Captain's Course is easier, taking players along the front edge of the pond before they climb the hill. Plaques along the way aid the theme as they tell the story of pirate William Kidd. Blackbeard's Challenge is more difficult and offers plenty of opportunities to lose a ball in the water, including a large water gap shot on hole #9. The holes get harder as you proceed, and the fairways contain lots of rolling hills and sloping greens.

Although the course is very clean and the maintenance crew does its best, the course has some worn spots due to the high volume of visitors who spot it from I-Drive. Crowds here can be an issue, especially at night. If you like pirates and don't mind driving, you may want to play one of the other two pirate-themed courses in Orlando, even if their theming is not quite as involved. If you do visit, don't forget to take a photo-op in the stockade.

Pirate's Cove Lake Buena Vista ★★★★
12545 FL 535, Lake Buena Vista; ☎ 407-827-1242;
piratescove.net

Hours Daily, 9 a.m.–11 p.m. **Cost** $10.95 + tax for adults; $9.95 + tax for children ages 4–12; free for children age 3 and under. The 36-Hole Special is $16.50 + tax for adults and $14.95 + tax for children ages 4–12.

DESCRIPTION AND COMMENTS You will see this course every time you take I-4 through Orlando. Located in the rear of the Crossroads Shopping Center, this Pirate's Cove location is less crowded than its I-Drive sibling, and the Buena Vista locale offers the same high-caliber theming and challenging courses.

The courses' names are, yet again, Captain's Course and Blackbeard's Challenge. Captain Kidd's is the easier course, taking players to the top of the mountain as well as through the caverns under the waterfalls on holes #13 and #14, two of the more scenic holes in Orlando. Blackbeard's Challenge has fine lies, which means the ball goes where you aim it. A few long downhill shots, however, make hitting par difficult. The greens are tidy, and excluding the I-4 traffic, the setting, with the palms and flora adorning the top of the rocky hill, is excellent.

Pirate's Cove US 192 ★★★½
**2845 Florida Plaza Blvd., Kissimmee; ☎ 407-396-7484;
piratesislandgolf.com**

Hours Daily, 10 a.m.–10 p.m. Call for seasonal hours. **Cost** $9.95 + tax for adults;
$8.95 + tax for children ages 4–12; free for children age 3 and under. All-Day
Play is available for $13.95 + tax per person.

DESCRIPTION AND COMMENTS One of three area Pirate's Cove mini-golf
courses is tucked behind a shopping center next to Old Town and Fun
Spot USA. Like the other Pirate's Cove courses nearby, this one has a
Captain's Course and a Blackbeard's Challenge course; however, a separate company owns and operates this golf location, and the theming is
not quite as strong.

But interesting holes—such as the 16th hole on the Captain's
Course inside a cave on top of a hill—give it the requisite piratical
ambience. The course is generally well shaded and the grounds are
absolutely spotless.

Because Pirate's Cove is hidden behind a Red Lobster, it gets little play.
It's a nice secret course to go to when all the others are overcrowded.

Pirate's Island ★★★½
**4330 W. Vine St., Kissimmee; ☎ 407-396-4660;
piratesislandgolf.com**

Hours Daily, 10 a.m.–10 p.m. Call for seasonal hours. **Cost** $9.95 + tax for adults;
$8.95 + tax for children ages 4–12; free for children age 3 and under. All-Day
Play is available for $13.95 + tax per person.

DESCRIPTION AND COMMENTS Located where US 192 meets West Vine.
Although it is not part of the Pirate's Cove franchise, Pirate's Island has all
of the necessary pirate theming, including a half-sunken ship in the pond.
There are two courses, Captain's Course and Blackbeard's Challenge, but
here Blackbeard's course is easier. Actually, most of the holes here are
easier than the holes at its pirate counterparts, and the theming is not
quite the same quality. What makes this course enjoyable is the elbow
room. Pirate Island has more acreage than the other pirate courses, making its layout open and uncluttered. The entire place is immaculate,
without even a leaf on the greens. Less overhead vegetation helps Pirate's
Island keep both this open feeling and clean grounds, but guests should
be sure to wear sunscreen if they come during the day.

The Putting Edge ★★★½
**5250 International Dr. (inside the Festival Bay Mall), Orlando;
☎ 407-248-0700; puttingedge.com**

Hours Monday–Thursday, 11 a.m.–9 p.m.; Friday–Saturday, 11 a.m.–11 p.m.;
Sunday, 11 a.m.–7 p.m. **Cost** $10.50 + tax for adults; $8.50 + tax for children age
12 and under.

DESCRIPTION AND COMMENTS Inside the Festival Bay Mall at the top of I-Drive, next to the Cinemark Theatres, is an underrated course. Although there is only one flat course, it is entirely under backlights. The theme here is aquatic. The music is also more tempered, with a mix of current Top 40 tunes. The edges of each hole are well marked, and each shot is moderately interesting. Younger players will enjoy both the easy shots and the charming theme, and the indoor location makes it a perfect rainy-day getaway.

Winter Summerland ★★★★
1548 W. Buena Vista Dr., Lake Buena Vista; ☎ 407-560-3000; disneyworld.disney.go.com

Hours Daily, 11 a.m.–11 p.m. Cost $12 + tax for adults; $10 + tax for children ages 3–9; repeat rounds within 24 hours of playing are half-price with receipt.

DESCRIPTION AND COMMENTS Inside Disney property, near the entrance to Blizzard Beach, you will find out what happens when the Imagineers set their minds to making an "ordinary" miniature golf course. There are two 18-hole courses, the Winter course and the Summer course. The play on each course is the same, but Winter features a snowy Christmas theme, while Summer features a sandy Christmas theme. Although Winter Summerland is small, the Imagineers have put in the effort to make each of the 36 holes unique. The in-course obstacles, such as sand and snow castles, all have interactive components. Some holes make noise, some blow air, and a few even attempt to block your shot! None of the holes are too difficult for children, making this an ideal family stop. One caveat: Winter Summerland's compactness may have you bumping elbows with other guests. The courses can be a mob scene during the day and unplayable at night.

PART ELEVEN

OLD TOWN *and* FUN SPOT USA

LOCATED SIDE BY SIDE ON US 192, Old Town and Fun Spot are in a heads-up competition for tourists who are in search of entertainment without the flat-rate ticket prices found at the major theme parks. Even though Old Town has been a staple on this section of highway for more than 22 years, the newer Fun Spot USA is gaining in popularity, helped in part by its sister location (Fun Spot Action Park) on International Drive.

Old Town and Fun Spot each have a unique feel, although the lack of a fence between the two may lead some guests to believe that the parks' tickets are interchangeable (they are not). Still, there's a bit of a synergy at work here. When you combine the rides at Fun Spot with the dining, shopping, and other activities at Old Town, they pose an interesting alternative for half-day touring, or an escape for those who don't want to spend their evenings within the confines of a major park.

OLD TOWN

THE PARK CELEBRATED ITS 25TH ANNIVERSARY in 2011 and is getting an updated look. The 1950s theme will remain, and new stores and eateries will be added. The longevity of this four-block Main Street relies upon its exclusive mixture of shopping, restaurants, carnival attractions, and thrill rides. Old Town is fashioned to be like a modern Mayberry with the fair in town. The atmosphere is akin to East Coast beach towns such as Ocean City, Maryland, or Myrtle Beach, South Carolina. Although the storefronts are attractive, Old Town has not undergone the Disney-styled whitewash of magic and charm.

As you walk down the street, you will pass storefronts ranging from trinket shops to spas, tattoo parlors to sunglass huts, and tobacco merchants to marionette dealers. Bars and restaurants are interspersed among the shops, and at either end of Old Town's Main Street are areas dedicated to carnival and thrill rides. Indeed, one of the more terrifying rides in Orlando—the Human Slingshot—is located on the property. There are also plenty of gentler rides for young children.

Old Town also offers events throughout the year, including its famous weekly automotive shows. Bikers congregate here on Thursday nights, classic cars roll in on Friday nights, and antique autos parade down Main Street on Saturdays. A live band, creating a spirited party atmosphere, accompanies most of these shows.

One of the fine features about Old Town is that these shows, and admittance in general, are all free. Parking is also gratis. These perks allow potential patrons to peruse the storefronts, restaurants, rides, and other attractions before committing any cash. Because all you have to invest to visit Old Town is your time, it becomes a hard deal to pass up.

GETTING THERE

OLD TOWN IS LOCATED on West US 192 (Irlo Bronson Memorial Highway), about 5 minutes from Walt Disney World. From I-4, take Exit 64 east onto 192. Old Town will be just over a mile ahead on your right.

ADMISSION PRICES

THE BUSINESS MODEL FOR OLD TOWN separates it from any amusement park in the area. Competing companies either lease or own each store and attraction, so one set of tickets or coupons is not valid for every experience (for example, carnival tickets will not get you into Grimm's Haunted House). The lack of a common currency frees you to spend as you see fit, but also bumps up the prices on all of the rides; it appears there is little profit sharing among companies.

Old Town tickets cost $1 apiece. The cheapest rides cost two tickets, while the most expensive rides on the ticket system cost five tickets. You can purchase a wristband or a Valuepak of 22 tickets for $20, 35 tickets for $30, or 60 tickets for $50 (tax not included). For other deals, see the Ticket Rides section farther along in this chapter.

ARRIVING

OLD TOWN IS OPEN EVERY DAY of the year 10 a.m.–11 p.m. Most of the rides are open noon–11 p.m. Every Friday and Saturday night, Old Town hosts a classic car show. The Friday show includes cars made between 1975 and 1989. It begins at 5 p.m. and lasts until 11 p.m., with a parade down Main Street at 9 p.m. On Saturday, cars of a pre-1975 vintage are on hand. The show begins at 1 p.m., and the cars cruise down Main Street at 8:30 p.m. A live band, weather permitting, accompanies the car shows. There is also a motorcycle show on Thursday nights. As with parking and admission to Old Town, the show is free.

CONTACTING OLD TOWN

FOR MORE INFORMATION, call ☎ 407-396-4888 or visit its website, **old-town.com.**

RIDES *and* ATTRACTIONS

OLD TOWN PROPER CONSISTS OF FOUR BLOCKS on Main Street. Located between US 192 and the first block of Old Town are the Human Slingshot and an area called the Swing Zone. At the other end of Old Town's Main Street, just behind the fourth block, are a myriad of carnival rides and the Windstorm Roller Coaster. The only attractions outside of these two main areas are the Old Town Bull and Grimm's Haunted House. They are each located between blocks two and three.

Because the admission system at Old Town is tricky to understand, we have divided the rides and attractions into ones that take cash and credit cards only, and ones that require Old Town tickets.

NONTICKET RIDES/ATTRACTIONS

Basketball Game   ★★

APPEAL BY AGE	PRESCHOOL ★	GRADE SCHOOL ★★½	TEENS ★★½
YOUNG ADULTS ★★		OVER 30 ★½	SENIORS ★½

What it is Shoot baskets for prizes. **Scope and scale** Minor attraction. **Authors' rating** ★★. **Cost** $5.

DESCRIPTION AND COMMENTS A carnival game in which you shoot basketballs through a hoop to win prizes. The more baskets you make, the better your prize. There's a mini-version for kids (also $5).

TOURING TIPS Unless you are a skilled player, you're better off taking your $5 and going to the gift shops.

Grimm's Haunted House   ★★★

APPEAL BY AGE	PRESCHOOL ★★½	GRADE SCHOOL ★★★½	TEENS ★★★½
YOUNG ADULTS ★★★		OVER 30 ★★½	SENIORS ★★

What it is Walk through a haunted house. **Scope and scale** Major attraction. **Authors' rating** ★★★. **Cost** $10 + tax for adults; $6.75 + tax for children age 9 and under.

DESCRIPTION AND COMMENTS Grimm's Haunted House is neither particularly frightening (unless you're being shadowed by a ghoulish character actor) nor well detailed. As you make your way through the rooms, the actor may attempt to scare you at each darkened turn. There is no plot, just moderately scary displays and dioramas. The grotesque has found a home here, and the final exhibit—we won't spoil it—is macabre and a bit tasteless. The designers attempted to lengthen the tour with a series of claustrophobic hallways, but even with the compact design, the house is not large enough to warrant the price tag.

TOURING TIPS　The haunting takes place on the second floor, so you must be able to climb stairs to participate. Leading up to Halloween, lines are as gruesome as the house, so try to stop in during the day if you're visiting in October. No running or flashlights are allowed at Grimm's.

Happy Days Bumper Cars　★★★

APPEAL BY AGE	PRESCHOOL ★★★	GRADE SCHOOL ★★★★	TEENS ★★½
YOUNG ADULTS ★★★	OVER 30 ★★★		SENIORS ★★½

What it is Disco-themed bumper cars. **Scope and scale** Minor attraction. **Special comments** Must be 48" tall to ride. **Authors' rating** No deductibles; ★★★. **Duration of ride** 8–10 minutes. **Cost** $5 for singles; $7 for double cars.

DESCRIPTION AND COMMENTS　The cars are in better shape than some of the competition's but are nothing particularly special. Although the interior has a 1970s disco theme, the music is 1980s hair metal—we suppose it's a subtle message about the timelessness of bumper cars.

TOURING TIPS　Not crowded; come anytime. Bumper cars do not have a reverse, so if you get stuck, just cock the wheel hard over and press the gas.

Happy Days Go-Karts　★★★

APPEAL BY AGE	PRESCHOOL —	GRADE SCHOOL ★★★★	TEENS ★★★½
YOUNG ADULTS ★★½	OVER 30 ★★½		SENIORS ★★½

What it is Small go-kart track. **Scope and scale** Major attraction. **Special comments** Must be 58" tall to drive; no height requirement for passengers. **Authors' rating** Small; ★★★. **Duration of ride** 8–10 minutes. **Cost** $6 per person; $2 for passengers in double carts.

DESCRIPTION AND COMMENTS　The go-kart track is one of the smallest in Orlando, but they did the best they could with the single oval track, having one of the longer sides bend inward to create two more turns and elevating the straightaway opposite. The simple shape allows you to pass other carts, but after 8 minutes, it becomes repetitive.

TOURING TIPS　The carts are in rather poor shape compared with other local tracks, but their condition does not affect their speed. Still, Fun Spot is the place to go for go-karts. Being the only track at Old Town, Happy Days Go-Karts becomes very crowded in the evenings, but a full track is more exciting than an empty one. Once you've begun the race, you are forced to continue until it is completely over because opening the gate to pit row would halt all the other carts.

Happy Days Laser Tag　★★★

APPEAL BY AGE	PRESCHOOL ★★½	GRADE SCHOOL ★★★★	TEENS ★★★
YOUNG ADULTS ★★½	OVER 30 ★★★		SENIORS ★★½

What it is Real-life shoot-'em-up. **Scope and scale** Major attraction. **Authors' rating** Good padding; ★★★. **Duration** 8–10 minutes. **Cost** $5.

DESCRIPTION AND COMMENTS　Forgoing the carpeted floor and many solid partitions in Lazerworks at WonderWorks, Laser Tag at Old Town is fully padded with large air sacks. The room is smaller than at WonderWorks, but the padding allows shooters to dive and roll around to avoid getting hit, and with less cover to hide behind, you'll find yourself fully prone more often than not.

TOURING TIPS Because the course is inflatable, shoes are not permitted inside. All participants must come with clean socks or wear a provided pair. The vests that register the tally are a bit cumbersome and the lasers are hard to aim. Your best bet is to sneak up on people and to keep moving.

Human Slingshot ★★★½

APPEAL BY AGE	PRESCHOOL †	GRADE SCHOOL †	TEENS ★★★★½
YOUNG ADULTS ★★★★		OVER 30 ★★★★	SENIORS ★★

† Sample size too small to develop rating.

What it is 180-foot slingshot. **Scope and scale** Major attraction. **Special comments** Must be 52" tall to ride. **Authors' rating** Scarier to watch than to ride; ★★★½. **Duration of ride** 4 minutes. **Loading speed** Slow. **Cost** $25 per person.

DESCRIPTION AND COMMENTS The Slingshot is a massive steel V shape with flashing rainbow lights located near the front of Old Town. Riders latch into a two-person cart at the base of the V, where a bungee-cord system runs down the legs of the V to the cart, like a slingshot. Once you're latched in, the tethered cart is pulled below the boarding area, then released, flinging riders 365 feet into the air, spinning head over feet the entire time. After the initial launch, the elastic cable makes for a smooth rise and fall. Surprisingly, the ride is almost peaceful, and less frightening than many of the major roller coasters in the area. Being more than 300 feet above the ground silences much surrounding noise, and the nighttime view is even better—for a few seconds at a time as you bob—than the SkyCoaster's. As with most rides, the thrill is in the anticipation, not in the event. For $25, however, you're better off taking a helicopter for sightseeing or, for thrill junkies, paying out a few more bucks for the SkyCoaster.

TOURING TIPS The cart must have two people in it to keep balanced; a ride operator will go with you if you can't convince any of your friends or family. Riding at night is more thrilling, but long lines begin after 7 p.m. During high season, the wait can be over an hour long. Watching everyone else is almost better than riding it yourself, though.

Old Town Bull ★★★

APPEAL BY AGE	PRESCHOOL —	GRADE SCHOOL ★★★	TEENS ★★½
YOUNG ADULTS ★★★½		OVER 30 ★★★½	SENIORS ★★

What it is Mechanical bull. **Scope and scale** Minor attraction. **Authors' rating** ★★★. **Cost** $10 for adults; $7 for children.

DESCRIPTION AND COMMENTS As any fan of the 1970's classic movie *Urban Cowboy* already knows, a mechanical bull is a machine with a saddle that bucks riders up, down, and around, attempting to knock the rider off. It's the gear-and-motor approximation of bull riding found in rodeos. Old

Town's bull is one and the same and has enough padding on the ground to minimize injuries, although you must sign a waiver before riding.

TOURING TIPS   The ride doesn't open until later in the day when crowds are heavier.

TICKET RIDES

ALL OF THE RIDES BELOW are on the Old Town ticket system. Tickets each cost $1; mild discounts are available in the Valuepak: 22 tickets for $20 and 35 tickets for $30. All-day ride wristbands are also available and make more sense than either of the Valuepaks. Wristbands cost $25 for adults and $15 for children under 42" tall. On Sunday, wristbands can be purchased for use from noon until 6 p.m. for $15, regardless of age. Tickets and wristbands may be purchased at the ticket booth in the front of the park. Wacky Wednesday currently offers buy-one-get-one-free bargains on some bracelets for Wednesday nights. Tiny Wristbands (not included in the Wacky Wednesday deal) are $15 and only cover the six kiddie rides, listed later in this section.

Rides before the First Block of Old Town

Old Town Ferris Wheel   ★★★

APPEAL BY AGE	PRESCHOOL ★★★★	GRADE SCHOOL ★★★★	TEENS ★★
YOUNG ADULTS ★★		OVER 30 ★★★★	SENIORS ★★★★

What it is Old-fashioned Ferris wheel. **Scope and scale** Minor attraction. **When to go** Anytime. **Special comments** You must be at least 42" tall to ride alone, or at least 52" tall to ride with a child. **Authors' rating** ★★★. **Duration of ride** 1 minute, 45 seconds; if there's no line, you can ride several times. **Loading speed** Moderate. **Cost** 4 tickets.

DESCRIPTION AND COMMENTS   A throwback to the early days of amusement parks, this Ferris wheel spins over US 192 under the gleam of its flashy, fast-moving neighbors. But it's a nice break from all the tummy-churning rides and a fun way to see the whole park, as you probably won't notice much at the top of the Super Shot. It might be too subtle for older kids, but preschoolers seem to appreciate its gentleness.

TOURING TIPS   Head to the Ferris wheel when your feet are tired or you need a moment to settle your stomach. The line is generally pretty short any time of day.

Pharaoh's Boat   ★½

APPEAL BY AGE	PRESCHOOL ½	GRADE SCHOOL ★★★½	TEENS ★★★½
YOUNG ADULTS ★★		OVER 30 ★½	SENIORS ½

What it is A sailor's worst nightmare. **Scope and scale** Major attraction. **When to go** Anytime. **Special comments** Must be at least 48" tall to ride, and at least 60" tall to ride with a child. **Authors' rating** Not for the easily nauseated; ★½. **Duration of ride** 1 minute, 45 seconds. **Loading speed** Slow; the ride can accommodate between 40 and 60 people at a time—if there's no line, you may have to wait as the ride fills up. **Cost** 4 tickets.

DESCRIPTION AND COMMENTS A large ship on a pendulum swings riders to and fro, reaching speeds of close to 80 miles per hour. The boat gains speed throughout the ride, and the last two tick-tocks are a doozy.

TOURING TIPS This is one attraction where a larger crowd waiting to ride is usually a good thing. The attendants may not run it if there are fewer than 20 people in line, but stop by and check. To get the most out of this ride, sit at either end of the boat. People often lose pocket contents.

The Scrambler ★★★

APPEAL BY AGE	PRESCHOOL ★★½	GRADE SCHOOL ★★★½	TEENS ★★★★
YOUNG ADULTS ★★★		OVER 30 ★★½	SENIORS ★★

What it is Two-person carts attached to a central hub. Scope and scale Major attraction. When to go Early. Special comments Must be at least 48" tall to ride alone, or must ride with an adult who is at least 60" tall. Authors' rating ★★★. Duration of ride 2 minutes. Loading speed Moderate. Cost 4 tickets.

DESCRIPTION AND COMMENTS Another carnival classic, The Scrambler has three arms with a set of spinning chairs attached to the end of each arm. The chairs whiz in close to one another as the entire apparatus spins around. Because riders move closer to and farther from the central axis, the experience is like being the ball tethered to a paddle in that childhood toy.

TOURING TIPS The Scrambler is on par with Pharaoh's Fury and Super Shot for the most extreme ticket rides at Old Town. It may make some riders a bit queasy.

The Super Shot ★★★½

APPEAL BY AGE	PRESCHOOL †	GRADE SCHOOL ★★★	TEENS ★★★★½
YOUNG ADULTS ★★★		OVER 30 ★★	SENIORS ½

† Preschoolers are generally too short to ride.

What it is Tummy tumbler. Scope and scale Headliner. When to go Before you eat dinner. Special comments Must be at least 42" tall to ride. Authors' rating ★★★½. Duration of ride 1½ minutes. Loading speed Fast. Cost 4 tickets.

DESCRIPTION AND COMMENTS A similar but better ride than Universal's Dr. Doom's Fearfall, the Super Shot is designed for pure terror. The operator straps you into a jump seat and, with your feet dangling, hoists you up a tower to a height of 120 feet. To add to the anticipation, your ascent is not only very slow, but a protrusion above your head blocks your view upward, so you have no idea when you've reached the top. Once you're there, it's an exhilarating free fall down, and at 47 miles per hour, not for the faint of stomach.

TOURING TIPS This is another big draw at Old Town, and the lines can get long in the evening. If the entire idea of an unexpected drop seems too scary, remember that if you sit on the side where you can see your shadow (during the day), you will be able to tell when you've reached the top. And if you don't want to know—grin—sit on the other side.

Wave Swinger ★★½

APPEAL BY AGE	PRESCHOOL ★★★½	GRADE SCHOOL ★★★	TEENS ★½
YOUNG ADULTS ★★	OVER 30 ★½		SENIORS ½

What it is Swings. **Scope and scale** Minor attraction. **When to go** Anytime.
Special comments Must be at least 42" tall to ride. **Authors' rating** ★★½.
Duration of ride 3 minutes. **Loading speed** Slow. **Cost** 4 tickets.

DESCRIPTION AND COMMENTS   A set of swings dangles from a central tower.
The tower spins around and raises the riders into the air. This attraction
doesn't hold much thrill for older kids.

TOURING TIPS   The ride has a high volume and a high turnover rate, although
the loading time is slow. Don't expect big lines.

Rides after the Fourth Block at Old Town

Kiddie Rides (Tiny Wristband Rides) ★★

APPEAL BY AGE	PRESCHOOL ★★★½	GRADE SCHOOL ★★★	TEENS ★½
YOUNG ADULTS ★	OVER 30 ★½		SENIORS ★★

What it is A bouncy bunch of small rides. **Scope and scale** Minor attraction. **When
to go** Anytime. **Special comments** Must be at least 36" tall to ride alone, or must
ride with an adult who is at least 60" tall. **Authors' rating** ★★. **Duration of ride**
2–3 minutes. **Loading speed** Moderate. **Cost** 2 tickets or $15 Tiny Wristband.

DESCRIPTION AND COMMENTS   There's a small collection of classic tot rides
located behind Block 4 in Old Town. They are **The Motorcycle Jump,
The Quad Runner, The Merry-Go-Round, The Frog Hopper, The Jump
Around,** and **The Flying Teacups.** The Motorcycle Jump and Quad
Runner are virtually the same ride, except that the carts are shaped like
motorcycles and four-wheelers, respectively. On each ride, kids sit on
the cart and spin around a central axis. The Merry-Go-Round has small
buggies attached to a tiny tower that turns, and the buggies bounce up
and down. The Frog Hopper is a miniature version of the The Super
Shot, found in the front of the park, while the Jump Around is merely a
trampoline with elastics to keep kids upright. The Flying Teacups is
another miniature of an original. Riders sit in teacups that they can spin
individually. All of the teacups rotate in a circle.

TOURING TIPS   These rides are meant for children under the age of 10. You
have to be at least 36" tall to ride any of them alone, and 42" high to
ride The Flying Teacups without an adult over 60". You must be
between 36" and 48" high to use The Jump Around.

Tilt-a-Whirl ★★★

APPEAL BY AGE	PRESCHOOL ★★★½	GRADE SCHOOL ★★★½	TEENS ★★★
YOUNG ADULTS ★★★	OVER 30 ★★½		SENIORS ★

What it is Spinning cars. **Scope and scale** Major attraction. **When to go**
Anytime. **Special comments** Must be at least 46" tall to ride alone, or must ride
with an adult who is at least 60" tall. **Authors' rating** ★★★. **Duration of ride** 2
minutes. **Loading speed** Fast. **Cost** 4 tickets.

DESCRIPTION AND COMMENTS This carnival classic consists of cars that rotate individually and spin around a circular track with two raised walls. You've ridden it before, but with its capacity to fit four adults and five children, you might as well introduce your children to it now.

TOURING TIPS The motion sickness is lower on the Tilt-a-Whirl than on most of Old Town's other rides. The ride's ability to move more than 500 people an hour keeps lines at bay.

Wacky Worm ★★

APPEAL BY AGE	PRESCHOOL ★★★½	GRADE SCHOOL ★★★	TEENS ★½
YOUNG ADULTS ★½		OVER 30 ★★	SENIORS ★★

What it is Tiny steel coaster. **Scope and scale** Minor attraction. **When to go** Anytime. **Special comments** Must be at least 42" tall to ride alone, or 36" tall with an adult who is at least 60" tall. **Authors' rating** ★★. **Duration of ride** 2 minutes. **Loading speed** Moderate. **Cost** 3 tickets.

DESCRIPTION AND COMMENTS Smaller even than Windstorm, this attraction is here primarily for children who are just a bit too short for the bigger coaster adjacent. The coaster track is almost identical but smaller. There are a few ups and downs but nothing thrilling.

TOURING TIPS Don't worry about lines here. This coaster is around only to placate children too short for Windstorm.

Windstorm Roller Coaster ★★★

APPEAL BY AGE	PRESCHOOL †	GRADE SCHOOL ★★★½	TEENS ★★½
YOUNG ADULTS ★★½		OVER 30 ★★½	SENIORS ★★

† Preschoolers are generally too short to ride.

What it is Small steel coaster. **Scope and scale** Major attraction. **When to go** Early. **Special comments** Must be at least 48" tall to ride alone, or at least 40" tall to ride with an adult who is at least 60" tall. **Authors' rating** ★★. **Duration of ride** 3 minutes. **Loading speed** Moderate. **Cost** 5 tickets.

DESCRIPTION AND COMMENTS The roller coaster in Old Town is smaller than other local coasters. This is no Kraken, but the small steel coaster does hold some thrills for smaller riders. Riders sit in cars on top of the track, ascend the drop hill, then descend around the large oval, up and down a series of bumps and rolls. The ride is unimpressive, and any of the equally compact coasters at the other parks offers a better ride.

TOURING TIPS Because this is the only real coaster at Old Town, the lines can be lengthy. Head here directly after purchasing tickets.

DINING

OLD TOWN HAS A WIDE VARIETY OF DINING OPTIONS. There is Chinese food at Spring Roll Chinese Gourmet, Mexican at Tex Mex, and fast food at A&W All American Food. Our pick for the best deal in the park is Flipper's Pizzeria, located near the front entrance. Diners can get a two-topping pizza and a soda for $5.99 plus tax. For pizza in an amusement park setting, this is an exceptional deal. Burger King and a slew of local restaurants are located just outside of Old Town.

SHOPPING

NO MAIN STREET WOULD BE COMPLETE without shops, and shops line all four blocks of Old Town. Although Old Town contains 75 specialty shops—more than we can mention here—there aren't very many bargains and don't expect flea-market prices. They've hooked you with the carnival rides, and now it's time to unload a barrage of souvenirs, but that's no different from any other Florida park.

On the first block, you'll find **Groovy Store,** packed with 1960s hippie memorabilia, **Old Town Leather** (a shop for bikers), **Annie's Gifts,** and the **Ocean Wave Surf Shop,** all on the right side of the street. **Puppets** sells marionettes; prices range from $8.50 for a small puppet to $50 for large puppets. Across the street is the **Toy Time** and a quirky shop called **Old Town Pet Palace,** where, among other things, you can purchase outfits for your dogs and cats.

Magic Max is on the second block. Here you can buy magic tricks and illusion kits, but you can see how they work only if you purchase them. **Kandlestix,** a candle outlet, is also on the second block.

On the third block, you will find **Vivian's Day Spa.** For $75 you can get a one-hour therapeutic massage and for $60 a French manicure. For $100, the Spa Serenity Package offers a one-hour full-body massage, a 20-minute foot treatment, and a paraffin hand dip. This is a perfect stop for Mom while Dad takes the kids around to the rides.

The fourth block hosts a **Made in the Shade Sunglasses** store, and a tattoo parlor that is open late, just in case you thought drinking was a good idea. **Old Town Candy Store** and **The General Store** are across the street. The General Store is themed to feel like a vintage hometown market, but instead of coffee cans and potatoes you'll find Coca-Cola memorabilia and fake road signs. On the same side of the street is **Black Market Minerals,** an African-themed store with a collection of rocks, sculptures, and wind chimes.

FUN SPOT USA

LOCATED DIRECTLY BESIDE OLD TOWN, Fun Spot USA offers more thrill rides than its competition, but less theming and things for the youngest children to do. Still, it seems to have a better grip on what will keep teenagers pleased, as well as a better pricing scheme.

The park, like its counterpart on International Drive called Fun Spot Action Park, contains both go-kart tracks and carnival rides. But with the addition of big-time thrills, such as the SkyCoaster, and a miniature golf course, it's clearly the superior choice for adventure seekers.

Also, as at neighboring Old Town, admission and parking are both free.

GETTING THERE

FUN SPOT USA IS LOCATED on West US 192 (Irlo Bronson Memorial Highway), about 5 minutes from Walt Disney World. From I-4, take

Exit 64 east onto 192. Fun Spot will be just over a mile ahead on your right.

ADMISSION PRICES

PRICES *Tickets:* $3 apiece; go-karts cost between three and four tickets while all other rides cost between one to two tickets.

Fun Spot offers three armbands. Each is good for the entire day. When selecting armbands, take the height and age of your group into consideration. There is no need to purchase armbands that are out of the height or age range of the rider.

- *Go-kart armband* $34.95 plus tax per person, unlimited go-kart tracks and rides.

- *Track Sampler armband* $20 per person, four rides on the tracks or attractions. It can be upgraded to the Go-kart armband for $15.

- *Rides armband* $24.95 plus tax per person, unlimited rides on the Screamer, Paratrooper, Bike Ride, Flying Bob's Bobsleds, Screamin' Eagle, Galaxy Spin, Double-Ferris Wheel, Hot Seat, Surf's Up, Tilt-A-Whirl, Bumper Kars, and all Kid Spot rides.

ARRIVING

FUN SPOT IS OPEN MONDAY–FRIDAY, 2–11 p.m.; Saturday–Sunday, 10 a.m.–midnight. Most of the rides are open noon–11 p.m. It's closed on occasion for private parties and holidays. Parking and admission are free.

CONTACTING FUN SPOT

FOR MORE INFORMATION, call ☎ 407-397-2509 or visit its website, **funspotusa.tutengraphics.com.**

RIDES *and* ATTRACTIONS

GO-KARTS The main draw at Fun Spot USA, as with Fun Spot Action Park, are the go-karts. Concrete tracks allow Fun Spot patrons to operate go-karts rain or shine and create a smoother ride than the wooden planks at places such as Magical Midway. There are four tracks here that are on par with Fun Spot's other tracks, but due to this park's location next to Old Town, these tracks tend to be more crowded.

The four tracks are the **Vortex,** the **Chaos,** the **Slick Track,** and the **Road Course.** All the tracks are color-coded to make them easy to distinguish.

The **Vortex** is the yellow, three-level, 800-foot track comprised of tight corkscrews at the back of the park. The biggest thrill occurs at its 36-foot apex where the track makes a sharp, 20-degree descent for 100 feet. The collection of skid marks at the bottom is proof of its wild design. If you can ride only one go-kart at Fun Spot, make it this one. Riders are usually allowed five laps, totaling about 9 minutes, and must be at least 10 years old and 54" tall. It costs three tickets.

The longest track at Fun Spot is the 820-foot, blue **Chaos** track. The course is steeper than the Vortex, but more timid due to the sharp twists and turns that make it difficult to pass other carts. There are plenty of hills and valleys, but after five laps and 8 minutes, you'll be ready to move along. As with the Vortex, riders must be at least 10 years old and at least 54" tall. The cost is three tickets.

The **Slick Track** course is red. It's a simple oval course and the dullest race available. Skip this unless you're a diehard NASCAR fan. Riders must be at least 8 years old and 56" tall. It costs two tickets.

The **Road Course** track is green, and if you really want to test your driving skills, this is the track on which to do it. It's completely flat and packed with hairpin turns and short straightaways. The variety of angles in the course, from slow bends to hairpins, will both test your skill as a driver and allow you the opportunity to pass other carts. The unassuming flat track will have shorter lines because most guests will be drawn to the multistoried Vortex and Chaos tracks. Riders must be at least 12 years old and 56" tall. It costs two tickets.

Other Rides and Attractions

Double-Ferris Wheel   ★★★

APPEAL BY AGE	PRESCHOOL ★★★	GRADE SCHOOL ★★★	TEENS ★★★
YOUNG ADULTS ★★½		OVER 30 ★★	SENIORS ★★½

What it is Two wheels in one. **Scope and scale** Major attraction. **Special comments** Must be at least 42" tall to ride. **Authors' rating** ★★½. **Duration of ride** 3 minutes. **Cost** 2 tickets.

DESCRIPTION AND COMMENTS One wheel not enough? Why not two? This Ferris wheel–style ride has hubs on either end that spin independently of the central hub. It's really no more thrilling than an ordinary Ferris wheel, but hey, the competition right next door already has one of those.

TOURING TIPS This attraction doesn't always run during the daytime. If you buy a ticket that includes it, be sure that it's running during the hours of your visit.

Extraordinary Bike Ride   ★★½

APPEAL BY AGE	PRESCHOOL ★★	GRADE SCHOOL ★★★	TEENS ★★½
YOUNG ADULTS ★★½		OVER 30 ★★	SENIORS ★½

What it is Bicycle swing set. **Scope and scale** Minor attraction. **Special comments** Must be at least 52" tall to ride. **Authors' rating** ★★½. **Duration of ride** 3 minutes. **Cost** 1 ticket.

DESCRIPTION AND COMMENTS A pedal-driven cart is suspended between two posts, like the Pharaoh's Fury ride. The faster you pedal, the higher you go, and if you pedal fast enough, you can spin the "bicycle" over the bar.

TOURING TIPS This ride is not crowded and much more work than fun.

Flying Bob's Bobsleds ★★★

APPEAL BY AGE	PRESCHOOL ★★	GRADE SCHOOL ★★★	TEENS ★★★
YOUNG ADULTS ★★½		OVER 30 ★★	SENIORS ★½

What it is Circular coaster. **Scope and scale** Minor attraction. **Special comments** Must be at least 42" tall to ride. **Authors' rating** ★★½. **Duration of ride** 3 minutes. **Cost** 2 tickets.

DESCRIPTION AND COMMENTS Located across from the Vortex track, Flying Bob's is another carnival standard. Cars, attached bumper-to-bumper, spin around a track, which is at an angle and shaped much like the tip of a lipstick. Disco beats blare, and when the ride starts spinning backwards, you'll remember why you haven't ridden one of these since you were a kid.

TOURING TIPS The spinning can be a little nauseating but falls just short of needing our motion sickness warning. The height requirement is 42" if the rider is unaccompanied by an adult.

Galaxy Spin ★★

APPEAL BY AGE	PRESCHOOL ★★½	GRADE SCHOOL ★★★½	TEENS ★★★
YOUNG ADULTS ★★		OVER 30 ★½	SENIORS ★

What it is Wild mouse coaster. **Scope and scale** Major attraction. **Special comments** Opened in March 2011; must be at least 42" tall to ride with an adult; 48" tall to ride alone. **Authors' rating** ★★. **Duration of ride** 5 minutes. **Cost** 1 ticket.

DESCRIPTION AND COMMENTS Purchased from Cypress Gardens and opened in March 2011 at Fun Spot, Galaxy Spin is one of two new rides at the park (the other being Screamin' Eagle). Individual cars, which can spin around 360 degrees, ascend to the top of the track and then wind down through a series of hairpin curves. At each curve, riders are thrust against each other as the car spins around. Not that the quick spin isn't fun once, but the repetition of slamming against each other wears thin by the third turn, and with around 15 turns in all, you'll be happy to get off. Riders can somewhat control how much their ride vehicle spins as it proceeds down the length of track.

TOURING TIPS Why amusement parks, including parks as big as Disney, continue to punish riders with these mouse coasters is beyond us. Skip this one if you have neck problems, or don't like quick stops and starts.

Hot Seat ★★★½

APPEAL BY AGE	PRESCHOOL ★★	GRADE SCHOOL ★★★	TEENS ★★★
YOUNG ADULTS ★★★		OVER 30 ★★	SENIORS ★½

What it is Big pendulum. **Scope and scale** Major attraction. **Special comments** Must be at least 42" tall to ride. **Authors' rating** ★★½. **Duration of ride** 3 minutes. **Cost** 2 tickets.

DESCRIPTION AND COMMENTS If you've ever wondered what's it like to be strapped to a giant's foot as he goes from a gentle walk to an all-out sprint, here's your chance. Side-by-side pendulums each have four seats attached to the bottoms. When they get swinging, riders get screaming. It's a fun, rather short, way to spook parents and the easily mortified.

TOURING TIPS The ride is very similar to the Pharaoh's Boat at Old Town, except that here you can see the ground beneath you. We're not sure why, but that makes this ride both more thrilling and less likely to turn your stomach.

Kid Spot (Kiddie Rides)   ★★★

APPEAL BY AGE	PRESCHOOL ★★★★	GRADE SCHOOL ★★★	TEENS ★
YOUNG ADULTS ★★	OVER 30 ★★		SENIORS ★★½

What it is Kiddie rides. **Scope and scale** Minor attraction. **Special comments** Must be at least 42" tall to ride alone. **Authors' rating** ★★★. **Duration of ride** 2–3 minutes. **Cost** 1 ticket.

DESCRIPTION AND COMMENTS A collection of classic kiddie rides sits near the parking lot in the front of the park. There are two sets of slides where you descend on burlap sacks, and four miniature carnival rides where you can either sit in a biplane (**Baron Planes**), a truck (**Convoy**), a flying car (**Cyber Jets**), or a train (**Train**) while circling a central hub.

TOURING TIPS This is on par with the kiddie rides at Fun Spot's I-Drive location. The only things missing are the bumper boats.

MiniGolf/Full Speed Race and Golf   ★★

APPEAL BY AGE	PRESCHOOL ★★★	GRADE SCHOOL ★★★	TEENS ★★½
YOUNG ADULTS ★★	OVER 30 ★★		SENIORS ★★

What it is Race-car-themed mini-golf. **Scope and scale** Minor attraction. **Authors' rating** Boring course; ★★. **Cost** Available only for birthday parties at $3 per person, per round.

DESCRIPTION AND COMMENTS A lesser mini-golf course, its claim to fame is being the only "indoor, black-light, race-car-themed 18-hole mini-golf course." With all of these qualifiers, we're not surprised to find a mediocre course. The carpeting is black, and under the black light, both your ball and the obstacles glow. The black carpet makes the small bumps and hills almost impossible to see, so many of your shots may go askew. There are no major hills or wild shots in this uninspired one-story course. The decor consists of airbrushed pictures of flaming cars, and the course obstacles are painted car parts made of hard foam. To complete the effect, 1980s hair metal plays over the sound system.

TOURING TIPS With plenty of other mini-golf courses in Orlando, there is no need to spend your money here, unless you buy a package deal with the NASCAR simulator.

NASCAR Simulators/Full Speed Race and Golf   ★★★½

APPEAL BY AGE	PRESCHOOL ★★★	GRADE SCHOOL ★★★★	TEENS ★★★★
YOUNG ADULTS ★★★½	OVER 30 ★★★★		SENIORS ★★★½

What it is Full-motion NASCAR race. **Scope and scale** Headliner. **Authors' rating** ★★★½. **Duration of ride** 6 minutes. **Loading speed** Slow. **Cost** Available only for birthday parties at $5 per person, per ride.

DESCRIPTION AND COMMENTS Each simulator is a four-fifths-scale representation of an actual racing stock car. You can choose from six cars: Bud, Dodge, DuPont, Home Depot, Miller, or Sony. Your group may also choose from six tracks: Atlanta, Bristol, Charlotte, Daytona, Daytona with no restricted weights, and Richmond. After you select manual or automatic transmission, an attendant furnishes you a brief tutorial on how to drive the car. Once you're inside, you will be immersed in the three screens that wrap around your car, allowing you peripheral vision as you race. The simulators are full-motion, meaning that when you hit another car, your car rattles and shakes. The graphics are Xbox quality, but not exceptional. Winning the race is challenging; we found ourselves skidding out more than passing other cars. Attempting to tell what place you are in is also difficult. The attendant will tell you periodically, but it is hard to hear him over the faux-engine noise.

TOURING TIPS The cars are not complete replicas of the stock cars, but for a simulator, the interior is fairly accurate. You will find the seats stiff and uncomfortable, but you aren't racing a 300-lap circuit. Four to ten laps, depending on the track, is all the 6-minute simulator allows. At the end of the race, the attendant hands each rider a sheet with his or her race statistics, leaving you a bit awed at the skill of real NASCAR drivers.

Paratrooper ★★

APPEAL BY AGE	PRESCHOOL ★★★	GRADE SCHOOL ★★★	TEENS ★★★
YOUNG ADULTS ★½		OVER 30 ★★	SENIORS ★★½

What it is Small, sideways Ferris wheel. **Scope and scale** Minor attraction. **Special comments** Must be at least 46" tall to ride. **Authors' rating** ★★½. **Duration of ride** 2 minutes. **Cost** 1 ticket.

DESCRIPTION AND COMMENTS A simplistic ride that spins around a central hub. Riders sit in carts that fit two people, and which dangle from an object that looks like a giant umbrella. The attraction is located directly across from the Chaos go-kart track.

TOURING TIPS This is a calm ride that is fine for older adults and younger children. The height requirement for all riders is 46".

Screamer ★★★

APPEAL BY AGE	PRESCHOOL ★★★	GRADE SCHOOL ★★★	TEENS ★★
YOUNG ADULTS ★★★		OVER 30 ★★	SENIORS ★★

What it is Spire drop. **Scope and scale** Minor attraction. **Special comments** Must be at least 42" tall to ride alone. **Authors' rating** ★★. **Duration of ride** 2 minutes. **Cost** 1 ticket.

DESCRIPTION AND COMMENTS This is yet one more rendition of a central spire where a group of riders goes to the top and then free-falls down. This ride holds eight guests at a time, and its height is in between that of Old Town's Frog Hopper and The Super Shot.

TOURING TIPS Perhaps the least thrilling ride in the park.

Screamin' Eagle

What it is Buckets revolving around a central axis. **Scope and scale** Minor attraction. **Special comments** Opened in February 2011. **Cost** 1 ticket.

DESCRIPTION AND COMMENTS A typical carnival ride with a nice view. Rudders allow the riders to control their up-and-down movement as the buckets fly in circles around the central axis.

TOURING TIPS While it's a minor attraction, it is new and slow-loading, so be prepared to wait if you want to ride.

SkyCoaster ★★★★½

APPEAL BY AGE	PRESCHOOL ★★	GRADE SCHOOL ★★★★	TEENS ★★★★½
YOUNG ADULTS ★★★★½		OVER 30 ★★★★	SENIORS ★★

What it is A 300-foot-tall pendulum. **Scope and scale** Headliner. **Special comments** Must be 42" tall to ride. **Authors' rating** Adrenaline; ★★★★½. **Duration of ride** 6 minutes. **Loading speed** Very slow. **Cost** $40 for single-person flight; $35 per person for double-person flight; $30 per person for triple-person flight; coupons available.

DESCRIPTION AND COMMENTS SkyCoaster is one of the most thrilling and expensive rides in Orlando. Situated over a pond, SkyCoaster looks like the buttress of a large suspension bridge. At 300 feet, the giant pendulum ride dwarfs many of the area's attractions; from the top, you can see Epcot.

After suiting up in a harness resembling a knee-length apron, you proceed to a wooden platform in the center of the pond. Ride operators then raise you up and attach your harness to two cables, one to pull you aloft and one from which to swing. You are attached so your head is toward the ground—you fly on your stomach like Superman—and then pulled backward to the top of the far tower. At the end of a 3-2-1 countdown, you pull your own rip cord (yipe!) and plummet toward the earth. After a 130-foot free fall, the pendulum action takes over and gently swings you across the pond at speeds up to 80 miles per hour, depending on the weight of the passengers. To disembark, you must grab a pole and stop yourself over the wooden platform.

TOURING TIPS Because SkyCoaster can handle only about 20 people an hour, the wait can be excruciating. We recommend coming during the middle of the day when crowds are fewer and the view from the top is better. The price is steep, but the three-person deal is not a bad call because increasing the mass of a pendulum increases its speed. If the ride were $15, we would ride it twice, but at $40 for a single rider for less than 1 minute of ride time, you'll need a disposable income. Remember, $40 is about half the price of an entire day at Disney.

PART TWELVE

INTERNATIONAL DRIVE

AT ITS INCEPTION, INTERNATIONAL DRIVE, also known as I-Drive, was nothing but a small road off I-4 serving local area hotels. After Disney came to town in 1971, developers were soon to follow. Now servicing Universal, SeaWorld, two smaller amusement parks, a host of roadside attractions, multitudes of hotels, eateries, bars, malls, and the Orlando Convention Center, International Drive has become its own attraction.

Of course, many attractions found on International Drive are covered in other parts of this book (SeaWorld, Universal, Water Parks, Miniature Golf, and the like), but there are still more attractions that are worthwhile and noteworthy. The two amusement parks, Fun Spot Action Park and Magical Midway, offer thrill rides, go-kart tracks, and top-notch arcades. WonderWorks, Ripley's Believe It or Not!, and Titanic: The Experience not only all have eye-catching edifices, but also can be categorized as museums. Although all three cater to entertainment instead of learning, WonderWorks is ostensibly a science museum, Ripley's a museum of natural history, and Titanic a museum of living history. And SkyVenture offer thrills you won't find at any of the parks.

There are so many options along International Drive that you may want to set aside a day just to explore this strip. Because International Drive contains an amalgamation of sideshow entertainments, each too large to fit into a major theme park but each too small to occupy a full or even half day of touring, picking three to four attractions is both a pleasant and paced way to experience what's roadside.

PLAN AHEAD

IN CONTRAST TO OTHER FAMOUS ROADS, such as the Strip in Vegas, you won't want to spend your vacation time cruising up and down this 7-mile drag. Because International Drive is just four lanes wide (only occasionally six), the influx of tourists clogs the road, creating waits that can exceed two hours. Because the wait time, especially 8 a.m–10 a.m. and 4 p.m.–8 p.m., is excessive, you should plan what sites you want to visit and what times you would like to visit them. Even if you plan your visits to avoid the rush hours, remember that traffic lights, pedestrians, and U-turning vehicles can make International Drive a hectic passage at anytime.

But don't let the traffic dissuade you from visiting the attractions of your choice. If you stay in a hotel in the area, you should be able to become one of those pedestrians slowing down the cars. The I-Drive Trolley is also an option for short hops. The fee is nominal, and schedules are available at its website at **iridetrolley.com.**

Because many of the attractions on International Drive are open late, most until midnight or afterward, visitors can spend their days at the major parks and, with any leftover energy, step out at night. Attractions will be more crowded in the evening than during midday, so you will need to schedule more time at night to experience them.

Most of the attractions along International Drive are enclosed, so when large thunderstorms threaten, many visitors choose to hop around International Drive instead of hoofing around major theme parks in the rain. Because crowds build during rainy days, make sure to arrive at least 30 minutes earlier than normal to any attraction you want to visit. Touring first thing in the morning is also advantageous and will keep both you and your umbrella dry.

GETTING THERE

INTERNATIONAL DRIVE EXTENDS from the Central Florida Parkway to a cul-de-sac at Prime Outlet Mall. You can reach International Drive from any exit between Exit 71 and Exit 75A off I-4.

▌▐ ATTRACTIONS

Fun Spot Action Park ★★★

APPEAL BY AGE	PRESCHOOL ★★	GRADE SCHOOL ★★★	TEENS ★★★★
YOUNG ADULTS ★★★		OVER 30 ★★★	SENIORS ★★

555 Del Verde Way, Orlando; ☎ 407-363-3867; fun-spot.com

Hours Daily (peak season), 10 a.m.–midnight; Monday–Thursday (off season), 2–11 p.m.; Friday, 2 p.m.–midnight; Saturday, 10 a.m.–midnight; Sunday, 10 a.m.–11 p.m. **Cost** *Tickets:* $3 apiece; go-karts cost 2 tickets while all other rides cost 1 ticket. Each armband is good for the entire day and includes the free-play arcade. *Go-kart armband:* $34.95 plus tax per person, unlimited go-kart tracks and rides. *Rides armband:* $24.95 plus tax per person, unlimited Cadet go-kart track only and rides. *Kid's Spot armband:* $14.95 plus tax per person, valid only for the Kid's Spot. *Free Play armband:* $4.95 plus tax per person, unlimited play in the Upstairs Free Play Arcade. **Authors' rating**★★★.

DESCRIPTION AND COMMENTS In late 2010, Fun Spot purchased 10 acres next door to expand the park, which would triple its current size when the expansion is complete in 2012 or 2013.

Past Magical Midway on I-Drive, you'll see Del Verde Way. Snuck in behind a shopping center is Fun Spot Action Park, visible from I-Drive by its enormous Ferris wheel. Fun Spot is a small amusement park, and like Magical Midway, its appeal rests in its go-kart tracks, carnival rides, and arcades. Fun Spot is larger than Magical Midway, and although Fun Spot does not contain rides on par with Magical Midway's Human Slingshot or StarFlyer, Fun Spot possesses superior go-kart tracks and better arcades.

Indeed, Fun Spot has the best go-kart tracks in Orlando. There is both free parking and free admission, so you can wander through the site and peruse the attractions before you purchase any tickets or wristbands.

GO-KARTS The main draw at Fun Spot is the go-karts. The go-karts cost two tickets per ride, unless you have an armband. In contrast to Magical Midway's wooden tracks, Fun Spot has concrete tracks that allow for both a faster and smoother ride. The concrete tracks also allow Fun Spot patrons to operate go-karts rain or shine. There are five tracks here, and collectively, they are better than any of the other local area tracks. Because Fun Spot is slightly hidden from the main drag, the tracks are often less crowded.

The four main tracks are the **Quad Helix,** the **Conquest,** the **Commander,** and the **Thrasher.** The fifth is a kiddie attraction called the **Cadet Track,** a short oval located in the back corner of the park that requires kids to be at least 4 years old and 42" tall. All the other tracks are color-coded to make them easier to distinguish.

The **Quad Helix** is yellow, and the longest track at 1,600 feet. As the name entails, the multistory track comprises four interlaced corkscrews. The lack of long straightaways or very sharp turns makes it difficult to pass other go-karts, but if you're not feeling very competitive, the banked turns and elevated layout are a good use of your ticket. Riders are usually allowed five laps, totaling about 9 minutes, and riders must be at least 10 years old and 52" tall.

The tallest track at Fun Spot is the blue **Conquest** track at 28 feet high, but with underpowered go-karts, height is not an advantage. The dawdling ascent through the long corkscrew is rewarded with a fast but short downhill leg, and the rest of the track winds slowly back to the starting gate. After five laps and 8 minutes, you'll be ready for something else. As with the Quad Helix, riders must be at least 10 years old and at least 52" tall.

The **Commander** track is green. The compact figure-eight design makes it the shortest of the four major tracks. The flatter track suggests use as a racetrack, although ride operators frown upon rigorous competition and strictly enforce the "no-bumping" rule. A moderate thrill, however, is still available when you head to the inside of the first corner at top speed, where you should be able to get a little air over the set of rolls. It's a little rough on your tailbone but should make you grin nonetheless. Riders must be at least 8 years old and 50" tall.

The **Thrasher** track is red and, if you're competitive, the best racetrack in Orlando. The track is completely flat and packed with hairpin turns and short straightaways. The variety of angles in the course will both test your skill as a driver and allow you the opportunity to pass other carts. Besides the intense ride, the unassuming flat track will have shorter lines because most guests will be drawn toward the multistoried Quad Helix and Conquest tracks. Riders must be at least 12 years old and 54" tall.

OTHER ATTRACTIONS The handful of rides at Fun Spot are quaint and generic, and each costs one ticket per ride. Tickets cost $3 each, but rides are included with the purchase of an armband. There are **bumper cars** in a small arena, **bumper boats** in a small pool, a large **Ferris wheel** called **Revolver,** and three common carnival rides. The carnival rides all spin you around a center axis, but do not invert you. They are the **Scrambler,** the **Sky Glider,** and the **Paratrooper** (riding the latter is akin to sitting on the side of a massive wobbly tire).

Also at a cost of one ticket per ride, and also included with armband purchases, are rides for the very young. Located in the **Kid's Spot,** these rides are recommended for kids ages 2–5. The tiny area contains a set of **miniature teacups,** a **carousel, kiddie swings,** and a few other minor rides, including a pair of the **oscillating trucks** commonly found outside shopping centers.

Although the ride selection at Fun Spot is meager, Fun Spot does boast central Florida's largest **arcade.** It's actually two arcades—a token arcade downstairs and a free-play arcade upstairs. Each token for the downstairs arcade costs $0.25, unless you buy the tokens in bulk. The three bulk-token options are: 120 tokens for $25 (a 16% discount), 400 tokens for $75 (a 25% discount), or 1,000 tokens for $175 (a 30% discount). Most of the games cost one token per turn, but a few take as many as four tokens to play.

While the downstairs arcade houses all of the newest arcade games, the upstairs free-play arcade is a collection of vintage games ranging from the more modern, such as The Simpsons and Tekken, to the classic games, such as Pac-man, Defender, and Centipede. The free-play arcade also has pinball machines and a few Xboxes. On its own, the free-play arcade costs $5.95 plus tax, but is included with the purchase of any of the armband deals. Because guests have no time restraint and unlimited replay on all of the games, you may find it difficult to play your favorite old-school games, but with more than 60 machines available, finding a comparable game shouldn't be difficult.

When the video games wear you out, you can pick up some food at the snack bar downstairs. A slice of cheese pizza costs $2.25, and a cheeseburger combo that includes small fries and a soda costs $6.25.

Ripley's Believe It or Not! Orlando Odditorium ★★★

APPEAL BY AGE	PRESCHOOL ★★	GRADE SCHOOL ★★★	TEENS ★★★
YOUNG ADULTS ★★★		OVER 30 ★★★	SENIORS ★★★

8201 International Dr.; ☎ 407-363-4418; orlando.ripleys.com

Hours Daily, 9 a.m.–1 a.m., with last entry at midnight. **Cost** $18.99 for adults; $11.99 for children ages 4–12; and free for children age 3 and under. **Authors' rating ★★★**.

DESCRIPTION AND COMMENTS With one side of the building slipping into a sinkhole (on purpose, of course), Ripley's is another of the odder buildings on I-Drive. Located just a few blocks from WonderWorks (the oddest building on I-Drive), Ripley's is open 9 a.m.–1 a.m., with the last entry available at midnight; parking is free. To tour the exhibits, you should need only about an hour. Even with the quick turnaround of guests, the lines for Ripley's can be monstrous, with wait times outside exceeding an hour. On rainy days, be sure to arrive at least 20 minutes before opening, or come very late in the evening.

Ripley's consists of a series of galleries, each with a different twist. Each gallery hosts a menagerie of odds and ends from around the world that fit with each room's general theme. The collection consists mainly of optical illusions, anthropologic oddities, genetic oddities, and some of the oddest objects built by man.

Once you enter, a hologram of Mr. Ripley greets you, one of the many optical illusions inside. Most of the other optical illusions are simple posters with questions such as, "Which line is longer: >—<, or <—>?" Others are on a grander scale, such as the billiards room, a room built to appear flat, but that is actually listing to one side. The Inversion Tunnel is another large-scale illusion, and just like the WonderWorks version, the tunnel can make you believe that you are spinning sideways.

The anthropologic and animal oddities may also set your head spinning. They include wax sculptures of deformities, Siamese piglets, ceremonial masks, and a shrunken head. After these galleries, guests can walk through the man-made oddities, from the strange—an authentic vampire-slaying kit—to the stranger—a replica of a Rolls-Royce made from 1,016,711 matchsticks, or the portrait of Elvis constructed from 600 smaller portraits.

Because Ripley's is more of an amusement than a museum, many of the descriptive plaques in front of each item contain factoids instead of in-depth accounts. You won't find any lengthy analysis of items to educate you inside the Odditorium. You will, however, be privy to a fine collection of some fringe aspects of nature and humanity.

Magical Midway ★★½

APPEAL BY AGE	PRESCHOOL ★★	GRADE SCHOOL ★★	TEENS ★★
YOUNG ADULTS ★★		OVER 30 ★	SENIORS ★

7001 International Dr.; ☎ 407-370-5353; magicalmidway.com

Hours Vary, but usually daily, 10 a.m.–midnight. **Cost** *Tickets:* $3 apiece; go-karts cost 2 tickets while all other rides cost 1 ticket. Admission does not include Human Slingshot or StarFlyer. *Three-hour armband:* $22.95 plus tax per person, includes 3 hours of unlimited go-karts and rides and one StarFlyer ride. Coupons are available on the website. **Authors' rating ★★½**.

DESCRIPTION AND COMMENTS Near the north end of I-Drive, well after WonderWorks but before SkyVenture, are the hard-to-miss signs for Magical Midway. The enormous towers of both the Human Slingshot and StarFlyer make them easy to find. The parking at the Midway is free but minimal. You can park across the street, but be wary of rubbernecking drivers while crossing I-Drive traffic. The I-Drive Trolley is also a sound option for arriving (**iridetrolley.com**).

Magical Midway's location, front and center on International Drive, draws many visitors, and their wear on the facility is apparent. The heavy traffic in the amusement park also makes riding the attractions during evening visits tedious at best.

Fortunately, the park offers free admission, so you can take a look around before you decide to purchase any wristbands or tickets.

GO-KARTS Magical Midway has three go-kart tracks called **Avalanche, Alpine Jump,** and **Fast Track.** You must be at least 12 years old and 58" tall to drive the single-seat carts, while the two-seat carts require the driver to be at least 16 years old with a valid driver's license and the passenger to be at least 5 years old and 36" tall. The two-seat carts are available only on the Avalanche and the Alpine Jump tracks.

On the multistory Avalanche and Alpine Jump tracks, be prepared for a very bumpy ride. Instead of concrete, slats of wood are laid across the tracks. Although the Midway attempts to keep the slats as flat as possible, the design flaw not only slows the carts as they clank over the seams, but the raised ridges of wood will leave your tailbone aching.

The **Avalanche** track is the largest track and the most popular. The track begins with a corkscrew and winds around in a figure eight as it descends. The conservative straightaways and slow bends did not impress us; neither did the long lines that build during the day and are unbearable at night.

The **Alpine Jump** track is a shorter version of the Avalanche and contains all the same construction problems. After driving up a long and tedious corkscrew, you are given a brief burst of speed down a straightaway, but the banked turns quickly cease any major thrills. The track is less crowded than the Avalanche, but the ride is shorter. With a lack of sharp turns and speed, passing other drivers is difficult. Your best bet is to wait until someone slows down to ease the jostling caused by the wooden slats, or to move on to the Fast Track.

The **Fast Track** is the best track for racing. A single concrete oval, the track is small, but large enough to allow you to accelerate your cart to top speed before making the turns. Because you are allowed the same amount of time on this track as on either of the others (about 8 minutes), you will have time to practice the turns and pass and re-pass your friends. Because the track is simplistic and small, many patrons will skip it for the long lines and slow, bumpy ride on the other tracks; don't be so hasty.

OTHER ATTRACTIONS As with Fun Spot Action Park, Magical Midway includes a small **bumper car arena** with a height requirement of 48" and an even smaller **bumper boat pool** with a height requirement of 42". However, Magical Midway's four rides—the **Tornado, Space Blast, StarFlyer,** and **Slingshot**—are all more thrilling than any found at Fun Spot.

The **Tornado** is a standard carnival ride with a height requirement of 48". Eight cars that rotate independently and each contain four seats are attached to the arms of a central spinning post. Although it is rather passé, it accomplishes what all centrifuge carnival rides are meant to: it makes you dizzy.

The **Space Blast** has a 48" height minimum and is similar to Universal's Dr. Doom FearFall ride, without any of the theming or grandeur. You sit in a seat that is launched 180 feet into the air, and then free-falls back to the ground. The ride is short, and the three g's of force are not dazzling.

The eye-catcher at Magical Midway is the **StarFlyer** with a height requirement of 44". Towering over I-Drive, the StarFlyer is a set of **rotating swings** that lifts riders up 230 feet and spins them at up to 54 miles per hour. To facilitate the thrill, the swing chains were built to be about one centimeter thick, forcing patrons to place their trust in Orlando's safety inspectors. Once you've overcome the vision of having your body flung onto I-Drive, you will have to resist the urge of having your stomach follow suit. Although the ride may induce motion sickness and mild terror, the view from the top of the StarFlyer is one of the best in Orlando. The ride is *not* included with the purchase of any of the armbands. It costs $7 for the first ride, and $5 for each additional ride.

The **Human Slingshot** is not included in any armband admissions and costs $25 per person, and you must be at least 52" tall to ride. The Human Slingshot is the same as the one at Old Town (the one at Magical Midway is actually taller by a foot or so, and only noticeable if you're bragging).

The structure is a massive V shape with flashing rainbow lights. Riders latch into a two-person cart at the base of the V, and a bungee-cord system stretches down the legs of the V to the cart—like a slingshot. Once you're latched in, the cart is pulled below the boarding area, then released, flinging riders 365 feet into the air, spinning head over feet the entire time. Surprisingly, the ride is almost peaceful and less frightening than many of the major roller coasters in the area. After the initial launch, the elastic cable makes for a smooth rise and fall. Being more than 300 feet above the ground silences much surrounding noise, and the nighttime view is even better—for a few seconds at a time as you bob—than even the StarFlyer's. As with most rides, the thrill is in the anticipation, not in the event. For $25, however, you're better off taking a helicopter for sightseeing or, for thrill junkies, paying out a few more bucks for the SkyCoaster at Old Town.

SkyVenture Orlando ★★★½

APPEAL BY AGE	PRESCHOOL ★★★★	GRADE SCHOOL ★★★★	TEENS ★★★
YOUNG ADULTS ★★★		OVER 30 ★★★	SENIORS ★★★

6805 Visitor Cir., Orlando; ☎ 407-903-1150 or 800-SKYFUN1 (759-3861; skyventureorlando.com

Hours Sunday–Thursday, 11:30 a.m.–9 p.m.; Friday–Saturday, 11:30 a.m.–10 p.m. **Cost**: $49.95 + tax for visitors age 3 and up. **Authors' rating** ★★★½.

DESCRIPTION AND COMMENTS SkyVenture is a high-velocity vertical wind tunnel that attempts to recreate the thrill of skydiving. While headed north on I-Drive, you will find the tunnel on the left-hand side after Magical Midway but before the Skull Kingdom and directly across the street from Wet 'n Wild. From I-4, just take Exit 75A and turn away from Universal. The tunnel resembles a large spaceship and is painted blue and yellow. The tunnel, when not floating tourists, is used for skydiving team-member training to coordinate stunts before they leap. Unlike jumping out of a plane, "skydiving" in the tunnel works by having five large fans at the top of the tunnel suck air upward. The balanced suction creates a wind tunnel for you to float around in, and although you won't experience the acceleration of free-falling from thousands of feet, you will be able to float around in relative safety. Although the price is steep, at $49.95 plus tax per person for only 2 minutes of actual flight time, it is still much cheaper than actually skydiving. Children under age 18 will need the signature of a parent or legal guardian on the waiver form in order to fly.

After purchasing your ticket, proceed up the staircase to the waiting room. The waiting room is a series of metal benches on one side of the flight chamber. The flight chamber is enclosed in Plexiglas, so if you arrive a few minutes early or are waiting for a member of your group to fly, you can watch other guests float around, and if you are lucky, you might see an instructor performing a few aerial stunts.

Once your time comes, an instructor will usher you upstairs, where you will be given all of the proper equipment, including a helmet, a flight suit, elbow and knee pads, earplugs, and proper footwear if you forgot it. You will also be allowed access to a locker where you can store the contents of your pockets, jewelry, and any other belongings that may be displaced during flight.

After you are suited up, you proceed to the preflight briefing room and watch a video on basic body positioning and hand signals. After the video, the instructor gives every student a chance to practice the in-flight pose. Remember, once you're in the flight chamber, you have only 2 minutes of flight time, so optimize your flight time by memorizing the hand signals and asking any questions beforehand. The hand signals are necessary because the wind tunnel is too loud for speech.

The hand signals are as follows:

- One finger pointed up—*raise your chin*
- Two fingers pointed straight out—*slowly straighten your legs*
- Two fingers curled in—*slowly bend your legs at the knees*
- Cupped hand facing downward—*arch your back*
- Spreading fingers—*spread your fingers*
- Raising hands—*raise your hands from the shoulder.*

Once your preflight briefing is finished, your instructor will take you down to the flight chamber. After the instructor signals the operator to fire up the wind tunnel, he will gesture you in one by one. When entering the chamber, put your hands by your head—as if you're surrendering—and slowly lean forward until the air catches you.

Your 2-minute flight time will be divided into 1-minute sections. The end of each session is marked with a loud alarm and a red flashing siren. When this occurs, make your way slowly to the exit door and the instructor will help you out. While you wait for your next turn you'll have time to reflect on what adjustments you'll need to make to improve your next flight.

The first thing you are apt to notice is that flying in the wind tunnel is very difficult. Unless your body posture is perfect, you will careen toward the Plexiglas or end up face first in the netting on the bottom. Thankfully, the instructors are very helpful and hands-on, keeping you from running headlong into the Plexiglas. But don't worry; if you can't get the hang of flying in 2 minutes and fail to find the right position, the instructor can take hold of you and fly you both into the air.

Safety in the wind tunnel is important, so avoid sudden movements. You'll find that very subtle changes in your posture can affect how you are flying. You do not have to worry about flying too high in the tunnel; you will not get sucked up into any massive fan. Go as high as you want to—if you are able—and for the best flight, watch and follow the instructor's hand signals.

After you have completed both of your flights, you will go back upstairs and remove your gear. After you change, you'll receive a certificate with your name on it. Before leaving, consider tipping your instructor. Tipping is not expected, but with an instructor in any sport, whether it is surfing, skating, or skiing, a "tip for tips" policy is generally a good practice.

Titanic: The Experience ★★★

APPEAL BY AGE	PRESCHOOL ★	GRADE SCHOOL ★★	TEENS ★★
YOUNG ADULTS ★★★	OVER 30 ★★★		SENIORS ★★★★

7324 International Dr., Orlando; ☎ 407-248-1166; titanictheexperience.com

Hours Daily, 9 a.m.–9 p.m., last tours Monday–Thursday at 8 p.m.; Friday–Sunday at 9 p.m. **Cost** $21.95 + tax for adults; $12.95 + tax for children ages 3–11. Children age 2 and under are free. **Authors' rating ★★★**.

DESCRIPTION AND COMMENTS The new and improved Titanic: The Experience has moved farther north on I-Drive, and is now near the intersection of Carrier Drive. Among the renovations at the new facility are a reconstruction of the vessel's bridge and an 8-foot model of the wreck. The museum also has more interactive exhibits.

Titanic is not an amusement park; rather, it is an overpriced museum filled with replicas of structures from the *Titanic* and period pieces from other ships. It is a fine museum, if you have a great interest in the *Titanic*, and comes complete with a guided tour. The tour guides assume the identity of a passenger who was onboard the *Titanic*. Depending on your guide, his or her narration can either save or sink your experience.

Your first tour guide greets you at the entrance and ushers you into the first room, where you watch a video on the building of the *Titanic*. The museum is set up chronologically, so after the video you are taken into rooms featuring ship schematics, details of the launch, and such. Your first tour guide leaves you in a room themed to look like the boarding dock in Southampton, England, complete with period luggage and ambient ship noise. When your second tour guide arrives, in the persona of a person who was on the ship, you enter the Titanic. The tour guide walks you through the preceding days' events, and then in a fit of melodrama relates the circumstances of the tragedy.

The theming at Titanic is excellent, and the museum's full-scale replications of living quarters, hallways, and the grand staircase are all well crafted, but can only be seen from behind velvet ropes. The last rooms contain low lighting to create a nighttime atmosphere, and the small replica of the ship's railing, with stars and cold air, makes you truly feel as if you are on board a ship.

A block of ice set to the temperature of the water the night the *Titanic* sank, as well as the presence of the guides, is meant to transport you back in time. The guides need to decide whether, as characters, they are still alive and taking guests on a tour of the ship while things begin to go wrong, or if they are talking to us posthumously. The blurred line only adds to our inability to suspend disbelief. We'd prefer if the guides were ghosts, able to answer questions about all aspects of the events at anytime, without having to break character.

The *Titanic*'s 100th anniversary is in 2012, so check to see if any special events are being offered.

WonderWorks ★★★½

APPEAL BY AGE	PRESCHOOL ★★★	GRADE SCHOOL ★★★★	TEENS ★★★
YOUNG ADULTS ★★★		OVER 30 ★★★	SENIORS ★★

9067 International Dr., Orlando; ☎ 407-351-8800; wonderworksonline.com

Hours Daily, 9 a.m.–midnight. **Cost** $24.99 + tax for adults; $19.99 + tax for seniors and children ages 4–12; free for children age 3 and under. **Authors' rating** ★★★½.

DESCRIPTION AND COMMENTS The unmistakable upside-down building is located on I-Drive in Orlando, between the Convention Center and Ripley's Believe It Or Not!. The interior of WonderWorks is stacked with small displays, a cross between a science museum and an arcade. Kids will enjoy this place more than adults, but even the older crowd can find a few exhibits to interest them. When the learning is completed, there is a laser-tag facility upstairs.

To enter WonderWorks, you must first pass through the Inversion Tunnel, a very effective optical illusion that gives you the sensation of spinning upside down. If you begin to get queasy, or fear you'll be hurled over the left-hand railing, simply close your eyes and walk forward. Once you've successfully cleared the tunnel and are fully inverted, you can watch other visitors wobbling their way into the first of the four rooms at WonderWorks.

Room 1 The main attractions in the first room are the **Hurricane Hole,** the **Earthquake Simulators,** the **Anti-Gravity Chamber,** the **Global VR,** and the **Famous Disasters** quiz center. **Hurricane Hole** is a small box with four metal poles, such as you'd find in a subway car. Before the 65-mile-per-hour winds start blowing, you'll receive safety glasses and a brief tutorial on hurricanes (part of that tutorial stating that the 65-mile-per-hour winds in Hurricane Hole are not slower than the requisite 75-mile-per-hour winds needed to call it a hurricane). The wind blows for less than a minute and, for its full impact, the best place to stand is directly in front of the fan.

The **Earthquake Simulators** are two small, open-sided boxes next to the Hurricane Hole. Each box contains seating for four adults at a booth you would find at a diner. Once you are seated, the "earthquake" begins with a series of tremors and jolts, replicating the effects of an earthquake of 5.3 on the Richter scale. The effect is equivalent to driving on a dirt road.

Next to the Earthquake Simulators is the **Famous Disasters** quiz center where you can play tic-tac-toe on a series of computers. If you get the question right, you get the square. The quiz center is a good place to sit and wait your turn to play the **Global VR,** a virtual reality video game, although the wait time is not worth the experience. There are two yellow helmets, but no time limit on how long each player is allowed to play this first-person shooter. The in-game experience is akin to sitting too close to your television and playing on an out-of-date video system. The graphics are low quality, but the concept of controlling your view by turning your head has potential. A better illusion is located in the **Anti-Gravity Chamber,** where water appears to run toward the ceiling. Take a minute to figure out how the illusion is created before heading upstairs to the second room.

Room 2 The second main room at WonderWorks contains the **Bed of Nails,** the **Bubble Lab, Virtual Hoops, Swim with the Sharks,** the **Velocity Tunnel,** and the **WonderWall.** The **Bed of Nails** sits in the center of the room and contains 3,497 nails. To keep your weight evenly distributed, you lie on a plastic plank and the nails rise from beneath you. Although lying on nails is uncomfortable, it makes a great photo op. Next to the Bed of Nails is the **WonderWall,** a human-sized example of pin art. People press their hands or faces into a screen of flat-tipped pins, raising the pins on the other side to make a cast. The WonderWall is a scaled-up version of most pin art, with 40,000 pins in all.

If using your entire body to play interests you, then both **Virtual Hoops** and **Swim with the Sharks** are worth a try. In both of these exhibits, you stand in front of a blue screen and your image is projected into a virtual world on a video screen in front of you. In Virtual Hoops, you can play basketball or block soccer shots, while in Swim with the Sharks, you collect gold coins and avoid predators. The graphics are bad in both games, and the on-screen play is two-dimensional (as well as difficult), but the technology is something at which to marvel.

Another exhibit that highlights technology is the **Velocity Tunnel,** where, after selecting a major league batter—choices include Barry Bonds—you throw actual baseballs at a slitted screen, giving you more respect for the real guys out on the mound.

If all the high-tech attractions are overcrowded or uninteresting to your children, there is always the **Bubble Lab,** an entire corner of the room dedicated to bubbles and bubble making. Just about every conceivable device for blowing bubbles is represented here, including the bubble screen and bubbles that can fit you inside.

Room 3 In the third room at WonderWorks, you will find most of the exhibits on sound, as well as a large collection of print illusions, including some by M. C. Escher. There is an oversize version of the Parker Brothers game **Simon** and a giant piano where you step on the keys to play the notes. The **3-D sound booths** are located in the corner near the entrance to the fourth room. In these booths, you sit in the darkness and listen to the effects of surround sound in a confined space.

Room 4 The fourth and final room in WonderWorks contains a small space exhibit, a selection of computer banks, and the full-motion **Max Flight Simulators.** The space exhibit includes a replica of the *Mercury* capsule with a fake control panel, a large astronaut suit, and a computer terminal where you can attempt to land a space shuttle by lining up the nose with the runway.

The computer banks around the perimeter of the room also hold another flight simulator where you can fly an F-18 fighter jet. The three computer-screen displays that cover your main peripheral vision, coupled with the quality of graphics, make this the best of the simulators, including the full-motion Max Flight Simulators. Other computer bank exhibits include the face-morpher that combines the faces of members of your party; WonderWorks **Tic-Tac-Toe,** where you answer Wonderfacts questions to gain your X or O; and the **Drum Machine,** where kids can smack and bang to their hearts' content and to the annoyance of anyone stuck standing in the Max Flight Simulator line.

The **Max Flight Simulators** are the main attraction in the fourth room. They are the only rides at WonderWorks and, as far as we're concerned, not worth the wait. The simulators have strict requirements for entry: riders must be 48" or taller, you must have two riders, and riders' weight must be within 100 pounds of each other with a maximum weight of 500 pounds. If your measurements are within the limits, you can enter the line and prepare to wait. Each ride takes 5 minutes and fits only two riders, so if only one of the two simulators is running—a distinct possibility—then 12 people ahead of you will mean a wait time of 30 minutes. We've seen lines of more than 40 people during off days, all listening to the children slamming away on the drum machine. To avoid the line, try to come to WonderWorks early on a weekday morning and head directly to the simulator. Of course, once you've made it to the head of the line, you'll find a very bad simulator. Although you can fully invert and rotate the cockpit of your fighter jet, and can toggle back and forth between who is piloting and who is shooting, the graphics are so terrible that you can barely tell what blips are the enemies. This ride is truly a letdown, and for the most part a drastic waste of time.

Lazerworks Once you've exited through the turnstile at the far side of the fourth room, the learning aspect of WonderWorks is gone. The fifth area at WonderWorks is upstairs, where there is a small arcade and a large laser-tag room. The arcade and the Lazerworks area are accessible without paying for WonderWorks (use the elevator in the lobby), a convenient alternative if you decide to return and play.

In laser tag, each player is given a laser gun to shoot other players and a vest that registers each shot, placing your scores on a large screen in the arcade. Once your vest has been activated, you may enter the Lazerworks room, where you can hide behind panels and shoot at other players. Once you've been shot, your gun stops firing and your vest stops accepting hits for a few seconds, and then restarts, allowing you time to run to another area of the room. Besides shooting other players, you can also shoot lights on the partitions for extra points. The key to winning is to keep moving and to aim well.

Ropes Course In the third level of WonderWorks, known as the basement, is a three-story (36-foot) indoor ropes course—the only one in Orlando. More than 20 different obstacles and activities await, including a tire traverse, suspension bridges, and swinging beams.

TICKETS

- $4.95 single game ($5.27 with tax); replay is an extra $3 plus tax
- $19.95 includes one 4-D ride, one ropes course, and one game of laser tag.

PART THIRTEEN

AIRBOAT TOURS, HORSE RIDES, ZOOS, *and* NATURE TOURS

DISNEY'S ANIMAL KINGDOM, SEAWORLD, and Busch Gardens all have unique and spectacular animal exhibits, yet, the massive scale of each of these parks prohibits some Orlando visitors from experiencing all three—or any—of the major animal attractions of central Florida. Because each of these parks requires an entire day to visit, costs upward of $50 per person, and is ostensibly a man-made re-creation of the natural environment, many visitors will opt for a smaller, cheaper, and more grassroots operation to fulfill their wonder for wild creatures. Orlando offers fulfillment in many forms. Airboat tours of the local lakes, nearby zoos, conservation projects, and horseback tours are all amenable answers to allow for animals in your itinerary. The quality of the attractions does vary drastically, and although none—or very few—are on par with an open-back truck ride on the Serengeti at Busch Gardens or a swim with the dolphins at Discovery Cove, they are all sound additions to a trip laden with animatronic creatures and miles of concrete.

AIRBOATS

AN AIRBOAT IS A FLAT-BOTTOMED BOAT POWERED by a large fan. The versatile machine, which can travel on both water and flat land, allows vacationers to explore the wetlands of central Florida. All the airboat tours near Orlando operate on lakes, so do not expect much of the swampy terrain common to the Everglades. You will see plenty of wildlife on these tours, and any ornithologists should have a field day. The two animals that awe most visitors are the bald eagle and the American alligator—you have a very good chance of seeing both on these tours, although neither animal is guaranteed. Some, but not all, bald eagles are migratory birds, flying north in the summer and returning in the winter. Migrating eagles do return to the same nest year after year, so clued-in tour guides will show you where their nests are located.

Bald eagles may be the animal icon of the United States, but the alligator is the animal icon of Florida (animated mice coming in a close second). You can see and feed baby alligators at Congo River Universal mini-golf, or marvel at the full-size gators at Gatorland. Wild alligators, on the other hand, are more difficult to spot, and you may see only their eyes and snout above the water. There are a few tricks to help you spot wild alligators. Alligators are exothermic, or cold-blooded, which means that they have a minimal amount of inner body temperature regulation and must rely on the outside sources of heat such as air and water to stay alive. Alligators are most active between 82°F and 92°F but seem to be easiest to spot when the air temperature outside is less than 84°F. During the winter, alligators stop feeding when the ambient temperature drops below 70°F, and become dormant, lying low in alligator holes, when the temperature drops below 55°F. Watch the weather during your visit and try to pick a day when the water is cool and the air temperature is around 84°F. Even if you follow none of our advice, chances are that you will see at least one alligator.

At a distance, telling an alligator from a clump of floating mud can be difficult unless you can see the alligator's eyes, or part of its tail. Some operators offer night tours with "gator shining." Like many nocturnal animals, alligators have a layer of cells below their retinas that reflect light back into their photoreceptors, increasing night vision. When you shine a flashlight into a nocturnal animal's eyes at night, this layer of cells (called *tapetum lucidum*) creates an eerie red glow. You will see more alligators on night tours—but only their eyes, and waterfowl are scarce.

A sign at Wild Willy's reads, "If you are seeking hype, sensationalism, or fantasy, there are many fine theme parks available nearby." We couldn't have said it better. Airboat tours are a great way to get out on the water on a hot afternoon, blast around a lake, and see much of the local wildlife. They aren't amusement rides, and you should have at least a hint of curiosity about the natural world before you go. Most tours require reservations, so plan ahead. Many of the airboat tours take coupons that can be printed online or found in any of the free magazines around town.

AIRBOAT TOURS

Big Toho Airboat Rides ★★★
In the public parking lot at 100 Lakeshore Blvd., Kissimmee;
☎ **888-937-6843; bigtohoairboatrides.com**

Hours 9 a.m.–5 p.m. or by reservation. **Cost** Daytime airboat tour, 1 hour: $45 for adults; $40 for children ages 3–10; free for children age 2 and under; minimum of 2 paying guests. Specialty airboat tours, around 80 minutes: Prices vary. **Authors' rating** ★★★.

DESCRIPTION AND COMMENTS Big Toho is the airboat tour closest to Orlando. They do not have a permanent ticket booth location, but launch from a public boat ramp on the north end of Lake Tohopekaliga (Lake Toho for short). The public boat ramp is easy enough to find, but be aware, a separate company called Big Toho Marina does have a permanent dock nearby; make sure to go to the public parking lot in front of the public dock.

The owner and operator, Brent, is a jovial character and happy to demonstrate the handiness of his airboat, popping over the reed beds and skimming through the lotus fields. Although he operates close to TJ's Airboats, his tour contains better scenery (the view, however, is still marred with industrial plants and power lines). The information on the tour is lackluster, but the boat's speed and handling should keep you entertained, and makes this the most thrilling airboat ride available. Big Toho specializes in night tours lasting about 80 minutes, and for anyone who felt comfy camping next to Florida lakes, the plethora of red eyes should install just the right amount of fear.

Coupons and advertisements are available in all the free local magazines and should be brought with you, but if you forget them, you should still be able to receive the stated prices above. There is a $1 discount per ticket if you purchase online.

Boggy Creek Airboat Tours ★★★
Two locations: 2001 E. Southport Rd., Kissimmee, and 3702 Big Bass Rd., Kissimmee; ☎ 407-344-9550; bcairboats.com

Hours 9 a.m.–4:30 p.m. Cost Airboat tours, 30 minutes: $25.95 + tax for adults; $19.95 + tax for children ages 3–12; free for children age 2 and under. Private airboat tour, 45 minutes: $54.95 per person, 2–6 people required. Night airboat tours, 1 hour: $49.95 + tax for adults; $45.95 + tax for children ages 3-12; free for gator-bait age 2 and under; reservations required weeks in advance, 6-person minimum. Authors' rating ★★★.

DESCRIPTION AND COMMENTS Boggy Creek Airboat Tours operates from two locations: one on Lake Toho and the other, a 45-minute drive from Walt Disney World, on West Lake Toho, a separate lake. Both locations offer very similar tours. The airboats each fit 18 people and have bench seating instead of height-staggered seating, so you should attempt to sit in the front row for the best view.

The 30-minute airboat tour leaves every half hour, beginning at 9 a.m., and takes you out onto the lake alongside open cow pastures. Herons, egrets, and a few other birds are visible here. Tours do not pass through reeds or much marsh but stick instead to the open water. Houses dot the landscape at both locations, but the development at both sites is not as pronounced as found on tours that operate from the north end of Lake Toho. The guides provide a moderate amount of information, including how to estimate an alligator's length (the number of inches between the eyes and the snout is equal to the alligator's length in feet). The ride is stop-and-go, pausing every time someone suspects a gator is present, and at only 30 minutes, it seems over before it has begun.

Boggy Creek is one of the most popular tours in the area due to their accessible locations and prolific advertising. They do not require reservations for the 30-minute airboat tours, although we strongly recommend making them. When you do make your reservation, find out if enough other guests have reserved spots for the boat to leave at the appointed time.

Cypress Lake Airboat Tours ★★★★
3301 Lake Cypress Rd., Kenansville; ☎ 407-957-2277;
cypresslakeairboattours.com

Hours 9 a.m.– 4:30 p.m.; night tours available by reservation. **Cost** Daytime airboat tour, 1 hour: $45 + tax for adults; $35 + tax for children ages 3–12; free for children age 2 and under. Private tours, 1 hour: $60 per person, minimum of 4 guests; reservations only. Daytime airboat tour, 30 minutes: $27.50 per person. **Authors' rating** Fantastic; ★★★★.

DESCRIPTION AND COMMENTS If you don't mind a longer drive, and have a bit more money to spend, Lake Cypress Airboat Tours are the best in the Kissimmee area. After a 1-hour drive from the Walt Disney World area, you make your way down a 2.3-mile dirt road to the edge of Lake Cypress. A small camp is set up at the end of the lake, complete with a big deck on which to picnic and plenty of shade under the live oaks (you can pick up picnic supplies at the Winn-Dixie about 10 miles before Lake Cypress).

Depending on the tour you decide on, your group can be as large as 20 people. The tours are aboard yellow airboats that are both faster and less deafening than any of their local counterparts. Each guest is lent a pair of binoculars, and ponchos (for afternoon showers) are also provided.

Beside the amenities and insightful narration (far and away the most informative in the area), what makes the tour special is the location. On Lake Cypress, unlike Lake Toho, there are no developments or any other houses besides the camp. The wildlife is abundant, and although the types of birds vary due to the season, kites, roseate spoonbills, a variety of ducks, and bald eagles are all regular visitors. According to Cypress Lake Airboats, the 60-minute tour passes through the highest concentration of bald eagles in Florida. The wildlife is astounding, but the terrain also sets this tour apart. Instead of sticking to the lake, you may go down a small canal, into the reed beds, and up and over the wetlands. The canal, during the cooler months, is a great place to see alligators basking on the banks.

TJ's Airboats ★★
Richardson's Fish Camp, 1550 Scotty Rd., Kissimmee;
☎ 407-846-4287 or 407-846-6540

Hours 9 a.m.–4:30 p.m. **Cost** Daytime airboat rides, 1 hour: $35 + tax for adults; $30 + tax for children ages 3–12; free for children age 2 and under; $100 minimum charge for each 6-person boat, but you can schedule a ride with others. **Authors' rating ★★**.

DESCRIPTION AND COMMENTS TJ's Airboats is located at Richardson's Fish Camp, a short drive from Kissimmee. The nearby location is TJ's greatest asset, although the friendly staff doesn't hurt it either. The fish camp is small but does include a store stocked with fishing gear and snacks. Smoking is permitted inside, so waiting at the tables is hazardous to your health.

The welfare of the passengers' hearing is also a secondary concern. TJ's is the only guided airboat tour in the area that does not require hearing protection—one can only wonder why. You cannot hear the driver's comments while the fan is spinning nor will you be able to hear much after the trip is over. We all came away with a mild case of tinnitus. They do offer earplugs, but you have to ask. Do not leave the dock without them.

Even when the guides talk, the tour is not very informative, stating few if any facts on alligators. You have a good chance of spotting alligators and an assortment of birds; however, the Kissimmee skyline dampens the natural wonder.

Wild Willy's Airboat Tours   ★★★½
4715 Kissimmee Park Rd., St. Cloud; ☎ 407-891-7955; airboatwilly.com

Hours 9 a.m.–5 p.m. or by reservation. **Cost** Daytime airboat tours, 1 hour: $35 + tax for adults; $32 + tax for children ages 3–12; free for children age 2 and under; bring the coupon found in any of the free local advertising magazines. **Authors' rating ★★★½**.

DESCRIPTION AND COMMENTS You can find Wild Willy's (it used to be called Glade Adventures) in a campground a few miles from Orlando. In the small office at the campground is a terrarium that is home to a few baby gators, and if you ask nicely, the staff will let you hold the toothy critters. The staff's knowledge of local wildlife, from the receptionists to the tour guides, is above average. When it's time for the tour, you board a six-passenger airboat and meander off onto the southern end of Lake Toho. This end of the lake has fewer developments than the north end, allowing you to encounter a more pristine Florida.

On your tour, your guide may reveal a few eagle nests. The eagle pairs here leave during the summer, but lone immature eagles are found year-round. Other wildlife includes anhingas, spoonbills, and, of course, alligators. The guides at Wild Willy's carry a pair of binoculars, so you may observe the birds even if they are perched up a distant tree. These tours are peaceful and can involve a bit of drifting under the Florida sun. Wear sunscreen and sit back with one eye closed and the other open to look for gators.

OTHER ANIMAL ATTRACTIONS

THERE IS A FINE ASSORTMENT of other creatures in the Orlando area that do not pose the threat of cleaving an arm. These attractions allow visitors to spend a half day away from the zoo of visitors on US 192 and I-Drive, and to come in contact with a more natural side of central Florida.

Audubon of Florida's Center for Birds of Prey ★★★½
1101 Audubon Way, Maitland; ☎ 407-644-0190; audubonofflorida.org

Hours Tuesday–Sunday, 10 a.m.–4 p.m. **Cost** $5 for adults; $4 for children ages 3–12. **Authors' rating** ★★★½.

DESCRIPTION AND COMMENTS With a mission to "conserve, protect, and restore Florida's natural resources," the Center for Birds of Prey is an outreach facility for rehabilitating injured or ill birds of prey. More than 12,000 birds have been treated here since its inception in 1979. For such a small center, with barely 2½ acres of land, this is quite a feat. The center is also the leading North American caretaker of bald eagles, with more than 250 birds treated. Of the birds treated here, 40% are released back into the wild. Those that are unable to be rehabilitated are kept here or sent to other care facilities.

The small grounds have quite a number of birds, including peregrine falcons, barred owls, burrowing owls, northern caracaras, red-tailed hawks, kestrels, and kites. You will not be allowed to hold any of the animals, but if you ask a keeper, he or she may give you an up-close look. Guided tours are available only to groups larger than ten people, cost $100, and require reservations. The guidebook rental for a self-guided tour is included in the normal admission price.

It is a great addendum to the nearby Orlando Science Museum or the Central Florida Zoo, and the price is right if you can find the place. Here are the directions from I-4: take Exit 87 headed east, to Fairbanks Avenue. Take a left on Fairbanks, then a right on Wymore. Cross Lee Road and continue to the next light (Kennedy Boulevard) and turn right. Continue to East Street. Make a left onto East Street. The center is just ahead at the three-way stop on your left. Even with the directions, we were forced to call multiple times. If that doesn't get you anywhere, just ask the locals; people walking dogs and jogging tend to know where they are going.

The Central Florida Zoo ★★★½
3755 NW Hwy., Sanford (off I-4 at Exit 104 on US 17-92);
☎ 407-323-4450; centralfloridazoo.org

Hours Daily, 9 a.m.–5 p.m.; closed Thanksgiving Day and Christmas Day. **Cost** $11.95 for adults; $9.95 for seniors (age 60+); $7.95 for children ages 3–12. **Authors' rating** ★★★½.

DESCRIPTION AND COMMENTS To see the animals at Busch Gardens or at Disney's Animal Kingdom, you have to buy admission to the entire park. If you were not able to spend an entire day of your trip at either of these destinations or found their prices overbearing, the Central Florida Zoo is worth a visit. It may be a slight drive from Orlando, taking about 30 minutes, but it is closer than Busch Gardens and makes a great half-day trip.

The zoo was founded in 1923 as the Sanford Zoo, moved to its current location in 1975, and has been growing ever since. The zoo bills itself as an educational center, and with the wide variety of animals and animal encounters on weekends and holidays, along with a purported 75,000 children visitors a year, it fulfills its purpose.

The variety of species is impressive for such a small zoo. Asian elephants, cheetahs, crocodiles, kangaroos, and zebus are some of the more interesting animals you will see as you traverse the boardwalks, etched with names of prior visitors.

Weekend visitors will be able to partake in the zoo's lectures and animal interactions. The current weekend schedule is as follows, but is subject to change at any time, so call ahead before the day of your visit: Elephant Demonstrations at 11 a.m. and 2 p.m., Bird Show at 11:30 a.m., Bug Encounter at 1 p.m., Primate Feeding at 2:15 p.m., Feline Feeding at 2:30 p.m., and Reptile Demonstrations at 3 p.m. A member of the zoo staff hosts each 15- to 30-minute exhibition and gives a short fact-laden lecture, then answers any questions. One of the best deals around is the Elephant Encounter at 2:15 p.m. on Saturdays and Sundays where, for $9.50 above the admission price, guests can touch and feed the elephants. Albeit a skewed comparison, a tour of the savanna to feed the giraffes and antelope at Busch Gardens costs $30 per person.

Because almost all the zoo's exhibits are outside, except for the Discovery Zone with its 10-centimeter millipedes and goliath tarantulas, you will need good weather. Sunscreen and water are also advisable, especially with the small aquatic play area called Tropical Splashdown (bring bathing suits and towels). A snack bar is on the premises, but you are better off bringing your own food; a comfortable picnic area is located inside.

Forever Florida ★★★½
Florida Eco-Safaris, 4755 N. Kenansville Rd., St. Cloud;
☎ **407-957-9794; foreverflorida.com**

Hours Vary; reservations required for horseback rides. Cost Horseback ride, 1 hour: $40 + tax per person, must be at least 12 years old; 2 hours: $60 + tax per person, must be at least 12 years old; 3 hours: $80 + tax includes lunch, must be at least 12 years old. Coach safaris, 2½ hours: $28 + tax for adults; $22 + tax for children ages 6–12; free for children age 5 and under. Zip line: $85 + tax per person, must be at least 10 years old and weigh 70–275 pounds. Departs daily at 10 a.m. and 1 p.m. Authors' rating★★★½.

DESCRIPTION AND COMMENTS A long drive from Walt Disney World at about 1½ hours, Forever Florida may fit into your plans if you are either headed to Miami or have just finished an airboat tour south of Kissimmee. Forever Florida is both a working cattle ranch and a nature conservancy. It offers hiking trails, a small petting zoo with pony rides, horseback safaris, eco-safaris, and a new zip line.

When you arrive, you should report to the main desk, located in the Cypress Lodge. The lodge is clean and modern, and contains the Cypress Restaurant, whose menu consists mostly of deep-fried food from the Deep South, with both okra and alligator gracing the menu. A cow burger with fries costs $5.95 plus tax.

The horseback safaris vary in length from 1 hour to multiday excursions and require reservations, close-toed shoes, and long pants. Trips over 2 hours require group reservations. Although 1 hour is all the time we need on a plodding horse, you will not see much on the 1-hour tour but scrub, dried-out pine trees, and open fields. Unlike the picture on the brochure, this is not swampland. The 2-hour tour is somewhat better, culminating in a stop at Bull Creek, a drastically different ecosystem from the rest of the ride's. A small promenade cuts out into the swamp with overhanging cypress and large live oaks. Unfortunately, the stop is all of 10 minutes, and then you're back in the open fields and scrub brush.

The Eco-Safari Tours are 2½ hours and comprise a preliminary presentation and then a tour that explores both the cattle ranch and the land conservation project. The tour begins with a narrated slide show depicting the history of Forever Florida. Dr. William Broussard owned and operated the Crescent J Ranch, where his children came to play. His eldest son, Allen, was fond of nature and went on to become a conservationist before his life was cut short due to Hodgkin's disease. The conservation project was Allen's last request, and the family has attempted to fulfill his dream. Thirty percent of all of the proceeds go to help purchase more land.

After the tragic and touching tribute, you are ushered onto a vehicle similar to the swamp buggy at Boggy Creek Airboat rides. This buggy, with its huge wheels, takes you first toward the cattle ranch, then past a small ditch with alligators, and then out into the conservation area. The tour is fully narrated, and although it will bore little kids to tears, it is one of the most educational attractions in central Florida. After a ride through the open fields, you arrive at Bull Creek and walk around the promenade, then return back to the lodge.

We support Forever Florida's commitment to preservation, and think it has a fine product, but we would be remiss if we didn't emphasize the barren and uninspiring landscape. Besides Bull Creek, the open plains and mild woodlands are not very scenic. We would like to see Forever Florida expand its operations to include a wider variety of terrain and ecosystems, and think it has tremendous potential. However, the zip line canopy tour that opened in 2009 increased the entertainment level for many guests.

The zip line tour lasts 2½ hours, but schedule at least 4 hours to be safe. Once everyone is accounted for, you are taken by jeep to the zip line area. The tour guide gives a brief tour of some caged animals on site, and then everyone enters the briefing area, where you begin putting on the safety gear. The provided harness keeps you in a sitting position while zipping across the trees. The gear does fit snugly, so wear knee-length or longer clothing; closed-toe shoes are a requirement. The zip line tour is open to anyone age 10 and up who weighs 70–275 pounds.

Once everyone has been outfitted in their snug safety devices, it is time to take a walk through the forest to the zip line. The walk is a little uncomfortable due to the amount of gear you are wearing, but soon you are looking at your first ladder to climb. During the course your tour guides will help you cross seven zip lines and two footbridges. At the highest point you will be 55 feet in the air and can zoom up to 25 miles per hour down the zips. Three tour guides are with you at all times. One tour guide will be the first to go across each zip and be on the other side ready to catch everyone. The tops of trees are the main scenery, but the fourth zip line features a small pond with one small alligator in it. The main thrill is gliding along the treetops.

There are two types of tours: the day tour and the moonlight tour. The moonlight tour is done in complete darkness with no lights to illuminate your way up the ladders that you must climb. Themed tours such as Haunted Halloween Zip Tours or Christmas Light Zip Tours are also offered. The tours operate in the rain, cold, or extreme heat but not during high winds or lightning. The summer is a busy season but also extremely hot. To ensure a pleasurable experience, try to book in the winter or fall, if possible, so the summer heat will not be a factor.

Horse World Riding Stables   ★½

3705 S. Poinciana Blvd., Kissimmee; ☎ 407-847-4343; horseworldstables.com

Hours 9 a.m.–5 p.m. Cost Nature trail ride, 1 hour: $43.95 + tax for visitors age 6 and up; $16.95 + tax for children age 3 and under if they ride with a paying adult. Intermediate trail ride, 1 hour: $52.95 + tax for visitors age 10 and up. Advanced trail ride, 1 hour: $74.95 + tax for visitors age 10 and up. The maximum total weight for all the rides is 250 pounds. Riders must wear closed-toed shoes, and long pants are recommended. Reservations are also required. Authors' rating ★½.

DESCRIPTION AND COMMENTS Twelve miles south of US 192 on Poinciana Boulevard, you will find Horse World. As romantic as riding a horse sounds, it is not for everyone. Horse World's featured ride is the nature ride, and although they may call it a "guided [ride] through the woods," what they mean to say is a guided ride with limited or no narration alongside the Poinciana Boulevard. After you've mounted the horse and headed off around the pond, the trail follows the side of the road, leaving its sight—but not the sound of its traffic—for very brief intervals. The walking pace, although suitable for very small children, is arduous for anyone older than 6 years of age. Sitting on top of a plodding horse in an uncomfortable saddle, with cars whizzing past, is not our idea of entertainment. As for the nature, this quote from our guide during one visit sums it up, "See those sticks on the top of that cell phone tower? That's an eagle's nest." The Intermediate Tour takes a similar path to the Nature Ride but goes slightly quicker and a bit farther. Poinciana Boulevard did not have the current high traffic flow it has now when Horse World opened. Horse World is attempting to build trails that head back into the woods, but it is not worth a visit until these trails are completed, so call ahead to see if these trails have opened.

Petting Farm at Green Meadows ★★½ /★★★★
1368 S. Poinciana Blvd., Kissimmee; ☎ 407-846-0770;
greenmeadowsfarm.com

Hours Tours operate continuously 9:30 a.m.–4 p.m. **Cost** $21 + tax; free for children ages 2 and under. **Authors' rating** ★★★★ (for preschoolers and grade schoolers); ★★½ for anyone older.

DESCRIPTION AND COMMENTS Six miles down Poinciana Boulevard off US 192, you will find the Petting Farm at Green Meadows on the right-hand side. The 40-acre "farm" features animal interactions. The animals include the standard barnyard fare of chickens and goats, but also more exotic animals such as llamas and zorses. After you buy your tickets, the attendant at the booth will show you where you can meet up with the rest of the tour. The tours are continuous, so once you've returned to the same site, you've seen the entire farm. Each station features a different animal, and takes 5–15 minutes to visit.

The farm is clean and well maintained. Although only a fence separates you from the highway, the traffic noise is slight, for the most part, and most of the attractions are set back from the road. Scattered tractors and other farm equipment add to the farm theme (no sharp equipment), and besides the smell of animals, the place is charming.

The animal interactions are as up-close as you can imagine. At the chicken, geese, and duck stations, you are allowed inside the pens and can pick up the animals. Watching guests attempt to catch geese may alone be worth the price of admission. You can pet and feed most of the other animals, including the sheep, goats, pigs, and donkeys, and everyone gets a turn to milk the cow and ride the pony. All of the animal feed is free, and hand-sanitizer locations are at every station. There are some larger animals here, and although you cannot pet all of them, they are worth seeing. These include ostriches, bison, llamas, a zebu, a zorse (a horse-and-zebra offspring), water buffalo, and the like.

Besides the animal exhibits, a small train takes guests around the perimeter of the park, and there is also a hayride. For in-park personal transportation, you can rent a small red wagon for $3 to pull diapers and tired children. Most children will love all of the animal interactions, although the geese can scare the very young. Children will find this place much more interesting than adults will, and you may get a bit restless. Expect to spend 2–4 hours here. Prying them away from the petting zoo, even if they've already seen everything, almost always results in tears, but these can be mended with the bribe of ice cream.

PART FOURTEEN

MUSEUMS *and* CULTURAL ATTRACTIONS

MANY VISITORS TO ORLANDO LIMIT THEIR VISITS to a few major theme parks, bypassing the local community. There is often no time allotted for days outside the major parks, and with a "run-till-you-drop" vacation mentality, many vacationers will find themselves worn out, in need of the proverbial vacation from their vacation.

Because the ride-to-ride shuffle of the major parks becomes monotonous after a few days, and that distinguishing line between individual attractions begins to blur, it becomes important to spark your brain before atrophy sets in. The museums and cultural attractions of central Florida all offer a convenient way to reactivate your mind, and surprisingly enough, most are very interesting. From Fantasy of Flight's exhibits on pre-jet aircraft, to the Morse Museum's collections of Tiffany glassware, central Florida contains museums and cultural attractions for all ages and tastes. The prices for many of the exhibits are also more affordable than their touristy competition, and crowds and lines are almost always less.

KIDS AND MUSEUMS

MENTION TO A CHILD THAT YOU ARE PLANNING a visit to a museum and you will receive the requisite groans of disgust. Mention that you plan on taking him with you, and you have a good chance of instigating a full-scale tantrum. Children's negative reactions to museums, gardens, and other cultural attractions are only heightened in Orlando, where the glitz of the major theme parks, with their cartoon-character mascots and patina of utter happiness, emblazons a glazed look in a child's eyes. And, don't forget, your children are on vacation as well, so instilling them with knowledge on their days away from school will be difficult.

Our best advice is to take note of the names of the Orlando Science Center and Fantasy of Flight and to avoid calling the attraction you are going to a museum. Another tactic is balancing your days' visits. If the

Historic Bok Sanctuary is on your list, contemplate leaving the children with your spouse and sending them to nearby Legoland Florida. Because attractions like the Cornell Museum and the Harry P. Leu Gardens are within blocks of the Orlando Science Center, try to balance your group's day by spending the morning playing at the Science Center and the afternoon viewing the gardens.

However you plan your itinerary, stay attuned to the likes and dislikes of your group. Most of the ticket prices are low, so don't be afraid to leave early if necessary. Dragging around bawling children is not only a hassle for you, but disobliges everyone else at an attraction.

ATTRACTIONS

Cornell Fine Arts Museum ★★★★

APPEAL BY AGE	PRESCHOOL ★★	GRADE SCHOOL ★½	TEENS ★★½
YOUNG ADULTS ★★★		OVER 30 ★★★½	SENIORS ★★★

100 Holt Ave., Winter Park; ☎ 407-646-2526; rollins.edu/cfam

Hours Tuesday–Friday, 10 a.m.–4 p.m.; Saturday–Sunday, noon–5 p.m. Closed Mondays. **Cost** $5 for adults, free for students and children. **Authors' rating** ★★★★.

DESCRIPTION AND COMMENTS A $4.5 million renovation of the museum, located on the Rollins College campus, has allowed this six-gallery museum to show more of its permanent collection. Unlike many small museums, the Cornell owns works by very substantial artists, including Winslow Homer, Henri Matisse, Pablo Picasso, Gilbert Stuart, and followers of Peter Paul Rubens. The low entrance fee, free parking, and lakeside location aren't bad visitor bait either.

TOURING TIPS Although the 9,000-square-foot facility was a major expansion, the museum still cannot display all 5,000 of its works at once. The collection rotates every few months, and two of the galleries regularly feature traveling exhibits. The Cornell is the best fine arts museum in central Florida, and even though it is small, the permanent collection dwarfs that of the Orlando Museum of Art.

kids Fantasy of Flight ★★★½

APPEAL BY AGE	PRESCHOOL ★★	GRADE SCHOOL ★★★½	TEENS ★★★½
YOUNG ADULTS ★★★½		OVER 30 ★★★★	SENIORS ★★★★

1400 Broadway Blvd. SE, Polk City; ☎ 863-984-3500; fantasyofflight.com

Hours Daily, 10 a.m.–5 p.m. **Cost** $28.95 + tax for adults; $26.95 + tax for seniors and children ages 6–15; free for children age 5 and under. **Authors' rating** ★★★½.

DESCRIPTION AND COMMENTS A 40-minute drive from Walt Disney World, Fantasy of Flight is dedicated to its namesake. The museum has two parts, the immersion environments and the hangars. We were a bit startled at the high-quality theming in the immersion environments. Guests walk through an exhibit on the birth of flight, flight in World War I, and then aerial warfare in World War II. Full sound and lighting are used to create atmosphere for each historic period. The birth of flight and World War I exhibits are both small, but the World War II exhibit houses an actual B-17 bomber amid the backdrop of an airfield. The immersion technique is very successful in the World War II exhibit, and the life-size figures only aid the effect.

Once you've finished the immersion environments, you enter the hangars where aircraft of pre-jet vintage have found a home. Most of the aircraft are set behind ropes, but a few are open to public inspection. Guided tours are available and meet regularly in the corners of the hangars under signs marked GUIDED TOURS. Besides the aircraft, the two hangars also contain a kids' area called Fun with Flight and flight simulators in Fighter Town. In the kids' area you can attempt to land a hang glider—a video simulation—or create paper airplanes to test for distance. The flight simulators in Fighter Town are World War II–era Corsair cockpits with screens inside. The graphics are not amazing, but on par with any of the flight simulators in Orlando.

Activities at Fantasy for Flight are printed out daily, so call ahead to check the schedule for the day you are visiting, because many tours are offered only once a day. Tours include a Tram Tour of the restricted areas, an Engine and Machine Shop Tour, a Woodshop Tour, and a Sheet Metal and Aircraft Assembly Tour. Daily aerial demonstrations are also a huge draw and usually include some aerobatics in vintage aircraft.

TOURING TIPS There is a direct corollary between your level of interest in aircraft and engineering and the amount of fun you will have here. Although the immersion environments are outstanding, they will take up only about 30 minutes of your visit. Fantasy of Flight makes a good half-day attraction, but children may get bored rather quickly, even with the kids' zone and flight simulators, so try to arrive for the aerial demonstration to give them a perspective on the aircraft at hand. The Rose Compass Diner is also located inside the complex and contains typical diner food at standard prices, a hamburger platter costing $5.95 plus tax.

Harry P. Leu Gardens ★★★½

APPEAL BY AGE	PRESCHOOL ★★	GRADE SCHOOL ★½	TEENS ½
YOUNG ADULTS ★★★½	OVER 30 ★★★★	SENIORS ★★★★	

1920 N. Forest Ave., Orlando; ☎ 407-246-2620; leugardens.org

Hours Daily, 9 a.m.–4 p.m.; closed Christmas Day. **Cost** $7 for adults; $2 for children attending K–12th grade; free for children in preschool and under. **Authors' rating** ★★★½.

DESCRIPTION AND COMMENTS Less isolated than the Historic Bok Sanctuary, the Harry P. Leu Gardens are situated in downtown Orlando, only a few blocks from the Science Center and the Orlando Museum of Art. Besides the location, the gardens' free parking and low admission prices are also appealing to visitors.

There are 50 acres' worth of smaller gardens situated within the Harry P. Leu Gardens. You enter through the Tropical Stream Garden, home to a variety of exotic equatorial plants. Continuing clockwise, you'll pass through the Home Demonstration Gardens, where you may pick up tips for landscaping your own yard. Next you will reach the Vegetable Garden and then the Butterfly Gardens, which both contain their respective namesakes.

In the bottom corner of the gardens is the Arid Garden (cacti and the like) and multitudes of camellias. Indeed, Harry P. Leu Gardens boast the largest camellia collection outside California. As you continue along the paths, you will pass more flowers at the Rose Garden and Floral Clock, before reaching the forest area. Here, you will find bamboo, pines, live oaks, cycads, and an array of deciduous and coniferous trees. The forest area also borders Lake Rowena. Stop at the small overlook before you make your way back to the entrance.

The Leu Museum House is located at the gardens and belonged to the benefactor Harry P. Leu before he donated the land to the city of Orlando in 1961. Tours of this refurbished house are available daily on the half hour 10 a.m.–3:30 p.m., but please note, the house is generally closed in July.

TOURING TIPS Children will be bored here, but adults over age 30 and seniors with a green thumb should find more than a few good ideas for their gardens at home. The palm trees and bamboo groves in the back of the gardens make a great place for a picnic, as does the outcropping deck on the lakefront.

Historic Bok Sanctuary   ★★½

| APPEAL BY AGE | PRESCHOOL ★★ | GRADE SCHOOL ★½ | TEENS ½ |
| YOUNG ADULTS ★★★ | OVER 30 ★★★½ | SENIORS ★★★★ | |

1151 Tower Blvd., Lake Wales; ☎ 863-676-1408; boksanctuary.org

Hours Daily, 8 a.m.–6 p.m., with last entrance at 5 p.m. **Cost** $10 for adults; $3 for children ages 5–12; free for children age 2 and under.; summers (June 1–September 30) are free for kids age 12 and under. **Authors' rating** ★★½.

DESCRIPTION AND COMMENTS A long, 55-mile drive away from the maelstrom of Orlando entertainment, the Historic Bok Sanctuary is a stately place for those seeking solace. Built on the top of Iron Mountain, the sanctuary offers some spectacular views of the plains 298 feet below—quite an altitude shift in central Florida. The chief attractions are the gardens, the tower, and the Pinewood Estate—although it is quite a trek on the hiking trails. The video at the visitor center and the Window by the Pond (a small cabin with a view of a pond) are mildly interesting.

The gardens were designed by the world-famous landscape architect Frederick Law Olmsted Jr., who, among other achievements, also designed the Rose Garden at the White House. The gardens sprawl over the entire hilltop, and a mixture of concrete and wood-chip walking paths allow you to see most of the landscaping. The design of the gardens is exceptional, but many of the flowers are seasonal, so plan your visit accordingly. There are few plaques to tell you what the plants are, so you will have to bring your keen personal knowledge, or a book.

In the center of the gardens, the Tower at Bok Sanctuary is the centerpiece of the estate. Built on the top of the mountain, this Neo-Gothic colossus dominates the landscape, made even more virile by the reflecting pool at its base. You cannot enter the tower or even cross the moat that surrounds it, so do not plan on getting the view from the top. Daily carillon concerts are played from the bells at the top of the tower, and although some prolonged tones can be discordant, many patrons seem to enjoy the music.

Away from the tower, Pinewood Estate, on the far side of the hill from the visitor center, joined the Historic Bok Sanctuary in 1970. Tours of this Mediterranean Revivalist mansion get under way at noon and 2 p.m. for the additional fee of $6 for adults and $3 for children ages 5–12. Kids age 12 and under get in free June 1–September 30.

TOURING TIPS Do not take kids to the Bok Sanctuary unless they need to be punished or enjoy studying botany in their free time. You will only disturb the other visitors and hand your children more retaliatory fodder for their teenage years.

The Historic Bok Sanctuary is a silent place, and time passes very slowly on the mountain. Self-reflection and boredom are the two chief results of a visit, so prepare your head before you come. Much of the serenity propagated at the visitor center seems forced, but if you are ready for a bit of solitude and don't want to shell out for a mud spa, this is a high-quality alternative.

The Mennello Museum of Art ★★½

APPEAL BY AGE		PRESCHOOL ★		GRADE SCHOOL ★½		TEENS ½
YOUNG ADULTS ★★			OVER 30 ★★★		SENIORS ★★★	

900 E. Princeton St.; ☎ 407-246-4278; mennellomuseum.org

Hours Tuesday–Saturday, 10:30 a.m.–4:30 p.m.; Sunday, noon–4:30 p.m. **Cost** $4 for adults; $3 for seniors; $1 for students with ID; free for children under age 12. **Authors' rating** ★★½.

DESCRIPTION AND COMMENTS When you walk in, your first question will be, "Where is the rest of the museum?" We're not sure, but the four rooms do hold a fine, if minor, collection of local Florida art. Most of the paintings are by Earl Cunningham, a St. Augustine resident and folk artist. The majority of his works are oil paintings on fiberboard. Most depict landscapes dotted with ships and houses, images ingrained from his upbringing in Edgecomb, Maine, and his travels up and down the East Coast. His use of vivid colors is unique and his ability to flatten three-dimensional shape is reminiscent of Cubism.

TOURING TIPS Check out an Earl Cunningham painting before arriving to see if it suits your taste. Some works may be found online at **mennello museum.org.** Behind the museum is a large grassy area on the side of Lake Formosa, a good place for a picnic.

Morse Museum of American Art ★★★★

APPEAL BY AGE	PRESCHOOL ★	GRADE SCHOOL ★★	TEENS ★★★
YOUNG ADULTS ★★★½		OVER 30 ★★★★	SENIORS ★★★★

445 N. Park Ave., Winter Park; ☎ 407-645-5311; morsemuseum.org

Hours Tuesday–Saturday, 9:30 a.m.–4 p.m.; Sunday, 1–4 p.m.; closed Mondays. **Cost** $5 for adults; $4 for seniors; free for children under age 12; free for everyone on Friday, 4–8 p.m., November–April. **Authors' rating★★★★.**

DESCRIPTION AND COMMENTS After watching the introductory video, make your way through one of the world's most extensive and astounding collections of Louis Comfort Tiffany. The collection includes his jewelry, but the real gems—pun intended—are found in his glasswork. Vases, jars, lamps, and stained-glass windows are all testament to his skill as a craftsman.

Also included at the Morse Museum is the Tiffany Chapel. Built in 1893 for the World's Exposition in Chicago, the chapel was almost destroyed multiple times before arriving in Florida in the mid-20th century. The porticos and stained glass are remarkable, but the chandelier, in the shape of a hypercube cross, will drop your jaw.

TOURING TIPS The one-story museum contains 19 small galleries. The layout is clean and every item is well marked. After walking through the galleries, stop by the gift shop. It does not contain any authentic Tiffany but does hock some fine glasswork.

Orange County Regional History Center ★★★

APPEAL BY AGE	PRESCHOOL ★★	GRADE SCHOOL ★★★½	TEENS ★★
YOUNG ADULTS ★★★		OVER 30 ★★★½	SENIORS ★★★½

65 E. Central Blvd., Orlando; ☎ 407-836-8500 or 800-965-2030; thehistorycenter.org

Hours Monday–Saturday, 10 a.m.–5 p.m.; Sunday, noon–5 p.m. **Cost** $9 for adults; $7 for seniors; $6 for children ages 5–12; free for children age 2 and under. **Authors' rating★★★.**

DESCRIPTION AND COMMENTS With an apropos location in the heart of downtown Orlando, the history center documents the growth of the Orlando area. Besides the myriad of facts and artifacts, the museum's layout and theming rival those found in other major metro areas. Instead of placing each artifact in a glass case with a small explanatory plaque, the museum has integrated many of them into re-creations, or has placed them in unorthodox positions, such as hanging from the ceiling.

Visitors start their chronological tour on the fourth floor with the Timucuan Native American exhibit and the pioneer exhibit. The Timucuan were the original inhabitants of the area, and the museum goes a long way to bring them back to life by displaying original canoes, wax sculptures of the people, and the remains of a massive shell pile. Skipping across the hall transports you a few hundred years into the future to a room dedicated to the first homesteaders. Re-creations of their lives and documents of their hardships fill this room. A replica of a cabin, complete with period tools, is the centerpiece of the exhibit.

Descending to the third floor, visitors will find a restored 1927 criminal court, which is worth a peek if meetings are not being held. Across from this is the exhibit on the area between 1900 and 1971, when Disney came to town. The second floor is home to modern regional history, ranging from the civil rights movement to the influence of Disney on the community. The positive economic impact of Disney is balanced against the displays highlighting the rise in crime and expansion of urban sprawl.

TOURING TIPS Although the theming is top-notch, the history lessons of Orange County are not very compelling. Florida residents and locals will find this museum much more entertaining than guests from other states. For a chronological tour, begin on the top floor and work your way down. Street parking is difficult to find, although there are plenty of parking garages in the neighborhood. If you do find street parking, the 2-hour time restraint should allow you enough time to peruse the museum and make it back to your car before you receive a ticket.

Orlando Museum of Art ★★

APPEAL BY AGE	PRESCHOOL ★★½		GRADE SCHOOL ★½		TEENS ★
YOUNG ADULTS ★★½		OVER 30 ★★★		SENIORS ★★	

2416 N. Mills Ave., Orlando; ☎ 407-896-4231; omart.org

Hours Tuesday–Friday, 10 a.m.–4 p.m.; Saturday–Sunday, noon–4 p.m.; closed Mondays. **Cost** $8 for adults; $7 for seniors; $5 for students ages 6–17; free for children age 5 and under. **Authors' rating** ★★.

DESCRIPTION AND COMMENTS We expected more from the permanent collection of the largest art museum in the area with the highest admission. A few exhibits, one on African art and another on art of the ancient Americas, along with a few paintings—including a few works by Andy Warhol—are the primary extent of the permanent collection. The museum's small collection is understandable when taking into account its dedication to traveling exhibits, such as the 2010 look at American Impressionism. The museum's size and donor-based fundraising allow it to display these traveling works, and many of these exhibits are first-rate. If you are not interested in the main traveling exhibit, the admission price is too high to make the rest of the museum worthwhile.

TOURING TIPS Call ahead to see what exhibit the museum is hosting. Free parking is available in front of the impressive building, and the museum is located within walking distance of both the Mennello Museum and the Orlando Science Center.

kids Orlando Science Center ★★★★½

APPEAL BY AGE	PRESCHOOL ★★★★	GRADE SCHOOL ★★★★½	TEENS ★★★½
YOUNG ADULTS ★★★		OVER 30 ★★★½	SENIORS ★★★½

777 E. Princeton St., Orlando; ☎ 407-514-2000 or 888-OSC-4FUN; osc.org

Hours Thursday–Tuesday, 10 a.m.–5 p.m.; closed Wednesdays and major holidays. **Cost** Tickets include all Cinedome (IMAX) presentations but not all visiting exhibits: $17 + tax for adults; $16 + tax for seniors age 55+ and students with ID; $12 + tax for children ages 3–11; free for children age 2 and under. **Authors' rating ★★★★½**.

DESCRIPTION AND COMMENTS When the thrill rides and shows have pounded your frontal lobe into slack-jawed submission, you may be ready for something more educational. In this case, a trip to the Science Center is a good idea, and not as boring as it might seem. Like WonderWorks, the Science Center contains a menagerie of scientific exhibits geared toward kids, a mixture of playtime and learning. Unlike WonderWorks, the Science Center provides more than a series of factoids that give a gist of the mechanics on hand. Almost every exhibit at the center contains an in-depth analysis of the history and physics behind the items on display. Most of the attractions found at WonderWorks are found at the Orlando Science Center—but with exponentially more attractions, a much larger complex, state funding, an IMAX theater, shorter lines, and cheaper tickets, the Orlando Science Center is the superior choice.

The first floor, located below the main entrance, contains the cafeteria, **NatureWorks, KidsTown,** and **Cinedome**—better known as the IMAX theater. Animals can be found at **NatureWorks** at the base of the elevator. NatureWorks is home to baby alligators, sea turtles, and fish. Check the daily schedule for feeding times.

Next to these natural exhibits is the **KidsTown,** which takes up most of the first floor. You must be less than 48" tall to enter, or accompanying your child. Some high points of the KidsTown are the tree house, the orange-picking simulator (we couldn't make that up), and the Water Table, where kids can build dams and channels.

The real draw on the first floor is not the KidsTown but the **Cinedome.** The eight-story screen acts as both an IMAX theater and a planetarium. Tickets are included in your entrance fee; however, you will need to stop by the main ticket counter on the second floor before each show—we recommend 45 minutes before—to claim a seat. The quality of the movies varies, but the towering screen makes even the dullest documentary tolerable, and the interesting shows spellbinding. Remember, with any theater attractions, adults with babies and children given to crying should sit in the back of the theater near the aisle. Bawling infants ruin more productions than cell phones ever could, and they don't, no matter how much you shush them, contain an off switch.

The other three floors of the museum contain nine massive halls with exhibits, science stations, and live programs that change seasonally. All of the exhibits are top-notch traveling exhibits, and if you didn't know better, you'd assume that they were part of an amazing permanent collection.

Call ahead or check the museum's website to see what shows are occurring during your visit. Recent exhibitions have included one that teaches kids how to take care of their bodies, with a virtual-reality tour of the immune system; and an area that features Curious George, complete with a construction area, galaxy, and fire escape.

The cafeteria, located on the first floor, has better deals than many Orlando restaurants, not to mention theme parks. A hamburger with fries is $4.50, a slice of cheese pizza is $1.75, and a large soda is $2. The cafeteria also has a great selection of healthy alternatives such as lean sandwiches, milk, juice, yogurt, and salads.

The gift shop is also cheaper than many Florida attractions. Most of the items are educational toys. Puzzles, space-shuttle models, books (one conspicuously titled *How to Go to the Bathroom in Space*), dayglow stars to decorate your ceiling, and construction helmets with lanterns are all on sale here. The gift shop is located on the second floor across from the front desk.

TOURING TIPS This museum is a fantastic mixture of learning and play. The building is laid out, like the Guggenheim in New York, around an open and circular center, with a glass elevator in the middle. There are four floors in the Science Center, and because it is rarely crowded, you may see them in any order, although starting on the second floor and working up, saving the first floor for last, is our preferred method. Maps are available at the front desk/ticket window.

Winter Park Boat Tours ★★★

APPEAL BY AGE	PRESCHOOL ★★	GRADE SCHOOL ★★½	TEENS ★½
YOUNG ADULTS ★★★	OVER 30 ★★★½		SENIORS ★★★★

312 E. Morse Blvd., Winter Park; ☎ 407-644-4056; scenicboattours.com

Hours Daily, 10 a.m.–4 p.m. Closed Christmas Day; tours depart on the hour. **Cost** $12 for adults; $6 for children ages 2–11; free for children age 1 and under; no credit cards accepted. **Duration of tour** 1 hour. **Authors' rating** ★★★.

DESCRIPTION AND COMMENTS Winter Park Boat Tours is located on Lake Osceola in Maitland, north of Orlando, a few miles from the Orlando Science Center and the Orlando Museum of Art, and near the Rollins College campus. The 1-hour tours begin on Lake Osceola.

The fully narrated tours take place on 18-passenger pontoon boats and review the history of Maitland County. After passing the summer house of oil tycoon Harry Sinclair, you squeeze through a thin canal into 223-acre Lake Virginia. Modern mansions adorn the east side of the lake, while Rollins College, and the home of the late Mr. Rogers of children's television fame, are to the west. Passing back through the canal and to the other side of Lake Osceola, you head through a longer and thinner canal into Lake Maitland. Here you will see more mansions, including one previously owned by basketball star Horace Grant. The tour is similar to being in the backyard of the very affluent.

TOURING TIPS The boat is a fine way to break up your day while touring museums, and the narration is very informative, although the tour guides are hesitant about revealing the names of the present owners of any of the houses. The boats have no bathrooms and are open to the sun, so be sure to use the facilities dockside and bring sunscreen and, if you own them, polarized sunglasses.

Zora Neale Hurston National Museum of Art ½
227 E. Kennedy Blvd., Eatonville; ☎ 407-647-3307; zoranealehurstonmuseum.org

Hours Monday–Friday, 9 a.m.–4 p.m.; Saturday, 11 a.m.–1 p.m. **Cost** Free. **Authors' rating** ½.

DESCRIPTION AND COMMENTS We were very disappointed with this one-room museum, although the price is right. Funded by a foundation in her name, the Zora Neale Hurston Museum exhibits focus on African culture and change frequently, but the one-room space is too small to house much of interest.

TOURING TIPS Unfortunately—doubly so for literary buffs—there is nothing here about the life and times of author Zora Neale Hurston. We are fans of Hurston's writings, but this museum does not do justice to her love of the creative arts. A self-guided walking tour of her hometown of Eatonville—the first all–African American town incorporated in the United States—is more substantial. You can find walking-tour brochures at the museum or at many of the local businesses.

PART FIFTEEN

AFTER DARK

DINNER SHOWS

CENTRAL FLORIDA PROBABLY HAS MORE dinner attractions than anywhere else on earth. The name *dinner attraction* is something of a misnomer because dinner is rarely the attraction. These are audience-participation shows or events with food served along the way. They range from extravagant productions where guests sit in arenas at long tables to intimate settings at individual tables. Don't expect terrific food, but if you're looking for something entertaining outside of Walt Disney World, consider one of these.

If you decide to try a non-Disney dinner show, scavenge local tourist magazines from brochure racks and hotel desks outside Disney World. These free publications usually have discount coupons.

THE SHOWS

Arabian Nights

APPEAL BY AGE	PRESCHOOL ★★★½	GRADE SCHOOL ★★★★½	TEENS ★★½
YOUNG ADULTS ★★★½		OVER 30 ★★★	SENIORS ★★★½

6225 W. US 192, Kissimmee; ☎ 407-239-9223; arabian-nights.com

Show times Sunday–Tuesday and Thursday, 6 p.m.; Wednesday, Friday, and Saturday, 8:30 p.m.; only 1 show nightly. **Reservations** Can usually be made through the day of the show. **Cost** $64.99 for adults; $41 for children ages 3–11. **Discounts** Coupons in local magazines, AAA, seniors, military; 25% discount available online. **Type of seating** Long rows of benches at tables flanking each side of a large riding arena. All seats face the action. **Menu** Salad, prime rib or chicken breast, mixed vegetables, garlic mashed potatoes, and sheet cake. Children's alternative is chicken fingers with mashed potatoes. **Vegetarian alternative** Lasagna. **Beverages** Unlimited Busch beer, blush wine, tea, coffee, and soft drinks.

DESCRIPTION AND COMMENTS Horses and riders present equestrian skills and trick riding with costumes, music, and theatrical lighting. The loose story line involves a princess who spots a handsome prince, who then disappears. A pair of genies, named Shararazad and Abra-Kadabra, grant her three wishes that, understandably, she uses to try to find the stud on the steed. For the sake of a plot, she doesn't just tell the genie to produce the guy front and center, so instead, they travel the world over—and back in time—to look for him. The search takes them anywhere they might find horses: the circus, the Wild West, the set of *Ben Hur,* and so on.

If you are an unbridled horse fan, or a little girl (we know of very few who don't like horses and magic-laden princess stories), you're going to think you've died and gone to heaven. Fifty horses, including Lipizzans, palominos, quarter horses, and Arabians, perform 22 acts. The stunts are impressive, and a great deal of skill and timing is employed to pull them off. All of the horse tricks found during an entire performance at Medieval Times, excluding jousting, are performed in just the opening of Arabian Nights. Yet after a while, the tricks start to look the same, and only the costumes and the music are different. However, the short run time of a little over an hour and a half keeps the tedium from setting in. The ending of the show has been changed from a pandering patriotic ploy to a beautiful snowy scene where the horses gambol about the arena. It's truly a lovely sight.

The prime rib is edible, and the lasagna alternative is fine. The salad is unappealing, as is the dessert. In a departure from other dinner theaters, the food here is served in the dark, making each bite a bit of a surprise.

Capone's Dinner & Show

APPEAL BY AGE	PRESCHOOL ★½	GRADE SCHOOL ★★★★	TEENS ★★★½
YOUNG ADULTS ★★★		OVER 30 ★★★	SENIORS ★★★½

4740 W. US 192, Kissimmee; ☎ 407-397-2378; alcapones.com

Show times Nightly, 7:30 p.m.; changes seasonally. **Reservations** Need to make reservations several days in advance. **Cost** $51.99 for adults; $31.99 for children ages 4–12 (does not include tax or tip). **Discounts** Florida residents, AAA, seniors, military, hospitality workers. **Type of seating** Long tables with large groupings facing an elevated stage; some smaller tables for parties of 2–6, balcony seating available. **Menu** Buffet with lasagna, baked ziti, spaghetti, baked chicken, baked ham, boiled potatoes, tossed salad, and brownies. **Vegetarian alternative** Spaghetti, ziti, pasta salad. **Beverages** Unlimited beer, wine, tea, coffee, and soft drinks.

DESCRIPTION AND COMMENTS The audience, attending a celebration for mobster Al Capone at a 1930s speakeasy in Chicago, enters through a secret door using a password. The show is a musical of sorts, with most songs from other sources sung by cast members to recorded accompaniment. The story revolves around two female leads. There is Miss Jewel—the speakeasy's hostess, who is enamored of Detective Marvel, the only cop in Chicago whom Capone can't buy—and one of the show's floozies and her gambling boyfriend. (Can you say *Guys and Dolls?*)

The audience parades through the buffet line before the show; seconds are invited. The food, which had been passable in the past, should now just be passed up. During a recent visit, the plastic flowers above the buffet were in dire need of dusting.

For a musical, this show employs a lot of nonsingers. Even the dancing is second-rate. The waiters—who speak with tough-guy accents and kid around with guests—did more to entertain the children than at any other show. Still, the theme is a bit too adult for families.

Two lines form before the show. You must go to the line on the left, directly into the box office, to pick up or purchase your tickets before joining the long line of guests leaning against the building. If you don't want to loiter outside, you can buy one drink per person and sit in the "office," which is a lounge upstairs.

Makahiki Luau

APPEAL BY AGE	PRESCHOOL ★★½	GRADE SCHOOL ★★½	TEENS ★★
YOUNG ADULTS ★★★		OVER 30 ★★★	SENIORS ★★★½

SeaWorld, 7007 SeaWorld Dr., Orlando; ☎ 800-327-2420; seaworld.com

Show times Nightly, 6 p.m. **Reservations** Need to make reservations at least 3 days in advance; reservations can be made online; payment is due at time of booking. **Cost** $46 for adults; $29 for children ages 3–9; free for children under age 3 with a reservation. **Discounts** Seasonally. **Type of seating** Long tables; no separation from other parties. **Menu** Fruit "pu pu" platter, salad, mahimahi in piña colada sauce, Hawaiian chicken, sweet-and-sour pork, fried rice, vegetables, and a seasonal dessert. **Vegetarian alternative** Salad, mixed vegetables, sticky rice. **Beverages** 1 complimentary mai tai; full cash bar. This is the only show to offer just one cocktail.

DESCRIPTION AND COMMENTS The Makahiki Luau has the appearance of a touring lounge act that might play the Ramada Inn circuit in the Midwest. Even the venue, a large, dark room with a very low ceiling, looks like a motel lounge. In this musical revue featuring singers, dancers, and fire twirlers, a Don Ho–esque singer is given way too much time. The dancers perform well, and the fire twirler who ends the show is impressive, but there is otherwise little excitement.

The food is more varied than at many shows. The mahimahi is good, but the fruit platter is fairly uninteresting. The food is served family-style, and you may share a platter with another family.

The service is not very attentive. Audience participation is minimal, and children probably will be bored.

kids Medieval Times Dinner and Tournament

APPEAL BY AGE	PRESCHOOL ★★★½	GRADE SCHOOL ★★★½	TEENS ★★★
YOUNG ADULTS ★★½		OVER 30 ★★½	SENIORS ★★

4510 E. US 192, Kissimmee; ☎ 800-229-8300;
medievaltimes.com/orlando.aspx

Show times Vary according to season and nights. **Reservations** Best to make reservations a week ahead. **Cost** $59.95 for adults; $37.95 for children ages 3–12 (does not include tax or tip). **Discounts** Seniors, military, AAA, hotel employees, travel agents. You get free admission on your birthday with 2 full-paying adults;

valid ID required for proof. **Type of seating** Arena style, in rows that face the riding floor. **Menu** Garlic bread, vegetable soup, whole roasted chicken, spare ribs, herb-basted potatoes, and strudel. Everything is eaten by hand. **Vegetarian alternative** Lasagna, or raw veggies with dip plate. **Beverages** 2 rounds of beer, sangria, or soft drinks; cash bar available.

DESCRIPTION AND COMMENTS A tournament set 900 years in the past pits six knights against one another. Audience members are seated in areas corresponding to the color of the knights' pennants and are encouraged to cheer for their knight and boo his opponents. Part of the tournament is actual competition. The knights perform stunts, including hitting a target with a lance or collecting rings on a lance while riding on horseback. After each event, successful knights receive carnations from the queen to toss to young ladies in their sections.

After a while, the tournament takes on a choreographed feel—and with good reason. It comes down to a fight to the finish until only one knight is left standing. Cheating knights pull others off their horses and have hand-to-hand combat with maces, battle-axes, and swords. The winning knight selects a fair maiden from the audience to be his princess.

In all, the show is mediocre, but the knights give 100% (the bruises they must get!). The sword fights are so realistic that sparks fly off the metal blades, but the kicking and punching choreography is worse than that found in professional wrestling. Even so, audience participation reaches a fevered pitch, with each section cheering for its knight and calling for the death of the dastardly opponents.

With all the horses, jousting, and fighting, children shouldn't be bored (although it does get repetitive), and parents of very young children might be concerned about the violence.

The food is remarkable only in that you eat it with your hands, including a whole chicken you must pull apart. The chicken is good, but the ribs are a little tough.

Outta Control Magic Show at WonderWorks

APPEAL BY AGE	PRESCHOOL ★★★½	GRADE SCHOOL ★★★★	TEENS ★★
YOUNG ADULTS ★★★½		OVER 30 ★★★½	SENIORS ★★★

9067 International Dr., Orlando; ☎ 407-351-8800; wonderworksonline.com

Show times Nightly, 6 p.m. and 8 p.m. **Reservations** Can be made up to the day of the show. **Cost** $24.99 for adults; $16.99 for seniors and children ages 4–12 (does not include tax or tip). **Discounts** Florida residents, AAA, AARP, military. **Type of seating** Communal tables. **Menu** Popcorn, unlimited pizza. **Vegetarian alternative** Cheese pizza. **Beverages** Unlimited beer, wine, and soft drinks.

DESCRIPTION AND COMMENTS For younger children, this is the funniest dinner show in Orlando. Two magicians and one assistant perform sleight-of-hand magic tricks coupled with a constant barrage of puns and sophomoric humor. A sound-effects board with a series of push buttons allows the magicians to add a version of morning radio show humor to their repertoire of jokes, all the while keeping the audience guessing, "What's in the box?!"

Although legerdemain, and a few other illusions, will awe young children, adults will find the tricks rather ordinary and will be unimpressed with the magicians' ability to make a sponge ball disappear. However, the magicians' repartee with the audience keeps the show alive and entertaining. Both magicians are gifted at improvising and toying with audience members. Almost every group of people that attends will have a member hauled up onto the stage. If you're brought up, the safest thing to do is just play along. You may get teased and hassled by the magicians, but only a fraction as much as you will be for refusing to come on stage.

The show is enjoyable and the food service is good, but the pizza is terrible and you may have to share the popcorn bowls with other people's children. Make sure yours wash their hands before the show.

Pirate's Dinner Adventure

APPEAL BY AGE	PRESCHOOL ★★★½	GRADE SCHOOL ★★★½	TEENS ★★
YOUNG ADULTS ★★½	OVER 30 ★★½		SENIORS ★★★

6400 Carrier Dr., Orlando; ☎ 407-248-0590; piratesdinneradventure.com

Show times Nightly, seasonal, 7:45 p.m. **Reservations** Can be made up to the day of the show. **Cost** $59.95 for adults; $54.95 for seniors; $39.95 for children ages 3–11 (does not include tax or tip). **Discounts** Florida residents, AAA, AARP, military, travel agents, Dollar rental car employees, police, firefighters, Girl Scouts. **Type of seating** Arena style. **Menu** Salad, beef and roasted chicken, fresh vegetables, ice cream, and apple cobbler; children's alternative is chicken fingers. **Vegetarian alternative** Lasagna. **Beverages** Unlimited beer, wine, and soft drinks.

DESCRIPTION AND COMMENTS Audience members are told to arrive long before the doors open to the auditorium. In the meantime, guests mill about and look over maritime memorabilia and nosh on assorted appetizers. The pirate museum, at the far end of the hall, is worth a visit and contains lengthy tales of pirates and their dastardly deeds. As show time approaches, a "host pirate" leads the audience members in song and dance, and a man demonstrates his fire-eating skills. Audience members will later recall that this man had the best meal of the evening. After a bit more preshow, guests are ushered into the dining area, which features a life-size pirate ship surrounded by water.

The set is impressive, and throughout the evening pirates swoop from overhead, race around the ship in boats powered by electric motors, toss balls into nets with the help of audience volunteers, and bounce on a trampoline that's part of the ship. What's mystifying is that there doesn't seem to be a reason for any of this. The sound system is poor, and it was difficult to tell what was going on and why. Audience members sit in color-coded sections and are encouraged to cheer for pirates wearing their colors as they compete against each other. There's plenty to interest kids. Adults might be interested too, if the story were easier to follow.

Sleuths Mystery Dinner Shows

APPEAL BY AGE	PRESCHOOL ★½	GRADE SCHOOL ★★★	TEENS ★★★½
YOUNG ADULTS ★★★★		OVER 30 ★★★★	SENIORS ★★★★

8267 International Dr., Orlando; ☎ 407-363-1985; sleuths.com

Show times Vary nightly; 6 p.m., 7:30 p.m., or 9 p.m. **Reservations** Can be made up to the day of the show. **Cost** $52.95 for adults; $23.95 for children ages 3–11 (does not include tax or tip). **Discounts** Florida residents, AAA, seniors, students, Disney employees, travel agents, military, hospitality employees. **Type of seating** Large, round tables that seat 8–10; some smaller tables. **Menu** Fruit platter and smoked salmon; assorted hot and cold hors d'oeuvres; tossed salad; choice of Cornish hen, prime rib (at an extra $3 charge), or lasagna; veggies and a baked potato; mystery dessert. **Vegetarian alternative** Cheese lasagna. **Beverages** Unlimited beer, wine, or soft drinks.

DESCRIPTION AND COMMENTS Sleuths enact a repertoire of murder mysteries that the audience must solve. Audience participation is key to the enjoyment. Guests are part of the show from the moment they enter the theater. Actors in character direct seating and try to drop clues as to who and what their parts are in the play. Although they work from a script, much of the show is ad-libbed. Fortunately, the cast tends to be very talented and capable of ad-libbing well. After the audience is seated, the first act occurs, and someone is murdered. During intermission, each table must choose a spokesman and prepare a question for the second act, where the collective audience interrogates the actors in an attempt (foolhardy as it seems, due to the actors' elusive responses) to solve the murder. Know that unless you come with a group of eight people, you will probably find yourself interacting with the strangers at your table.

You'll probably have more fun if you go with a large group and occupy your own table. Older children might find the show interesting, but younger ones will be bored and may disturb the other guests who are trying to follow the show.

The food has improved drastically from the old cheese spread and crackers. Guests who arrive early will be able to nibble on a platter of fresh fruit and smoked salmon. The prime rib was tough during our visit, but the Cornish hen was excellent.

FAMILY-FRIENDLY COMEDY SHOW

SAK Improv Comedy

APPEAL BY AGE	PRESCHOOL ★★½	GRADE SCHOOL ★★★½	TEENS ★★★★½
YOUNG ADULTS ★★★★		OVER 30 ★★★★	SENIORS ★★★½

29 S. Orange Ave., Orlando (downtown, off Exit 82 from I-4);
☎ 407-648-0001; sak.com

Show times Vary for different shows; *Duel of Fools,* Thursday–Saturday at 7:30 p.m. with periodic performances at 9:30 p.m. Calling ahead for reservations is strongly encouraged. **Cost** $15 per person; $12 for seniors, students, and military.

DESCRIPTION AND COMMENTS   SAK is an improv comedy troupe whose graduates include daytime talk show host Wayne Brady, and writers for shows such as *SNL, Mad TV,* and *Everybody Loves Raymond.*

SAK offers a variety of shows, which in the past has included an improv opera, but their baseline show is the long running *Duel of Fools.* The show features two teams competing in a series of improv sketches, very much like the television show *Whose Line Is It Anyway?* (that also featured Wayne Brady). Because shows besides the *Duel of Fools* change frequently, call or check the website for a list of other available shows.

The *Duel of Fools* is a clean show with no cursing, and the humor relies on absurd situations. The types of improv sketches vary throughout the evening from on-the-spot songs based on audience suggestion to raw pantomime. Each sketch is about 5 minutes, so any that are mundane are over quickly, while the funnier ones continue until the scenario becomes too absurd to comprehend. Because there is no script, the performance varies each show, but the quality of actors remain the same, and their ability to integrate any suggestions into a humorous scene is outstanding.

Parking for SAK is available on the street for free or in the nearby Plaza Cinema Garage ($4 validated parking). In 2010 the theater moved to a new location with 200 seats and an expanded concession and lounge area, where popcorn, candy, and sodas are offered.

UNIVERSAL ORLANDO CITYWALK

CITYWALK IS A SHOPPING, DINING, AND ENTERTAINMENT venue that doubles as the entrance plaza for the Universal Studios and Islands of Adventure theme parks. Situated between the parking complex and the theme parks, CityWalk is heavily trafficked all day but truly comes alive at night.

CityWalk offers a number of nightclubs to sample, and many of those entertainment and restaurant venues depend on well-known brand names. At CityWalk you'll find a Hard Rock Cafe and concert hall; Jimmy Buffett's Margaritaville; a Bubba Gump Shrimp Co.; NBA City, a sports bar; a NASCAR Sports Grille; a branch of New Orleans's famous Pat O'Brien's club; and a reggae club that celebrates the life and music of Bob Marley. Places that operate without big-name tie-ins include The Red Coconut Club, a lounge and nightclub; the groove, a high-tech disco; CityWalk's Rising StarJazz, a karaoke club with a live backup band; and the Latin Quarter, a space dedicated to food, music, and culture of all 21 Latin nations.

Another CityWalk distinction is that most of the clubs are also restaurants, or alternatively, most of the restaurants are also clubs. Although there's a lot of culinary variety, restaurants and

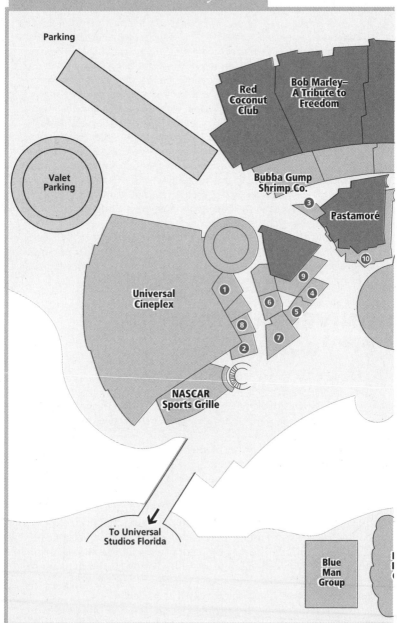

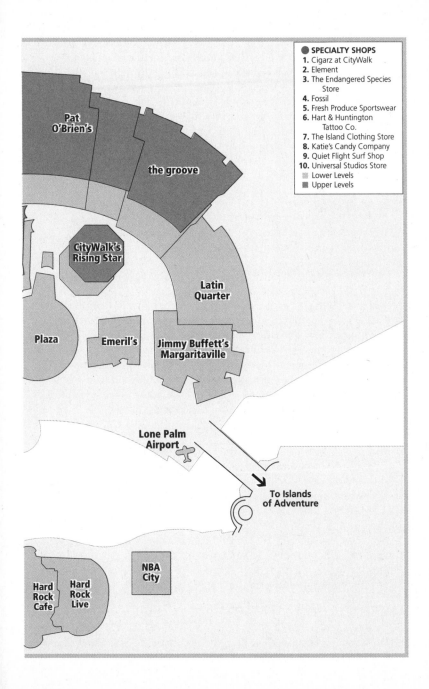

SPECIALTY SHOPS
1. Cigarz at CityWalk
2. Element
3. The Endangered Species Store
4. Fossil
5. Fresh Produce Sportswear
6. Hart & Huntington Tattoo Co.
7. The Island Clothing Store
8. Katie's Candy Company
9. Quiet Flight Surf Shop
10. Universal Studios Store
   Lower Levels
   Upper Levels

Pat O'Brien's

the groove

CityWalk's Rising Star

Latin Quarter

Plaza

Emeril's

Jimmy Buffett's Margaritaville

Lone Palm Airport

To Islands of Adventure

NBA City

Hard Rock Cafe

Hard Rock Live

nightclubs are different animals. Sight lines, room configuration, acoustics, intimacy, and atmosphere—important considerations in a nightclub—are not at all the same in a venue designed to serve meals. Although it's nice to have all that good food available, the club experience is somewhat dulled. Working through the lineup, Pat O'Brien's, the groove, and CityWalk's Rising Star are more nightclub than restaurant, whereas Margaritaville is more restaurant than club. Bob Marley's and the Latin Quarter are about half and half. The Hard Rock Cafe, NASCAR Sports Grille, NBA City, Emeril's, and Pastamoré are restaurants.

GETTING THERE

THE UNIVERSAL FLORIDA COMPLEX can be accessed via Kirkman Road from I-4, Exit 75B. Driving from the Walt Disney World area, take I-4 Exit 74A onto Sand Lake Road heading north (away from International Drive) and turn right onto Turkey Lake Road. Follow the signs to the Turkey Lake Road entrance.

ADMISSION PRICES

CITYWALK'S PARTY PASS ALL-CLUB ACCESS is $11.99, which gets you into all the clubs (you can also pay $15.98 and add a movie). The Party Pass is complimentary with the purchase of any multiday theme-park admission. Otherwise, you can pay individual cover charges at each club; these tend to run $4–$8 apiece. Given this price range, getting the all-access pass makes the most sense unless you intend to visit just one club. Not into the club scene? The Meal and Movie Deal is $21.95 and includes—what else?—dinner at one of the CityWalk restaurants (you choose from a special menu) and a movie.

ARRIVING

ONCE WITHIN THE UNIVERSAL COMPLEX, you'll be directed to park in one of two multitiered parking garages. Parking runs $15 for cars and $20 for RVs. Be sure to write down the location of your car before heading out of the garages—the evening will end on a considerably brighter note if you avoid wandering about the garages searching for the rental car. An alternative: if you're out for a special occasion or just want to have everything taken care of, Universal also offers valet parking (2 hours) for $15; $25 for more than 2 hours. After 6 p.m., parking is $3, with the exception of valet services. From the garages, moving sidewalks transport you directly to CityWalk.

CONTACTING CITYWALK

CONTACT CITYWALK GUEST SERVICES AT ☎ 407-224-2691, or visit its website at **citywalk.com**. Keep in mind, though, that CityWalk personnel may not be up on individual club doings, so your best bet may be to contact specific clubs directly when you reach the Orlando area.

CITYWALK CLUBS

Bob Marley—A Tribute to Freedom

What it is Reggae restaurant and club. **Hours** Daily, 4 p.m.–2 a.m. **Cuisine** Jamaican-influenced appetizers and main courses. **Entertainment** Reggae bands in the outdoor gazebo every night. **Cover** $7 after 9 p.m. nightly (more for special acts).

COMMENTS This club is a re-creation of Marley's home in Kingston, Jamaica, and contains a lot of interesting Marley memorabilia. The courtyard is the center of action. Must be age 21 or older after 9 p.m.

CityWalk's Rising Star

What it is Karaoke club with live band and backup singers Tuesday–Saturday (Sunday–Monday, sing to recorded tracks with live backup singers). **Hours** Nightly, 8 p.m.–2 a.m. **Cuisine** Appetizers. **Entertainment** Karaoke. **Cover** $7.

COMMENTS With a live band backing you up, you can pretend that you've hit the big time at this karaoke club.

the groove

What it is High-tech disco. **Hours** Nightly, 9 p.m.–2 a.m. **Cuisine** No food. Entertainment DJ plays dance tunes. Sometimes there are live bands. **Cover** $7.

COMMENTS Guests must be age 21 or older to enter this très-chic club designed to look like an old theater in the midst of restoration. There are seven bars and several themed cubbyholes for getting away from the thundering sound system. Dancers are barraged with strobes, lasers, and heaven knows what else.

Hard Rock Live

What it is Live music concert hall and club. **Hours** Nightly, 7 p.m. until closing. **Cuisine** Limited menu. **Entertainment** House band performs weekdays with big-name groups taking over on weekends. **Cover** $10 for house band; cover varies for name acts.

COMMENTS Great acoustics, comfortable seating, and good sight lines make this the best concert venue in town. House band is excellent. By the by, the Hard Rock Live concert hall and the Hard Rock Cafe restaurant are separate facilities.

Jimmy Buffett's Margaritaville

What it is Key West–themed restaurant and club. **Hours** Daily, 11:30 a.m.– 2 a.m. **Cuisine** Caribbean, Florida fusion, and American. **Entertainment** Live rock and island-style music after 10 p.m. **Cover** $7 after 10 p.m.

COMMENTS Jimmy's is a big place with three bars that turns into a nightclub after 10 p.m. If you eat dinner here, you'll probably want to find another vantage point when the band cranks up.

Latin Quarter

What it is Latin salsa-themed restaurant and live music hall. **Hours** Sunday–Wednesday, 5–10 p.m. (dinner only); Thursday–Saturday, 5 p.m.–2 a.m. (dinner served until 10 p.m.) **Cuisine** Latin American. **Entertainment** Spanish guitar nightly and a DJ Thursday–Sunday after 10 p.m. **Cover** $7 after 10 p.m.

COMMENTS Primarily a restaurant with entertainment on the side. Live music (and sometimes dancing) is performed in sets throughout the night. After 10 p.m. Thursday–Saturday, the restaurant turns into a nightclub with a DJ playing Latin and Reggaeton music.

Pat O'Brien's Orlando

What it is Dueling pianos sing-along club and restaurant. **Hours** Daily, 4 p.m.–2 a.m. **Cuisine** Cajun. **Entertainment** Dueling pianos and sing-alongs. **Cover** $7 after 9 p.m. for piano bar only.

COMMENTS A clone of the famous New Orleans club of the same name. You can dine in the courtyard or on the terrace without paying a cover. You must be age 21 or older to hang out here.

The Red Coconut Club

What it is Modern lounge and nightclub. **Hours** Sunday–Thursday, 8 p.m.–2 a.m; Friday–Saturday, 6 p.m.–2 a.m. **Cuisine** Expensive appetizers. **Entertainment** Lounging and dancing. **Cover** $7 after 9 p.m.

COMMENTS This nightspot is billed as a nightclub and "ultra-lounge," although what that means is anyone's guess. There is a lounge and a dance floor, and the bar features signature martinis. Happy hour is 8–10 p.m. Sunday–Thursday and 6–9 p.m. Saturday, and the signature drinks are half-priced.

DOWNTOWN ORLANDO/ CHURCH STREET STATION AREA

VISITORS IN THEIR 20S AND EARLY 30S may find the experience at CityWalk a bit contrived. Indeed, any nighttime entertainment that attempts to bring in families and individuals between the ages of 18 and 80 will have a hard time indulging the "hip" demographic. When you attempt to offer a select amount of evening entertainment over large age and taste ranges, you compromise your selections of music, theming, and prices, usually settling for the most generic solutions possible. For people in their 20s, downtown Orlando makes no compromises in taste. This is a hip urban center, and although it is not New York or Miami, the nearby University of Central Florida provides plenty of other young people to party with over a whole swath of different bars and dance clubs.

Once you're there, remember that bars in the Orlando area close at 2 a.m. The bars below represent a cross section of what is available, but there are many more bars on and around Church Street for you to find and explore. You must be age 21 and older (and have a valid photo ID) to enter any of the bars, although some nightclubs may let you in if you are between 18 and 21 years old, but you will not be allowed to drink. Call ahead for details.

GETTING THERE

TAKE I-4 TO EAST ANDERSON STREET, Exit 82C. Turn right onto West Anderson and go a few blocks until you reach South Rosalind Avenue. Turn left on South Rosalind and look for parking. All of the bars are located only a few blocks apart, so if you drive, you can park as long as you want in the garages along Pine Street, just north of Church Street, for $5. If you do not have a designated driver, you must take a taxi. A cab ride one-way to Universal costs around $25, while a trip to Disney will cost around $55. There are no good reasons to drive drunk, and Orlando police set up frequent sobriety checkpoints to catch inebriated drivers (if you think we are just being cautious, take a sober drive around downtown or along I-4 at night). When taking a cab, try to go with a group of people—if you're not with one, check your hotel lobby—to spread the cost.

BARS AND CLUBS

Antigua

What it is Dance club. **Hours** 8 p.m.–2 a.m. **Entertainment** Latin-flavored music and Miami vibe. **Cover** $5–$8. **Location** 41 W. Church St. **Contact** ☎ 407-649-4270; **churchstreetbars.com.**

COMMENTS Antigua attempts to replicate a stereotypical slice of Miami's South Beach district inside a bar. The bar is set up around an enclosed courtyard complete with fake rocks, waterfalls, pinkish lighting, and—just like every street in Miami—window ledges with cages for dancers. A large dance floor is in the center, but it may be difficult to spot with all of the machine-made fog. The music is mostly rap and dance music, with salsa music on Sundays.

Chillers

What it is Nightclub. **Hours** 7 p.m.–2 a.m. **Entertainment** Small dance floor. **Cover** $5–$8 on Friday and Saturday. **Location** 33 W. Church St. **Contact** ☎ 407-649-4270; **churchstreetbars.com.**

COMMENTS Chillers is a frat boy's fantasy. This compact bar is rather dirty, with the unmistakable scent of stale beer. Young adults in collared shirts make use of the myriad of frozen daiquiri machines that line the wall behind the bar. Upstairs is a small balcony with booth seating. College students will appreciate the $1 well drinks on Wednesday.

Cleo's Lounge

What it is Lounge with pool tables. **Hours** 5 p.m.–2 a.m. **Entertainment** Pool tables, great atmosphere. **Cover** None. **Location** 11 S. Court Ave. **Contact** ☎ 407-841-4545.

COMMENTS Cleo's is near the Wall Street bars at the corner of Court Street and Pine Street. This is one of our favorite hangouts. Live DJs often spin underground records, but the music is not so loud as to drown out conversation. The place is cozy and home to "the most inconvenient bathrooms" in Orlando, not that they are terribly hard to get to. Domestic bottles cost $3.50, and they have a large collection of wines. Cleo's is not to be confused with the other Cleo's, a "gentlemen's club" on Orange Blossom Drive.

Dragon Room

What it is VIP Lounge. **Hours** 7 p.m.–2 a.m. **Entertainment** Other VIPs. **Cover** $20. **Location** 25 W. Church St. **Contact** ☎ 407-843-8600; **dragonroom orlando.com.**

COMMENTS When you go out in black shoes and a collared shirt with a large fold of cash, you might be able to get into this chic nightspot, but odds are you're not on the guest list. The crowd here is older, in their early 30s, and don't be surprised when you receive a $12 tab for a vodka and soda. The music is mostly electronic.

The Lodge

What it is Bar made to feel like a ski lodge. **Hours** Monday–Friday, 4 p.m.– 2 a.m.; Saturday, 7 p.m.–2 a.m.; Sunday, 8 p.m.–2 a.m. **Entertainment** Beer and talk. **Cover** None. **Location** 49 N. Orange Ave. **Contact** ☎ 407-650-8786; **downtownlodge.com.**

COMMENTS Located a short walk up Orange Avenue, The Lodge is where people in their late 20s and early 30s congregate. The bar has a ski-lodge vibe, and for the whole month of July, it celebrates "Christmas in July," decorating the interior with snowmen, Christmas lights, and candy canes. The music is generally 1980s rock ballads.

Wall Street Plaza Bars

What it is 8 bars together, 1 cover on weekends. **Hours** Vary. **Entertainment** Some dancing, normal bar activities. **Cover** $5 for entry to area with all bars on Friday and Saturday after 9 p.m. **Location** 18 Wall Street Plaza. **Contact** ☎ 407-849-0471; **wallstplaza.net.**

COMMENTS These eight bars are the hub of weekend nightlife in downtown Orlando. The bars that put on the weekly block party are the Globe, the Wall Street Cantina, WaiTiki, Slingapour's, the Tuk Tuk Room, the Loaded Hog, One Eyed Jack's, and the Monkey Bar. Most of the bars have outside seating; guests can carry drinks from one bar to another. Some serve food into the evening, and the Tuk Tuk Room offers sushi. Slingapour's has a dance floor, but there are better dance clubs to visit on Church Street. This area really takes off around 10:30 p.m.—our pick for the place to go on the weekends.

PART SIXTEEN

DINING

DINING *outside* WALT DISNEY WORLD

UNOFFICIAL GUIDE RESEARCHERS love good food and invest a fair amount of time scouting new places to eat. And because food at Walt Disney World is so expensive, we (like you) have an economic incentive to find palatable meals outside the World. Unfortunately, the area surrounding Disney World is not exactly a culinary nirvana. If you thrive on fast food and the fare at chain restaurants (Denny's, T.G.I. Friday's, Olive Garden, and the like), then you'll be as happy as an alligator at a chicken farm. If, however, you're in the market for a truly superlative dining experience, you'll find the pickings outside the World of about the same quality as those inside, only less expensive. In addition, some ethnic cuisines aren't represented in Walt Disney World restaurants.

Among specialty restaurants both in and out of the World, location and price will determine your choice. There are some decent Italian restaurants in Walt Disney World as well as in adjoining tourist areas—which one you select depends on how much money you want to spend and how convenient the place is to reach. Our recommendations for specialty and ethnic fare served outside of Disney World are summarized in the table that starts on the next page.

Better restaurants outside Walt Disney World cater primarily to adults and aren't as well equipped to deal with children. If, however, you are looking to escape children or want to eat in peace and quiet, you're more likely to find such an environment outside the World.

TAKE OUT EXPRESS

IF YOU'RE STAYING IN A HOTEL outside Disney World, **Take Out Express** (7111 Grand National Dr.; ☎ 407-352-1170; **orlandotakeout express.com**) will deliver a meal from your choice of more than 20

Where to Eat outside Walt Disney World

AMERICAN

Everglades Restaurant Rosen Centre, 9840 International Drive, Orlando; ☎ 407-996-2385; **evergladesrestaurant.com;** moderate to expensive. Seafood and steaks and unusual creations such as gator chowder and buffalo tenderloin.

Hue* 629 East Central Boulevard, Orlando; ☎ 407-849-1800; **huerestaurant.com;** moderate to expensive. Chic hot spot in trendy Thornton Park, but the food is still star of the show—try the sea bass.

Luma on Park* 290 South Park Avenue, Winter Park; ☎ 407-599-4111; **lumaonpark.com;** moderate to expensive. New American cuisine in a cool dining room on Winter Park's trendy Park Avenue.

Seasons 52 7700 West Sand Lake Road, Orlando; ☎ 407-354-5212; **seasons52.com;** moderate to expensive. Delicious, creative New American food (and low in fat and calories). Solid wine list.

BARBECUE

Bubbalou's Bodacious Bar-B-Que 5818 Conroy Road, Orlando (near Universal Orlando); ☎ 407-295-1212; **bubbalous.com;** inexpensive. Tender, smoky barbecue; tomato-based killer sauce.

CARIBBEAN

Bahama Breeze 8849 International Drive, Orlando; ☎ 407-248-2499; **bahamabreeze.com;** moderate. A creative and tasty version of Caribbean cuisine from the owners of the Olive Garden and Red Lobster chains.

CHINESE

Ming Court 9188 International Drive, Orlando; ☎ 407-351-9988; **ming-court.com;** moderate to expensive. Wok-fired dishes, sushi.

CUBAN/SPANISH

Columbia 649 Front Street, Celebration; ☎ 407-566-1505; **columbiarestaurant.com;** moderate. Authentic Cuban and Spanish creations, including paella and the famous 1905 Salad.

Numero Uno* 2499 South Orange Avenue, Orlando; ☎ 407-841-3840; **numero-uno-restaurant.com;** inexpensive. No trip to Florida is complete without a sampling of Cuban food.

EASTERN EUROPEAN

Chef Hans Cafe* 3716 Howell Branch Road, Winter Park; ☎ 407-657-2230; **chefhanscafe.com;** moderate. Family-run cafe with authentic and delicious dishes. Don't leave without having a slice (or five) of the apple strudel.

ETHIOPIAN

Nile Ethiopian Restaurant 7040 International Drive, Orlando;
☎ 407-354-0026; **nile07.com;** moderate. Small space in a strip mall;
authentic stews and delicious vegetarian dishes. Open for dinner only.

FRENCH

Le Coq au Vin* 4800 South Orange Avenue, Orlando; ☎ 407-851-6980;
lecoqauvinrestaurant.com; moderate. A perennial local favorite featuring
country French cuisine in a relaxed atmosphere. Reservations suggested.

INDIAN

Memories of India 7625 Turkey Lake Road, Orlando; ☎ 407-370-3277;
moderate. A quiet atmosphere with some of the best Indian cuisine in the
area. A bit more reasonable than some other I-Drive–area Indian restaurants.

Passage to India 6129 Westwood Boulevard, Orlando; ☎ 407-351-3456;
passagetoindiarestaurant-orlando.com; moderate. A lot of locals brave
International Drive just to dine here.

ITALIAN

Antonio's Sand Lake 7559 West Sand Lake Road, Orlando;
☎ 407-363-9191; **antoniosonline.com;** moderate to expensive.
Upscale Italian that's a popular choice among locals.

Bice Loews Portofino Bay Hotel, 5601 Universal Blvd., Orlando;
☎ 407-503-1415; **biceorlando.com;** expensive. Authentic Italian;
great wines.

JAPANESE/SUSHI

Amura 7786 West Sand Lake Road, Orlando; ☎ 407-370-0007; **amura.com;**
moderate. A favorite sushi bar for locals. The tempura is popular too.

Hanamizuki 8255 International Drive, Orlando; ☎ 407-363-7200;
hanamizuki.us; moderate to expensive. Usually filled with Japanese visitors;
pricey but very authentic.

Nagoya Sushi 7600 Dr. Phillips Boulevard, in the very rear of the Dr. Phillips
Market Place; ☎ 407-248-8558; **nagoyasushi.com;** moderate. A small,
intimate restaurant with great sushi and an extensive menu.

MEXICAN

Chevys Fresh Mex 12547 State Road 535, Lake Buena Vista;
☎ 407-827-1052; **chevys.com;** inexpensive to moderate.
Conveniently located across from the FL 535 entrance to WDW.

Don Pablo's 8717 International Drive, Orlando; ☎ 407-354-1345;
donpablos.com; inexpensive. Good food but can be a bit noisy.

20 minutes or more from the tourist areas

Where to Eat outside Walt Disney World (continued)

MEXICAN (CONTINUED)

Vallarta Mexican Grill   12167 South Apopka–Vineland Road, Orlando; ☎ 407-238-5300; inexpensive. Family-owned restaurant serving freshly prepared Mexican dishes. Full bar.

NEW WORLD

Norman's   4012 Central Florida Pkwy., in the Ritz-Carlton Orlando; ☎ 407-393-4333; **normans.com;** expensive. Norman Van Aken, patron of New World cuisine, offers a menu that changes often—but you'll always find his sinfully delicious conch chowder. World-class wine menu. Open for dinner only.

SEAFOOD

Bonefish Grill   7830 West Sand Lake Road, Orlando; ☎ 407-355-7707; **bonefishgrill.com;** moderate. Casual setting along busy Restaurant Row on Sand Lake Road. Choose your fish, and then choose a favorite sauce to accompany. Also steaks and chicken.

McCormick & Schmick's   4200 Conroy Road, Mall at Millenia, Orlando; ☎ 407-226-6515; **mccormickandschmicks.com;** expensive. Menu changes often based on freshness. Raw oysters are a big hit.

STEAK/PRIME RIB

The Capital Grille   Pointe Orlando, 9101 International Drive, Orlando; ☎ 407-370-4392; **thecapitalgrille.com;** expensive. Dry-aged steaks, extensive wine list, and classic decor.

Charley's Steak House   6107 South Orange Blossom Trail, Orlando; ☎ 407-851-7130; moderate to expensive. There are other locations for this small chain, including one just east of the Interstate 4 interchange on US 192.

Texas de Brazil   5259 International Drive, Orlando; ☎ 407-355-0355; **texasdebrazil.com;** expensive. All-you-care-to-eat in an upscale Brazilian-style *churrascuria*. Filet mignon, sausage, pork ribs, chicken, lamb, and more. Kids under age 6 free, ages 7 to 12 half price. Salad bar with more than 40 options.

Vito's Chop House   8633 International Drive, Orlando; ☎ 407-354-2467; **vitoschophouse.com;** moderate. Surprisingly upscale meat house with a taste of Tuscany.

THAI

Red Bamboo   6803 South Kirkman Road at International Drive, Orlando; ☎ 407-226-8997; **redbamboothai.com;** moderate. Housed in an unassuming strip-mall location and acclaimed by Orlando dining critics for its authentic Thai dishes. Delicious vegetarian options; impressive wine list. The *Unofficial* research team agrees that this is some of the best Thai food anywhere. Try the fried cheesecake for dessert.

restaurants, including **T.G.I. Friday's, Toojay's Deli, Passage to India,** and **Kim Wu Chinese Restaurant.** The delivery charge is $5 per restaurant, with a minimum $15 order. Gratuity is added to the bill. Cash, traveler's checks, MasterCard, Visa, American Express, and Discover are accepted. Hours are 4:30–11 p.m.

ONE MAN'S TREASURE

A MAN FROM RICHLAND, WASHINGTON, URGES:

> I think that you should in future editions promote the Crossroads at Buena Vista [Shopping Center] a little stronger. There are plenty of non-WDW restaurants at non-WDW prices. The Crossroads is nothing less than a small city that can service all your needs.

CROSSROADS SHOPPING CENTER is on FL 535, directly across from the entrance to Walt Disney World Village and the Downtown Disney Resort Area. As the reader suggests, it offers about everything you might need. Fast food is sold at **McDonald's** and **Taco Bell.** Up a notch are **Chevys, T.G.I. Friday's,** the pizzeria **Uno,** and **Red Lobster.** For a more upscale meal, pick **Johnnie's Hideaway,** featuring steaks and seafood. When you finish eating, shop for sportswear, swimwear, and athletic shoes.

BUFFETS AND MEAL DEALS OUTSIDE WALT DISNEY WORLD

BUFFETS, RESTAURANT SPECIALS, and discount dining abound in the area surrounding Walt Disney World, especially on US 192 (known locally as the Irlo Bronson Memorial Highway) and along International Drive. The local visitor magazines, distributed free at non-Disney hotels among other places, are packed with advertisements and discount coupons for seafood feasts, Chinese buffets, Indian buffets, breakfast buffets, and a host of combination specials for everything from lobster to barbecue. For a family trying to economize, some of the come-ons are mighty appealing. But are these places any good? Is the food fresh, tasty, and appealing? Are the restaurants clean and inviting? Armed with little more than a roll of Tums, the *Unofficial* research team tried all the eateries that advertise heavily in the free tourist magazines. Here's what we discovered.

CHINESE SUPER BUFFETS Whoa! Talk about an oxymoron. If you've ever tried preparing Chinese food, especially a stir-fry, you know that split-second timing is required to avoid overcooking. So it should come as no big surprise that Chinese dishes languishing on a buffet lose their freshness, texture, and flavor in a hurry.

For the past few editions of this guide, we were able to find several Chinese buffets that were a cut above the rest and that we felt comfortable recommending. Unfortunately, however, our endorsements seem to be the kiss of death: we return the next year to discover that quality has slipped precipitously. We attempted to find a new buffet to replace the ones we deleted from the guide, and we can tell you that wasn't fun work. At the end of the day, **Mei Asian Bistro** (8255 International Dr.; ☎ 407-352-0881) is the only Chinese buffet we've elected to list. To call it a *super* buffet might be stretching things, but aside from a lackluster dessert selection, it's pretty good.

INDIAN BUFFETS Indian food works much better on a buffet than Chinese food; in fact, it actually improves as the flavors marry. In the Walt Disney World area, most Indian restaurants offer a buffet at lunch only—not too convenient if you plan on spending your day at the theme parks. If you're out shopping or taking a day off, here are some Indian buffets worth trying:

Aashirwad Indian Cuisine   5748 International Dr., at the corner of International Drive and Kirkman Road; ☎ 407-370-9830

Punjab Indian Restaurant   7451 International Dr.; ☎ 407-352-7887

BRAZILIAN BUFFETS A number of Brazilian buffets have sprung up along International Drive. The best of these is **Vittorio's** (5159 International Dr., near the outlet malls at the northern end of I-Drive; ☎ 407-352-1255; **vittoriosrestaurant.com**).

GENERAL BUFFETS **Bill Wong's** (5668 International Dr.; ☎ 407-352-5373) offers fair value. The restaurant represents itself as a Chinese buffet but shores up its Asian selections with peel-and-eat shrimp, prime rib, and a nice selection of hot and cold vegetables.

SEAFOOD AND LOBSTER BUFFETS These affairs don't exactly fall under the category of inexpensive dining. The main draw (no pun intended) is all the lobster you can eat. The problem is that lobsters, like Chinese food, don't wear well on a steam table. After a few minutes on the buffet line, they make better tennis balls than dinner. If, however, there's someone in the kitchen who knows how to steam a lobster, and if you grab your lobster immediately after a fresh batch has been brought out, it will probably be fine. There are three lobster buffets on US 192 and another two on International Drive. Although all five do a reasonable job, we prefer **Boston Lobster Feast** (6071 W. US 192; ☎ 407-396-2606; and 8731 International Dr., five blocks north of the Convention Center; ☎ 407-248-8606; **bostonlobsterfeast.com**). Both locations are distinguished by a vast variety of seafood in addition to the lobster. The International Drive location is cavernous and insanely noisy, which is why we prefer the US 192 location, where you can actually have a conversation over dinner. There's ample parking at the International Drive location, while parking places are in short supply at the US 192 restaurant. At about $35 for early birds (4–6 p.m.) and $40 after 6 p.m., dining is expensive at both locations.

unofficial **TIP**
Discount coupons for many of the buffets are available in local visitor magazines.

SALAD BUFFETS The most popular of these in the Walt Disney World area is **Sweet Tomatoes** (6877 S. Kirkman Rd.; ☎ 407-363-1616; **sweet tomatoes.com**). During lunch and dinner, you can expect a line out the door, but fortunately one that moves fast. The buffet features prepared salads and an extensive array of ingredients to build your own. In addition to the rabbit food, Sweet Tomatoes offers a variety of soups, a modest pasta bar, a baked-potato bar, an assortment of fresh fruit, and ice-cream sundaes. Dinner runs $9.89 for adults, $5 for children ages 6–12, and $3.49 for children ages 3–5. Lunch is $8.49 for adults and the same prices as dinner for children (all prices are without tax).

BREAKFAST AND ENTRÉE BUFFETS Entrée buffets are offered by most chain steak houses in the area, such as **Ponderosa, Sizzler,** and **Golden Corral.** Among them, they have 18 locations in the Walt Disney World area. All serve breakfast, lunch, and dinner. At lunch and dinner, you get the buffet when you buy an entrée, usually a steak. Generally speaking, the buffets are less elaborate than a stand-alone buffet but considerably more varied than a salad bar. Breakfast service is a straightforward buffet (that is, there is no obligation to buy an entrée). As for the food, it's chain-restaurant quality but decent all the same. Prices are a bargain, and you can get in and out at lightning speed—important at breakfast when you're trying to get to the theme parks early. Some locations offer lunch and dinner buffets at a set price without your having to buy an entrée.

Though you can argue about which chain serves the best steak, Golden Corral wins the buffet contest hands down, with at least twice as many offerings as its three competitors. While buffets at Golden Corral and Ponderosa are pretty consistent from location to location, the buffets at the various Sizzlers vary a good deal. The pick of the Sizzlers is the one at 7602 W. US 192 (☎ 407-397-0997). In addition to the steak houses, area **Shoney's** also offer breakfast, lunch, and dinner buffets. Local freebie visitor magazines are full of discount coupons for all of the above.

MEAL DEALS Discount coupons are available for a wide range of restaurants, including some wonderful upscale-ethnic places such as **Ming Court** (Chinese; 9188 International Dr., Orlando; ☎ 407-351-9988; **ming-court.com**). Our favorite prime-rib joint is **Wild Jack's Steaks & BBQ** (7364 International Dr.; ☎ 407-352-4407). The decor is strictly cowboy modern, but the beef is some of the best in town, and the price is right.

unofficial **TIP**
Many Chinese dishes simply do not work on a buffet. The exception might be a busy local Chinese lunch spot where buffet items are replenished every 5 or so minutes. Even then, however, the food doesn't measure up to dishes that are cooked to order and served fresh out of the wok. At the Chinese super buffets, the food often sits a long time. We've tried the buffets advertised in the visitor magazines (and a few that weren't), and while many had great eye appeal, the food was often ho-hum.

At the **Black Angus Steak House,** the beef is served with salad, a choice of vegetables or potato, and bread, and it's available at two locations convenient to Disney: 7516 W. US 192, ☎ 407-390-4548; and 6231 International Dr., ☎ 407-354-3333. Another meat eater's delight is the Feast for Four at **Sonny's Real Pit Bar-B-Q,** a Florida chain that turns out good barbecue. For $40 per family of four, you get sliced pork or beef plus chicken, ribs, your choice of three sides (beans, slaw, or fries), garlic bread or cornbread, and soft drinks or tea, all served family-style. The closest location to the Walt Disney World and Universal tourist areas is at 7423 S. Orange Blossom Trail in Orlando (☎ 407-859-7197); for a listing of other locations within a wider radius, visit **sonnysbbq.com.** No coupons are needed or available for Sonny's, but they are available for the other "meateries."

FAST FOOD IN THE THEME PARKS

BECAUSE MOST MEALS DURING vacation are consumed on the run while touring, we'll tackle counter-service and vendor foods first. Plentiful in all theme parks are hot dogs, hamburgers, chicken sandwiches, salads, and pizza. They're augmented by special items that relate to the park's theme or the part of the park you're touring. Counter-service prices are fairly consistent from park to park. Expect to pay the same for your coffee or hot dog at Busch Gardens as at SeaWorld.

Getting your act together in regard to counter-service restaurants in the parks is more a matter of courtesy than necessity. Rude guests rank fifth among reader complaints. A mother from Fort Wayne, Indiana, points out that indecision can be as maddening as outright discourtesy, especially when you're hungry:

> Every fast-food restaurant has menu signs the size of billboards, but do you think anybody reads them? People waiting in line spend enough time in front of these signs to memorize them, and still don't have a clue what they want when they finally get to the order taker. If by some miracle they've managed to choose between the hot dog and the hamburger, they then fiddle around another 10 minutes deciding what size Coke to order. Tell your readers, PULEEEZ get their orders together ahead of time!

Cutting Your Dining Time at the Theme Parks

Even if you confine your meals to vendor and counter-service fast food, you lose a lot of time getting food in the theme parks. When it comes to fast food, *fast* may apply to the time you spend eating it, not the time invested in obtaining it.

Here are suggestions for minimizing the time you spend hunting and gathering food:

1. Eat breakfast before arriving. Don't waste touring time eating breakfast at the parks. Besides, many restaurants offer some

outstanding breakfast specials. Some hotels furnish small refrigerators in their guest rooms, or rent them. If you can get by on cold cereal, rolls, fruit, and juice, having a fridge in your room will save a ton of time. If you can't get a fridge, bring a cooler.

2. After a good breakfast, buy snacks from vendors in the parks as you tour, or stuff some snacks in a fanny pack. This is very important if you're on a tight schedule and can't spend a lot of time waiting in line for food.

3. All theme-park restaurants are busiest between 11:30 a.m. and 2:15 p.m. for lunch and 6 p.m. and 9 p.m. for dinner. For shorter lines and faster service, don't eat during these hours, especially 12:30–1:30 p.m.

4. Many counter-service restaurants sell cold sandwiches. Buy a cold lunch (except for drinks) before 11:30 a.m. and carry it until you're ready to eat. Ditto for dinner. Bring small plastic bags in which to pack the food. Purchase drinks at the appropriate time from any convenient vendor.

5. Most fast-food eateries have more than one service window. Regardless of time of day, check the lines at all windows before queuing. Sometimes a window that's manned but out of the way will have a much shorter line or none at all. Note, however, that some windows may offer only certain items.

6. If you're short on time and the park closes early, stay until closing and eat dinner later. If the park stays open late, eat dinner about 4 or 4:30 p.m. at the restaurant of your choice. You should miss the last wave of lunchers and sneak in just ahead of the dinner crowd.

Beyond Counter Service: Tips for Saving Money on Food

Though buying food from counter-service restaurants and vendors will save time and money (compared with full-service dining), additional strategies can bolster your budget and maintain your waistline. Here are some suggestions our readers have made over the years:

1. Go on vacation during a period of fasting and abstinence. You can save a fortune and save your soul at the same time!

2. Wear clothes that are slightly too small and make you feel like dieting (no spandex allowed!).

3. Whenever you're feeling hungry, ride attractions that induce motion sickness.

4. Leave your cash and credit cards at your hotel. Buy food only with money your children fish out of fountains and wishing wells.

A Missouri mom writes:

I have shared our very successful meal plan with many families. We stayed six nights and arrived after some days on the beach south of Sarasota. We shopped there and arrived with our steel Coleman cooler well stocked with milk and sandwich fixings. I froze a block of ice in a milk bottle, and we replenished it daily with ice from the resort ice machine. I also froze small packages of deli-type meats for later in the week. We ate cereal, milk, and fruit each morning, with boxed juices. I also had a hot pot to boil water for instant coffee, oatmeal, and soup.

Each child had a belt bag of his own, which he filled from a special box of goodies each day. I made a great mystery of filling that box in the weeks before the trip. Some things were actual food, such as packages of crackers and cheese and packets of peanuts and raisins. Some were worthless junk, such as candy and gum. They grazed from their belt bags at will throughout the day, with no interference from Mom and Dad. Each also had a small, rectangular plastic water bottle that could hang on the belt. We filled these at water fountains before getting into lines and were the envy of many.

We left the park before noon; ate sandwiches, chips, and soda in the room; and napped. We purchased our evening meal in the park at a counter-service eatery. We budgeted for both morning and evening snacks from a vendor but often did not need them. It made the occasional treat all the more special. Our cooler had been pretty much emptied by the end of the week, but the block of ice was still there.

We interviewed one woman who brought a huge picnic for her family of five packed in a large diaper/baby paraphernalia bag. She stowed the bag in a locker (offered by all theme parks and swimming parks) and retrieved it when the family was hungry. A Pennsylvania family adds:

Despite the warning against bringing food into the park, we packed a double picnic lunch in a backpack and a small shoulder bag. Even with a small discount, it cost $195 for the seven of us to tour the park for a day, and I felt that spending another $150 or so on two meals was not in the cards. We froze juice boxes to keep the meat sandwiches cool (it worked fine) and had an extra round of juice boxes and peanut-butter sandwiches for a late-afternoon snack. We took raisins and a pack of fig bars for sweets, but didn't carry any other cookies or candy to avoid a "sugar low" during the day. Fruit would have been nice, but it would have been squashed.

Note: Some parks have a rule against bringing your own food and drink into the park. Although after 9/11 all packs, purses, diaper bags, and such are searched, security usually does not enforce this ban.

Finally, a mom from Whiteland, Indiana, who purchases drinks in the parks, offers this suggestion:

One must-take item if you're traveling with younger kids is a supply of small paper or plastic cups to split drinks, which are both huge and expensive.

DINING *at* UNIVERSAL ORLANDO

ONE OF OUR CONSTANT GRIPES about theme parks is the food. To many guests hustling through the parks, dining is a low priority—they don't mind the typically substandard fare and high prices because their first objective is to see the sights and ride the rides. This is certainly understandable, but the *Unofficial Guide* team is made up of big fans of big eating. We feel there's no reason not to expect high-quality food and service when theme parks invest so much elsewhere in design, production, and development.

The good news is that food in Universal is almost always a cut above and a step ahead of what you can find at Walt Disney World and other parks. More variety, better preparations, and more current trends are generally the rule at Universal. Counter-service and fast-food offerings are comparable to Disney. To help you make choices for sit-down meals at breakfast, lunch, or dinner, we've provided profiles of Universal's full-service places, most of which are located in the CityWalk complex.

Universal rolled out its answer to Downtown Disney with a vengeance in 1999. Like Downtown Disney, CityWalk is a combination of entertainment and dining with a focus on adults. Restaurant tastes run the gamut, from the elegant (**Emeril's Orlando**) to the basic (**NASCAR Sports Grille**)—or, if you prefer, from the sublime to the ridiculous. All the restaurants share one common trait: they are loud. But there is good food to be found inside some of them. Most of the eateries are partners with Universal's culinary team. For information about CityWalk's nightclub scene, see the Universal Orlando CityWalk section in Part Fifteen, After Dark.

In addition to these restaurants, the three Loews hotels on Universal's property offer various full-service dining opportunities. At the Portofino Bay resort, you'll find Mama Della's, with Italian comfort food served in a casual dining space where Mama is in charge.

unofficial **TIP**
You may be pleasantly surprised by the quality of the food at Universal Studios Orlando.

Trattoria del Porto offers many of the same types of dishes but without Mama's interference. For more upscale dining, there's Bice, serving Italian specialties in a romantic atmosphere that includes a strolling guitarist. Across the way is the Hard Rock Hotel's The Palm, a link in the chain of steak houses based on the original in New York and its characteristic wall caricatures. The Hard Rock also hosts Beach Club, a casual bar and grill.

The Royal Pacific brings the second Orlando restaurant from Emeril Lagasse, this one called Emeril's Tchoup Chop. The name is pronounced "chop chop" ("Tchoup" is short for Tchoupitoulas, the street that Lagasse's main New Orleans restaurant is on), and the cuisine is a stylized version of Hawaiian dishes. The food gets mixed reviews, but most people love the decor. Royal Pacific also has good light bites at Jake's American Bar, as well as in the Islands Dining Room, the hotel's version of a coffee shop.

Counter-service fast food is available throughout Universal Studios Orlando. The food compares in quality to McDonald's, Arby's, or Taco Bell, but is more expensive, though often served in larger portions.

UNIVERSAL ORLANDO RESTAURANT PROFILES

BELOW ARE PROFILES for full-service restaurants found in Universal Studios, Islands of Adventure, CityWalk, and the Universal hotels.

Bice   ★★★★½

ITALIAN	EXPENSIVE	QUALITY ★★★★	VALUE ★★★★

Portofino Bay; ☎ 407-503-1415

Customers Locals and tourists. **Reservations** Recommended. **When to go** Dinner. **Entrée range** $16–$49. **Payment** AE, D, DC, MC, V. **Service rating** ★★★★★. **Friendliness rating** ★★★★. **Parking** $25 valet or $20 self-parking. **Bar** Full service. **Wine selection** Very good. **Dress** Resort dressy. **Disabled access** Good. **Hours** Sunday–Saturday, 5:30–10:30 p.m.

SETTING AND ATMOSPHERE Wood and marble floors, crisp white linens, opulent flower arrangements, and waiters in black suits give Bice ("beach-ay") the feeling of a formal restaurant, but there is nothing stiff or fussy about the space or the staff. It is immaculately clean, beautifully lit, and relatively quiet even when it's crowded.

HOUSE SPECIALTIES Menu changes seasonally; selections may include prosciutto with fresh melon and baby greens; homemade braised beef spare-rib ravioli with spinach in mushroom-marsala sauce; veal Milanese with cherry tomatoes and arugula; pistachio semifreddo.

ENTERTAINMENT AND AMENITIES Piano in bar.

SUMMARY AND COMMENTS This is part of a chain of very upscale and quite impressive restaurants found in New York, Tokyo, and Las Vegas and other international locales. The food is incredibly fresh, well prepared, and elegant, and the service is top-notch. But be prepared: even a modest meal will put a dent in your wallet, and even though the food and service are definitely worth it, it may be too expensive for many vacationers. If you want to try a variety of things on the menu, split a salad, appetizer, or pasta dish between two people for a starter; portions are large enough for sharing and the staff is more than happy to accommodate.

Bob Marley—A Tribute to Freedom   ★★½

JAMAICAN/CARIBBEAN	MODERATE	QUALITY ★★★½	VALUE ★★★

CityWalk; ☎ 407-224-2262

Customers Locals and tourists. **Reservations** Not accepted. **When to go** Early evening. **Entrée range** $8–$17. **Payment** AE, D, MC, V. **Service rating** ★★.

Friendliness rating ★★★. **Parking** Universal Orlando garage. **Bar** Full service. **Wine selection** Poor. **Dress** Casual; dreadlocks if you have them. **Disabled access** Good. **Hours** Monday–Friday, 4:30 p.m.–2 a.m.; Saturday–Sunday, 2 p.m.– 2 a.m.

SETTING AND ATMOSPHERE   The space, said to be fashioned after Bob Marley's island home, gives one the feeling of sitting on a porch or verandah and watching entertainment on a backyard stage. Most of the area is open to the elements, although there are shelters from the occasional rainstorm.

HOUSE SPECIALTIES   Jerk-marinated chicken breast; smoky white-cheddar cheese fondue; Jamaican vegetable patties; beef patties.

ENTERTAINMENT AND AMENITIES   Live reggae; cover charge after 8 p.m.

SUMMARY AND COMMENTS   There is much more emphasis put on the music than the food here, although you can manage a palatable bite to eat while listening to some good tunes. Sure, you're allowed to get up and dance.

The Bubba Gump Shrimp Co. Restaurant
& Market   ★★

SOUTHERN/SEAFOOD	MODERATE	QUALITY ★★★	VALUE ★★

CityWalk; ☎ 407-903-0044

Customers Tourists. **Reservations** Not accepted. **When to go** Anytime. **Entrée range** $10–$23. **Payment** AE, D, MC, V. **Service rating ★★★**. **Friendliness rating ★★★★**. **Parking** Universal Orlando garage. **Bar** Full service. **Wine selection** Minimal. **Dress** Casual. **Disabled access** Good. **Hours** Daily, 11 a.m.– midnight.

SETTING AND ATMOSPHERE   The movie that inspired the chain, *Forrest Gump,* plays on TVs throughout, but without sound, just subtitles. Movie memorabilia decorates the wooden walls of this seafood shanty. License plates that say RUN FORREST RUN on one side and STOP FORREST STOP on another help signal a waiter when you need service, and the waiters will ask you trivia questions from the movie.

HOUSE SPECIALTIES   Fried, stuffed, or grilled shrimp (and shrimp cooked almost every other way); burgers; salads; grilled salmon; fried chicken; baby back ribs. A gluten-free menu is also offered.

SUMMARY AND COMMENTS   The theme may seem a little cheesy, but it's a fun and festive atmosphere to bring the kids. The food is done fairly well here and is not too spicy.

Confisco Grille   ★★½

AMERICAN	MODERATE	QUALITY ★★★½	VALUE ★★★

Islands of Adventure/Port of Entry; ☎ 407-363-8000

Customers Park guests. **Reservations** Accepted. **When to go** Anytime. **Entrée range** $9–$18. **Payment** AE, D, DC, MC, V. **Service rating ★★**. **Friendliness rating ★★**. **Parking** Universal Orlando garage. **Bar** Full service. **Wine selection**

Moderate. **Dress** Casual. **Disabled access** Good. **Hours** 11 a.m. until park closing; also hosts a character breakfast featuring Spider-Man several mornings throughout the year. Call for details.

SETTING AND ATMOSPHERE A way station on the road to Morocco, perhaps? Actually, it's meant to look like a customs house.

HOUSE SPECIALTIES Pizza; selection of salads; beef and chicken fajitas; grilled sandwiches.

SUMMARY AND COMMENTS It's clear that the Universal food gurus put all their efforts into the counter-service eateries located throughout the park. Confisco is fine when you just can't stand in another line.

Emeril's Orlando ★★★½

AMERICAN	EXPENSIVE	QUALITY ★★★	VALUE ★★★

CityWalk; ☎ **407-224-2424**

Customers Locals and park guests. **Reservations** Required. **When to go** Early or late evening. **Entrée range** $19–$75. **Payment** AE, D, DC, MC, V. **Service rating** ★★★★. **Friendliness rating** ★★★★. **Parking** Universal Orlando garage; valet parking available; check with restaurant about validation. **Bar** Full service. **Wine selection** Very good. **Dress** Casual to dressy. **Disabled access** Good. **Hours** Sunday–Thursday, 11:30 a.m.–2:30 p.m. and 5:30–10 p.m.; Friday–Saturday, 11:30 a.m.–2:30 p.m. and 5:30–11 p.m.

SETTING AND ATMOSPHERE Chief among your dining options here, this is Emeril Lagasse's Florida version of his New Orleans restaurant. The main dining room is two stories high and features hardwood floors, wooden beams, and stone walls, all of which act as sounding boards for the noisy dining room. Sliding glass doors lead to the kitchen, where Emeril probably won't be cooking. Part of the kitchen is open, and there are eight seats at a food bar—some of the best seats in the house

HOUSE SPECIALTIES The menu changes frequently. Signature items that might be available include oyster stew; farm-raised quail; "a study of duck"; and lobster cheesecake.

SUMMARY AND COMMENTS Owner Emeril Lagasse gained popularity from his show on Food Network, and his restaurants were instant hits. But the food proves he's more than a flash in the proverbial pan. Lagasse also has restaurants in New Orleans and Las Vegas, so it's unlikely he will be on the premises, though he does visit sometimes. But even when he's not there, you're in for some good eating. *Note:* Reservations can be hard to come by unless booked weeks in advance. To get a table on the same day as your visit, call the restaurant at 3:15 p.m.

Finnegan's ★★

IRISH	MODERATE	QUALITY ★★★	VALUE ★★

Universal Studios/New York; ☎ **407-363-8757**

Customers Park guests. **Reservations** Priority seating. **When to go** Anytime. **Entrée range** $11–$22. **Payment** AE, D, DC, MC, V. **Service rating** ★★.

Friendliness rating ★★. **Parking** Universal Orlando garage. **Bar** Full service. **Wine selection** Ireland is not really known for its wines; good beer selection, though. **Dress** Casual. **Disabled access** Good. **Hours** Daily, 11 a.m. until park closing.

SETTING AND ATMOSPHERE Fashioned after an Irish pub, albeit one built as a movie set. Along with the requisite publike accoutrements—such as the tin ceiling and belt-driven paddle fans—are movie lights and half walls that suggest the back of scenery flats.

HOUSE SPECIALTIES Shepherd's pie; fish-and-chips; Irish stew; bangers and mash; shrimp Scargo; Irish coffee.

ENTERTAINMENT AND AMENITIES Singer.

SUMMARY AND COMMENTS The fare is modest, but the entertainment is fun and the beer is cold. Add to that the fact that this is only one of two spots in Universal Studios park where you can get a waiter to bring food to you, and the pub fare starts to look a bit more attractive.

Hard Rock Cafe ★★★

AMERICAN	MODERATE	QUALITY ★★★½	VALUE ★★★★

CityWalk; ☎ 407-351-7625

Customers Locals and tourists. **Reservations** Not accepted. **When to go** Afternoon or evening. **Entrée range** $10–$22. **Payment** AE, D, DC, MC, V. **Service rating** ★★★. **Friendliness rating** ★★. **Parking** Universal Orlando garage. **Bar** Full service. **Wine selection** Moderate. **Dress** Casual. **Disabled access** Good. **Hours** Daily, 11 a.m.–2 a.m.

SETTING AND ATMOSPHERE This is the biggest HRC in the world (or in the Universe, as they like to say in this part of town). Shaped like the Coliseum, the two-story dining room is a massive museum of rock art memorabilia. The circular center bar features a full-size Cadillac spinning overhead. If you need to be told this is a noisy restaurant, you've never been to a Hard Rock Cafe before. Everyone, however, should visit a Hard Rock at least once.

HOUSE SPECIALTIES Pig sandwich; charbroiled burgers; barbecued ribs; rock-and-roll pot roast; grilled fajitas; T-bone steak.

OTHER RECOMMENDATIONS Hot fudge brownie; chocolate-chip cookie pie.

ENTERTAINMENT AND AMENITIES Rock 'n' roll records and memorabilia.

SUMMARY AND COMMENTS Most people complain about a burger that costs $10. But this is a good burger—half a pound—and it comes with fries. And all the rest of the food is equally as good, which is why Hard Rock Cafe remains the theme restaurant that everyone else wants to imitate.

Islands Dining Room ★★★

CARIBBEAN	MODERATE	QUALITY ★★★	VALUE ★★★

Royal Pacific Hotel; ☎ 407-503-DINE (3463)

Customers Hotel guests. **Reservations** Suggested for character dining and during holiday weekends. **When to go** Breakfast, character dinners. **Entrée**

range Breakfast, $8–$19.50; Lunch, $12–$17; Dinner, $10–$33. **Payment** AE, D, DC, MC, V. **Service rating** ★★★. **Friendliness rating** ★★★. **Parking** $25 valet or $20 self-parking. **Bar** Full service. **Wine selection** Average. **Dress** Casual. **Disabled access** Good. **Hours** Daily, 7 a.m.–11 p.m.

SETTING AND ATMOSPHERE Pretty standard hotel dining room; big and open, and always spotless.

HOUSE SPECIALTIES Guava-barbecue shredded pork on goat-cheese grits; roasted almond and mixed-berry pancakes; Tahitian French toast à l'orange; herb-crusted ahi tuna; panko-crusted chicken breast; Islands sushi sampler for two.

ENTERTAINMENT AND AMENITIES Character dining available on Monday, Tuesday, and Saturday evenings. Other entertainment such as face painters and hula dancers appear other nights; call ahead to confirm.

SUMMARY AND COMMENTS Breakfast here is a treat—the specialties are all tasty and (surprisingly) moderately priced. Lunch and dinner are good too, but with all the other restaurants around, especially if you're spending the day in the parks, we suggest having a hearty breakfast here and a lighter lunch elsewhere.

Jake's American Bar ★★

AMERICAN	MODERATE	QUALITY ★★	VALUE ★★

Royal Pacific Hotel; ☎ 407-503-DINE (3463)

Customers Hotel guests. **Reservations** Not accepted. **When to go** Early evening. **Entrée range** $10–$20. **Payment** AE, D, DC, MC, V. **Service rating** ★★. **Friendliness rating** ★★★. **Parking** $25 valet or $20 self-parking. **Bar** Full service. **Wine selection** Average. **Dress** Resort casual. **Disabled access** Good. **Hours** Daily, 2–11 p.m.; bar, 2 p.m.–2 a.m.

SETTING AND ATMOSPHERE Run-of-the-mill hotel bar and restaurant.

HOUSE SPECIALTIES Pu Pu platter; Brandi's BBQ baby back ribs; steak sandwich; Fly Away Roaster.

ENTERTAINMENT AND AMENITIES Thursday and Sunday, karaoke from 8:30 p.m.–12:30 a.m.; Friday and Saturday, live music from 8:30–11:30 p.m.

SUMMARY AND COMMENTS This is a viable option if you're staying in the hotel, but as far as special meals go, this place doesn't deliver—and really isn't meant to. For a quick meal, this spot is convenient but doesn't merit a visit if you're not already in the area.

Jimmy Buffett's Magaritaville ★★★

CARIBBEAN/AMERICAN	MODERATE	QUALITY ★★★½	VALUE ★★★

CityWalk; ☎ 407-224-2155

Customers Local and tourist Parrotheads. **Reservations** Not accepted. **When to go** Early evening. **Entrée range** $10–$25. **Payment** AE, D, DC, MC, V. **Service rating** ★★★. **Friendliness rating** ★★★. **Parking** Universal Orlando garage. **Bar** Full service. **Wine selection** Minimal. **Dress** Flowered shirts, flip-flops. **Disabled access** Good. **Hours** Daily, 11:30 a.m.–2 a.m.

SETTING AND ATMOSPHERE Two-story dining space with many large-screen TVs playing Jimmy Buffett music videos and scenes from his live performances. A volcano above one of the bars occasionally erupts to spew margaritas down the slope into a giant blender. The Lone Palm Airport next door features a seaplane and offers quick bites and drinks.

HOUSE SPECIALTIES Cheeseburgers, of course; conch fritters; Yucatán quesadillas with whole-wheat tortillas; New Orleans nachos; Key lime pie.

ENTERTAINMENT AND AMENITIES Live music on the porch early; band on inside stage late evening.

SUMMARY AND COMMENTS This is a relaxing, festive place, but it's not always worth the wait (especially if it's 2 hours, which it has been known to be). The atmosphere, though, is like a taste of the beach without having to travel to the coast. If the line for a table is outrageous, see if you can sidle up to the bar for a margarita and appetizers, which is just as much—if not more—fun than actually having a full meal. None of the food, including the cheeseburger, will make you think that you're in paradise, but fans don't seem to care. This place is wildly popular with Jimmy Buffett fans standing in line just to get a beeper so they can stand in line some more and wait for a table.

The Kitchen ★★★★

AMERICAN	MODERATE	QUALITY ★★★	VALUE ★★★

Hard Rock Hotel; ☎ 407-503-DINE (3463)

Customers Tourists. **Reservations** Recommended. **When to go** Dinner. **Entrée range** $10–$32. **Payment** AE, D, DC, MC, V. **Service rating** ★★½. **Friendliness rating** ★★★★. **Parking** $25 valet or $20 self-parking. **Bar** Full service. **Wine selection** Good. **Dress** Casual. **Disabled access** Good. **Hours** Daily, 7 a.m.–10 p.m.

SETTING AND ATMOSPHERE With the appearance of a spacious kitchen in a rock megastar's mansion, The Kitchen's walls are adorned with culinary-themed memorabilia from the Hard Rock Hotel's many celebrity guests.

HOUSE SPECIALTIES Seared ahi tuna; chicken chorizo quesadillas; Kobe beef burger; maple-glazed cedar-plank salmon; meatloaf; Key lime tart.

ENTERTAINMENT AND AMENITIES Rock stars occasionally visit to cook their specialties; signed aprons and rock memorabilia on the walls.

SUMMARY AND COMMENTS Though we must admit that our expectations weren't too high for this Hard Rock venture, we were pleasantly surprised with the food and service here. Though expensive, the food is actually quite good and the setting is pretty fun. The Kobe beef burger will set you back about $18, but the regular version is just as tasty and much less expensive. Visiting rock stars often perform cooking demonstrations of their favorite dishes at the Chef's Table, so call ahead to see if any rock stars will be in the kitchen—you may find yourself having dinner with Joan Jett or Bob Seger. If dinner is a little out of your price range but you still want the experience, go for the $15.95 breakfast buffet, which includes a host of fresh, yummy selections and an omelet station.

Latin Quarter ★★★

NUEVO LATINO	MODERATE	QUALITY ★★★	VALUE ★★★

CityWalk; ☎ 407-224-FOOD (3663)

Customers Tourists. **Reservations** Accepted. **When to go** Sunday–Wednesday if you're not looking for a nightclub scene. **Entrée range** $10–$27. **Payment** AE, D, MC, V. **Service rating** ★★★. **Friendliness rating** ★★★★. **Parking** Universal Orlando garage. **Bar** Full service. **Wine selection** Minimal. **Dress** Casual. **Disabled access** Good. **Hours** Sunday–Wednesday, 5–10 p.m.; Thursday–Saturday, 5 p.m.–2 a.m.

SETTING AND ATMOSPHERE Aztec, Incan, and Mayan ruins influenced the architecture here, and a sky is painted on the ceiling. Lanterns hang above the outdoor patio, where music plays every night. The restaurant turns into more of a nightclub Thursday–Saturday.

HOUSE SPECIALTIES Chilean sea bass; churrasco skirt steak; paella; fajitas; roast pork loin; cheese flan.

ENTERTAINMENT AND AMENITIES Spanish guitar on the patio nightly; dancing to Latin and Reggaeton Thursday–Saturday after 10 p.m..

SUMMARY AND COMMENTS Most of the patrons come here to dance and drink. The specialty drinks feature selections from all 21 Latin American countries. Meat lovers will be happy here, and the restaurant has an assortment of seafood dishes. Order carefully—the food can be hit or miss.

Lombard's Seafood Grille ★★½

SEAFOOD	MODERATE	QUALITY ★★★½	VALUE ★★★

Universal Studios/San Francisco; ☎ 407-224-6401

Customers Park guests. **Reservations** Accepted. **When to go** Anytime. **Entrée range** $11–$20. **Payment** AE, D, DC, MC, V. **Service rating** ★★★. **Friendliness rating** ★★. **Parking** Universal Orlando garage. **Bar** Full service. **Wine selection** Good. **Dress** Casual. **Disabled access** Good. **Hours** Daily, 11:30 a.m. until 2 hours before park closes or until park closing, depending on park attendance. Call to verify hours, as there is no set schedule.

SETTING AND ATMOSPHERE Situated on the park's main lagoon, Lombard's looks like a converted wharfside warehouse. The centerpiece of the brick-walled room is a huge aquarium with bubble-glass windows. A fish-sculpture fountain greets guests.

HOUSE SPECIALTIES Shrimp cioppino ratatouille; ravioli with five cheeses; fried shrimp; fresh fish selections.

SUMMARY AND COMMENTS Lombard's Seafood Grille is now more casually focused. Unfortunately, so is the kitchen. There are arguably better food options in the park, but as one of only two full-service restaurants in Universal Studios park, the place can be crowded.

Mama Della's ★★★

ITALIAN	EXPENSIVE	QUALITY ★★★	VALUE ★★★

Portofino Bay Hotel; ☎ 407-503-DINE (3463)

Customers Hotel guests. **Reservations** Suggested during high season. **When to go** Dinner. **Entrée range** $17–$32. **Payment** AE, D, DC, MC, V. **Service rating** ★★★. **Friendliness rating** ★★★★. **Parking** $25 valet or $20 self-parking. **Bar** Full service. **Wine selection** Good. **Dress** Nice casual. **Disabled access** Good. **Hours** Daily, 5–10 p.m.

SETTING AND ATMOSPHERE Just like being in the dining room of a home in Tuscany, with hardwood floors, provincial printed wallpaper, and wooden furniture.

HOUSE SPECIALTIES Baked clams with garlic and oregano; gnochetti with Bolognese sauce; grilled shrimp, scallops, and grouper on cappellini; seared rib-eye steak; chocolate praline crunch cake; lemon cheesecake; and panna cotta.

ENTERTAINMENT AND AMENITIES Strolling musicians on select nights.

SUMMARY AND COMMENTS This falls on the fancy scale somewhere in between Bice and Trattoria del Porto. Traditional Italian food is served in a comfortable atmosphere conducive of a special meal, but not quite as extravagant as its lavish neighbor, Bice. If you want food (almost) as tasty but for (a bit) less dough, Mama Della's is a great choice.

Mythos ★★★

STEAK/SEAFOOD	MOD/EXP	QUALITY ★★★★	VALUE ★★★

Islands of Adventure/The Lost Continent; ☎ 407-224-4533

Customers Park guests. **Reservations** Accepted. **When to go** Early evening. **Entrée range** $10–$19. **Payment** AE, D, DC, MC, V. **Service rating** ★★. **Friendliness rating** ★★★. **Parking** Universal Orlando garage. **Bar** Full service. **Wine selection** Good. **Dress** Casual. **Disabled access** Good. **Hours** Daily, 11:30 a.m.–3 p.m. or until park closing; call ahead for closing time.

SETTING AND ATMOSPHERE A grottolike atmosphere suggests that you're eating in a cave. Large picture windows look out over the central lagoon to the Incredible Hulk roller coaster. You can time your meal by coaster launchings.

HOUSE SPECIALTIES Tempura shrimp sushi; coq au vin; cedar-plank salmon; beef filet; risotto of the day.

SUMMARY AND COMMENTS This was originally the park's one stab at fine dining, but few guests seem to be looking for this sort of dining experience, especially after getting soaked on one of the water-based rides. Things are now more casual. The food is above-average theme-park eats, and the setting provides a pleasant retreat. Make your reservation early if you want to dine here.

NASCAR Sports Grille ★★

AMERICAN	MODERATE	QUALITY ★★★	VALUE ★★

CityWalk; ☎ 407-224-7223

Customers Racing fans. **Reservations** Not accepted. **When to go** Anytime. **Entrée range** $10–$28. **Payment** AE, D, DC, MC, V. **Service rating** ★★.

Friendliness rating ★★. **Parking** Universal Orlando garage. **Bar** Full service. **Wine selection** Modest. **Dress** Casual; grease-stained jumpsuits OK. **Disabled access** Good. **Hours** Daily, 11 a.m.–midnight.

SETTING AND ATMOSPHERE The dining area is on the second level of this two-story building. As you might expect, the room is decorated with a myriad of memorabilia from the world of NASCAR. A full-size replica of a race car hangs overhead and occasionally revs up, its wheels spinning, and speakers roar with trackside noise (at a too-realistic sound level).

HOUSE SPECIALTIES Bill France pork chop; filet; rib eye; Smoky Mountain barbecued ribs.

SUMMARY AND COMMENTS This is strictly for serious NASCAR fans who can't get enough of it. And the food? With all those signs for motor oil hanging all over the place, do you have to ask?

NBA City ★★★

AMERICAN	MODERATE	QUALITY ★★★	VALUE ★★★

CityWalk; ☎ 407-363-5919

Customers Basketball fans. **Reservations** Not accepted. **When to go** Anytime. **Entrée range** $10–$20. **Payment** AE, D, DC, MC, V. **Service rating** ★★★. **Friendliness rating** ★★★. **Parking** Universal Orlando garage. **Bar** Full service. **Wine selection** Modest. **Dress** Casual. **Disabled access** Good. **Hours** Daily, 11 a.m.–11 p.m.

SETTING AND ATMOSPHERE A giant statue of Logoman, the official NBA figure, guards the entrance to the restaurant. The building is designed to resemble an older arena, complete with an overhead track that circles the main dining floor. Booths line the walls, and each has a TV that plays videos of famous basketball players and key moments in round-ball history.

HOUSE SPECIALTIES Grilled salmon; double-thick pork chops; chicken stuffed with mozzarella and spinach; New York strip steak.

SUMMARY AND COMMENTS This was originally another concept from the next-door neighbor, Hard Rock Cafe, but the two entities split soon after this prototype opened. But some of HRC's theme-restaurant quality rubbed off. As themes go, this one is done well. Basketball fans will enjoy the videos and the arcade games in the outer lobby.

The Palm ★★★

STEAK	VERY EXPENSIVE	QUALITY ★★★★	VALUE ★★

Hard Rock Hotel; ☎ 407-503-7256

Customers Tourists. **Reservations** Recommended. **When to go** Dinner. **Entrée range** $22.50–$58. **Payment** AE, D, MC, V. **Service rating** ★★★. **Friendliness rating** ★★★. **Parking** $25 valet or $20 self-parking; validation available. **Bar** Full service. **Wine selection** Very good. **Dress** Resort, business casual, smart casual. **Disabled access** Good. **Hours** Monday–Thursday, 5–10 p.m.; Friday–Saturday, 5–11 p.m.; Sunday, 5–9 p.m.

SETTING AND ATMOSPHERE Despite the celebrity caricatures drawn on the wall, the restaurant exudes sophistication due to the dark woods and white tablecloths. The chain's flagship location is in New York, and the decor reflects this. Waiters wear long, white aprons.

HOUSE SPECIALTIES New York strip; Porterhouse; veal parmigiana; Alaskan king crab legs; Atlantic salmon; salads.

SUMMARY AND COMMENTS The crowd here can get noisy, so The Palm may not be the best place for a romantic night out. However, if you're looking to celebrate with friends or family, this is a good, if very expensive, choice. The steaks are done well, while some of the other dishes could be better. The side dishes are meant for sharing.

Pastamoré ★★★½

ITALIAN	MODERATE	QUALITY ★★★★	VALUE ★★★★

CityWalk; ☎ 407-224-2244

Customers Park guests. **Reservations** Priority seating. **When to go** Anytime. **Entrée range** $15–$28. **Payment** AE, D, MC, V. **Service rating** ★★. **Friendliness rating** ★★★. **Parking** Universal Orlando garage. **Bar** Full service. **Wine selection** Good Italian wines. **Dress** Casual. **Disabled access** Good. **Hours** Daily, 5 p.m.–midnight.

SETTING AND ATMOSPHERE A very hip sort of neoclassic design with high walls of green, purple, and yellow. The ceiling is tiered and features angles and curves that flow through the large space. Romanesque statues and artistic depictions of Italian landscapes dot the room. An open kitchen is at the rear of the restaurant. Outdoor seating is available.

HOUSE SPECIALTIES Veal parmigiana; chicken piccata; veal Marsala; fettuccine Alfredo; mussels marinara; calamari.

SUMMARY AND COMMENTS The kitchen puts forth a decent effort, even though the food is not quite authentic Italian. Family-style dinners—including antipasti, soup, salad, two entrées, and dessert—are available for $20 per person. Not a bad deal if you're really hungry. For an even better deal, book the Chef's Table, which is actually a counter overlooking the open kitchen. For a relatively modest fee, you'll have your own personal chef who will create a special menu.

Pat O'Brien's ★★★

CAJUN	INEXPENSIVE	QUALITY ★★★½	VALUE ★★★★

CityWalk; ☎ 407-224-2106

Customers Tourists. **Reservations** Not accepted. **When to go** Anytime. **Entrée range** $8–$17. **Payment** AE, D, DC, MC, V. **Service rating** ★★. **Friendliness rating** ★★★. **Parking** Universal Orlando garage. **Bar** Full service. **Wine selection** Modest. **Dress** Casual. **Disabled access** Good. **Hours** Daily, 4 p.m.–closing varies.

SETTING AND ATMOSPHERE A fairly faithful rendition of the original Pat O'Brien's in New Orleans, right down to the fire-and-water fountain in the courtyard. The outdoor dining area is the most pleasant place to eat; inside areas feature a noisy bar and another room with dueling pianos. It's mostly a music venue that also serves food.

HOUSE SPECIALTIES Shrimp gumbo; jambalaya; muffuletta; red beans and rice.

SUMMARY AND COMMENTS The food is surprisingly good, and surprisingly affordable. Be careful about ordering a Hurricane, the restaurant's signature drink. You are automatically charged for the souvenir glass, and if you don't want it, you must turn it in at the bar for a refund.

Trattoria del Porto ★★★

ITALIAN	MODERATE	QUALITY ★★★	VALUE ★★

Portofino Bay Hotel; ☎ 407-503-DINE (3463)

Customers Hotel guests. **Reservations** Suggested for dinner. **When to go** Lunch. **Entrée range** Lunch, $10–$17; dinner, $15–$30. **Payment** AE, D, DC, MC, V. **Service rating** ★★★. **Friendliness rating** ★★★. **Parking** $25 valet or $20 self-parking. **Bar** Full service. **Wine selection** Average. **Dress** Resort casual. **Disabled access** Good. **Hours** Daily, 7 a.m.–11 p.m., but closed for dinner Tuesday and Wednesday.

SETTING AND ATMOSPHERE Like a boisterous down-home Italian kitchen.

HOUSE SPECIALTIES Gnocchi verdi; grouper Milanese; filet mignon; open-faced ravioli with gulf shrimp; pizza Bianca; meatball sandwich.

ENTERTAINMENT AND AMENITIES Character dining available on select evenings; call ahead to confirm.

SUMMARY AND COMMENTS Where Mama Della's succeeds in not feeling like a hotel restaurant, Trattoria del Porto does not. The food is perfectly fine and moderately priced (relatively speaking), but lunch is your best option here. Omelets at breakfast can set you back more than $10, and dinner options are limited. If the poolside snack bar isn't your thing, or if you must try a meal here, lunch is your best bet.

Wantilan Luau ★★★★

HAWAIIAN	MODERATE	QUALITY ★★★	VALUE ★★★

Royal Pacific Hotel; ☎ 407-503-DINE (3463)

Customers Tourists. **Reservations** Accepted. **When to go** Dinner only. **Buffet** $58 adults; $32 children ages 3–11. (Prices include tax, gratuity for everyone, and mai tais, wine, and beer for guests age 21 and older.) **Payment** AE, D, DC, MC, V. **Service rating** ★★★. **Friendliness rating** ★★★★. **Parking** $25 valet or $20 self-parking. **Bar** Mai tais, wine, and beer available. **Dress** Flowered shirts, beachy casual. **Disabled access** Average. **Hours** Every Tuesday and Saturday night year-round; an additional Friday-night show runs from May through the end of August.

SETTING AND ATMOSPHERE A typical luau setting with tiki torches and wooden tables.

HOUSE SPECIALTIES Buffet includes pit-roasted suckling pig with spiced rum-soaked pineapple purée; guava-barbecued short ribs; whole roasted South Pacific wahoo; *lomi lomi* chicken with Maui onions; tropical fruits.

ENTERTAINMENT AND AMENITIES Polynesian dancing, storytelling, hula dancers, live music.

SUMMARY AND COMMENTS This is a fun diversion and a change of scenery from the other restaurants offered on Universal property. Though dinner is a bit expensive, the entertainment is worth it. A separate children's buffet keeps kids happy with offerings such as chicken fingers, macaroni, and pizza.

ACCOMMODATIONS INDEX

Note: Page numbers of hotel profiles are in **bold face** type.

RESTAURANTS INDEX

Note: Page numbers of restaurant profiles are in **bold face** type.

SUBJECT INDEX

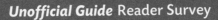

If you'd like to express your opinion about traveling in Central Florida or this guidebook, complete the following survey and mail it to:

> *Unofficial Guide* Reader Survey
> P.O. Box 43673
> Birmingham, AL 35243

Inclusive dates of your visit:_____

Members of your party:

	Person 1	Person 2	Person 3	Person 4	Person 5
Gender:	M F	M F	M F	M F	M F

Age:_____

How many times have you been to Central Florida? _____
On your most recent trip, where did you stay?_____

Concerning your accommodations, on a scale of 100 as best and 0 as worst, how would you rate:

The quality of your room?   The value of your room?
The quietness of your room?   Check-in/checkout efficiency?
Shuttle service to the airport?   Swimming pool facilities?

Did you rent a car?_____   From whom?_____

Concerning your rental car, on a scale of 100 as best and 0 as worst, how would you rate:

Pickup-processing efficiency?_____   Return processing efficiency?____
Condition of the car?_____   Cleanliness of the car?_____
Airport shuttle efficiency?_____

Concerning your dining experiences:

Estimate your meals in restaurants per day? _____
Approximately how much did your party spend on meals per day? ____

Favorite restaurants in Central Florida: _____
_____

Did you buy this guide before leaving? _____ While on your trip?_____

How did you hear about this guide? (check all that apply)

☐ Loaned or recommended by a friend   ☐ Radio or TV
☐ Newspaper or magazine   ☐ Bookstore salesperson
☐ Just picked it out on my own   ☐ Library
☐ Internet

What other guidebooks did you use on this trip? _____

_____

_____

_____

On a scale of 100 as best and 0 as worst, how would you rate them?

_____

_____

_____

Using the same scale, how would you rate the *Unofficial Guide*(s)?

_____

Are *Unofficial Guides* readily available at bookstores in your area? _____

Have you used other *Unofficial Guides*? _____

Which one(s)? _____

_____

_____

Comments about your Central Florida trip or the *Unofficial Guide*(s):

_____

_____

_____

_____

_____

_____

_____

_____

_____

_____

_____

_____

_____

_____

_____

_____

_____

_____

_____

_____